WOMEN OF MATHEMATICS

WOMEN OF MATHEMATICS

A Biobibliographic Sourcebook

Edited by
Louise S. Grinstein and Paul J. Campbell

With a Foreword by Alice Schafer

Greenwood Press
New York • Westport, Connecticut • London

To Jack and to Lois

Library of Congress Cataloging-in-Publication Data

Women of mathematics.

Bibliography: p.
Includes index.
1. Women mathematicians—Biography. 2. Women
mathematicians—Bibliography. I. Grinstein, Louise S.
II. Campbell, Paul J.
QA28.W66   1987   510′.92′2 [B]   86–25711
ISBN 0–313–24849–4 (lib. bdg. : alk. paper)

Library of Congress Catalog Card Number: 86–25711
ISBN: 0–313–24849–4

First published in 1987

Greenwood Press, Inc.
88 Post Road West, Westport, Connecticut 06881

Printed in the United States of America

∞

The paper used in this book complies with the
Permanent Paper Standard issued by the National
Information Standards Organization (Z39.48–1984).

10 9 8 7 6 5 4 3 2 1

CONTENTS

FOREWORD

In the past fifteen years, many individuals and many organizations in the United States have worked long and hard to ensure that women have the same opportunities for education, for professional careers, and for advancement in their careers as men. This has not been an easy task, and much remains to be done; but there has been some progress. One of the fields in which women have been little represented in this country, or in any country, is mathematics.

In fact, it is possible to read most histories of mathematics and find little or no mention of women mathematicians, even of the few there were. Who were those few who did succeed? Why were there so few? What were the barriers they faced in becoming mathematicians, barriers which men of far less ability did not have to face? For example, why was it necessary for Sofia Kovalevskaia to arrange a fictitious marriage as a means to leave Russia and go to Germany, where she hoped she would be able to study mathematics? Why were Sophie Germain and Emmy Noether, in France and Germany, respectively, barred from attending the schools which prepared men for the universities? Why was Mary Fairfax Somerville not allowed to buy an algebra book in a bookstore in Scotland, as her brother would have been allowed to do? Why did Christine Ladd-Franklin find it necessary to change her field of study from physics to mathematics and then to psychology? Why was she forced to wait to receive her doctorate in mathematics from Johns Hopkins University for forty-two years after she had completed the work for the degree?

What were the barriers faced by women for the first seventy years of this century when they sought to be mathematicians and to have the same opportunities in the mathematical community as men? What progress has been made since 1970 in ensuring that women will have true equality in the mathematical community? What obstacles still stand in the way of this equality? What can be done to eliminate these obstacles? What brought about the drive of the last fifteen years to change the status of girls and women in mathematics: to encourage them to continue the study of mathematics, to seek careers in mathematics and mathematically related fields, and to participate in the mathematical community on a basis equal to that of their male colleagues?

By the 1920s women in the United States could gain admission to the graduate schools of all the universities with outstanding research departments in mathematics (except Princeton University, which did not admit women to its graduate program in mathematics until the late 1960s). Although women could gain admission, they did not necessarily feel welcomed into the department as bona fide graduate students. For example, at Harvard University some professors refused to allow women to sit in their classrooms. They were, however, allowed to sit in chairs placed just outside the classroom doors so that they could hear the lectures.

Until the 1970s the employment situation for women mathematicians remained much as Anna Pell Wheeler described in a letter written in 1910, soon after she received her doctorate in mathematics from the University of Chicago: "I had hoped for a position in one of the good universities like Wisconsin, Illinois, etc., but there is such an objection to women that they prefer a man even if he is inferior both in training and in research. It seems that Professor E. H. Moore [her thesis advisor] has also given up hope for he has inquired at some of the Eastern Girls' Colleges." Women mathematicians found employment mainly at the women's colleges and small liberal arts colleges, where salaries were low and teaching loads heavy, and where there was little or no money for help with paper grading. Seldom were there funds for sabbaticals or for travel to professional meetings. At these institutions, duties having no connection with teaching were often required of the women members of the faculty; for example, living in the dormitories, acting as advisors to students in the dormitories and to student groups, and even teaching Sunday School. The result was that there was little time for research and little money for travel to centers of mathematical research.

As women students moved through their courses of study, they saw fewer and fewer women as classmates or instructors in mathematics courses. Except at the women's colleges, women frequently received little or no encouragement—indeed they often received discouragement—to continue their mathematical studies; had little or no knowledge of possible careers in mathematics or in fields that depend upon mathematics; had little or no contact with or knowledge of women mathematicians. There is ample evidence that women role models are important. Therefore, it is not surprising that many women who early in their schooling had shown an affinity for mathematics and a commitment to pursue study of it were soon discouraged from doing so because they knew little or no precedent for the serious participation of women in mathematical activities.

Women were as invisible in other parts of the mathematical community as they were on the faculties of universities. Seldom did women's names appear on the lists of officers of mathematical organizations, or on membership lists of their committees, which set the policy for those organizations. Seldom did women's names appear on the lists of invited speakers at professional meetings, on lists of colloquium speakers at universities, on the lists of editors of research journals in mathematics, or on lists of holders of prestigious fellowships. Until very recently the National Science Foundation listed no women mathematicians as Program Directors or as members of the Advisory Board for the Mathematical Sciences. In 1970, at the five mathematics departments usually considered by mathematicians to be the leading ones in research in the country, no women had tenure. The 1979 National Research Council report on the status of women in the sciences showed that in 1975–1976, at the twenty-five institutions in the country that received the largest amounts in federal expenditures for research and development, the number of women on the mathematics faculties at the rank of associate or full professor was 13, while the number of men in those ranks was well over 500.

It was clearly time for a change. Probably no one event triggered it: the student revolts of the 1960s, the beginning of the women's movement, or perhaps women mathematicians finally saying, "Enough is enough." By 1970 some women mathematicians were talking openly about discrimination faced by women in the mathematical community. In the Boston area, women mathematicians and women graduate students in mathematics were meeting to discuss common problems and possible solutions. In the Washington area, Mary W. Gray of American University was among those disturbed by the treatment of women in the mathematical community. In January 1971, at a meeting of the American Mathematical Society (AMS), she and other women decided to form an association with the purpose of improving the status of women in mathematics. In the summer of 1972, the Boston group joined forces with the new association, which became the Association for Women in Mathematics (AWM). The AWM, incorporated in 1973, was the first of the organizations and committees appointed by mathematical organizations to combat discrimination against women in mathematics. Today the AWM has grown to a membership of approximately 1,500 members throughout the world, with many academic institutions holding institutional memberships, and with 80% of the individual members being women.

In the past fifteen years, undoubtedly due primarily to the influence of these organizations and committees, some progress has been made by women in the mathematical community: more girls are continuing their study of mathematics in secondary schools; there has been an increase in the number of women majoring in mathematics in college; the percentage of the doctorates awarded to women has increased from approximately 6% to 15%; instead of no tenured women on the mathematics faculties in the five most outstanding mathematics departments in the United States, there are now four; more women are receiving appointments to university faculties than previously; more invited talks by women are being given at mathematics meetings; a few mathematical organizations have had their first woman president; more women are appointed to important committees of the mathematical organizations; a few of the editors of mathematical journals are women; and students, as well as male mathematicians, now see and hear about more women mathematicians.

With the increased participation of women in the mathematical community has come an interest in knowing more about women mathematicians of the past and the present. It is gratifying to be able to pick up a high school mathematics text today that has been written by a woman mathematician and contains a picture of Emmy Noether. Some teachers are now assigning papers to be written about women mathematicians. In the past half dozen years, I have been called on several occasions by parents asking if there are books about women mathematicians—and if so, where can they be found—for their children need them for their assignments. It has been good to see the list grow from one book to several; this volume is a happy addition to that list.

Among the books already in print is the excellent one by Ann Hibner Koblitz, *A Convergence of Lives,* about Sofia Kovalevskaia. Beatrice Stillman has translated Kovalevskaia's *A Russian Childhood* into English, and Roger Cooke has written a very good book on her mathematics, *The Mathematics of Sonya Kovalevskaya.* Auguste Dick's *Emmy Noether* was finally translated into English in 1981. James W. Brewer and Martha K. Smith have edited *Emmy Noether: A Tribute to Her Life and Work,* which consists of ten chapters, written by different people, some of whom knew her personally, with an eleventh chapter containing a copy of the address which she delivered at the 1932 International Congress of Mathematicians. *Emmy Noether in Bryn Mawr* is a collection of talks about her work and its influence on mathematical research; it resulted from a 1982 symposium sponsored by AWM in honor of the centennial of Noether's birth. Teri Perl has written *Math Equals: Biographies of Women Mathematicians + Related Activities,* which has been used by both high school and beginning college students. The *AWM Newsletter* since its beginning has carried occasional articles about women mathematicians, including those already mentioned. Some of the other women about whom articles have appeared in the *Newsletter* are Augusta Ada Byron Lovelace, Charlotte Angas Scott, and Grace Chisholm Young. All of these women are represented in this volume.

The present volume contains biographies and bibliographies of more than forty women mathematicians, with the majority of the chapters written by women mathematicians. There is no book of the scope of the present one. This volume is an especially important contribution to our knowledge of women mathematicians. Apart from its value as a reference work, the book will be inspirational reading for high school and college students. All of it will interest mathematicians. Anyone interested in the history of mathematics or in the history of women will find it enjoyable and informative reading.

Alice Schafer

PREFACE

This volume originated with the idea that a biographical reference source of women in the mathematical sciences was needed. Histories of mathematics rarely devote much coverage to the work of women per se, and only a handful of women are likely to be noted—perhaps Agnesi, Châtelet, Germain, Hypatia, Kovalevskaia, Noether, and Somerville.

Within the past two decades the situation has improved somewhat. In 1973 the Association for Women in Mathematics (AWM) was founded. Its bimonthly *Newsletter* has offered biographical sketches and scientific biographies—either original or reprinted—of women mathematicians. Several survey books have also been devoted exclusively to the topic: *Women in Mathematics* by Lynn M. Osen, and *Math Equals: Biographies of Women Mathematicians + Related Activities* by Teri Perl. These books concentrate primarily on the above-mentioned women, although Perl also includes Lovelace and Young. Both books are primarily for the general reader; as a consequence, the lives of the women have been highlighted and their mathematics necessarily minimized.

Two other recently published works are outside the mainstream of the mathematical literature: *Notable American Women* and the *Dictionary of Scientific Biography*. Both of these scholarly sources present well-researched profiles of the individuals considered. The first is restricted to American women (and foreign-born women who have done important work in the United States), and the only mathematicians noted are Geiringer, Ladd-Franklin, Scott, and Wheeler. Each entry contains an outline of the salient aspects of the individual's life, plus a very general and concise assessment of her achievements. The *Dictionary of Scientific Biography* contains longer entries; still, the only women accorded individual entries are Agnesi, Châtelet, Germain, Hypatia, Kovalevskaia, and Noether. Mention is made of Young's work in the entry on her husband. Even taken together, these two reference sources provide an extremely limited picture of the role women have played in the growth and development of the mathematical sciences.

Our first inclination was to try to reprint in one book many of the less accessible articles that have appeared over the years about a wider variety of individuals. Conversations with Greenwood Press produced the more ambitious goal of an archival collection of original essays on a larger group of individuals—including many about whom little had yet been published—featuring their work as well as their lives. Such is the present work.

It was clear that no such reference source could be complete without the inclusion of the women mentioned above. The process of deciding who else should be included was more difficult. Representative women were selected from different countries who have gained recognition through (a) attainment of advanced degrees despite extensive familial and societal pressures; (b) innovative research results in some aspect of the mathematical sciences; (c) influence exerted in teaching and guidance of students both at the undergraduate and graduate levels; (d) active participation and leadership in professional societies; (e) extensive scholarly publications; (f) participation on journal editorial boards. A woman was deemed eligible for inclusion if her work satisfied several of these criteria, even though in terms of any one she may not have been particularly outstanding. To provide the volume with a certain historical dimension, the scope was limited to those deceased or else born before 1925.

The list of women to be considered began with the editors' files, representing a cumulation of nearly fifteen years of research on the history of women in the mathematical sciences. Those on the list that were primarily physicists and astronomers were eliminated as being possible subjects for a companion volume. The resultant list was circulated. Scholars knowledgeable in the area suggested additional women for inclusion or indicated that some women did not really merit treatment. In some instances where no adequate coverage was possible without the cooperation of the living subject, we were forced with regret to omit a woman who was unwilling to be included.

The entries are arranged in alphabetical order. Where a woman has been known by more than one name, we have tried to use the name under which much of her professional work has been published.

For purposes of stylistic uniformity and consistency in the volume as a whole, contributors were asked to follow a set format. Each entry has three sections—biography, work, and bibliography. Cross-reference to other women discussed in the volume is given by an asterisk following the first mention in a chapter of the individual's name. Since space limitations have forced us to shorten some contributors' essays, the reader is cautioned not to interpret the length of any contribution (or part of it) as a measure of the fame of the individual portrayed or the importance of her work.

The biography section includes known information about the subject's family background, education, and career. Particular attention is given to any circumstances and influences that affected her career.

In the work section, an estimate is made of the individual's career and its significance. Every attempt has been made to present the relevant mathematics in language as nontechnical as possible without destroying its flavor.

The bibliography section is divided into listings of "works by" and "works about" the subject. The listing of "works by" is chronological. Space limitations forced us to abridge the lists supplied by the contributors. If a substantial bibliography of the individual's work is easily available elsewhere, we refer the reader to that source. In addition, we omit nonmathematical works and such minor works as abstracts of lectures and unpublished papers, book reviews, unpublished technical reports, and the like. The listing of "works about" is alphabetical by author. Omitted from the individual listings, but collected in an appendix at the end of the volume, are citations to standard reference works and other compilations.

Two other appendices are included. One presents the subjects in chronological order by birthdate and graphically depicts the timespan of their lives. The other summarizes in tabular form the data on place of birth, highest education attained, place of work, and specific field of mathematical interest.

This volume could not have been brought to fruition without the efforts of our contributors. We wish to express to this community of scholars our thanks and appreciation for their suggestions, advice, and participation. Their work required in many cases deep commitment and compassion. We also wish to thank the editorial staff at Greenwood Press for their guidance, encouragement, and patience in producing this work. We wish to acknowledge the assistance of Brenda Michaels in cross-checking bibliographic entries. Finally, we wish to thank David Heesen of Beloit College for skilled typing and formatting, which accommodated the intentions of the contributors, the deadlines of the publisher, and the high hopes of the editors.

Note: Readers interested in the work of the Association for Women in Mathematics may contact the organization at its office at Wellesley College, Wellesley, MA 01281.

INTRODUCTION

Jeanne LaDuke

The present collection of essays is an important beginning. In the nature of any opening, it suggests questions rather than themes, issues rather than syntheses. Recognizing that it is impossible to present only the best, or the typical, or some representative sample, the editors have selected essays that describe the personal histories and work of some women who have already been studied extensively; and they introduce many women whose work may not be well known to most readers. The stories we have before us are sometimes depressing, frequently inspiring, always informative. They hint at the variety and richness of the individual personal and intellectual experiences of many women in mathematics. Geographically, the subjects of the essays are restricted to certain women from the United States, Great Britain, part of Western Europe, and Russia. All but one of the women lived during the last 300 years.

The forty-three essays fall fairly naturally into three chronological groups. Members of the first group, largely active before the 1860s, may be characterized as "women mathematicians as exceptions." Few formal means for obtaining an education were available, so development and achievement by these women depended largely on the confluence of special circumstances. A second group may be seen as "pioneers," especially in the area of graduate education for women. Often they themselves opened doors; frequently they were active and effective advocates of equal educational opportunities for women. Finally, with respect to education, a third group may be characterized as "mainstream." Members of this group have access to institutions within which they can obtain professional training roughly equal to that available to men. They do not necessarily have equal access to all educational opportunities, nor are professional career opportunities necessarily open or available without discrimination. To be sure, there is overlapping of the groups, and virtually all of the so-called mainstream women share many individual traits characteristic of the pathbreaker; few of any group could be called unexceptional.

The first six, in order of birth, are Hypatia, Châtelet, Agnesi, Germain, Somerville, and Lovelace. Their stories have been frequently popularized and even romanticized; they were truly instances of women mathematicians as exceptions. They were women of unusual talent with special opportunities for developing that talent. In the long span of 1,500 years from Hypatia to Lovelace, they appear, as women mathematicians, isolated and exotic. The essays in this volume generally provide a more balanced and less romantic image of these six and their work than one frequently sees.

Of the remaining thirty-seven women treated here, all except Stott received some formal higher education, most a doctorate. Kovalevskaia can be seen as a transition between the first two groups. In the essays about her and her contemporary Litvinova, Koblitz treats us to a fine introduction to the historical setting in Russia and part of Europe for the beginning of formal educational opportunities for women at the graduate level. Although much of Kovalevskaia's work was done privately and her Göttingen Ph.D. was granted in absentia, without examination, in 1874, she and Litvinova were part of a Russian community of women actively seeking and attaining higher education. Litvinova's Ph.D. from Bern in 1878 marked the beginning of the regular granting of such degrees to women in mathematics. We see parallels in the United States, especially with Ladd-Franklin's work at Johns Hopkins, which should have led to a doctorate there in 1882. Litvinova, Kovalevskaia, Ladd-Franklin, and Hayes, holder of an A.B. from Oberlin and one of the earliest members of the mathematics faculty at Wellesley College, all worked consciously and energetically for improvements in women's educational and professional opportunities.

Doors to graduate education continued to be pushed open. Scott received a D.Sc. from the University of London in 1885, while the first Ph.D. in mathematics granted to a woman in the United States was earned by Winifred Edgerton (Merrill) at Columbia a year later. Scott was head of the mathematics department for forty years at Bryn Mawr College, the only one of the newly opened women's colleges in the United States to grant Ph.D.'s in mathematics (until Radcliffe did so in 1917). Her compatriot Maddison became one of the first two Bryn Mawr Ph.D.'s in mathematics in 1896.

As part of the agitation for equal educational opportunities for women in Europe and with the aid of Felix Klein, the Englishwoman Young and two Americans, Newson and a young woman in physics, entered in 1893, attended lectures and seminars, and took degrees from the university at Göttingen, the first to do so in a Prussian university. This is just one instance where women in mathematics were among the first to break down barriers for women in other fields.

All of the women mentioned in the last three paragraphs pioneered in establishing access to graduate education for women. By the turn of the century such opportunities existed throughout most of Western Europe, Great Britain, and the United States.

In reading of these women and the "mainstream" group one is struck by the size and diversity of the larger group from which they have been chosen. For example, of the thirty-seven "non-exceptions," twenty-four were or are active primarily in the United States. Of these twenty-four, twelve are members of the group of nearly 230 American women who received Ph.D.'s prior to 1940, a group which has been identified and studied by this author and Judy Green. Thus, omissions can and must be seen as a happy state of affairs, since they are a consequence of the impossibility of presenting in a single volume a comprehensive picture of "women in mathematics."

We can round out the picture somewhat for women in the United States. Ten Ph.D.'s were granted to American women or women studying in the United States in the nineteenth century, the first in 1886. During the first four decades of this century, more than 14% of the Ph.D.'s in mathematics in the United States were granted to women. In this period, the Wellesley College mathematics department, largely under the direction of Hayes and then Merrill, was the largest producer of undergraduate women who eventually received Ph.D.'s in the field. Sinclair, who received her doctorate at Chicago in 1908, was the first of forty-six women to do so there before 1940. The University of Chicago was by far the leading producer of Ph.D.'s by women in mathematics in that period, accounting for 20% of the total. However, the percentage of U.S. degrees going to women plunged from more than 14% before 1940 to about 5% in the 1950s. It has taken until the early 1980s to again attain the relative proportions that existed throughout the first four decades of this century. These figures are sobering, for they suggest that the drive for equality and opportunity by one generation may well be followed by a forgetting and a subsequent loss.

Most of the remarks so far have focused on the acquisition of educational opportunities, since they are so critical for the creation of entire communities of women in mathematics. However, after women acquire professional training, what do they do? From these essays we can conclude that they may do just about anything. They may function as amateurs or as professionals, although antinepotism rules, prejudice, tradition, and ignorance may make entry into many institutions difficult or impossible. If they function professionally, it may be in academic or nonacademic settings, on a full-time or part-time basis. If in academic circles, they may emphasize teaching—because they want to or because they are pushed in that direction—or they may emphasize mathematical research—often because they have gained entrance to a community that provides vital interaction. The picture of what may constitute mathematical scholarship is broad and appealing; it may consist of creating new directions of research; or it may involve decades of delightful interweaving of threads of ideas to create a rich tapestry. Some have systematized and organized; others have taken pleasure in the exposition of mathematical ideas. The administrative skills of some have shaped policy at important levels, and the innovative, imaginative skills of others have led to major creations in fields outside of mathematics. In these essays we see possibilities; further study is required before we can see patterns.

This collection of essays may serve many ends. The individual stories may entice and inspire. They may introduce the reader to new personalities and experiences. They may provide entry to certain mathematical areas. They raise questions and suggest areas of study that should be pursued and issues that should be addressed; and they provide substantial bibliographical material for doing so. Most important, perhaps, they provide counterexamples to the many negative and limiting stereotypes about both mathematics and women which continue to exist in some circles. That is, they remind us of the potential for breadth and richness in the mathematical experience. By helping us remember, they fire the imagination, sharpen the wits, and expand possibilities.

REFERENCE

Green, Judy, and Jeanne LaDuke. "Women in the American Mathematical Community: The Pre-1940 Ph.D.'s." *The Mathematical Intelligencer*, 9 (1) (1987):11–21. Preliminary report on a forthcoming longer study.

WOMEN OF MATHEMATICS

MARIA GAETANA AGNESI (1718–1799)

Hubert Kennedy

BIOGRAPHY

Maria Gaetana Agnesi was born on May 16, 1718, the first of the twenty-one children of her father, Pietro Agnesi. Her mother, Anna Fortunata (Brivio) Agnesi, died on March 13, 1732, after giving birth to her eighth child; Pietro Agnesi later remarried. Both of Agnesi's parents were of wealthy merchant families of Milan, so that Pietro Agnesi could afford to lead the life of a cultured nobleman; indeed, he eventually purchased a title.

Agnesi's intellectual ability—particularly her excellent memory—was discovered early. She was trained in several languages and first exhibited by her father at the age of nine at one of his "academic evenings," where she recited, in Latin, a scholastic exercise on the topic: The study of the liberal arts by women is by no means to be rejected. Having discovered that his second daughter, Maria Teresa (1720–1795), had musical talent, Pietro Agnesi had her specially trained also; and his academic evenings, at which Maria Agnesi debated learned guests on philosophic and scientific topics, and her sister entertained at the harpsichord, became famous in Milan. These evenings continued until 1739, when Agnesi expressed a wish to retire to a convent of nuns. Her father opposed this; always obedient to him, she agreed not to do so. In return, he agreed to three wishes: (1) that she be allowed to dress simply and modestly, (2) that she might go to church whenever she wished, and (3) that she not be required to attend balls, the theater, and so on.

There followed a decade in which Agnesi concentrated her studies on mathematics. As early as 1735, she had corresponded with her teacher Carlo Belloni about a difficulty in Guillaume François de L'Hôpital's treatise on conic sections; she also had two teachers of mathematics and science: Francesco Manara (Pavia) and Michele Casati (Turin), both of whom later became university professors. From 1740 she was directed in her studies by Ramiro Rampinelli, professor of mathematics at the University of Pavia. This more systematic study included Charles René Reyneau's *Analyse démontré* (1708), which was an early attempt to bring order to the new mathematical discoveries of the seventeenth century. The result of her study was the publication in 1748 of the *Instituzioni Analitiche* (Foundations of Analysis), which was modeled on Reyneau's book and is the work on which Agnesi's fame as a mathematician rests.

The *Instituzioni Analitiche* is a systematic presentation, in two volumes, of algebra, analytic geometry, calculus, and differential equations. Already before its publication she had been elected, on Rampinelli's recommendation, a member of the Accademia delle Scienze (Bologna); the book made her widely known, as evidenced by a scene from Carlo Goldoni's play *Il medico olandese* (1756), in which the maid Carolina says to Monsieur Guden:

You wonder that my mistress likes the sweet study of geometry? You should rather be astonished that you don't know that a woman has produced such a profound and great book. Its author is Italian, not Dutch, an illustrious and learned lady, an honor to her country.

Agnesi dedicated her book to the Empress Maria Theresa of Austria (to whom Agnesi's musical sister had earlier dedicated a volume of songs), and in return she received a crystal box with diamonds and a diamond ring. But the pious Agnesi was probably most pleased by the response of Pope Benedict XIV, who not only sent her a gold wreath set with precious stones and a gold medal, but also named her honorary professor at the University of Bologna; the diploma to this effect is dated October 5, 1750.

This was the period of the Enlightenment, and both Maria Theresa and Benedict XIV were relatively enlightened monarchs. Indeed, Italy had a long tradition of women professors. Nevertheless, Agnesi never lectured in Bologna, despite being urged to do so by, among others, the physicist Laura Bassi Verati (1711–1778), who had taught there since 1732 and whose first philosophical disputation had been heard by Benedict XIV while he was archbishop of Bologna.

Following the death of her father on March 19, 1752, a new phase of Agnesi's life began that lasted until her death. She restricted her study to theology and gave her time, effort, and money to devotional and charitable activities. Although continuing to live with her family, she kept a separate apartment, where she cared for a few poor, sick people. From 1759 she lived in a rented house with four of her poor people; and when money was needed for her charitable activity, she sold her gifts from the Empress Maria Theresa to a rich Englishman. Besides caring for the sick and indigent, she often taught catechism to working-class people.

In 1771 Prince Antonio Tolemeo Trivulzio gave his palace to be a home for the aged, named Pio Albergo Trivulzio. At the request of Cardinal Pozzobonelli, Agnesi assumed the position of visitor and director of women. The home was soon expanded to house 450 people. Agnesi herself moved there permanently in 1783 and devoted her last twenty-eight years to this institution.

The early years of intense study appear to have affected Agnesi's health as an adolescent, for her doctor at the time prescribed more physical exercise, including dancing and horseback riding, and these were followed by seizures of chorea, or St. Vitus's dance. But despite her delicate health and the voluntary privations of her later life, she continued to be physically active, although there was a decline in her last years, when she gradually grew blind and deaf. Fainting spells were followed by attacks of dropsy of the chest (hydrothorax); and the latter appears to have been the immediate cause of her death on January 9, 1799. She was buried in a common grave of poor people.

WORK

Agnesi not only wrote but also supervised the printing of the *Instituzioni Analitiche*. It was completed near the end of 1748 on the presses of the publishing house Richini, which had been installed in her house! The typesetters gave credit for their later good work to the experience gained there. The book is in two quarto volumes of 1,020 pages, with an additional 59 pages of figures engraved by Marc'Antonio Dal Rè, which may be folded out to view while reading the text. The pages are of handmade paper and printed in large type with wide margins.

The two volumes contain the analysis of finite and infinitesimal quantities, respectively. Although Agnesi made no claim to original mathematical discoveries, nevertheless she revised the material considerably in an attempt to put into their "natural order" the discoveries that are "separated, without order, and scattered here and there in the works of many authors, and principally in the *Acta* of Leipzig, in the *Mémoires* of the Academy of Paris, and in other journals. . . . Then in the act of handling the various methods, there occurred to me several extensions and a number of other things, which by chance are not without novelty and originality." With a charming frankness, she also notes that she at first intended to publish the work in Latin; but having written it in Italian, she decided to avoid the effort of translation. Nor did she lay claim to purity of language, "having had in mind more than anything else the necessary possible clarity." It is just this clarity that has been praised by later commentators.

As an illustration of how contemporary mathematicians viewed this work, we cite the conclusion of the report of Jean d'Ortous de Mairan and Étienne Mignot de Montigny, who reviewed it for the Académie des Sciences (Paris):

Obviously it covers all the analysis of Descartes and almost all of the discoveries which have been made up to the present in the differential and integral calculus. It takes a good deal of knowledge and skill to reduce to an almost always uniform method, as indeed was done, the various discoveries in the works of modern geometers, where these are often explained by methods quite different one from another. Order, clarity, and precision reign in every part of this work. Up to now we have seen no work, in any language, which allows the student to penetrate so quickly and so far into mathematical analysis. We regard this treatise as the most complete and well written of its kind. (Anzoletti 1900, 479–480)

That the work continued to be useful is shown by its later translation into French (second volume only) and English. It was widely used in Italy. Joseph Louis Lagrange listed it among the books he thoroughly studied, after Euclid's *Elements* and Alexis Claude Clairaut's *Algèbre,* and before he read Leonhard Euler and Johann Bernoulli. It was soon overshadowed, however, by the series of systematic texts published by Euler, beginning with his *Introductio in Analysin Infinitorum* in 1748.

The name of Agnesi is most often recalled today in connection with the Curve of Agnesi, known in English texts as the Witch of Agnesi. This last term appears to be John Colson's mistranslation of *versiera,* the Italian form of the Latin name *versoria,* both used for this curve by Guido Grandi as early as 1718. The curve itself had already been described by Pierre de Fermat and Isaac Newton. Although the metric properties of the Curve of Agnesi continued to interest mathematicians, physical applications have been found only recently.

Agnesi first presented the *versiera* as an exercise in analytic geometry (*Instituzioni Analitiche,* 380–382), where the problem is to find the equation of a curve described geometrically. This equation is usually given today as $y(a^2 + x^2) = a^3$, which is the inverse of the function given by Agnesi; but its graph (Table 35, Figure 162) looks the same, since she considers the x-axis to be the vertical axis and the y-axis to be the horizontal axis. She later presented an algebraic method for finding the curve's point of inflection (pp. 427–428), returning again to the curve to illustrate the method of derivatives for finding points of inflection (pp. 561–562).

BIBLIOGRAPHY

Works by Maria Gaetana Agnesi

Mathematical Works

Instituzioni Analitiche ad uso della gioventù italiana. 2 vols. Milan, 1748. 1020 pp. in quarto. 59 foldout tables. French translation of vol. 2 by Pierre Thomas Antelmy, under the title *Traités Élémentaires de Calcul. . . .* Paris: Claude-Antoine Jombert, 1775. Translated by John Colson, under the title *Analytical Institutions.* London: Taylor and Wilks, 1801.

Works about Maria Gaetana Agnesi

Anzoletti, Luisa. *Maria Gaetana Agnesi.* Milan: L. F. Cogliati, 1900. In Italian.
        Corrects and completes Frisi's essay of a century earlier. Includes genealogical
        table.
Frisi, Antonio Francesco. *Elogio storico di Donna Maria Gaetana Agnesi milanese, dell'Accademia dell'Instituto delle Scienze, e Lettrice Onoraria di Matematiche nella Università di Bologna.* Milan: Galeazzi, 1799. Reprint. Milan, 1965. French translation by Antoine Marie Henri Boulard. Paris, 1807.

Published four months after Agnesi's death by a family friend, this work is the basis for Anzoletti's more extensive biography.

Kennedy, Hubert. "The witch of Agnesi—exorcised." *Mathematics Teacher* 62 (1969): 480–482.

Gives Agnesi's presentation of the *versiera* and calls attention to two widely repeated errors about Agnesi: that she and/or her father taught at the University of Bologna and that she became a nun.

Kramer, Edna A. "Maria Gaetana Agnesi." In *Dictionary of Scientific Biography,* edited by C. C. Gillispie. Vol. 1, 75–77. New York: Charles Scribner's Sons, 1970.

Mistakenly reports that Agnesi's father was a professor at the University of Bologna, but is otherwise good.

Loria, Gino. *Curve piane speciali algebriche e transcendenti: Teoria e storia.* 2 vols. Milan: 1900.

See pp. 93–99 for the Curve of Agnesi.

Masotti, Arnaldo. "Maria Gaetana Agnesi." *Rendiconti del seminario matematico e fisico di Milano* 14 (1940): 89–127.

Updates Anzoletti's biography, without finding errors in it. The appendix (pp. 122–127) has an annotated list of the twenty-five volumes of manuscripts of Agnesi in the Biblioteca Ambrosiana (Milan).

Mulcrone, T. F. "The names of the curve of Agnesi." *American Mathematical Monthly* 64 (1957): 359–361.

Rebière, A. *Les femmes dans la science.* 2nd ed. Paris: Nony, 1897.

Mistakenly says that Agnesi joined an order of nuns, but is otherwise good.

Spencer, Roy C. "Properties of the witch of Agnesi—application to fitting the shapes of spectral lines." *Journal of the Optical Society of America* 30 (1940): 415–419.

States that the curve is "of importance to physicists because it approximates the spectral energy distribution of x-ray lines and optical lines, as well as the power dissipated in sharply tuned resonant circuits" (p. 416).

Tenca, Luigi. "La versiera di . . . Guido Grandi." *Bollettino dell'Unione Matematica Italiana* (3) 12 (1957): 458–460.

Thomas à Kempis, Sister Mary. "The walking polyglot." *Scripta Mathematica* 6 (1939): 211–217.

Pleasant hagiography; but despite a reference to Anzoletti's work, it apparently was not read, for the error that Agnesi and her father taught at the University of Bologna is again repeated.

NINA KARLOVNA BARI (1901–1961)

Joan Spetich and Douglas E. Cameron

BIOGRAPHY

Nina Karlovna Bari was born November 19, 1901, the daughter of Olga Ed-
uardovna and Karl Adolfovich Bari, a doctor. She attended L. O. Vyazemska's
private high school for girls, and it is said that even in those days she showed
great mathematical ability (Lyusternik 1970). In 1918 she passed the examination
for a boy's high school graduation certificate. She entered the Faculty of Physics
and Mathematics at Moscow State when it first reopened in 1918 after the
Revolution. Throughout its history the university had existed as an institution
of higher learning exclusively for men, but after the Revolution women were
allowed to enter.

The immediate post-Revolutionary years were a time of rapid growth for the
Moscow school of mathematics. But, more important, this was the era of "Luzitania." Luzitania was the nickname given to the group of students who clustered
around Nikolai Nikolaevich Luzin (1883–1950) in the early 1920s. The term
"Luzitania" arose in the autumn of 1920 (Lyusternik 1967, 58), when Luzin
shifted his main activities from Ivanovo-Voznesensk Polytechnic Institute (where
he and other members of the faculty had moved because of the war) back to
Moscow State.

The original Luzitanians were V. V. Stepanov (1889–1950), P. S. Alexandrov
(1896–1982), P. S. Urysohn (1898–1924), and Bari herself (Lyusternik 1967,
59). Many others, including L. A. Lyusternik, joined later. Luzitanians tended
to reject studying any area other than function theory (Luzin's specialty), and
many worshipped their leader. Bari was certainly not the least ardent among
them. While many of the others later broke the bond with Luzin and went on
to study other branches of mathematics, she made function theory the topic of
her life's research. It was as a student of Luzin that she first encountered the
uniqueness problem of trigonometric series, a study which would become the
main interest in her life's work.

The Luzitanians were a very close group socially as well as mathematically.

They often had parties, more often than not meeting in Luzin's apartment; and many times it was Bari who organized these events. They also took over a group known as the Students' Mathematics Circle. Luzin was made honorary president and Bari was elected vice-president. The group flourished under their leadership (Lyusternik 1967, 177) until the end of 1921.

Bari was clearly a very active and very good student, for she graduated from Moscow State in 1921 earlier than normal. In those difficult years following the Revolution, there were essentially no fixed examination periods; Bari chose to take her exams early. Because she was the first woman to enroll at Moscow State University, she was undoubtedly the first female graduate.

Most graduates at that time went into teaching; so did Bari. She lectured at the Moscow Forestry Institute (1921–1925), the Moscow Polytechnic Institute (1921–1923), and the Sverdlov Communist Institute (1921–1922). But shortly after she began teaching, Moscow State opened its Research Institute of Mathematics and Mechanics. Bari decided to continue her own schooling while teaching and became one of the first aspirants (research students) at the Research Institute. She was probably the first female research student at Moscow State (Lyusternik 1967, 79). In 1922 there were ten postgraduate students at the Research Institute, but only one official appointment was available. Since her last name was first in alphabetical order, the appointment was given to Bari. Although she received the only official stipend, she shared it equally with her fellow students (Lyusternik 1967, 183).

Under the tutelage of Luzin, Bari continued her research into current problems in the theory of trigonometric series. These problems dealt with the uniqueness of a trigonometric expansion for a function, and this area became her thesis topic. In 1922 she presented the main results of her research to the Moscow Mathematical Society; she was the first woman to deliver a lecture to the society (Lyusternik 1967, 80). In 1923 she published these results in her first research paper.

In 1925 Bari completed her postgraduate work and in January 1926 defended her thesis. The thesis contained solutions to several very difficult problems from the theory of trigonometric series. For her effort she was awarded the Glavnauk Prize. (Glavnauka was the acronym for the Central Administration of Scientific, Scholarly, Artistic and Museum Institutions, 1922–1930.) After receiving the equivalent of a Western Ph.D., she worked at Moscow State, first as a calculator, then as a research associate at the Institute of Mathematics and Mechanics.

In the spring of 1927, she was given the opportunity to study abroad. She spent six months studying and working at the Sorbonne and the Collège de France in Paris, and attended the seminars of Jacques Hadamard (1865–1963), "the leading French mathematician of this century" (Kline 1972, 703). Bari took an active role in Hadamard's seminars and was occasionally asked to give lectures.

The next stop in her travels was Lvov, Poland, where she attended the Polish Mathematical Congress in September 1927. In 1928 she went on to Bologna,

Italy, where she lectured at the International Congress of Mathematicians. She was then awarded a Rockefeller grant, which enabled her to continue studying in Paris until the end of 1929. In the midst of all this travel, Bari remained a faculty member at Moscow State. In 1932 she was made a full professor.

By 1935 Bari had established herself, through her lectures as well as sixteen published works, as a leading mathematician in the theory of functions of a real variable. In 1935 she was awarded the degree of Doctor of the Physical-Mathematical Sciences (a higher research degree than a Western Ph.D.).

By the 1940s she had also become a well-respected professor at Moscow State, and her clear, precise lectures were popular with undergraduate and research students alike. Together with D. E. Men'shov, she was in charge of all work done at the university in the area of function theory. Each year she directed various seminars and gave a course on a topic from the theory of functions.

During the 1950s Bari continued to teach at Moscow State University and to participate in various mathematical societies and seminars. She attended major mathematical events, such as the International Congress of Mathematicians in Edinburgh in 1958 (Bari and Men'shov 1959). She presented at the Third All-Union Congress in Moscow in 1956 a survey of the state of the theory of trigonometric series (Bari 1956, 1957).

Bari's energy did not diminish with the years, and her enthusiasm carried over to her students. Her popularity as a professor continued, and she was very successful in encouraging students in various areas of research.

Bari wrote a widely used textbook on the theory of series (1936 [2nd ed.], 1938), as well as one on higher algebra (1932). She also helped in the publication of various books and journals. She translated and edited Henri Lebesgue's *Lecons sur l'integration et la recherche de fonctions primitives;* and she edited a complete collection of the works of Luzin, as well as his book *Integral i trigonometricheskii ryad* (1951), adding several appendices. For some time she was editor-in-chief of the mathematical series of the journal *Uchenye Zapiski Moskovskogo Universiteta* and was also one of the editors of the journal *Vestnik Moskovskogo Universiteta.*

While mathematics was the center of Bari's life, it was certainly not her only interest. She loved literature and is said to have been very good at writing comic verse (Lyusternik 1967, 79). She found great pleasure in music, the ballet, and the arts in general, and on several occasions she acted as a judge at amateur art competitions. But her greatest hobby appears to have been a much more rugged pastime: she loved to hike in the mountains.

Her introduction to this sport was probably due to her husband, the distinguished Soviet mathematician Viktor Vladmirovich Nemytski. Nemytski, a year older than Bari, entered Moscow State as Bari graduated (1921), and he too eventually became a full professor there.

Nemytski was not only a great mathematician, he was also a great explorer of the mountains of the Soviet Union. One of the passes in the Caucasus was discovered by him and the mathematician A. N. Tikhonov and thus is named after them. Bari eventually became Nemytski's constant companion on these excursions. Information is not available as to when the two were married, although Lyusternik indicates that it was long after their student days at Moscow State (Lyusternik 1967, 79). Nevertheless, together they hiked in many of the country's mountains, including the Caucasus, Altai, Lamir, and Tyan'shan' ranges. Bari was very courageous on these hikes and often encouraged her companions when conditions were rough (Lyusternik 1967, 80). Shortly before her death, she completed a walking tour across Kamchatka, the farthest eastern region of the Soviet Union.

On July 15, 1961, a tragic accident took Bari's life. It has been reported that Bari was killed by falling in front of a train in the Moscow Metro. It is also reported that it was not an accident but a successful suicide attempt, brought on by despondency over the death ten years before of her teacher and reported lover, Luzin. She was not yet sixty years old. Her friend and colleague D. E. Men'shov and her former student P. L. Ul'yanov wrote (1962, 79–80):

The untimely death of N. K. Bari is a great loss for Soviet mathematics and a great misfortune for all who know her. The image of Bari as a lively, straightforward person with an inexhaustible reserve of cheerfulness will remain forever in the hearts of all who knew her.

WORK

In the early 1920s, when Bari was an undergraduate, a great transition was taking place in Soviet mathematics. Classical mathematics was giving way to more abstract areas of set theory, topology, abstract algebra, and, of course, function theory. Quite naturally there were those who opposed the new mathematics. They called it "philosophy" rather than mathematics, claiming that it had no application in the real world and that it existed only for the enjoyment of mathematicians themselves. The idea of wanting to know the characteristics of functions, sets, etc., seemed too introspective, and some laughingly called it "descriptive mathematics or mathematics for ladies" (Lyusternik 1967, 85).

The latter nickname was used in reference to the number of women members of Luzitania. But although it was meant as a derogatory title, Bari certainly showed that it was no insult. She was a master of this "descriptive mathematics" and lived to see it solve many concrete problems, including some famous ones from that period (Lyusternik 1967, 86).

Her ability in this type of mathematics came from her great talent for using the constructive method of proof. The constructive technique grew out of the school of function theory (Lyusternik 1967, 87). It was with this method, which she learned from Luzin, that Bari excelled.

During the 1920s Bari was interested in the uniqueness problem of trigonometric series. The basic question in her thesis is, Under what condition is a trigonometric development of a given function unique? From a 1916 work by D. E. Men'shov, she knew that such developments were not unique in general. In particular, she was searching for the necessary and sufficient conditions for a given nondense perfect set to be either an *M*-set or a *U*-set. An *M*-set (set of multiplicity) is a set for which there exists a trigonometric series, with not all coefficients zero, that converges to zero everywhere outside of the set. A *U*-set (set of uniqueness) is a set such that every trigonometric series that converges to zero everywhere outside of the set must have all zero coefficients. It was believed at the time that all uncountable sets of measure zero were *M*-sets. In 1921 Bari used constructive techniques to show the existence of a perfect *U*-set of measure zero (Bari 1923). Several years later she obtained some surprising results in this area ("Sur la nature . . . ," 1936, 1937).

She was considered an expert in the area of trigonometric series, and in 1949 she wrote a survey article on the uniqueness problem. The article has been the starting point for much research and has been a great aid in the training of young research students.

In 1952 Bari published an outstanding article on primitive functions and trigonometric series converging almost everywhere. A *primitive* of a function $f(x)$, defined on an interval $[a, b]$, is any continuous function $F(x)$ for which $F'(x) = f(x)$ almost everywhere on $[a, b]$. The purpose of the paper was to prove the following result: every function that is measurable and finite almost everywhere has a primitive whose Fourier series, differentiated term by term, converges to the function almost everywhere.

During the 1950s Bari continued her research in trigonometric series. The topic of interest during those years was subsequences converging everywhere to zero of partial sums of trigonometric series (Bari 1959, 1960). Bari also obtained major results in several other areas, most notably in the superpositions of absolutely continuous functions and functions of bounded variation, orthogonal systems, bases, biorthogonal systems, and in the approximation of functions.

At the time of her death, Bari had fifty-five publications. Her final publication, appropriately, was a 900-page monograph on her favorite topic, trigonometric series. In it she presented the state of the theory at that time. The range and depth of topics covered is quite extensive, and most of her work in the field is included. But even within so long a monograph, the subject could not be completely exhausted. Thus she notes in the preface that she has completely excluded any discussion of Fourier integrals or trigonometric series of several variables, and only briefly touches upon best approximations of functions by trigonometric polynomials and orthogonal systems. Other than these few omissions, the monograph covers all major areas in the theory of trigonometric series. It has become a standard reference for mathematicians specializing in the theory of functions and the theory of trigonometric series. It is a fitting culmination to a fine mathematical career.

BIBLIOGRAPHY

Works by Nina Karlovna Bari

Space does not permit a full listing of the works of N. K. Bari; Men'shov et al. (1962) give such a list. We give here references for works we have cited, together with updates on reprinting and translation of Bari's works.

Mathematical Works

"Sur l'unicité du developpement trigonométrique." *Comptes rendus hebdomadaires des séances de l'Académie des Sciences* 177 (1923): 1195–1197.

Vysshay algebra (Higher algebra). Isd. zauchnogo sektora Ped. in-ta im. V. I. Lenina, 1932.

"Sur la nature diophantique du problème d'unicité du developpement trigonométrique." *Comptes rendus hebdomadaires des séances de l'Académie des Sciences* 202 (1936): 1901–1903.

Teoriya ryadov (Theory of series). Moscow: Ushpedgiz., 1936. 2nd ed., 1938.

"Sur le rôle des lois diophantiques dans le problème d'unicité du developpement trigonométrique." *Matematicheskii Sbornik* 2 (44) (1937): 699–724.

"The uniqueness problem of the representation of functions by trigonometric series" (in Russian). *Uspekhi Matematicheskikh Nauk* 4 (3) (31) (1949): 3–68. Supplement, 7 (5) (51) (1952): 193–196. Translation: American Mathematical Society Translation no. 52 (1951).

(with V. V. Golubev) "Biography of N. N. Luzin" (in Russian). *Integral i trigonometricheskii ryad* (Integral and trigonometric series) by N. N. Luzin, 11–21. Moscow-Leningrad, 1951. Reprinted in *Collected Works* (in Russian) by N. N. Luzin, vol. 3, 468–483. Moscow: Izdat. Akad. Mauk SSSR, 1959. Reprinted in *Nikolai Nikolaevich Luzin: On the 100th Anniversary of His Birth* (in Russian), edited by P. I. Kuznetsov, 8–26. Novoe Zhizni Nauke Teklinike Seria "Matematika Kibernetika" No. 83. Moscow: "Znanie," 1983.

"On primitive functions and trigonometric series converging almost everywhere" (in Russian). *Matematicheskii Sbornik* 31 (73) (1952): 687–702.

"Trigonometric series" (in Russian). *Trudy III Vzesoyuznogo Matematicheskoga S'ezda* 2 (1956): 25–26.

"Trigonometric series" (in Russian). *Trudy III Vzesoyuznogo Matematicheskoga S'ezda* 3 (1957): 164–177.

"On subsequences convergent to zero of partial sums of a trigonometric series" (in Russian). *Doklady Akademii Nauk SSSR* 129 (1959): 482–483.

(with D. E. Men'shov) "On the international mathematical congress in Edinburgh" (in Russian). *Uspekhi Matematicheskikh Nauk* 14 (2) (1959): 235–238.

"Subsequences converging to zero everywhere of partial sums of trigonometric series" (in Russian). *Izvestiya Akademii Nauk SSSR. Seriya Matematika* 24 (1960): 531–548.

Trigonometricheskie ryady. Moscow: Gosudarstv. Izdat. Fiz. Mat. Lit., 1961. Authorized English translation by Margaret F. Mullins, under the title *A Treatise on Trigonometric Series*. 2 vols. New York: Macmillan, 1964.
Review: *Mathematical Reviews* 30 (1965): #1347.

Works about Nina Karlovna Bari

Lavrent'ev, M. A., and L. A. Lyusternik. "Nina Karlovna Bari" (in Russian). *Uspekhi Matematicheskikh Nauk* 6 (6) (46) (1951): 184–185.

Lyusternik, L. A. "The early years of the Moscow mathematical school" (in Russian). *Uspekhi Matematicheskikh Nauk* 22 (1) (133) (1967): 137–161; 22 (2) (134) (1967): 199–239; 22 (4) (136) (1967): 147–185; 25 (4) (154) (1970): 189–196. Translation. *Russian Mathematical Surveys* 22 (1) (1967): 133–157; 22 (2) (1967): 171–211; 22 (4) (1967): 55–91; 25 (4) (1970): 167–174.

Men'shov, D. E., S. B. Stechkin, and P. L. Ul'yanov. "Nina Karlovna Bari—Obituary" (in Russian). *Uspekhi Matematicheskikh Nauk* 17 (1) (103) (1962): 121–133. Translation by Roy O. Davies. *Russian Mathematical Surveys* 17 (1) (1962): 119–131.

Men'shov, D. E., and P. L. Ul'yanov. "Professor N. K. Bari: In memoriam" (in Russian). *Vestnik Moskovskogo Universiteta. Seriya I Matematika. Mekhanika* 1962 (1) (1962): 74–80.

Other References

Alexandrov, P. S., M. M. Vainberg, R. E. Vinograd, and B. P. Demidovich. "Viktor Vladimirovich Nemytskii—Obituary." *Russian Mathematical Surveys* 23 (2) (1968): 167–179.

Kline, M. *Mathematical Thought from Ancient to Modern Times.* New York: Oxford University Press, 1972.

RUTH AARONSON BARI (1917–   )

Florence D. Fasanelli

BIOGRAPHY

Ruth Aaronson Bari is the daughter of Polish immigrants, Israel Aaronson and Becky Gursky, who met shortly after their arrival in New York. "Isser" Aaronson had a religious education usual for Jewish boys in Poland at the Torah school; as a child, Becky Gursky had not been encouraged in her education. Aaronson worked for a wholesaler in butter and eggs and as a grocer; Mrs. Aaronson often worked in the family stores. Bari was born in Brooklyn on November 17, 1917. Her only sibling, Ethel, was born in 1921.

Bari attended several public schools in Brooklyn until the eighth grade, finishing at Bay Ridge High School. At that girls' school, the administrators did not feel that it was important to offer much mathematics. However, Bari's father was pleased at her interest in mathematics and sometimes would reason through algebra problems she brought home. As a senior Bari wanted a higher algebra course; she was given a book and told to read it without supervision. A medal was presented to her at graduation for excellence in mathematics.

Brooklyn College, at that time a small, fairly selective institution, where books and tuition were provided free, accepted Bari. She had always anticipated college education; in Jewish families of the time, it was felt that an education was important. Bari decided to study mathematics, which she liked, although she saw no prospects for employment in that field.

Since she attended college during the Depression years, Bari included a course in accounting in her program, thinking she could be a bookkeeper if no other work was available. After she graduated in 1939, she took graduate courses in the evening and worked as a summer playground director in Staten Island. During this period she met her future husband, Arthur Bari, a diamond setter who had studied engineering. She abandoned her coursework when she passed a civil service exam and worked as a statistical clerk in the 1940 census in Washington, D.C. She was married on November 22, 1940.

Bari went back to school, taking a master's degree at Johns Hopkins in 1943, where she was a junior instructor. Her chairman, Francis D. Mernghan, told Bari and Yaëla Naim (later Dowker) that they could continue for the Ph.D.; but since it was difficult to attract men toward advanced mathematics degrees during the war, he could not offer them any teaching work. The teaching was to attract men; he could offer Bari and Naim only paper grading, at $25 a month. Bari received another $25 a month from her husband, who was in the marines in the South Pacific; but the rent was $40. Unable to find any work in Baltimore (after writing many companies without reply), she was hired by Bell Telephone Laboratories in New York City as a technical assistant. There she made breadboard models of engineers' designs. When the job ended, the unemployment office in Baltimore set up an interview for her at the University of Maryland. Hired as an instructor there, she took a course in combinatorial topology. Although she was not officially a student, Professor D. W. Hall thought that she had promise and asked if she would like to write a thesis with him. However, being pregnant, she thought that the university would not allow her to go on as a teacher and a mother, so she resigned.

Gina, the first of her three daughters, was born in 1948, followed by Judi (1949) and Martha (1951). When the eldest was eight and the youngest four, so that all three were in school, Bari went back to Johns Hopkins University with the constant encouragement of her husband. She was able to reconcile her personal and professional life, in part because she preferred to stay up very late and could study while her family slept. When she resumed her studies in 1955, at age thirty-eight, Bari was placed on probation because of her twelve-year absence. After one year she became a regular degree candidate. In the 1960s she became a full-time instructor at the University of Maryland because the pay was better than that of a teaching assistant at Johns Hopkins.

Her thesis advisor was Daniel C. Lewis, who had done his Ph.D. with George Birkhoff. It took a long time to finish her thesis; all the while she worked full-time and took care of home and children. She received her Ph.D. in 1966.

In turn, she has patiently encouraged and advised three Ph.D. candidates at George Washington University, where she has been since 1966. The famous graph theorist Frank Harary termed her their "doctoral mother."

Bari sees her teaching as a valuable counterpart to research, for the lecturer must think through unfamiliar concepts and thus avoid stagnation. Similarly, activity in professional organizations is a source of stimulation. She chaired sessions of the American Mathematical Society in 1975 and 1981. In 1972 she was co-director of a conference in combinatorics at George Washington University, and in 1973 co-director of another. For the benefit of high school teachers, she directed in-service institutes for five years under National Science Foundation grants.

WORK

Bari's research has been recognized as influential, as typified by requests for her papers and invitations to speak at conferences in many countries. She spent two weeks at the University of Waterloo at the invitation of W. T. Tutte, where she spoke on "Chromatically equivalent graphs" and "Graphs with the same chromials." She also spoke at the Mathematical Institute at Oxford in 1974, in Cambridge in 1982, and in Denmark in June 1985. Harary has called her the world expert on chromatic polynomials. She showed how broken circuits and broken cocircuits could be used to define and compute the chromatic polynomial from the Tutte polynomial, using Whitney's theorem on broken circuits.

Homomorphism polynomials originated with Bari while speaking to Alan Hoffman of Yale University. He asked the question: Can you find the achromatic number of a graph from the chromatic polynomial? The answer was no, but Bari realized that it may be useful to construct a polynomial to give the result. She experimented with this idea, finally concluding that with each graph we may associate a polynomial, the homomorphism polynomial, which counts all the homomorphisms and determines the chromatic number and achromatic number.

BIBLIOGRAPHY

Works by Ruth Aaronson Bari

Mathematical Works

"Absolute reducibility of maps of at most 19 regions." Ph.D. diss., The Johns Hopkins University, 1966.

"The four leading coefficients of the chromatic polynomials $Q_n(u)$ and $R_n(x)$ and the Birkhoff-Lewis conjecture." In *Recent Progress in Combinatorics*, edited by W. T. Tutte, 217–219. New York: Academic Press, 1969.

"Coefficients of u^{n-5} and u^{n-6} in the Q-chromial $Q_n(u)$." *Annals of the New York Academy of Sciences* 175 (1970): 25–31.

"Maximal m-gons in 4-regular major maps." In *Recent Trends in Graph Theory*, edited by M. Capobianco et al., 5–8. New York: Springer-Verlag, 1971.

"Regular major maps of at most 19 regions and their Q-chromials." *Journal of Combinatorial Theory* B 12 (1972): 132–142.

"Minimal regular major maps with proper 4-rings." In *Graph Theory and Applications*, edited by Y. Alavi and A. T. White, 13–20. New York: Springer-Verlag, 1972.

"Chromatically equivalent graphs." In *Graphs and Combinatorics*, edited by R. A. Bari and F. Harary, 186–200. New York: Springer-Verlag, 1974.

(edited with F. Harary) *Graphs and Combinatorics*. New York: Springer-Verlag, 1974.

"Recent results on chromatically equivalent graphs." *Annals of the New York Academy of Sciences* 319 (1977): 37–46.

(with D. W. Hall) "Chromatic polynomials and Whitney's broken circuits." *Journal of Graph Theory* 1 (1977): 269–275.

"Chromatic polynomials and the internal and external activities of Tutte." In *Graph Theory and Related Topics*, edited by J. A. Bondy and U.S.R. Murty, 41–52. New York: Academic Press, 1979.

"A combinatorial approach to graphical polynomials and spanning subgraphs." *Annals of the New York Academy of Sciences* 328 (1979): 21–29.

"Homomorphism polynomials of graphs." *Journal of Combinatorics, Information &
     System Sciences* 7 (1982): 56–64.
"Line graphs and their chromatic polynomials." In *Graph Theory*, edited by Bela Bol-
     lobás, 15–21. Annals of Discrete Mathematics 13. New York: North-Holland,
     1982.

Works about Ruth Aaronson Bari

Harary, Frank. "Academic Roots." *The Mathematical Intelligencer* 7 (1) (1985): 7.

DOROTHY LEWIS BERNSTEIN (1914–   )

Ann Moskol

BIOGRAPHY

Dorothy Lewis Bernstein, born on April 11, 1914, in Chicago, Illinois, was the eldest child of Jacob and Tillie Lewis Bernstein. Bernstein's parents were poor Jewish Russian emigrants who had no formal education, but who encouraged all of their four daughters and one son to seek education; Bernstein's father even remortgaged the family house to help pay for her undergraduate education. Of the five children, four earned Ph.D.'s and the fifth an M.D. degree.

Bernstein attended North Division High School, a public school in Milwaukee, Wisconsin, and entered the University of Wisconsin at Madison in 1930. She intended to major in journalism but was encouraged by Professor Mark Ingraham to take mathematics courses. Bernstein decided to major in mathematics and spent her junior and senior year in Wisconsin under the system of advanced independent study. Under this plan, Bernstein studied mathematics on her own, attending lectures and conferring with department members as she wished; she took no exams and received no grades. During 1933–1934 she held a University Scholarship and was elected to Phi Beta Kappa. In 1934, at the age of twenty, Bernstein, on the basis of her thesis and comprehensive examination, received both a B.A. degree, summa cum laude, and an M.A. degree in mathematics.

In 1934–1935 Bernstein did further graduate work at the University of Wisconsin and taught freshmen as a University Fellow. In 1935 she obtained a scholarship to attend Brown University, where she taught and studied for the next two years. While at Brown Bernstein became a member of the scientific society Sigma Xi. After a year at Brown, she took her Ph.D. qualifying examination, a grueling eight-hour (two afternoons) oral examination conducted by the entire mathematics faculty. Although she passed, she later discovered that some of her fellow graduate students had examinations that lasted only two and a half hours. When she asked her advisor, J. D. Tamarkin, about this, he admitted that her examination was extra long because she was a woman and because she had taken most of her courses at a midwestern university.

While at Brown Bernstein experienced other examples of prejudice against females in mathematics. The mathematics chairman, C. R. Adams, forbade her to teach male students because he felt that they would never tolerate being taught by a woman instructor. As a result, she taught only three female students, while Hugh Hamilton, a male graduate student, taught the same course to forty-five male students. When Bernstein was looking for a teaching job, she asked advice from Roland G.D. Richardson, who was dean of the Brown Graduate School and secretary of the American Mathematical Society (AMS) for many years; he took out a map of the United States and told her she could not get a job west of the Mississippi because she was a woman, and she could not teach south of the Ohio River because she was Jewish. That advice made her so angry that she attended the spring AMS meeting; after numerous inquiries, she learned about a job at Mount Holyoke College, which she later obtained. When Bernstein told Richardson that she got a college teaching position at Mount Holyoke, he was miffed because he had intended that job for Hamilton.

Bernstein was an instructor at Mount Holyoke from 1937 to 1940. Although she taught full-time, she continued to do research and received her Ph.D. from Brown in 1939. In 1941 Bernstein returned to Wisconsin as an instructor and worked with Stan Ulam on general integration and measure theory. In June 1942, after the United States had entered World War II, Bernstein became a research associate to Jerzy Neyman at the Statistical Laboratory of the University of California at Berkeley. There she worked on theoretical problems in probability and taught a graduate course in probability theory.

In 1943 Bernstein began teaching at the University of Rochester, where she stayed until 1959. During that time she taught both undergraduate and graduate courses, directed several Ph.D. and master's theses, rose to full professor, and was acting chairman of the mathematics department during 1955–1957. Bernstein spent sabbatical years at the Institute for Advanced Study in Princeton (1950) and at the Institute for Numerical Analysis at UCLA (1957).

In 1959 Bernstein was appointed professor of mathematics at Goucher College, where she remained until her retirement in 1979. She was chairman of the mathematics department for most of that time. She spent sabbatical years at Brown University (1966 and fall 1973) and at the University of Tennessee (spring 1974).

WORK

Bernstein's major research interests were in applied mathematics. She did her master's thesis research on finding complex roots of polynomials by an extension of Newton's method. In her Ph.D. thesis, she studied the Laplace integral for functions of two variables. While she found that some of the results were direct generalizations of the one-variable theory, other results were quite different. The problem had many ramifications for functions of several complex variables, functions of bounded variation in higher dimensions, and partial differential equations.

When Bernstein was at the University of Rochester, she worked on existence theorems in partial differential equations at the request of C. B. Tompkins of Engineering Research Associates, who held a contract for this work from the Office of Naval Research (ONR). After World War II, the ONR was especially concerned about the computational power of digital computers for solving complex partial differential equations. Bernstein's careful analysis of theorems included concise formulation of the various boundary problems, clarification of hypotheses under which the solutions held, and specification of the regions where the solutions were valid. In 1950 Princeton University Press published her results in *Existence Theorems in Partial Differential Equations*.

Bernstein gave numerous mathematical talks at universities and conferences throughout the United States. She refereed papers for various journals and served on the editorial board of the *Two Year College Mathematics Journal*.

As chairman of the mathematics department of Goucher College, Bernstein was instrumental in revising the mathematics curriculum to include the use of computers and applications of mathematics. Under Bernstein's leadership, Goucher was one of the first women's colleges to use computers in instruction. In 1961 Goucher received a National Science Foundation (NSF) grant to purchase an IBM 1620 computer. Bernstein, who served as director of Goucher's computer center for six years (1961–1967), introduced computer programming into her statistics courses. She believed that applied mathematics not only made material more relevant to students, but it also motivated them to understand the axioms and theorems of pure mathematics, which could then be used in applied problems. To this end she incorporated applications into her courses and encouraged her faculty to follow her lead.

To provide students with practical work experience, Bernstein developed an internship program. During Goucher's four-week January term, mathematics students worked in companies that were carefully selected to give them meaningful employment experience.

Bernstein was concerned with maintaining high standards and preparing students for possible graduate work in mathematics. She was also interested in helping integrate the computer into secondary school mathematics. In 1968 Bernstein directed an NSF grant to help teach programming to local high school students. Under another NSF grant in 1969, Bernstein directed a summer institute which taught secondary school teachers how to incorporate the computer into statistics and calculus courses. In 1972 she helped found the Maryland Association for Educational Use of Computers and served on its board of directors until 1975.

Although Bernstein belonged to a variety of professional societies, including the AMS, the Society for Industrial and Applied Mathematics, and the American Association of University Professors, she was particularly active in the Mathematical Association of America (MAA). Bernstein was especially concerned that few women were represented on MAA committees, and she worked hard to remedy that problem. She served on numerous committees herself. As chairman of the buildings site committee in 1975, Bernstein was instrumental in finding a permanent home for the MAA in Washington, D.C. Bernstein was on the board of governors (1965–1968) and served as first vice-president (1972–1973). From 1979 to 1981 she was president, the first woman elected to that office.

BIBLIOGRAPHY

Works by Dorothy Lewis Bernstein

Mathematical Works

"The double Laplace integral." *Duke Mathematical Journal* 8 (1941): 460–496.
    Doctoral thesis.
Existence Theorems in Partial Differential Equations. Annals of Mathematics Studies,
    no. 23. Princeton, N.J.: Princeton University Press, 1950.
(with Geraldine A. Coon) "Some properties of the double Laplace transformation."
    Transactions of the American Mathematical Society 74 (1953): 135–176.
———. "Some general formulas for double Laplace transformations." *Proceedings of
    the American Mathematical Society* 14 (1963): 52–59.
———. "On the zeros of a class of exponential polynomials." *Journal of Mathematical
    Analysis and Applications* 11 (1965): 205–212.
"The role of applications in pure mathematics." *American Mathematical Monthly* 86
    (1979): 245–253.

Works about Dorothy Lewis Bernstein

Bernstein, Dorothy L. Transcript of panel address. In "Women mathematicians before
    1950." *Association for Women in Mathematics Newsletter* 9 (4) (July–August
    1979): 9–11.
Coon, Geraldine A. "Coon on Bernstein." *Goucher Quarterly* 57 (Fall 1979): 16–17.
    A short summary of Bernstein's life, written at the time of her retirement by a
    Goucher colleague.

GABRIELLE-ÉMILIE LE TONNELIER DE BRETEUIL, MARQUISE DU CHÂTELET (1706–1749)

Garry J. Tee

BIOGRAPHY

Gabrielle-Émilie Le Tonnelier de Breteuil, the marquise du Châtelet (to be referred to as Châtelet), was born at Paris, France, on December 17, 1706. Her mother was Gabrielle Anne de Froulay, daughter of a French noble of the sword; and her father was Louis-Nicolas Le Tonnelier de Breteuil, baron of Preuilly, who was the chief of protocol at the French court. He was a powerful official and one of the effective rulers of France. He recognized his daughter's intellect, and he engaged tutors who trained her in many languages and also in mathematics, which became her major interest.

In 1725 she married Florent-Claude, the marquis du Châtelet and count of Lomont, who was then aged thirty. He was then governor of the city of Semur-en-Auxois, and the couple spent five years there. He was a bluff and amiable military man; after he became a regimental colonel in 1730, he concentrated his interests on his regiment and visited his wife only occasionally. During that period she bore two children: Gabrielle-Pauline in 1726 and Louis-Marie-Florent in 1727.

In 1730 Châtelet returned to Paris, where she led a gay life in the frivolous high society of the French capital. After the birth of her third child, Victor-Esprit, in 1733, she settled down, at the age of twenty-seven, to the serious study of mathematics. She became a close friend of the mathematician Alexis Claude Clairaut, who was an important supporter of the physics of Isaac Newton against that of Descartes, which was still fashionable in France. Her principal lover at that period was the physicist Pierre Louis Moreau de Maupertuis (1698–1759), who was another powerful supporter of Newton.

Voltaire (1694–1778) had been exiled in England from 1726 to 1729 for insulting a young nobleman. He went to England as a poet and returned to France as a philosopher, worshipping the achievement of Newton. In 1733 he met Châtelet, and they quickly announced their love. Châtelet declared that she was planning to spend the rest of her life with Voltaire, which she did (although she still continued ardently to pursue Maupertuis). The marquis was well satisfied to have such a uniquely distinguished man as his wife's acknowledged lover, and when the marquis visited her, he was happy to dine with her children while she and Voltaire continued their philosophical discussions over dinner.

Châtelet was handsome rather than beautiful, and richly dressed rather than elegant; but Voltaire compared her mind with that of Newton, master of his thought. His *Mémoires* begin by reporting their meeting, which he regarded as the turning-point of his life. She directed him to a serious study of metaphysics and a critical study of religion. She guided him in studying the physics of Leibniz and of Newton. He made her an ardent Anglophile, and they frequently conversed in English.

Voltaire was frequently in danger of being arrested, and in June 1734 he withdrew to the marquis's isolated estate of Cirey in Champagne. Châtelet soon joined Voltaire there, and he rebuilt the decayed mansion. They remained there for most of the rest of her life, with occasional periods in Paris, Versailles, Brussels, and Lunéville. She became renowned throughout Europe as Voltaire's love Émilie. They made their philosophical retreat at Cirey into one of the important intellectual centers of Europe, admired greatly by their few visitors, and the target of much malicious gossip. They studied intensely and wrote prodigiously. They jointly studied the Bible and wrote skeptical commentaries, which were of course unpublishable.

In 1735 Francesco Algarotti visited Cirey. He was writing *Il newtoniasmo per le dame*, an elementary account of Newton's optics, which was first published in 1737. His work inspired Voltaire, assisted by Châtelet, to write *Éléments de la philosophie de Newton*, which was published in 1738.

In 1748 Châtelet acquired a new young lover, the Marquis J. F. de Saint-Lambert, and she became pregnant again at the age of forty-two. Both she and her lover agreed ruefully with Voltaire's remark that their child would have to be listed under her "miscellaneous works" (Mitford 1957, 257). She dedicated herself to completing her edition of Newton and made arrangements for it to be published if she should not live. At the palace at Lunéville on September 2, 1749, she was sitting at her desk and writing on Newtonian theory when she suddenly gave birth to a daughter (Mitford 1957, 269). Châtelet appeared to be making an excellent recovery, but on September 10, 1749, she died very suddenly. Voltaire, her lover, and her husband were all heartbroken by the unexpected tragedy.

Her edition of Newton was finally published in 1759, with the assistance of Clairaut and with a eulogistic preface by Voltaire. It was reprinted in 1966, and it remains the only French translation of Isaac Newton's *Philosophiae naturalis principia mathematica*.

WORK

When Châtelet began her scientific studies, Cartesian philosophy was favored by most French philosophers, and Newton had few supporters in Europe. She collaborated with Voltaire in writing the *Éléments de la Philosophie de Newton* (1738), and she published her "Lettre sur les élémens de la philosophie de Newton" in 1738 as a defense of the treatment of Newtonian attraction in the *Éléments*, against criticism from followers of Leibniz.

In 1736 the Académie des Sciences organized a prize contest on the nature of fire, and Châtelet and Voltaire independently submitted memoirs. The prize was awarded in 1738 to Leonhard Euler and two minor writers, but Voltaire arranged for the memoirs by Châtelet and himself to be published in 1739, with the three prize-winning memoirs. Those memoirs by Châtelet and by Voltaire are of interest mainly for demonstrating that, in eighteenth-century Europe, the role of air in combustion could be overlooked even by highly intelligent scientists.

Châtelet began to write a textbook of physics for her son, and in 1739, assisted by Samuel König, she made a careful study of Leibniz's physics. As a consequence, she became much more appreciative of Leibniz's views than she had been. In 1740 she dismayed Voltaire by publishing her textbook of physics on Leibnizian principles, *Institutions de physique*. That book gave a careful and detailed historical and philosophical account of physics, and it was acclaimed as an extraordinarily lucid exposition of Leibniz's physics. Four editions of her book were published, but Voltaire considered that she had wasted her time by expounding Leibniz's ideas rather than those of Newton. She engaged in an extensive debate about Leibniz's concept of *vis viva* (Σmv^2) with Euler, Maupertuis, Clairaut, Willem J. S. van s'Gravesande, Petrus van Musschenbroek, Jean d'Ortous de Mairan, and other leading physicists.

In the controversy over *vis viva*, although she was unable to resolve the problem, she did play a significant role in directing the attention of many scientists to the importance of that concept. A detailed account of the controversy over *vis viva*, including the role of Châtelet, was given by J. F. Montucla ([1802] 1966, 637–640).

Her book *Institutions de physique* (1740) remains one of the clearest accounts of Leibnizian physics, rejecting Newton's concept of action at a distance. Her commentary on the Bible, the *Examen de la Genèse*, circulated clandestinely in manuscript copies, as did other unorthodox works on theology before the French Revolution.

After the publication of *Institutions de physique*, she returned to Newtonian physics. From 1745 her major efforts were devoted to translating Newton's *Philosophiae naturalis principia mathematica* from Latin into French. She provided a detailed commentary, inspired by that provided by François Jacquier and Thomas Leseur for their Latin edition (1739). She provided extensive supplements, derived largely from works of Clairaut. In 1746 Clairaut became her consultant and advisor, and the printing of her translation was commenced. But Clairaut became concerned over difficulties in the theory of the motion of the moon, which suggested to him that Newton's theory of universal gravitation might require modification. Accordingly, from 1747 until 1749, he advised caution over completing the commentaries.

Her major work was her translation of Newton's *Philosophiae naturalis principia mathematica,* which made the Newtonian system accessible to French readers. The second volume contains her commentary, in two parts. The first part (pp. 1–116) is an exposition of the system of the world according to Newton's principles. It is effectively a version of the *Éléments de la philosophie de Newton,* rewritten after she had attained much deeper insight into Newton's ideas. After a historical introduction on the development of understanding of the structure of the solar system, there are chapters on:

1. The principal phenomena of the system of the world
2. The success of Newton's theory in explaining the major planetary phenomena
3. The shape of the Earth, according to Newton's principles
4. Newton's explanation of the precession of the equinoxes
5. The ebb and flow of the tides
6. Newton's explanation of the motion of planetary satellites, and in particular of the moon.

The second part of volume 2 (pp. 117–280) is devoted to analytical solutions of some major problems concerning the system of the world, based largely on work by Clairaut. The complicated bibliographic history of her version of Newton's masterpiece, with preliminary publication in 1756, full publication in 1759, and a modified edition in 1966, has been analyzed by I. Bernard Cohen.

Châtelet had a strong influence on Voltaire, guiding his studies of metaphysics, biblical criticism, and the physics of Newton and of Leibniz. Her publications and her correspondence contributed significantly to the development of scientific thought in Europe. Her flamboyant personal life provided entertaining material for gossip throughout Europe, yet her actions at the end of her life demonstrated her sincere dedication to science.

Although she was not a creator of original science, her work of translation, commentary, and synthesis was a valuable contribution to the triumph of Newtonian science in the eighteenth century.

BIBLIOGRAPHY

Works by Châtelet

Mathematical and Physical Works

de Voltaire, F. M. *Éléments de la philosophie de Newton.* Paris, 1738. Translated by John Hanna, under the title *The Elements of Sir Isaac Newton's Philosophy.* London, 1738. Facsimile reprint. London: Cass, 1967.
    Châtelet collaborated with Voltaire on this work.

"Lettre sur les élémens de la philosophie de Newton." *Journal des sçavans* (September 1738): 534–541.

Dissertation sur la nature et la propagation du feu. Paris, 1739 and 1744. Reprinted in *Recueil de pièces qui ont remporté le prix de l'Académie royale des sciences....* Vol. 4. Paris, 1752.

Institutions de physique. Paris, 1740. London, 1741. Revised edition. Amsterdam, 1742. Italian translation. Venice, 1743.

Reponse de Madame... à la lettre que M. de Mairan... lui a écrite... sur la question des forces vives. Brussels, 1741. New edition, with author's name. Brussels, 1741 and 1744.

"Mémoire touchant les forces vives adressé en forme de lettre à M. Jurin...." In *Memorie sopra la fisica & istoria naturale....* Edited by C. Giuliani. Vol. 3, 75–84. Lucca, 1747.

Principes mathématiques de la philosophie naturelle. Preliminary edition. Paris, 1756. Full publication. 2 vols. Paris, 1759. Modified edition. 2 vols. Paris: Albert Blanchard, 1966.

"Réflexions sur le bonheur." In *Opuscules philosophiques et littéraires.* Edited by J.-B. Suard and J. Bourlet de Vauxcelles, 1–40. Paris, 1796. Critical edition by R. Manzi. Paris, 1961.

T. Besterman, ed. *Les lettres de la marquise du Châtelet.* 2 vols. Geneva: Institut Voltaire, 1958.

Works about Châtelet

Cohen, I. Bernard. "The French translation of Isaac Newton's Philosophiae Naturalis Principia Mathematica (1756, 1759, 1966)." *Archives internationales d'histoire des sciences* 21 (1968): 261–290.

Mitford, Nancy. *Voltaire in Love.* London: Hamish Hamilton, 1957.

Detailed and sympathetic biography of Châtelet, concentrated on her association with Voltaire. Based on published material and manuscripts, including some unpublished letters by Voltaire.

Montucla, J. F. *Histoire des mathématiques.* 2nd ed. Vol. 3, 637–640. Paris: Henri Agasse, An 10 (May 1802). Facsimile reprint. Paris: Albert Blanchard, 1966.

Newton, Isaac. *Isaac Newton's Philosophiae naturalis principia mathematica.* The third edition (1726) with variant readings. Assembled and edited by Alexander Koyré and I. Bernard Cohen, with the assistance of Anne Whitman. Vol. 2, 876–881. Cambridge, England: Cambridge University Press, 1972.

Analyzes the complicated bibliographic history of Châtelet's version.

Wade, Ira O. *Voltaire and Mme. du Châtelet; an Essay on the Intellectual Activity at Cirey.* Princeton: Princeton University Press, 1941. Facsimile edition. New York: Octagon Books, 1967.

Presents evidence that Châtelet played a much more significant role in Voltaire's intellectual development than previous writers suggested.

Walters, R. L. "Mme du Châtelet and Leibnizianism. The genesis of the *Institutions de physique.*" *Studies on Voltaire and the Eighteenth Century* 58 (1967): 1807–1827.

GERTRUDE MARY COX (1900–1978)

Maryjo Nichols

BIOGRAPHY

Gertrude Mary Cox was born on January 13, 1900, in Dayton, Iowa. She was the daughter of John William Allen and Emmaline (Maddy) Cox. She graduated from Perry High School, Perry, Iowa, in 1918 and spent several years preparing to become a deaconess in the Methodist Episcopal Church, including some time caring for children in a Montana orphanage. But in 1925 she entered Iowa State College in Ames, where she received her B.S. in 1929 and, in 1931, the first master's degree in statistics given by the department of mathematics. Her work at Iowa State was guided by George W. Snedecor, who had recognized the need for better statistical methods to deal with the practical problems of agricultural research.

Cox was a graduate student at the University of California (Berkeley) from 1931 to 1933, where she studied psychological statistics. In 1933 Snedecor asked her to be his assistant in his new Statistical Laboratory at Iowa State, the first statistical center of its kind in the United States. Cox worked there until 1939, when she became an assistant professor at Iowa State. Her teaching and consulting duties were so extensive that she was unable to find time to write a dissertation. But at its centennial celebration on March 22, 1958, Iowa State conferred on Cox the honorary degree of Doctor of Science. In presenting the award, Iowa State's dean said, "Her influence is worldwide, contributing to the development of national and international organizations, publications, and councils of her field. One of our graduates, she has helped to build the accomplishments of our first century."

In October 1940, Cox accepted the newly created position of head of the department of experimental statistics at North Carolina State College in Raleigh. The search committee had asked Snedecor for his recommendations, and he had replied, after naming several statisticians, " . . . but if you would consider a woman for this position I would recommend Gertrude Cox of my staff." L. D. Bavor, director of the Agricultural Experiment Station, had arranged for North

Carolina State to train the staff of the Crop Reporting Service of the United States Department of Agriculture (USDA) in statistics. Three qualifications made Cox the ideal person to head this program: her training in psychology, her work for the M.S. degree under Professor Snedecor, and her experience in the Statistical Laboratory.

Cox also turned out to be the ideal choice for this new program because she managed to get sizable grants from the General Education Board for a program in statistics. She also organized the department of experimental statistics, with programs in training and in consulting. Her first faculty included Jack Rigney, Richard L. Anderson, and Al L. Finkner.

In 1941 Cox organized a summer session in Raleigh, North Carolina. Some of the people who attended this session later led in developing programs in statistics throughout the South. The participants included Harold Hotelling of Columbia, C. I. Bliss of Yale, and Snedecor. Hotelling later joined Cox at North Carolina in 1946.

In 1945 Cox organized and became director of the Institute of Statistics, which combined the teaching of statistics at the University of North Carolina under Hotelling and at North Carolina State College under W. G. Cochran. The university taught the courses in statistical theory and the state college taught the courses in methodology.

Cox organized a series of work conferences on such topics as plant science, quality control, agricultural economics, animal sciences, plant genetics, and taste testing; and she sponsored two summer conferences in the mountains of North Carolina (Junaluska in 1946 and Blue Ridge in 1952). These conferences established the Institute of Statistics as an international center for statistics.

However, Cox believed that the main objective for the institute was to develop strong statistical programs throughout the South, referred to as "spreading the gospel according to St. Gertrude." She persuaded the Southern Regional Education Board to establish a committee on statistics, and this committee decided that its job was (1) to develop a series of summer sessions to upgrade the basic level of statistical competence in the South; (2) to provide consulting help; and (3) to encourage the development of more statistics departments in the South. One of the most important outcomes of this committee has been a camaraderie among southern statisticians.

In 1960 Cox resigned from the university to become director of the Statistics Section of the Research Triangle Institute in Durham, North Carolina, where she remained until 1964. She died of leukemia in Durham on October 17, 1978.

WORK

When Cox was working at the Statistical Laboratory at Iowa State College, she established herself as an expert in the design of experiments. She and Cochran assembled a collection of mimeographed notes and expanded it into *Experimental*

Designs (1950), recognized as the classic textbook on design and analysis of replicated experiments.

Cox believed that the faculty at the Institute of Statistics should be free to pursue their academic and scientific interests, and therefore she raised needed money and developed appropriate administrative procedures. Graduate programs originated from ties with the Agricultural Experiment Station at Raleigh and the USDA in Washington. Research ranged from statistical genetics to multivariate analysis.

After her retirement from the Research Triangle Institute in 1964, she served as a consultant for the development of statistical programs in Egypt and Thailand, and as a consultant to government agencies, trade associations, and other groups.

Cox was the recipient of the Oliver Max Gardner award in 1959 and the distinguished service award of Gamma Sigma Delta in 1960. She was a member of the American Association for the Advancement of Science and the American Statistical Association, and president of the latter in 1956. She was one of the founders of the Biometrics Society in 1947 and editor of the *Biometrics Bulletin* and *Biometrics* from 1945 until 1955. She was an honorary member of the Biometrics Society and its president in 1969–1970; her vision and energetic dedication are credited with helping it become a viable organization. She was a fellow of the Institute of Mathematical Statistics and the American Public Health Association, and an honorary fellow of the Royal Statistical Society. She was a member of the International Statistical Institute and its treasurer from 1955 to 1961. She was honorary president of the Statistical Society of the Union of South Africa and an honorary member of the Société Adolphe Quetelet of Brussels, Belgium.

BIBLIOGRAPHY

Works by Gertrude Mary Cox

Statistical Works

"The multiple factor theory in terms of common elements." *Psychometrika* 4 (1939): 59–68.

"Enumeration and construction of balanced incomplete block configurations." *Annals of Mathematical Statistics* 11 (1940): 72–85.

(with R. C. Eckhardt and W. G. Cochran) "The analysis of lattice and triple lattice experiments in corn varietal tests." *Iowa Agricultural Experiment Station Research Bulletin* 281 (1940): 1–66. Reprinted in *Contributions to Statistics* by William G. Cochran, 20.1–20.66. New York: Wiley, 1982.

(with H. McKay) "Length of the observation period as a factor in variability in calcium retentions." *Journal of Home Economics* 34 (1942): 679–681.

"Statistics as a tool for research." *Journal of Home Economics* 36 (1944): 575–580.

"Opportunities for teaching and research." *Journal of the American Statistical Association* 40 (1945): 71–74.

(with W. G. Cochran) "Designs of greenhouse experiments for statistical analysis." *Soil Science* 62 (1946): 87–98. Reprinted in *Contributions to Statistics* by William G. Cochran, 36.87–36.98. New York: Wiley, 1982.

"A proposed statistical plan for the Southeastern States." *Proceedings of the Auburn Conference of Statistical Applications Research in Social Science, Plant Science and Animal Science* (1948): 26–36.

"Experimental designs (1) A survey of types of experimental designs." *Biometrics* 6 (1950): 301–302.

"The function of designs of experiments." *Annals of the New York Academy of Science* 52 (1950): 800–807.

"Organization and functions of the Institute of Statistics of the University of North Carolina." *Journal of the Royal Statistical Society* Series B 12 (1950): 1–18.

(with W. G. Cochran) *Experimental Designs.* New York: Wiley, 1950. 2nd ed., 1957.

"Elements of an effective inter-American training program in agricultural statistics." *Estadística* 11 (1953): 120–128.

"Statistical frontiers." *Journal of the American Statistical Association* 52 (1957): 1–12.

(with W. S. Connor) "Methodology for estimating reliability." *Annals of the Institute of Statistical Mathematics* 16 (1964): 55–67.

(with Paul G. Homeyer) "Professional and personal glimpses of George W. Snedecor." *Biometrics* 31 (1975): 265–301.

Works about Gertrude Mary Cox

Anderson, R. L. "My experience as a statistician from the farm to the university." In *The Making of Statisticians,* edited by J. Gani, 129–148. New York: Springer-Verlag, 1982.

Anderson, R. L., et al. "Gertrude M. Cox—A modern pioneer in statistics." *Biometrics* 35 (1979): 3–7.

Cochran, William G. "Gertrude Mary Cox 1900–1978." *International Statistical Review* 47 (1) (April 1979): 97–98.

———. "Some reflections." *Biometrics* 35 (1979): 1–2.

"Gertrude Mary Cox—1900–1978." *Biometrics* 34 (4) (1978): 718–720.

Harshbarger, Boyd. "History of the early developments of modern statistics in America (1920–1944)." In *On the History of Statistics and Probability,* edited by D. B. Owen, 131–145. New York: Dekker, 1976.

Monroe, Robert J., and Francis E. McVay. "Gertrude Mary Cox (1900–1978)." *American Statistician* 34 (1) (1980): 48.

Rao, Poduri S.R.S., and Joseph Sedransk, eds. *W. G. Cochran's Impact on Statistics.* New York: Wiley, 1984.
    Contributions by Richard L. Anderson (pp. 121–160) and Nell Sedransk (pp. 161–188) on Cox's collaboration with Cochran on their book.

Yates, Frank. "Obituary: Gertrude Mary Cox (1900–1978)." *Journal of the Royal Statistical Society,* Series A 142 (1979): 516–517.

KÄTE FENCHEL (1905–1983)

Else Høyrup

BIOGRAPHY

Käte Fenchel was born December 21, 1905, in Berlin. Her father, Otto Sperling, worked in the public relations department of a newspaper publishing house, and her mother, Rusza, born Angress, was a bookkeeper. Fenchel had a sister who was a year older than she. Their mother left their father when Fenchel was a few years old, and they met him seldom after that. Fenchel spent most of her childhood and youth during the war, postwar, and inflation periods, and her family was poor, like almost everybody else.

As a child, Fenchel was not interested in playing with dolls. She learned to read and write by herself during her sister's first year in school. She skipped first grade, and for six years, the sisters were classmates in a private girls' school, where they studied on scholarships. Afterwards, Fenchel went to high school for six years. She studied Latin, modern languages, mathematics, and physics. Her mother, who herself had felt the need of a better education, encouraged the two girls to study, both in school and later on. Fenchel did well in school, but she was not at the top. In high school she liked mathematics and decided to become a mathematician.

From 1924 to 1928 she studied mathematics, philosophy, and physics at the University of Berlin. She was supported by a schoolmate's father. Her main interest was pure mathematics. At the Mathematics Institute of the University of Berlin, there were three professors in pure mathematics and one in applied mathematics. Each had an assistant, and one of those was a woman. A few other women were studying there. Fenchel found the atmosphere very friendly, and she felt no discrimination against women. Later, however, when a gifted woman friend received no job offers, Fenchel wondered whether the friend was being discriminated against because of her sex. Subsequently, Fenchel also experienced discrimination against herself because she was a woman.

She was asked to write a thesis but could not afford to continue her studies; furthermore, it would be difficult to get a research job afterwards. Instead, for the next two years, she supplemented her theoretical education with pedagogical training, qualifying herself as a high school teacher. In 1931 she got a high school job, and for two years she taught mathematics and liked it.

In 1933 Hitler came to power, and the Nazis started racial persecutions. Fenchel was dismissed from her job because she was a Jew. Later, in the 1950s, West Germany passed a "Restitution Act" giving pensions to those who had lost their jobs because of their race; Fenchel was given a pension according to the supposed promotion level she would have reached if she had not been dismissed.

For a short time after her dismissal, she earned her living by private teaching, especially by helping nuns get their master's degrees. In November 1933 she immigrated to Denmark with a former fellow student, Werner Fenchel, who was also a Jew; they married in December. Fenchel did research in pure mathematics (algebra) in her spare time and published her first mathematical paper in 1937. But she did not find a job as a mathematician for many years to come.

From 1933 to 1943 Fenchel worked for a Danish mathematics professor as a part-time secretary. She did this not only because it augmented the small family income, but also because part of the work was correspondence helping other German Jews to emigrate.

In 1940, when she was thirty-five years old, she and her husband had a son, Tom. From 1940 to 1945 Denmark was occupied by Germany, and in 1943 Jews in Denmark were to be deported to German concentration camps. Therefore, Fenchel and her husband, like many other Danish Jews, escaped to Sweden; their son was sent to them later. During the war and while her son was small, Fenchel did no research but read the new literature in algebra and attended mathematics lectures at the university.

After the end of the war in Europe, the family returned to Denmark. Fenchel was offered a regular high school teaching job; but being now forty years old, she felt too old to start working under supervision.

In 1962, after a research pause of twenty-five years, she published two papers in pure mathematics. She got a part-time lecturer's job in 1965 at Aarhus University, which she held till she turned sixty-five in 1970. She liked the contact there with students and colleagues. In 1978, at age seventy-three, she published another paper.

Fenchel did not have the opportunity to become a very productive mathematician, but she was an extraordinary person who made her mark in the mathematical life of Denmark. Fenchel died the night of December 18–19, 1983.

WORK

Most of Fenchel's work deals with finite nonabelian groups, particularly the nature of groups of odd order.

In Fenchel (1937) she is concerned about what were called "vectormodules," that is, subgroups of R^n with $+$, $n \geq 2$. She shows that already in R^2 there exists an everywhere-dense subgroup intersecting each one-dimensional subspace in a discrete lattice.

In one of her papers ("Eine Bemerkung. . . . " 1962) she finds some conditions which characterize groups of odd order, and she looks at the decompositions of a group into residue classes that come from the centralizer corresponding to an element of the group. She then proves various results concerning such decompositions.

In another paper ("Beziehungen. . . . " 1962), she uses an $(n-1) \times (n-1)$ "structure matrix" for a finite group with n elements. She is interested in the greatest common divisor d_{n-1} of the subdeterminants of order $n-1$; and the central result of her paper is that $d_{n-1} = 1$ if and only if the group is identical with its commutator subgroup. Group representation theory is used in the proofs.

Her last paper, in 1978, concerns a theorem of Frobenius. Let G be a finite group of order $|G|$, n a divisor of $|G|$. Let $L_n = \{x \epsilon G | x^n = 1\}$, then L_n is a multiple of n (Frobenius's theorem). Frobenius conjectured that if $|L_n| = n$, then L_n is a subgroup of G. Fenchel proves this conjecture in case n and $|G|/n$ have no common divisor.

BIBLIOGRAPHY

Works by Käte Fenchel

Mathematical Works

"An everywhere dense vectormodule with discrete one-dimensional submodules" (in Danish). *Matematisk Tidsskrift B* (1937): 94–96.
"Eine Bemerkung über Gruppen ungerader Ordnung" (A remark on groups of odd order). *Mathematica Scandinavica* 10 (1962): 182–188.
"Beziehungen zwischen der Struktur einer endlichen Gruppe und einer speziellen Darstellung" (Relations between the structure of a finite group and a special representation). *Monatshefte für Mathematik* 66 (1962): 397–409.
"On a theorem of Frobenius." *Mathematica Scandinavica* 42 (1978): 243–250.

IRMGARD FLÜGGE-LOTZ (1903–1974)

John R. Spreiter and Wilhelm Flügge

BIOGRAPHY

Irmgard Lotz was born in Hameln, Germany, on July 16, 1903, the older of two sisters. Her father, Oskar Lotz, was a traveling journalist. The family of her mother, Dora (Grupe) Lotz, had been in the construction business for several generations. By visiting construction sites with members of her family and also by watching airship tests being conducted near her home by Count von Zeppelin, Lotz developed a fascination with the art of construction.

Lotz went to an elementary school in Frankenthal. By 1912 she was at the Lyceum in Mönchen-Gladbach. In 1914 her father accepted a position at one of the large city newspapers in Hanover. He enrolled his daughter in a high school for girls, there being no coeducation there then. The day he was to report to his new job, World War I began. He was promptly conscripted into the German army, and, being too old for the combat troops, he was assigned to occupied Belgium for the next four years. With the loss of the breadwinner, hard times came upon the family, and Lotz began as soon as she could to contribute to the family budget, by tutoring in mathematics and Latin.

Her father returned after the war with broken health and was no longer able to keep up with the demands of journalistic work. He held various jobs, none of which seemed to provide adequate income. It fell upon Lotz, now in high school, to provide a major part of the family's financial needs. Her interest in mathematics was encouraged by her father; but, as she was fond of saying, her final decision to choose an engineering career was made because "I wanted a life which would never be boring—a life in which new things would always occur."

After graduating from high school in 1923, Lotz enrolled in the Technical University in Hanover to study applied mathematics, with the clear intention of applying her knowledge to engineering problems. There she found herself the only woman in most classes, in a school with more than a thousand engineering students. In 1927 she acquired the degree of *Diplom-Ingenieur,* the usual conclusion of a study of engineering, and in 1929 she became a *Doktor-Ingenieur,* the equivalent of an American Ph.D. degree in engineering, with a thesis on the mathematical theory of heat conduction in circular cylinders. During the last two years, she held a full-time job as an "assistant" for practical mathematics and descriptive geometry, in which she served as the conductive and insulating medium (as the need may be) between the professor and the students.

In those times it was difficult for a young woman to find a job in engineering. Lotz had two offers, one from the steel industry and one from the Aerodynamische Versuchsanstalt (AVA) in Göttingen, a research institute. She chose the latter, where she was received with caution. To make sure that the institute would get something for its money, she was to devote half her time to cataloguing its vast collection of separate reprints, leaving the other half for research more or less of her own choosing. It soon developed that the second half was by far the more useful.

She worked closely with the leading German aerodynamicists of the time, Ludwig Prandtl and Albert Betz, director of the institute. More than a decade before, Prandtl had formulated the integro-differential equation for his lifting line theory for the spanwise lift distribution of an airplane wing; but there had been little success in solving the equation, except for certain special cases. Applying her mathematical skill to the problem, Lotz both solved the problem for the general case and developed a relatively convenient and rapidly convergent method for practical use. That accomplishment put an end to her cataloguing duties, and she was made head of a fast-growing group dealing with theoretical aerodynamics.

Her life was not simple, being the head of a group of young men, mostly with doctoral degrees from Göttingen University, and a staff of computing women, the precursors of today's electronic machines. She mastered the situation with tact and determination.

In 1938 Lotz married Dr. Wilhelm Flügge and joined his name to hers to become Irmgard Flügge-Lotz. They had no children. Wilhelm Flügge, a civil engineer, had been in Göttingen for many years and had just accepted a position as a department head at the Deutsche Versuchsanstalt für Luftfahrt (DVL) in Berlin. It was not long before the leaders of the DVL found what a talented mathematician-engineer had come within reach, and Flügge-Lotz was offered a position as consultant in aerodynamics and flight dynamics. There she commenced her career in automatic control theory, developing at first the theory of discontinuous, or on-off, control systems. Such controls, having only two or three input settings, are simple and inexpensive to manufacture and rugged and reliable in service. However, a theory for their performance had to be developed before design could be undertaken with confidence; and she set about the task immediately.

In the spring of 1944, the Flügges moved most of their DVL activity to Saulgau, a town of 4,000 in the hills north of the Bodensee. When Germany collapsed a year later, the Flügges found themselves in the French zone of occupation. They became part of the Centre Technique de Wasserburg, where the French gathered the aeronautical intelligentsia of the region. In 1947 the Flügges both accepted offers to join the newly established ONERA (French National Office for Aeronautical Research) in Paris. Flügge-Lotz served there as chief of a research group in theoretical aerodynamics from 1946 to 1948 and published papers in both automatic control theory and aerodynamics. Among the latter is her first paper in which the compressibility of air is taken into account, as it was becoming necessary to deal with problems arising from the increased speed of aircraft.

The time in Paris was an enjoyable period for both the Flügges. They became fluent in the language, the people were friendly, and the city was superb. However, their positions did not appear permanent, and they left Paris for the United States in October 1948 to accept invitations from Stanford University.

At Stanford, Flügge was appointed professor; but, because of antinepotism rules, Flügge-Lotz was appointed only as lecturer in engineering mechanics and research supervisor. Lack of an appropriate title did not deter her from embarking upon a full and useful life of teaching and research. She immediately undertook the guidance of Ph.D. dissertation research in aerodynamic theory, with one of the present authors, John R. Spreiter, as her first student.

In the spring of 1949, Flügge-Lotz taught her first Stanford course, a graduate course in boundary-layer theory. Before long, she introduced a new year-long sequence of courses in mathematical hydro- and aerodynamics for first-year graduate students.

At that time there were few full-time graduate students interested in fluid mechanics at Stanford; but there was a substantial number of young research engineers from the nearby National Advisory Committee for Aeronautics (NACA, now NASA) Ames Research Center, who were using vacation leave sparingly to attend Stanford part-time to acquire M.S. and Ph.D. degrees. By her constant willingness to conduct research consultations late in the day or in the evenings at her home, she gained the lasting gratitude of many of these students. By 1951 the number of students had grown sufficiently that she established the weekly fluid mechanics seminar, at which Spreiter was the first speaker. This seminar continues to this day to be an active and unifying forum at which faculty and students from many departments meet and exchange information and ideas on all aspects of fluid mechanics.

As the years passed, she continued to have a strong interest in fluid mechanics, particularly in boundary-layer theory and numerical methods. Not long after her arrival, Flügge-Lotz also began building a second role for herself at Stanford, in the theory of automatic controls. She developed new courses in this important subject and began guiding the research of a steady succession of Ph.D. students. She typically published results of these studies in reports coauthored with her students. Since automatic control devices were often of an electrical nature, this work led also to an increasingly close contact with faculty and students in electrical engineering.

By the middle 1950s, it seemed evident to almost everyone at Stanford that Flügge-Lotz was carrying on all the duties of a full professor but without official recognition. In fact, it was hard for students to understand why she was a lecturer rather than a professor. The same question arose on the international scene in the summer of 1960, when she was the only woman delegate from the United States at the First Congress of the International Federation of Automatic Control in Moscow. By then the disparity had become apparent to all. Before school opened for the autumn quarter, she was appointed full professor in both engineering mechanics and aeronautics and astronautics. Stanford had been in existence for seventy years, but she was its first woman professor in engineering.

Throughout Flügge-Lotz's busy career of teaching and research at Stanford, she always exhibited great interest in knowing her students well. This extended to frequent invitations to her home, where carefully selected mixes of faculty, students, and visitors were brought together for evenings of good food, tea, and conversation. While her classroom teaching stopped with retirement in 1968, her research on problems of satellite control, heat transfer, and drag of high-speed vehicles continued actively right to the end of her life. This was the more remarkable because of the constant pain and discomfort with which she lived for many years, as disabling arthritis attacked first one part and then another of her body. Through it all, she kept her good spirits and maintained frequent contacts with friends and colleagues, all of whom were sadly shocked by her sudden death at Stanford Hospital on May 22, 1974, at the age of seventy.

WORK

Flügge-Lotz was internationally renowned for her many important mathematical contributions to aerodynamics and to automatic control theory. Within Stanford, Dean of Engineering William M. Kays considered her to be "one of our most distinguished professors by any standard of measure." Honors accorded her include an honorary Doctor of Science degree by the University of Maryland in 1973, the Achievement Award by the Society of Women Engineers in 1970, and selection by the American Institute of Aeronautics and Astronautics (AIAA) to give the prestigious annual von Kármán Lecture in 1971. She is the only woman to present a von Kármán Lecture, and she was the first woman elected to the grade of fellow by the AIAA. She was also a senior member of the Institute of Electrical and Electronic Engineers, a member of the scientific society Sigma Xi, and member of advisory boards of several scientific journals. She published over fifty technical papers in three languages and authored two books.

During her tenure at the AVA in Göttingen from 1929 to 1939, she produced a steady stream of significant contributions to aerodynamic theory. Her first publication there presented a method for the calculation of the spanwise lift distribution on wings that soon became a standard procedure used throughout the world ("Berechnung der Auftriebsverteilung. . . . " 1931). It has been known since as the "Lotz method." Subsequent publications presented a number of further advances in wing theory, including effects of control surfaces, slots, propellor slipstream, and wind-tunnel wall interference. During this period she also developed a considerably improved theory for the calculation of the pressures and lift on airships, in which the mathematical sources and sinks used to simulate the flow field were placed at the true position of the airship surface rather than along the centerline of the airship, thereby increasing both the accuracy and generality of such predictions. In a sense, this could be considered to be the forerunner of the panel methods widely used today for the calculation of pressure and flow about complicated shapes, such as complete aircraft.

Flügge-Lotz continued her contributions to aerodynamic theory through the 1940s, but her subsequent work at Stanford extends over a longer period of time and is of greater significance. From her arrival in 1948 to her retirement in 1968, her work in fluid mechanics was directed toward developing numerical methods for the accurate solution of problems in compressible boundary-layer theory. She pioneered the use of finite-difference methods for such purposes and was quick to employ the emerging capability of computers to deal with the large computations inherent in the use of these methods. Working with a succession of students, she applied these methods to solve a series of important and previously unsolved problems in compressible boundary-layer theory. By the time of her retirement, she and her students had published accounts of a wide range of applications, extending from ordinary compressible boundary-layer and wake flows to those with intersecting shock waves, and to hypersonic flow around blunt bodies. Evidence of her reputation in the application of finite-difference methods to boundary-layer problems is provided by Hermann Schlichting, who states in his book (1968) that he is "indebted to Professor I. Flügge-Lotz and to Doctors R. T. Davis and T. K. Fanneloep [two of her students] who kindly provided me with the ensuing presentation"—the entire account—on finite-difference methods in boundary-layer theory.

Flügge-Lotz's studies of automatic control theory, which began at the DVL in Berlin, resulted in *Discontinuous Automatic Control* (1953), setting forth in one place many of the details of over a decade of her own work as well as that of others. Further developments and extensions were summarized in a second book, *Discontinuous and Optimal Control* (1958). Her work with her Stanford students was characterized by incorporating higher-order and nonlinear effects into the analysis, thereby providing more accurate predictions than possible previously.

A succinct and independent evaluation of her career is provided by the citation for her honorary doctorate:

Professor Flügge-Lotz has acted in a central role in the development of the aircraft industry in the Western world. Her contributions have spanned a lifetime during which she demonstrated, in a field dominated by men, the value and quality of a woman's intuitive approach in searching for and discovering solutions to complex engineering problems. Her work manifests unusual personal dedication and native intelligence.

BIBLIOGRAPHY _____

Works by Irmgard Flügge-Lotz

Mathematical Works

"Die Wärmeleitung im endlich langen Kreiszylinder unter besonderen Randbedingungen." *Zeitschrift für angewandte Mathematik und Mechanik* 9 (1929): 498–499. Abstract of her doctoral dissertation.

"Berechnung der Auftriebsverteilung beliebig geformter Flügel." *Zeitschrift für Flugtechnik und Motorluftschiffahrt* 22 (1931): 189–195.

"Zur Berechnung der Potentialströmung um quergestellte Luftschiffkörper." *Ingenieur-Archiv* 2 (1931): 507–527.

"Theorie von Flügeln mit Ausschnitten." *Zeitschrift für Flugtechnik und Motorluftschiffahrt* 23 (1932): 410–413.

"Neuere Probleme der Tragflügeltheorie." *Proceedings of the International Congress of Mathematicians, Zurich,* 1932, vol. 2, 253–254.

(with A. Betz) "Verminderung des Auftriebes von Tragflügeln durch den Widerstand." *Zeitschrift für Flugtechnik und Motorluftschiffahrt* 23 (1932): 277–279.

"Korrektur des Abwindes in Windkanälen mit kreisrunden oder elliptischen Querschnitten." *Luftfahrtforschung* 12 (1935): 250–264.

"Beeinflussung der Auftriebsverteilung durch den Schraubenstrahl." *Jahrbuch der Lilienthal-Gesellschaft für Luftfahrtforschung* 1936, 57–74.

"Der Abwind." *Ringbuch der Luftfahrttechnik* 1937.

(with W. Fabricius) "Die Berechnung des Abwindes hinter einem Tragflügel mit Berücksichtigung des Aufwickelns der Unstetigkeitsfläche." *Luftfahrtforschung* 14 (1937): 552–557.

(with F. Riegels) "Der zusätzliche Abwind am Ort eines Eindeckers in einem dreieckigen Freistrahl." *Luftfahrtforschung* 14 (1937): 550–551.

(with A. Betz) "Berechnung der Schaufeln von Kreiselrädern." *Ingenieur-Archiv* 9 (1938): 486–501.

(with F. Keune) "Druckverteilungen von Kármán-Trefftz-Profilen bei hohen Auftriebsziffern." *Jahrbuch der deutschen Luftfahrtforschung* 1938, I–39.

(with D. Küchemann) "Zusammenfassender Bericht über Abwindmessungen ohne und mit Schraubenstrahl." *Jahrbuch der deutschen Luftfahrtforschung* 1938, I–172.

(with I. Ginzel) "Die ebene Strömung um ein geknicktes Profil mit Spalt." *Ingenieur-Archiv* 11 (1940): 268–292.

(with K. Solf) "Strömungsaufnahmen eines durch einen Tragflügel gestörten Schraubenstrahls." *Luftfahrtforschung* 17 (1940): 161–166.

(with H. F. Hodapp et al.) "Über Bewegungen eines Schwingers unter dem Einfluss von Schwarz-Weiss Regelungen." *Zeitschrift für angewandte Mathematik und Mechanik* 25/27 (1947): 97–113.

(with K. Klotter) "Über Bewegungen eines Schwingers unter dem Einfluss von Schwarz-Weiss-Regelungen. I. Bewegungen eines Schwingers von einem Freiheitsgrad; Regelung mit Stellungszuordnung ohne Schaltverschiebungen." *Zeitschrift für angewandte Mathematik und Mechanik* 28 (1948): 317–337.

Discontinuous Automatic Control. Princeton: Princeton University Press, 1953.

(with A. F. Johnson) "Laminar compressible boundary layer along a curved, insulated surface." *Journal of the Aeronautical Sciences* 22 (1955): 445–454.

(with W. S. Wunch) "On a nonlinear transfer system." *Journal of Applied Physics* 26 (1955): 484–488.

Discontinuous and Optimal Control. New York: McGraw-Hill, 1958.

(with G. Baxter) "Compressible laminar boundary layer behavior studied by a finite difference method." *Zeitschrift für angewandte Mathematik und Physik* 9b (1958): 81–96.

"Discontinuous automatic control." *Applied Mechanics Reviews* 14 (1961): 581–584.

(with M. Yin) "The optimum response of second-order, velocity controlled systems with contactor control." *Journal of Basic Engineering (= Transactions of the American Society of Mechanical Engineers Series D)* D–83 (1961): 59–64.

(with H. A. Titus) "The optimum response of full third-order systems with contactor control." *Journal of Basic Engineering (= Transactions of the American Society of Mechanical Engineers Series D)* D–84 (1962): 554–558.

(with F. G. Blottner) "Finite-difference computation of the boundary layer with displacement thickness interaction." *Journal de Mécanique* 2 (1963): 397–423.

(with M. D. Maltz) "Attitude stabilization using a contactor control system with a linear switching criterion." *Automatica* 2 (1963): 255–274.

(with R. T. Davis) "Second-order boundary-layer effects in hypersonic flow past axisymmetric blunt bodies." *Journal of Fluid Mechanics* 20 (1964): 593–623.

(with A. J. Craig) "A choice of time for zeroing a disturbance in a minimum-fuel consumption control problem." *Journal of Basic Engineering (= Transactions of the American Society of Mechanical Engineers Series D)* D–87 (1965): 29–38.

(with A. J. Craig) "Investigation of optimal control with a minimum-fuel consumption criterion for a fourth-order plant with two control inputs: Synthesis of an efficient suboptimal control." *Journal of Basic Engineering (= Transactions of the American Society of Mechanical Engineers Series D)* D–87 (1965): 39–57.

(with H. D. Marbach) "On the minimum effort regulation of stationary linear systems." *Journal of the Franklin Institute* 279 (1965): 229–245.

(with T. K. Fannelöp) "Viscous hypersonic flow over simple blunt bodies: Comparison of the second-order theory with experimental results." *Journal de Mécanique* 5 (1966): 69–100.

(with Y. Kashiwagi) "Periodic solutions of differential-difference equations with relay control." *International Journal of Control* 6 (1967): 1–25.

(with Y. Kashiwagi) "Stability indicative function and its application to systems with time delay." *Ingenieur-Archiv* 35 (1967): 332–339.

(with K. A. Hales and B. O. Lange) "Minimum-fuel attitude control of a spacecraft by an extended method of steepest descent." *International Journal of Nonlinear Mechanics* 3 (1968): 413–438.

(with Jose L. Garcia Almuzara) "Minimum time control of a nonlinear system." *Journal of Differential Equations* 4 (1968): 12–39.

(with A. Plotkin) "A numerical solution for the laminar wake behind a finite flat plate." *Journal of Basic Engineering (= Transactions of the American Society of Mechanical Engineers Series E)* E–35 (1968): 625–630.

(with T. A. Reyhner) "The interaction of a shock wave with a laminar boundary layer." *International Journal of Nonlinear Mechanics* 3 (1968): 173–199.

(with D. W. Ross) "An optimal control problem for systems with differential-difference equation dynamics." *SIAM Journal of Control* 7 (1969): 609–623.

(with W. Boykin) "High accuracy attitude control of satellites in elliptic orbits." *Journal of Optimization Theory and Its Applications* 5 (1970): 197–224.

(with R. E. Foerster) "A neighboring optimal feedback control scheme for systems using discontinuous control." *Journal of Optimization Theory and Its Applications* 8 (1971): 367–395.

"Trends in the field of automatic control in the last two decades." *AIAA Journal* 10 (1972): 721–726.

(with W. Flügge) "Ludwig Prandtl in the nineteen-thirties: Reminiscences." *Annual Review of Fluid Mechanics* 5 (1973): 1–7.

Works about Irmgard Flügge-Lotz

"Emerita Professor Flügge-Lotz (16 July 1903–22 May 1974)." *Automatica* (1975): i.

"A life full of work—the Flügges." *Stanford Engineering News* 68 (May 1969).

Obituary. *New York Times* (23 May 1974): 44.

Spreiter, John R., et al. "In memoriam Irmgard Flügge-Lotz (1903–1974)." *IEEE Transactions on Automatic Control* AC–20 (1975): 183a–183b.

Stanford Engineering News 91 (November 1973).

Other References

Schlichting, Hermann. *Boundary Layer Theory*. New York: McGraw-Hill, 1968.

HILDA GEIRINGER VON MISES (1893–1973)

Joan L. Richards

BIOGRAPHY

Hilda Geiringer was born to a middle-class family in Vienna on September 28, 1893. She was the second of four children and the only girl. Her father, Ludwig, was born in Hungary but was a textile manufacturer in Vienna when he married her mother, Martha Wertheimer.

Like her father, Geiringer had a prodigious memory, especially for numbers, and by the time she was in the gymnasium, it was clear that mathematics was her major interest. With her parents' support, Geiringer studied pure mathematics with Wilhelm Wirtinger at the University of Vienna and received her doctorate in 1917.

For the next two years, Geiringer worked under Leon Lichtenstein editing the *Jahrbuch über die Fortschritte der Mathematik,* a major reviews journal. At the end of her life, Geiringer remembered Lichtenstein as one of several men who were her teachers in "the most essential sense." In 1921 she went to the Institute of Applied Mathematics at the University of Berlin, as first assistant under Richard Martin Edler von Mises. This was a critical move for Geiringer, both personally and professionally. In Berlin she was married for about two years to another mathematician, Felix Pollaczek, and they had a child, Magda Pollaczek, in 1922. After their divorce Geiringer brought up the girl while pursuing professional interests. Under the influence of von Mises, these interests moved away from pure mathematics; for the rest of her life, Geiringer focused on applied areas.

Geiringer remained as first assistant to von Mises until 1927, when she was made *Privatdozent* at the University of Berlin. In 1933 the faculty proposed her as an extraordinary professor. No action was taken, however, because Hitler came to power in that year, and, like other Jewish academics, Geiringer lost her job. She left Germany with her child and went to Belgium as a research associate at the Institute of Mechanics in Brussels, where she studied the theory of vibrations. In 1934 she moved to the University of Istanbul, where she stayed for five years as professor of mathematics.

In Turkey, Geiringer was part of a larger German community that was seeking refuge from Hitler's regime. Despite the obvious difficulties associated with this exile—for example, she had to learn Turkish in order to give her lectures— Geiringer continued to pursue her mathematical interests, particularly in plasticity.

After the death of Kemal Atatürk in 1938, Geiringer was among those who feared that their refuge was no longer safe and so left Turkey for the United States. She and her daughter went to Bryn Mawr College, where she was a lecturer from 1939 until 1944. Here she made friends with Anna Wheeler*, who supported and encouraged her in the task of learning English and adjusting to what Geiringer called "the American form of teaching" (von Mises Papers, HUG 4574.105, Box 2, folder 1946–1948). During this period she did classified research work for the Applied Mathematics Panel of the National Defense Research Council. In addition, she spent the summer of 1942 teaching in a program for advanced instruction and research in mechanics at Brown University. For this program, which was intended to raise the technological knowledge of American scientists to the level of their German counterparts, Geiringer wrote a series of lectures at a very advanced level on the geometrical foundations of mechanics. These were widely circulated in mimeograph.

In 1943 Geiringer married von Mises, whose flight from Germany by way of Turkey had paralleled hers. At the time of their marriage, von Mises was a lecturer in mathematics at Harvard University. Motivated in part by a desire to be closer to her husband, Geiringer left Bryn Mawr in 1944 to become professor and chairman of the mathematics department at Wheaton College in Norton, Massachusetts. She maintained an apartment at Wheaton, where she lived and worked during the week. On weekends she came into Cambridge to be with her husband.

Geiringer was a hardworking, dedicated teacher; a number of her Wheaton students went on to pursue careers in mathematics. However, teaching in a small college that had only two mathematics faculty members was not adequate to encompass her mathematical energies. Geiringer repeatedly tried to find employment in a larger university in the Boston area, but she was unsuccessful. Several times the reasons given for not considering her seriously were explicitly tied to her sex. For example, one attempt was met with the response, "I am quite sure that the President will not approve of a woman. We have some women on our staff, so it is not merely prejudice against women, yet it is partly that, for we do not want to bring in more if we can get men" (von Mises Papers, HUG 4574.105, Box 2, folder 1946–1948). Geiringer was "pretty discouraged by this rather open discrimination" but did not allow it to deflect her from her work. "I hope there will be better conditions for the next generation of women," she wrote. "In the meantime one has to go on as well as possible" (von Mises Papers, HUG 4574.105, Box 2, folder 1946–1948). This she did, taking the time after 5 P.M. each day for her own research. At Wheaton, as everywhere, her work served to sustain her. As she explained in a 1953 letter to a Wheaton College administrator: "I have to work scientifically, besides my college work. This is a necessity for me; I never stopped it since my student days, it is the deepest need in my life" (von Mises Papers, HUG 4574.105, Box 2, Wheaton folder).

On July 14, 1953, Richard von Mises died, and Geiringer felt it was incumbent upon her to complete and edit his unfinished works. In 1954 she was awarded a grant from the Office of Naval Research and came to Harvard as a research fellow in mathematics. Although she did not formally retire from Wheaton until July 1959, Geiringer spent as much time as she could afford in Cambridge finishing von Mises's work and developing her own interests. From 1955 until 1958, she worked with G. S. Ludford to finish an incomplete von Mises manuscript, which was published as *Mathematical Theory of Compressible Fluid Flow* (1958). At the same time, she was pursuing her interest in plasticity in collaboration with A. M. Freudenthal. This work culminated in the mathematical part of a joint article (Geiringer and Freudenthal 1958).

Geiringer's work received increasing recognition. In 1960 Wheaton awarded her an honorary degree of Doctor of Science. The University of Berlin elected her professor emeritus with full salary in 1956, and in 1967, on the occasion of the fiftieth jubilee of her graduation, she was given a special presentation by the University of Vienna. She was also a member of the scientific society Sigma Xi and a fellow of the American Academy of Arts and Sciences.

Geiringer's broad range of interests, noticeable in the breadth of her professional work, also extended beyond the field of mathematics. She was an avid mountain climber and had an impressive knowledge and love of literature, poetry, and classical music. She died of influenzal pneumonia at the age of seventy-nine in Santa Barbara, California, while visiting her brother, Karl Geiringer, a noted musicologist.

WORK

Geiringer's thesis on double trigonometric series was a seminal contribution to the theory of multiple trigonometric series associated with the names of Godfrey Harold Hardy, Martin Krause, Walter Wolleben Küstermann, and W. H. Young, as well as a contribution to the twentieth-century development of Fourier series (Geiringer 1918).

During the Berlin years (1921–1933), Geiringer made important contributions to probability theory. She also developed an interest in the mathematical theory of plasticity which led her to the fundamental Geiringer equations for plane plastic distortions (Geiringer 1931).

While at Wheaton, a large part of Geiringer's research interest focused on biometrical problems, which had first caught her interest while in Berlin. As early as 1908, G. H. Hardy had mathematically investigated the transmission of Mendelian traits in a highly special case. It became clear, however, that his simplifying assumptions were unrealistic and the actual situation significantly more complex. Geiringer viewed these biological issues from the most abstract reaches of probability theory, which allowed her to move beyond the specific cases treated by Hardy into more broadly defined questions (Geiringer 1936, 1939). Her interest in these problems illustrates Geiringer's mathematical style. She summed it up by writing, "While the mathematical problems arising as a consequence of Mendel's biological principles are of great interest from the point of view of probability theory, it is one more challenge that they are in a certain way inaccessible to most biologists" (von Mises, HUG 4574, Box 1, folder 1945–1947). Toward the end of the 1940s, she began to be attracted again to problems of plasticity.

Underlying a great deal of Geiringer's work was an abiding interest in probability theory, an interest she shared with von Mises, who had considered the foundations of probability theory while he was still in Berlin. One interpretation of probability theory would ground it axiomatically, leaving its applications to be discovered later. Rather than thus splitting the pure science of probability from the applied science of statistics, von Mises tried to unite them by grounding probability theory in the objective study of frequency. Although these ideas proved to be highly suggestive, von Mises all but ceased working on them when he came to the United States. At the end of his life, however, he reaffirmed his conviction that probability theory was inductively based. Upon his death, Geiringer took up this work and edited new editions of his *Probability, Statistics and Truth* (1957) and *Mathematical Theory of Probability and Statistics* (1964). Particularly in the second work, which is "edited and complemented by Hilda Geiringer," Geiringer significantly reworked the first edition, incorporating material from von Mises's lectures. While keeping to the basic natural philosophic spirit of von Mises's original work, Geiringer incorporated new results of Erhard Tornier and Abraham Wald to strengthen its basic structure. In the last decade of her life, she lectured frequently and published a number of articles developing and supporting this important and controversial view of the foundations of probability theory.

BIBLIOGRAPHY

Works by Hilda Geiringer

Space does not permit the listing of the complete works of Hilda Geiringer. The Cumulative Author Index to vols. 1–25 of *Zentralblatt der Mathematik und ihre Grenzgebiete* (covering 1930–1940) lists two articles under "Pollaczek-Geiringer," one under "Pollazek *[sic]*-Geiringer," and sixteen under "Geiringer." The Cumulative Author Index volumes for *Mathematical Reviews* (for 1940–1959, 1960–1964, 1965–1972, and 1973–1979) list more than thirty other works. Listed below are works not included in those indexes, plus works cited in the text.

Mathematical Works

"Trigonometrische Doppelreihen." *Monatshefte für Mathematik und Physik* 29 (1918): 65–144. Doctoral thesis.

"Die nichteuklidischen Geometrien und das Raumproblem." *Die Naturwissenschaften* 6 (1918): 635–641, 653–658.

Die Gedankenwelt der Mathematik. Berlin: Verlag der Arbeitsgemeinschaft, 1922.

"Über eine Randwertaufgabe der Theorie gewöhnlicher linearer Differentialgleichungen zweiter Ordnung." *Mathematische Zeitschrift* 12 (1922): 1–17.

"Zur expliziten Lösung nicht orthogonaler Randwertprobleme." *Mathematische Annalen* 90 (1923): 292–317.

"Rückschluss auf die Wahrscheinlichkeit seltener Ereignisse." *Zeitschrift für angewandte Mathematik und Mechanik* 5 (1925): 493–501.

"Beitrag zu den Fundamentalsätzen der Wahrscheinlichkeitsrechnung." *Mathematische Zeitschrift* 24 (1926): 684–705.

"Culmansche Gerade und ebene Ausnahmefachwerke." *Zeitschrift für angewandte Mathematik und Mechanik* 6 (1926): 48–58.

"Stereoskopische Bilder von Kristallgittern." *Zeitschrift für angewandte Mathematik und Mechanik* 6 (1926): 70–73.

"Über die Gliederung ebener Fachwerke." *Zeitschrift für angewandte Mathematik und Mechanik* 7 (1927): 58–72.

"Theorie der Statistik seltener Ereignisse." *Zeitschrift für angewandte Mathematik und Mechanik* 7 (1927): 445–446.

(translator) Boutroux, P. *Das Wissenschaftsideal der Mathematiker.* Leipzig: Teubner, 1927.

"Zur Praxis der Lösung linearer Gleichungen in der Statik." *Zeitschrift für angewandte Mathematik und Mechanik* 8 (1928): 446–447.

"Statistik seltener Ereignisse, I, II." *Naturwissenschaften* 16 (1928): 800–807, 815–820.

"Die Charliersche Entwicklung willkürlicher Verteilungen." *Skandinavisk Aktuarietidskrift* 11 (1928): 98–111.

"Praktische Verfahren der Gleichungsauflösung, I, II." *Zeitschrift für angewandte Mathematik und Mechanik* 9 (1929): 58–77, 152–164.

"Beitrag zum vollständigen ebenen Plastizitätsproblem." In *Verhandlungen des 3. Internationalen Kongresses für Technische Mechanik Stockholm 24–29 August 1930,* vol. 2, 185–190. Stockholm: A. B. Sveriges Litografiska Tryckerier, 1931.

"Bemerkungen zur Korrelationstheorie." *Proceedings of the International Congress of Mathematicians,* Zurich, 1932, vol. 2, 229–230.

"Zur Gliederungstheorie räumlicher Fachwerke." *Zeitschrift für angewandte Mathematik und Mechanik* 12 (1932): 369–376.

"Internationaler Mathematiker-Kongress Zürich 1932." *Blätter für Versicherungsmathematik und verwandte Gebiete* 2 (1934): 350–354.

"Zur Weinbergschen Probandenmethode." *Revue de la Faculté des Sciences de l' Université d'Istanbul (= Istanbul üniversitesi Fen fakültesi mecmuasi. Ser. A Revue.)* (2) 1 (3) (1936): 10–36.

Fondements mathématiques de la théorie des corps plastiques isotropes. Paris: Gauthier-
    Villars, 1937.
"La repartition des groupes sanguins de deux races en cas de croissements." *Revue de
    la Faculté des Sciences de l'Université d'Istanbul (=Istanbul üniversitesi Fen
    fakültesi mecmuasi. Ser. A. Revue.)* (2) 4 (1939): 1–12.
Geometrical Foundations of Mechanics. Mimeographed. Providence, R.I.: Brown Uni-
    versity, 1942.
von Mises, Richard. *Probability, Statistics and Truth.* 2nd rev. English ed. Prepared by
    Hilda Geiringer. New York, 1957. 4th German ed. Library of Exact Philosophy,
    vol. 7. New York: Springer-Verlag, 1973.
Mathematical Theory of Compressible Fluid Flow. Completed by Hilda Geiringer and
    G. S. Ludford. New York: Academic, 1958.
(with Alfred Freudenthal) "The mathematical theories of the inelastic continuum." *Hand-
    buch der Physik (=Encyclopedia of Physics),* edited by S. Flügge, vol. 6, 229–
    432. Heidelberg: Springer, 1958.
von Mises, Richard. *Mathematical Theory of Probability and Statistics.* Edited and com-
    plemented by Hilda Geiringer. New York: Academic, 1964.
"Ideal plasticity." *Handbuch der Physik (=Encyclopedia of Physics).* Vol. 6a/3, 403–
    533. New York: Springer-Verlag, 1973.
    Revised version of second part of Geiringer and Freudenthal (1958).

Works about Hilda Geiringer

"Applied mathematics at Brown: A description and history of the division of Applied
    Mathematics at Brown University on the occasion of its 25th Anniversary Cele-
    bration. September 7–10, 1971." Pamphlet.
    This and Richardson (1943) provide background about the summer program to
    which Geiringer contributed in 1942.
Fermi, Laura. *Illustrious Immigrants.* Chicago: University of Chicago Press, 1968.
Fleming, Donald, and Bernard Bailyn, eds. *The Intellectual Migration Europe and Amer-
    ica, 1930–1960.* Cambridge, Mass.: Harvard University Press, 1969.
    This and Fermi (1968) provide background against which to understand Geiringer's
    American experience and contributions.
Geiringer, Hilda. Papers. Schlesinger Library, Radcliffe College, Cambridge, Mass.
    Includes a German-language analysis of her mathematical contributions.
"Hilda Geiringer." *Wheaton Newsletter* (September 1959).
von Mises, Richard. Papers. Harvard University Archives, Cambridge, Mass.
    Contains a considerable collection of Geiringer manuscripts and correspondence.
Obituary. *Boston Sunday Globe* (25 March 1973): 95.
Obituary. *New York Times* (24 March 1973): 36.
Richardson, Dean R.G.D. "Advanced instruction and research in mechanics." *American
    Journal of Physics* 11 (1943): 67–73.

SOPHIE GERMAIN (1776–1831)

Mary W. Gray

BIOGRAPHY

Marie-Sophie Germain was born on April 1, 1776, in a house on Rue St. Denis in Paris. Her father, Ambroise-François, was a silk merchant, a prosperous member of the bourgeoisie, whom he was elected to represent in the États-Généraux in 1789. The Germain home was a meeting place for those interested in liberal reforms, and the young mathematician-to-be must have heard exciting political and philosophical discussions swirling around her. Despite the shifting trends of French politics, the family continued to be sufficiently prosperous that Germain could devote herself to research and writing without worrying about means of support.

Of Germain's mother we know little other than her name, Marie-Madeleine Gruguelin. Germain had an older sister, Marie-Madeleine, whose son Armand-Jacques Lherbette was his aunt's literary executor; and a younger sister, Angé-lique-Ambroise, who outlived her two physician husbands and died in 1874 at the age of ninety-five. The coincidence in mother's and daughters' first names perhaps accounts for Germain's use of "Sophie."

Retreating from the turmoil of the Parisian streets of the Reign of Terror to her father's library, Germain resolved to find a serious occupation for herself. In Montucla's *L'Histoire des Mathématiques*, Germain found the story of Archimedes, struck down at the siege of Syracuse as he meditated over his diagram in the sand. Much moved, she determined that she, too, would be a geometer, the term "geometry" at that time encompassing all of pure mathematics.

Although there was a tradition in France of women's engaging in intellectual pursuits, there was also an adverse reaction, typified by the satire of Molière's *La Femme Savante*, an attitude apparently shared by Germain's parents. That a woman could make use of mathematics seemed improbable; but Germain relentlessly pursued her interest, even when her family took away her fire, her light, and her clothes to force her from her books to the needed sleep. She simply waited until everyone else was asleep, and, wrapping herself in her covers, studied by the light of contraband candles. Étienne Bézout's *Traité d'Arithmé-tique* was a favorite text; to read Isaac Newton and Leonhard Euler, she taught herself Latin.

Eventually, her parents lessened their opposition to her studies; her mother even provided secret support. Germain absorbed Jacques Antoine-Joseph Cousin's *Le Calcul Différential,* and the author's visit to her home provided much-needed encouragement. Her interests were not confined to mathematics; she explored the works of Diderot and Condorcet and maintained throughout her life an interest in the developing subject of psychology.

This was an exciting period in French mathematics, with great developments soon to come. Instrumental in this flowering was the establishment of the École central des travaux publics, later to become the École polytechnique. Among the first professors were Joseph Louis Lagrange, Gaspard Monge, Antoine de Fourcroy, and Claude Berthollet. This splendid opportunity for an eighteen-year-old eager for knowledge was denied to Germain because of her sex. However, one of the innovations in this new scheme of education was to make lecture notes available to all who asked, among them Germain. Another innovation was the practice of having students submit written observations, which she sent to Lagrange using the name of a student acquaintance, M. LeBlanc. Germain's originality and insight moved Lagrange to want to meet "LeBlanc." His respect for her work was not diminished when he learned that the notebooks were produced by a woman, and Lagrange continued for many years to provide support and encouragement.

When Adrien Marie Legendre's *Essai sur le Théorie des Nombres* was published in 1798, Germain turned with great intensity to its study, beginning an extensive correspondence with him concerning her work on number theory and later on elasticity. Her most famous correspondence was with Carl Friedrich Gauss, whose 1801 *Disquisitiones arithmeticae* had been enthusiastically received at the École polytechnique and was recommended to Germain. Again adopting the pen name "M. LeBlanc," in 1804 she wrote to Gauss of several number-theoretic problems on which she was working. Several exchanges of correspondence followed, with Gauss giving her work high praise, an evaluation repeated in letters to his colleagues. He also asked for her help in trying to collect royalties in arrears from his Paris publisher; unfortunately, Germain's researches found that the publisher had declared bankruptcy, and no money was to be had.

Germain's true identity was revealed to Gauss only at the time of the French occupation of his hometown of Braunschweig. Germain apparently feared that Gauss would suffer a fate similar to that of Archimedes; she contacted a family friend with the French forces, who sent a battalion chief to Braunschweig to see how Gauss was faring. When the chief reported to Gauss that his mission was due to the intervention of Mlle. Germain, the mathematician truthfully replied that he knew no one of that name. Germain later wrote to clear up Gauss's confusion, citing as the reason for her earlier deception the fear of ridicule attached to *femmes-savantes*. Gauss continued to praise her work, and he gave her credit for inspiring his return to investigations in number theory.

Although Germain's work on Pierre de Fermat's Last Theorem was her soundest, that she is remembered at all is due to her work in elasticity. After demonstrations by a visiting German scientist, Ernest Chladni, impressed Parisians, including Napoleon, the Institut de France set a prize competition on the mathematical theory of elastic surfaces. The difficulty of the problem was generally recognized, and Germain's anonymous submission was the only entry in the original competition of 1811, as well as in the reopened competitions of 1813 and 1815. In the second contest, her work received honorable mention; and her third try was declared worthy of the prize, though deficiencies in its mathematical rigor remained. To public disappointment, she did not appear as anticipated at the award ceremony on January 8, 1816.

Germain had difficulty in having her work taken seriously, particularly because it was not in the spirit of the molecular theory of matter then in vogue. Nevertheless, when her prize memoir was published in 1821, Augustin Louis Cauchy wrote that it "was a work for which the name of its author and the importance of the subject both deserved the attention of mathematicians" (Harlor 1953, 141). In what was apparently intended as a tribute to the complexity of the mathematics, not a comment on the incomprehensibility of her prose, Claude Navier wrote, "It is a work which few men are able to read and which only one woman was able to write" (Harlor 1953, 141).

Although her work in elasticity did lead other researchers in the correct direction, when the Eiffel tower was built, her name was not among those researchers in elasticity listed at its base as making possible its construction.

Germain continued to work in mathematics and philosophy until her death. She was stricken with breast cancer in 1829. Undeterred by that and by the sound of the guns of the 1830 revolution, she completed retrospective papers on number theory and on the curvature of surfaces (1831). She died at 11 A.M. on June 27, 1831, in a house at 13 rue de Savoie. This house has been designated as a historical landmark and is marked by a commemorative plaque.

Her grave in the Père Lachaise cemetery in Paris is marked with a simple stone; her other monuments in the city are the École Sophie Germain and rue Germain. She died before the honorary degree from the University of Göttingen that Gauss recommended could be conferred upon her; in fact, she never met her esteemed correspondent.

In her obituary, Guillaume Libri wrote:

[Her] forgetfulness of self, she carried throughout everything; in the science which she cultivated with entire self denial, without dreaming of the advantages that success would procure, applauding even, on occasion, the sight of her ideas fertilized by others who had seized them; saying it was not important where an idea came from but only how far it could go, and [she was happy], as long as her ideas bore their fruit for science without furthering the reputation, which she disdained; and [she] proclaimed ludicrous the glory of the bourgeois, [calling fame] the small place which we occupy in the mind of others. (Raphael 1978, 46)

However, her death certificate listed her not as mathematician or scientist, but as *rentier* (property holder).

In fact, Libri's evaluation suffers from the usual tendency of obituaries to see only the good. Germain was denied easy access to scientific circles and the benefit of the free exchange of ideas. The inclination of sympathetic mathematicians to praise her work rather than to provide substantive criticism from which she might learn was crippling to her mathematical development. Moreover, Germain did show resentment of Siméon Denis Poisson's appropriation of her work without attribution, and she expressed skepticism that he and others whose approach differed fundamentally from hers would be disinterested judges of her prize submissions (Bucciarelli and Dworsky 1980, 65–84).

Germain's achievements, recognized as remarkable by her contemporaries, have secured her a place in the roll of women scientists. Christine Ladd-Franklin*, a later entry to this group, paid tribute to her (Ladd-Franklin 1894), and H. J. Mozans characterized her as "probably the most profoundly intellectual woman that France had yet produced" (Mozans 1913, 156).

WORK

Germain's major work falls naturally into three fields: number theory; elasticity, including curvature of surfaces; and philosophy. There is no doubt that her research is the most significant done by a woman mathematician before Sofia Kovalevskaia*. Both her number theory and elasticity results marked contributions to the advancement of knowledge in those fields and have stood the test of time.

Many of Germain's early research results were contained in letters to other mathematicians, in particular Legendre and Gauss. Her letters to Legendre, detailing her work on Fermat's Last Theorem, have not been published separately; several letters were published in her *Oeuvres philosophiques*. Fermat's theorem states that $x^n + y^n = z^n$, x, y, z nonzero integers, cannot be solved for n greater than 2. It is usually divided into two cases. Case 1 asserts that $x^n + y^n + z^n = 0$ has no solutions in integers $x,y,$ and z not divisible by n. Germain proved Case 1 of Fermat's Last Theorem for all primes n greater than 2 and less than 100. The proof is based on what has come to be known as Germain's Theorem:

Let n be an odd prime. If there is a second ("auxiliary") prime p with the properties that

$$(1) \ x^n + y^n + z^n \equiv 0 \ (\mathrm{mod} \ p) \text{ implies } x \equiv 0 \text{ or}$$
$$y \equiv 0 \text{ or } z \equiv 0 \ (\mathrm{mod} \ p), \text{ and}$$
$$(2) \ x^n \equiv n \ (\mathrm{mod} \ p) \text{ is impossible,}$$

then Case 1 of Fermat's Last Theorem is true for n.

The proof of Germain's Theorem appears in different forms in several sources (Edwards 1977). Her table of auxiliary primes appears in the second supplement to Legendre's work on number theory. Her work was a considerable advance at that time, as Fermat's Last Theorem had fascinated mathematicians for centuries; prior to Germain's work Euler had proved it for the case $n = 3$ and Legendre for $n = 5$. Her proof was used by L. E. Dickson in 1908 to generalize her work to $n < 1700$ and later to $n < 7000$. More recently, J. Barkley Rosser used her theorem to prove Case 1 for $n < 41,000,000$ (1940).

In 1910 E. Dubouis paid tribute to Germain's work by defining a "sophien" of a prime to be a prime p of the form $kn + 1$ where n is also prime such that $x^n \equiv y^n + 1 \pmod{p}$. He proved that for any given n there exists a finite number of sophiens.

In Germain's correspondence with Gauss in the first decade of the 1800s, she also provided solutions for several problems in number theory (Boncompagni 1880). One of these, a generalization of one of Gauss's results, she published much later (1831). She also referred to a proof of Fermat's Last Theorem for $n = p - 1$, p a prime of the form $8k + 7$; but this result has never been published. She also provided a solution to a problem that baffled Lagrange (Boncompagni 1880). She used Gauss's method to reduce the formula $s^{10} - 11(s^8 - 4s^6r^2 + 7s^4r^4 - 5s^2r^6 + r^8)r^2$ to $t^2 - 11u^2$.

There was also considerable discussion between Gauss and LeBlanc/Germain concerning binary, ternary, and quaternary forms. Germain came up with a result equivalent to the theorem later proved by Cauchy: Let $A = (a_{ij})$ be a square matrix with determinant D. If $\epsilon \pm a_{11}a_{22} \ldots a_{nn} = D$, then $\epsilon \pm A_{11}A_{22} \ldots A_{nn} = D^{n-1}$, A_{ik} being the coefficient of a_{ik} in D^2. She also produced proofs for several of Gauss's unsolved problems in cubic and biquadratic residues. At the same time, Germain did some work in astronomy. Her correspondence with Gauss reflects a thorough understanding of the astronomical work of Laplace and Lagrange.

Germain's work in elasticity suffered generally from an absence of rigor, which might be attributed to her lack of formal training in the rudiments of analysis. The difficulty of the problems she tackled, in view of the gaps in her background and her mathematical isolation, did not discourage her. J. Fang wrote of her approach:

[She] never hesitated to compete with her contemporary [mathematical] giants, all male, for the most difficult problems. The harder, the better or the more significant. Her unerring instinct, as it were, would always direct her to such "significant" problems. And, of course, there was always her magnificent talent to solve them somehow or other. (Fang 1976/77, 54)

The interest in the mathematical theory of elastic surfaces resulted from demonstrations of Chladni in Paris in 1808. He sprinkled sand on a metal plate and transferred the nodal figures formed during vibration to a wet sheet of paper.

The problem as posed by the Academy was: To give the mathematical theory of the vibration of an elastic surface and to compare the theory to experimental evidence. Germain's was the only entry in the 1811 competition, for Lagrange had frightened off all other contenders by his pronouncement that a solution would require the invention of a whole new system of analysis. Unfortunately, although Germain's approach was correct, her mathematics were not. However, from Germain's hypothesis, Lagrange was able to derive an equation that is correct under special assumptions and which was used by Poisson and others in subsequent work on elasticity.

The competition was reopened, with a closing date of October 1813. Germain's entry again suffered from mathematical errors, due to a lack of understanding of variational techniques, in particular the misuse of double integrals; but she did receive an honorable mention. In 1816 she won the third competition, although there was lingering doubt as to the rigor of her work. In the published version which appeared in 1821, Germain herself pointed out some errors; Gustav Robert Kirchhoff pointed out others; others remained uncorrected. In 1814 Poisson had published his own work on elasticity, not acknowledging his indebtedness to Germain; as a judge of the 1813 competition, he had had access to her entry. Poisson's work was based on the molecular theory of Laplacian mechanics, a view which dominated French science at the time. Germain's work, although shaky mathematically, did not suffer from reliance on any such theory; but it took some years for the Laplace-Poisson view to be discredited. The subsequent work on elasticity by Jean Baptiste Joseph Fourier, Navier, and Cauchy relied to some extent on the Germain-Lagrange model. Germain's work was fundamental in the development of a general theory of elasticity.

In 1821 Germain published her prize memoir, still not free from the mathematical weaknesses. Subsequently, she attempted to extend her research, in a paper submitted in 1825 to a commission of the Institut de France comprised of Poisson, Gaspard de Prony, and Laplace. The work suffered from a number of deficiencies, but rather than reporting them to the author, the commission apparently simply ignored the paper. It was recovered from Prony's papers and published in 1880.

Germain wrote a more philosophical paper on the subject of elasticity; it appeared in 1828. There she referred to her earlier criticism of the molecular theory, but went on to condemn the confusion of mathematical theory with causal conjectures.

Significantly, although it was Germain who first attempted to solve a difficult problem, when others of more training, ability, and contacts built on her work, and elasticity became an important scientific topic, she was closed out. Women were simply not taken seriously.

The remainder of Germain's scientific work consisted of two more or less retrospective papers, one on the concept of mean curvature of a surface in three-space, developed by her in her work on elasticity, and the other revisiting some topics in number theory.

Germain did not intend to publish her work in philosophy; but her nephew, Armand-Jacques Lherbette, compiled her writings for publication to fulfill what he considered to be his duty to her memory. The primary thrust of the main essay is to show the similarities in exact sciences, philosophy, literature, and the fine arts. In her applications of stable and unstable equilibria and related concepts to political and mechanical phenomena, one can see a hint of the principles underlying catastrophe theory.

Whereas the school of Descartes believed that laws governed the inorganic world, Germain believed that the living world also has its governing principles, which could be discovered and used to calculate events. Alexis Claude Clairaut, Euler, Jean Baptiste Le Rond d'Alembert, the Bernoullis, Lagrange, and Laplace had presided at the last great period of celestial discoveries and systemization; Henry Cavendish, Joseph Priestley, Antoine-Laurent Lavoisier, and Berthollet had discovered the composition of earth, air, and water; Antoine-Laurent de Jussieu, Carl von Linné, Georges-Louis Buffon, Johann Wolfgang von Goethe, and others developed botanical classifications. Consequently, there was optimism about similar progress in the study of human behavior.

Germain observed that science results from the classification of observed facts, the abstraction and concomitant simplification from these, and finally the idealization in a system as Leibniz had done in mathematics, Laplace in astronomy, and Jussieu in biology. She hoped to do the same in what we now know as psychology and, in particular, sociology. Her philosophy emphasized the unity of the physical and moral orders of things and anticipated many of the features of the positivism of Auguste Comte, by whom her work was highly regarded (Comte 1869, 415).

BIBLIOGRAPHY

Works by Sophie Germain

Mathematical Works

"Remarques sur le mémoire d'Euler: 'Investigatio motuum quibus laminae et virgae elasticae constremiscunt,' *Acta Acad. Petrop. Ann.* (1779): 103 et seq." Manuscript, Bibliothèque Nationale, MS Fr. 9114 f. 155–194.
Recherches sur la théorie des surfaces élastiques. Paris: Huzard-Courcier, 1821.
Remarques sur la nature, les bornes et l'étendue de la question des surfaces élastiques. Paris: Huzard-Courcier, 1826.
"Examen des principes qui peuvent conduire à la connaissance des lois de l'équilibre et du mouvement des solides élastiques." *Annales de chimie et de physique* 8 (1828): 123–131.
"Mémoire sur la courbure des surfaces." *Journal für die reine und angewandte Mathematik* 7 (1831): 1–29.
"Note sur la manière dont se composent les valeurs de y et z dans l'équation $4(x^p - 1)/$

$(x-1) = y^2 \pm pz^2$ et celles de Y' et Z' dans l'equation $4(x^p - 1)/(x-1) = Y'^2$ $\pm pZ'^2$." *Journal für die reine und angewandte Mathematik* 7 (1831): 201–204.
"Mémoire sur l'emploi de l'épaisseur dans la théorie des surfaces élastiques." *Journal de Mathématiques pures et appliqués* 6 (1880) Supplement: S5–S64.

Other Works

"Considérations générales sur l'état des sciences et des lettres aux différentes époques de leur culture." Edited by Armand-Jacques Lherbette. Paris: 1833.
Oeuvres philosophiques de Sophie Germain (suiviés de pensées et de lettres inédités et précédées d'une notice sur sa vie et ses oeuvres). Edited by H. Stupuy. Paris: Paul Ritti, 1879. New ed. Paris: Firmin-Didot, 1896.

Works about Sophie Germain

Bell, E. T. *Men of Mathematics,* 253, 261–263. New York: Simon & Schuster, 1965.
Biedenkapp, Georg. *Sophie Germain, ein weiblicher Denker.* Jena: H. W. Schmidt, G. Tauscher, 1910.
Boncompagni, B. *Cinq Lettres de Sophie Germain à Charles-Frédéric Gauss.* Berlin: Gustave Schade, 1880. Also published in *Archiv der Mathematik und Physik* 65 (1880): 259. Original Italian edition, Firenze: 1871.
    Contains the text of Germain's letters to Gauss, but not all of the mathematical papers that accompanied them.
———. "Intorno ad una lettera di Carlo Frédérico Gauss al Dr. Enrico Guglielmo Mattia Olbers: Memoria." *Atti dell'Accademia Pontificia de Nuovi Lincei* 36 (1884): 201–295.
    Gauss speaks highly of Germain's talents in correspondence with his colleague Olbers.
———. *Lettera inedita di Carlo Frédérico Gauss à Sofia Germain.* Firenze, Paris: 1879. Also in *Werke,* by Carl Friedrich Gauss, vol. 10.1. Göttingen: 1917.
    Here is collected the other side of the Germain-Gauss correspondence.
Bucciarelli, Louis L., and Nancy Dworsky. *Sophie Germain: An Essay in the History of the Theory of Elasticity.* Dordrecht, Holland: D. Reidel Publishing Company, 1980.
    A biography centered around Germain's work on elasticity. Emphasizes the deficiencies in her work and the hardships imposed by her relative isolation from the contemporary scientific community, as well as the controversy surrounding the early development of elasticity theory. Review: *American Mathematical Monthly* 92 (1985): 64–70.
Comte, Auguste. *Cours de philosophie positive.* Vol. 2. Paris: J. B. Baillière et Fils, 1869.
Dickson, L. E. *History of the Theory of Numbers.* Vol. 1, 382–383; vol. 2, 732–769. New York: G. E. Stechert, 1934.
Dubouis, E. "Sur les nombres premiers." *Intermédiaire des Mathématiciens* 17 (1910): 103–104.
Dunnington, G. Waldo. *Carl Friedrich Gauss: Titan of Science.* New York: Hafner, 1955.
    Detailed account of Gauss's exchanges with Germain and his evaluation of her work.

Edwards, Harold M. *Fermat's Last Theorem: A Genetic Introduction to Algebraic Number Theory*, 61–65. New York: Springer-Verlag, 1977.

Fang, J. "Mathematicians, man or woman: Exercises in a Verstehen-approach." *Philosophia Mathematica* 13/14 (1976/1977): 15–72.
Analyzes Germain's general approach to mathematics.

Fère, Guyot de. "Sophie Germain." *Nouvelle Biographie Générale*. 1842 ed. Edited by Jean Chrétien Ferdinand Hoefer. Paris: Firmin-Didot, 1842.
Appears to be the earliest reference to Germain in a biographical reference book.

Genocchi, Angelo. "Alcune asserzioni di C. F. Gauss circa le forme quadratiche $Y + nZZ$." *Bollettino di bibliografia e di storia delle scienze matematiche e fisiche* 17 (1884): 245–247.

———. "Ancora un cenno dei residui cubici e biquadratici." *Bollettino di bibliografia e di storia delle scienze matematiche e fisiche* 18 (1885): 231–234.

———. "Il carteggio di Sofia Germain e Carlo Frédérico Gauss." *Atti della Reale Accademia Delle Scienze di Torino* 15 (1880): 795–808.

———. "Intorno ad una proposizione inesatta di Sofia Germain." *Bollettino di bibliografia e di storia delle scienze matematiche e fisiche* 17 (1884): 315–316.

———. "Sur la loi de reciprocité de Legendre étendue aux nombres non premiers." *Bollettino di bibliografia e di storia delle scienze matematiche e fisiche* 18 (1885): 235–237.

———. "Teoremi di Sofia Germain intorno ai residui biquadratici." *Bollettino di bibliografia e di storia delle scienze matematiche e fisiche* 18 (1885): 248–251.
This series of papers discusses Germain's contributions to number theory.

Göring, Hugo. *Sophie Germain und Clotilde de Vaux: Ihr Leben und Denken*. Zurich: 1889.
A comparative biography, attempting to place Germain in terms of cultural influences.

Gray, Mary. "Sophie Germain, a bicentennial appreciation." *Association for Women in Mathematics Newsletter* 6 (6) (September–October 1976): 10–14.

Harlor. "Sophie Germain: mathématicienne et philosophe." *Revue des deux mondes: littérature, histoire, arts et sciences* (1 September 1953): 134–145.

Henry, Charles. "Les manuscrits de Sophie Germain—documents nouveaux." *Revue philosophique* 8 (1879): 627–636.

Ladd-Franklin, Christine. "Sophie Germain: An unknown mathematician." *Century* 48 (1894): 946–949. Reprinted in *Association for Women in Mathematics Newsletter* 11 (3) (May–June 1981): 7–11. "Postscript." *Century* 49 (1894): 157.

Legendre, A. M. "Recherches sur quelque object d'analyse indeterminée et particulièrement sur le théorème de Fermat." 2nd suppl. to *Essai sur la Théorie des Nombres*, 2nd ed. Paris: Courcier, 1808. Also in *Mémoires de l'Académie Royale des Sciences de l'Institut de France*, vol. 6. Paris: Firmin-Didot, 1821.
Legendre reports Germain's work on Fermat's Last Theorem.

Libri, Guillaume. "Sciences Mathématiques—Mlle. Germain." *Journal des Débats* (18 May 1832).

Mordell, L. J. *Le Dernier Théorème de Fermat*. Paris: Les Presses Universitaires de France, 1929.
Germain's work is included.

Mozans, H. J. *Woman in Science*. New York: D. Appleton & Co., 1913, 154–157. Reprint. Cambridge, Mass.: MIT Press, 1974.

Noguera, Rodrigo. "Generalizacion de la identidad de Sofia Germain." *Studia revista de la universidad del Atlantico* 1 (1956): 131–135.

Raphael, Ellen. *Sophie Germain, Mathematician: A Biographical Sketch.* Senior thesis, Brown University, 1978.

> The most complete discussion in English of Germain's life; contains much anecdotal material and the text of the Germain-Gauss correspondence.

Ravaisson-Mollien, Félix. *La Philosophie en France au XIX^{ieme} Siècle.* Paris: Librairie Hachette, 1904.

> Germain's philosophy is discussed.

Scripta Mathematica 19 (1953): 189.

> Photo of a bust of Germain.

"Sophie Germain und Gauss." *Das Weltall* 26 (1926): 8–11. Reprinted in *Kölnische Zeitung* (1 April 1927); also in *Neue Züricher Zeitung* 3 (1966).

Terquem, M. "Sophie Germain." *Bulletin de bibliographie, d'histoire et biographie mathématique* 6 (1860): 9–12. Appended to *Nouvelles Annales de Mathématique* 19 (1860).

Todhunter, Isaac, and Karl Pearson. *A History of the Theory of Elasticity and of the Strength of Materials.* Vol. 1, 147–160. Cambridge, England: Cambridge University Press, 1886. Reprint. New York: Dover, 1960.

> Germain's theorem on elastic surfaces and its importance to later developments are described.

Vandiver, H. S. "Fermat's Last Theorem." *American Mathematical Monthly* 53 (1946): 557–578.

EVELYN BOYD GRANVILLE (1924–)

Patricia Clark Kenschaft

BIOGRAPHY

No doctorate in mathematics was granted to a black woman until 1949, when two were awarded in the United States, to Marjorie Lee Browne and Evelyn Boyd Granville. There were no more during the next decade (Kenschaft 1981). Browne, who was ten years older than Granville, devoted her remaining thirty years to North Carolina Central University and died a few months after her retirement in 1979 (Kenschaft 1980). She and Granville never met.

Granville, who had just passed her twenty-fifth birthday when she received her doctorate from Yale University, had a varied and interesting career. She was born in Washington, D.C., on May 1, 1924, to William and Julia Walker Boyd, when her older sister Doris, her only sibling, was less than twenty months old. Her father's job was maintaining the apartment building in which they lived, but he did not remain with them through their childhood. His checkered career included stints as a chauffeur and as a messenger in the FBI office. Granville does not know where he grew up or the extent of his schooling.

She was raised by her mother and her mother's twin sister, Louise Walker, who never married. They had grown up in Orange, Virginia, and were high school graduates. For over thirty-five years both were examiners with the U.S. Bureau of Engraving and Printing. Eventually, Louise Walker, who had earlier been graduated from Miner Normal Teachers College with certification to teach kindergarten, became a supervisor. They raised the girls as Episcopalians. Granville's sister left college in 1942 to begin a career as a statistical assistant in the U.S. Census Bureau.

Although the public schools of Washington, D.C., were racially segregated during Granville's youth, the academic high school that she attended had high standards. Several of Dunbar High School's teachers had degrees from top colleges, and they pushed their students to excellence, encouraging them to apply to the best colleges. Her mathematics teachers included Ulysses Basset, a Yale graduate, and Mary Cromwell, a graduate of the University of Pennsylvania, who was also her homeroom teacher. Cromwell's sister, Otelia Cromwell, had earned a doctorate from Yale in English around the turn of the century and campaigned to send blacks to Ivy League institutions. Granville cites Basset, Cromwell, and Mary Hundley (who taught French) as "outstanding teachers," and says, "We looked up to our teachers as people to emulate." She describes her family and teachers as "very supportive" of her academic aspirations.

Money was not as plentiful as encouragement. She won a small partial scholarship for her first year at Smith College, but her mother and aunt had to make many sacrifices in order to pay the rest of her bills. During her last three years she lived in a "co-op house" where there were no maids and the students waited on tables and helped the cooks. During her summers she worked for the National Bureau of Standards in Washington.

She studied astronomy under Miss Marjorie Williams and wanted to be an astronomer, but did not relish the prospect of the isolation of the great observatories where astronomers had to live in those days. Now she reflects that if she had foreseen the space program and her role in it, she would have majored in astronomy. However, she enjoyed studying mathematics under Neal McCoy and Susan Rambo. In 1945 she graduated summa cum laude and was elected to Phi Beta Kappa.

She then won awards for graduate study from Yale University. During her first year these were supplemented by a fellowship from Smith College. She earned an M.A. in mathematics and physics in one year. Then for two years she held a Julius Rosenwald Fellowship, designated to enable the most promising American blacks to develop their research potential. During her third and last year of doctoral work, she was an Atomic Energy Commission Predoctoral Fellow. She specialized in functional analysis, writing her dissertation under Einar Hille, a former president of the American Mathematical Society. She received her doctorate in 1949, at which time she was elected to membership in the scientific honorary society Sigma Xi.

After a postdoctoral year at New York University, she had interviews for a more permanent position, including one at a college not far away. Years later a woman adjunct on that faculty told this author that when the interviewing committee discovered she was black, "they just laughed." Later a male mathematician familiar with the situation said, "It was not her race that was the problem. The mathematicians wanted to hire her, but the dean said they would have to change the plumbing." Whether it was due to racial or sexual discrimination, the refusal to hire her was totally inconsistent with her superb academic credentials.

She obtained instead a position at Fisk University, where she was a much-loved associate professor from 1950 to 1952. There she taught and inspired Vivienne Malone Mayes and Etta Zuber Falconer, who later themselves earned doctorates in mathematics. Then she spent sixteen years in government and industry doing applied mathematics, numerical analysis, celestial mechanics, trajectory and orbit analysis and computation, and digital computer programming in the "space race." She describes these years as "very rewarding."

About her personal life she observes: "I never encountered any problems in combining career and private life. Black women have always had to work." She never had the complication of giving birth to children, but her sentiments echo those of most professional black women, who claim that they do not have the schizophrenic feelings that afflict middle- and upper-class white women; black women were raised to expect that they would always earn money and the only question was how. In 1960 Granville married the Reverend Gamaliel Mansfield Collins, whose three children occasionally lived with them. The marriage ended in divorce in 1967 because of incompatibility.

In 1970 she married Edward V. Granville, a real estate broker in Los Angeles. His two daughters were already grown. In 1984 she retired from California State University in Los Angeles after teaching there for seventeen years. She and her husband bought a house on sixteen acres in Texas. With 800 chickens they then went into the business of selling "fresh country eggs." Concerns such as the 275 frightened chickens that smothered when an owl entered the coop provide diversion from teaching mathematics and computer science full-time at Texas College in Tyler. She spent a couple of months teaching eighth grade nearby but discovered that she much prefers the college level.

Looking back she wrote, "I feel that I have had a very rich life. I have been blessed with a fine family, an excellent education, many friends that I have gathered over the years, and last, but by no means least, a happy (second) marriage."

WORK

After her two years at Fisk University, Granville was a mathematician for three and a half years with the Diamond Ordnance Fuze Laboratories of the U.S. Army. She was a consultant to ordnance engineers and scientists on the analysis of the mathematical problems arising in the development of missile fuzes. From January 1956 to November 1960, she was a mathematician and staff assistant for IBM. During this time she worked on the formulation of orbit computations and computer procedures for the Project Vanguard and Project Mercury space probes. She was also a consultant in numerical analysis and a programmer of the IBM 650 and 704 computers.

Then for almost two more years she participated in research studies on the methods of orbit computation with the Computation and Data Reduction Center of the U.S. Space Technology Laboratories. From August 1962 to October 1963, she was a research specialist providing technical support to the Apollo engineering departments in celestial mechanics, trajectory and orbit computation, numerical analysis, and digital computer techniques at the North American Aviation Space and Information Systems Division. Her final four years outside academia were again with IBM as a senior mathematician continuing this type of work.

In September 1967 she joined the mathematics faculty of California State University in Los Angeles, obtaining the rank of full professor. However, her teaching ranged beyond college classrooms. During the 1968–1969 school year she taught a supplemental mathematics program half-time in an elementary school under the State of California Miller Mathematics Improvement Program. In the following school year, she directed an after-school program in mathematics enrichment for kindergarten through fifth grade and taught the upper four grades herself. During the summer of 1972, she was an instructor at a National Science Foundation Institute for Secondary Teachers of Mathematics at the University of Southern California, culminating eleven years as a senior lecturer in mathematics at that university.

She was a member of several important boards, including the U.S. Civil Service Panel of Examiners of the Department of Commerce (1954–1956), the Psychology Examining Committee of the Board of Medical Examiners of the State of California (1963–1970), an advisory committee of the National Defense Education Act Title IV Graduate Fellowship Program of the Office of Education (1966–1969), the Advisory Committee of Project One of the Los Angeles County Schools Mathematics Television Project (1974–1975), and the Board of Trustees of the Center for the Improvement of Mathematics Education in San Diego (1975–1979). She has been active in the National Council of Teachers of Mathematics, the California Mathematics Council, and the American Association of University Women, serving as president of the Beverly Hills Branch of the last from 1968 to 1970.

Her major publication is the text *Theory and Application of Mathematics for Teachers,* published in 1975 and used at over fifty colleges. It was coauthored with Jason Frand.

BIBLIOGRAPHY

Works by Evelyn Boyd Granville

Mathematical Works

"On Laguerre series in the complex domain." Ph.D. diss., Yale University, 1949.
(with Jason Frand) *Theory and Application of Mathematics for Teachers.* Belmont, Calif.:
    Wadsworth Publishing Co., 1975, 1978.

Works about Evelyn Boyd Granville

Dannett, Sylvia G.L. *Profiles of Negro Womanhood.* Negro Heritage Library, vol. 2,
    82–86. Yonkers, N.Y.: Educational Heritage, 1966.
    A winsomely personal account of her life before her divorce, with many cheerful,
    idealistic quotes from her own letters.

Davis, Marianna W., ed. *Contributions of Black Women to America,* vol. 2, 455–456, 458. Columbia, S. C.: Kenday Press, 1982.

Refers to Granville by her first husband's name (Collins).

Kenschaft, Patricia. "Black men and women in mathematical research." To appear in the *Journal of Black Studies* (December 1987).

———. "Black women in mathematics in the United States." *American Mathematical Monthly* 88 (1981): 592–604. Reprinted and expanded with photographs added. *Journal of African Civilizations* 4 (1) (April 1982): 63–83.

Provides brief biographies of twenty-one of the twenty-four American black women who received doctorates in pure or applied mathematics by the end of 1980.

———. "Marjorie Lee Browne: In memoriam." *Association for Women in Mathematics Newsletter* 10 (5) (September–October 1980): 8–11.

ELLEN AMANDA HAYES (1851–1930)

Ann Moskol

BIOGRAPHY

Ellen Amanda Hayes was born on September 23, 1851, the first child of Charles Coleman and Ruth Rebecca (Wolcott) Hayes. As was the custom for first-born children, Hayes was born at the home of her maternal grandparents, who lived across the road from her parents in Granville, Ohio. Hayes's maternal great-grandparents had traveled six weeks on horseback in 1805 from Granville, Massachusetts, to form the new colony of Granville, Ohio.

As a child, Hayes enjoyed spending time on her grandparents' farm, where she developed a lifelong interest in gardening. Hayes's later interest in woman suffrage had its origin in a political meeting that she attended with her grandfather, where she observed the injustice of only men being allowed to vote on matters concerning the whole state.

Hayes grew up in a family that encouraged education of both males and females. Her grandfather, Horace Wolcott, was a friend, supporter, and trustee of the Granville Female Academy. His wife, Rebecca, was a literate woman who read Horace Greeley's *Tribune* as well as her Bible. Hayes's mother was a teacher who had graduated from the Granville Female Academy; there she had studied logic, elementary botany, and religion. Ellen Hayes learned how to read from her mother. Hayes's father, though not an educated man, supported her learning; one of Hayes's fondest memories was when she awoke to find a copy of McGuffey's *First Reader* on her pillow, given to her by her father.

Hayes's father, also descended from Ohio pioneers, was a tanner. He was wounded as an officer in the Civil War. In 1866 he moved the family to Hanover, Ohio, fourteen miles east of Granville, to start a new tannery.

Hayes attributed her adult self-reliance and independence to a childhood spent in a pioneer midwestern town. As the oldest of four girls and two boys (in order: Anna, Orlena, Mariquita, Willard, and Stanley), Ellen Hayes described her childhood role as that of a leader. Life in a midwest pioneer town was difficult because childhood diseases and death were common. When Hayes was only eleven, her four-year-old brother Willard nearly died of diphtheria. When Hayes was thirteen, her nine-year-old sister Orlena died suddenly from a fatal brain disease that was probably meningitis; Hayes deeply mourned her loss.

Hayes's family allowed their daughters much more freedom than was customary. While "proper" girls of the time stayed indoors and sewed, Hayes and her sisters participated in outdoor activities, such as climbing trees, swimming, and skating, and wore their hair short rather than in customary tight braids. Despite these freedoms, Hayes resented those restrictions that her family did impose upon her because of her sex, such as forbidding her to ride a horse and requiring her to wear a sunbonnet.

Hayes's interest in science began when she was very young. Her mother taught all the children the Latin names for plants, the parts of a flower, and how to compare different flowers. She also taught her children the names of some of the stars. Hayes also learned astronomy from her copy of Smith's *Primary Geography*. In 1858, at the age of seven, she watched Donati's comet from her home.

Hayes's formal education began at the age of seven, when she was sent to the Centerville school, a one-room ungraded public school. At the age of sixteen, Hayes taught at a country school to earn money to study. In 1872 she entered Oberlin College as a student in the preparatory department; she was admitted as a freshman in 1875. Although her main studies at Oberlin were mathematics and science, Hayes also studied English literature, Greek, Latin, and history, and was a member of Aeolian, the college literary society.

After obtaining an A.B. from Oberlin in 1878, she took a position as principal of the women's department at Adrian College in Michigan. In 1879 she accepted a position as teacher of mathematics at Wellesley College, where she worked until her retirement in 1916. In 1882 she became assistant professor, and in 1883 associate professor. In 1888 Hayes became professor and head of the mathematics department. In 1897 she was made head (and sole member) of a new department of applied mathematics; she had the difficult task of teaching all seven applied mathematics courses.

Hayes was a very strong-willed individual whose views often clashed with those of others. According to one of her colleagues, the Wellesley College administration removed Hayes as head of the mathematics department because of complaints that she admitted graduates from some preparatory schools while refusing admission to others who graduated from schools of comparable or higher standards. Relations between Hayes and the pure mathematics faculty were strained, according to reports from a former student and from a colleague (Brown 1932, 25; Merrill 1944, 43–44). When she retired in 1916 after thirty-seven years of teaching at Wellesley College, the trustees did not appoint her professor emeritus.

Hayes was a very controversial mathematics professor because of her unorthodox views and manner. Although she had attended Methodist Sunday school as a child, she did not affiliate with any religion as an adult and was regarded by her colleagues as an unbeliever. She rarely attended college chapel, and she shocked colleagues and students by questioning the truth of the Bible. Defying fashion, she wore comfortable thick-soled shoes and practical skirts with many pockets instead of the long, cumbersome skirts that were in fashion.

Hayes had a variety of social concerns. In 1888 she wrote a regular editorial column for the college newspaper, in which she discussed women's causes such as suffrage and dress reform. In the 1890s she founded a chapter of the temperance movement at Wellesley.

Hayes was considered a political radical because she espoused socialist causes. She supported the union movement and the right of workers to share in profits. At the height of the Lawrence strike in 1912, Hayes addressed a crowd of 2,000 people in the Colonial Theatre in Boston and urged them to continue their strike. In that same year, she was the Socialist Party candidate for Secretary of State in Massachusetts, the first woman in Massachusetts to be nominated for a state office. Ironically, although no women were allowed to vote for her, she won more votes than any other Socialist candidate on the ballot and 2,500 more votes than the Socialist candidate for governor. She also wrote a socialist novel for young people.

Hayes spent her retirement writing and speaking on a variety of social causes. During the Russian Revolution, when anti-Red mania was sweeping the country, she helped raise money for Russian orphans and defended socialist causes, despite threats on her life. From 1924 until 1930, she wrote and published *The Relay,* a monthly that discussed current events, education, nature, geology and geography, and astronomy. She worked for the Socialist Party and in an intercollegiate socialist organization. She supported the work of the Rationalist Society; in 1930 she read a paper entitled "Is Science Becoming Religious?" at its New York meeting.

In 1927, at the age of seventy-six, Hayes was arrested for marching in protest against the execution of Nicola Sacco and Bartolomeo Vanzetti. She became a defendant in the American Civil Liberties Union's test case concerning the legality of the arrests, which was won on appeal.

In the fall of 1929, Hayes moved to West Park, New York, to help teach at the newly founded Vineyard Shore School for women workers in industry. Her pain from arthritis did not prevent her from actively participating in the new school; she taught geology and shared her learning and thoughts at informal gatherings of the faculty and the fourteen students. On October 27, 1930, she died. According to her will, her brain was sent to the Wilder Brain Collection at Cornell University; her ashes were buried in Granville, Ohio.

WORK

Hayes had very high standards of instruction. As head of the mathematics department, she wrote the examination questions for all the courses; many of the instructors found these problems too difficult for the students. During the first year that Hayes's trigonometry book was used, over half of the students received a grade of D or below. Nevertheless, she had a loyal following of students who appreciated her serious teaching style. After these students graduated, Hayes often corresponded with them, offering suggestions and encouragement in their own teaching.

Hayes was especially interested in astronomy. In 1887–1888 she studied at the Leander McCormick Observatory at the University of Virginia, where she determined the definite orbit of the newly discovered Minor Planet 267. In her 1904 *Science* article, Hayes suggested that the newly discovered Comet *a* could possibly be an asteroid. She based her assertion on a comparison of its elliptic elements with those of Mars and Jupiter. In that same year, Hayes delivered a paper on the path of the shadow of a plummet bead at a meeting of the American Association for the Advancement of Science. Hayes developed an equation for describing the shadow and showed mathematically how to determine the latitude and time of year in which the shadow would form various conic curves.

Hayes was concerned that females take sufficient mathematics and science courses. Hayes (1910) argued that the reasons for the small number of women scientists included (1) social pressures that rewarded females for spending time on their appearance, rather than on science; and (2) the scarcity of good employment opportunities for females. She advised college girls to study science and mathematics, especially the fundamental sciences of physics and chemistry. She was particularly critical of the elective system, which allowed females to avoid studying science and mathematics (1909).

Hayes taught a diversity of applied courses, such as mechanics, thermodynamics, geodynamics, and mathematical astronomy, and her college textbooks in algebra, calculus, and trigonometry stressed mathematical applications.

BIBLIOGRAPHY

Works by Ellen Amanda Hayes

Mathematical Works

Lessons on Higher Algebra. Boston: Press of F. I. Brown, 1891. Rev. ed. Boston: J. S. Cushing & Co., 1894.
Elementary Trigonometry. Boston: J. S. Cushing & Co., 1896.
Algebra for High Schools and Colleges. Norwood, Mass.: J. S. Cushing & Co., 1897.
Calculus with Applications: An Introduction to the Mathematical Treatment of Science. Boston: Allyn & Bacon, 1900.
"Comet *a* 1904." *Science* 19 (27 May 1904): 833–834.
"The path of the shadow of a plummet bead." *Popular Astronomy* 16 (1908): 279–286.

Other Works

Letters to a College Girl. Boston: Geo. H. Ellis Co., 1909.
"Women and scientific research." *Science* 32 (16 December 1910): 864–866.

Works about Ellen Amanda Hayes

Brown, Louise. *Ellen Hayes: Trail-Blazer*. West Park, N.Y., 1932.
 Detailed pamphlet on Hayes's life, written by a former Wellesley College student and friend. Proceeds were to be used to fund the Ellen Hayes Laboratory in the Vineyard Shore School.

Gordon, Geraldine. "Ellen Hayes: 1851–1930." *The Wellesley Magazine* (February 1931): 151–152.
 Short summary of Hayes's life, written at the time of her death.

Merrill, Helen A. "Ellen A. Hayes." In Scrapbook of the History of the Department of Mathematics, 1944: 41–46. Archives, Wellesley College.

GRACE BREWSTER MURRAY HOPPER (1906–   )

Amy C. King with Tina Schalch

BIOGRAPHY

Grace Brewster Murray Hopper was born in New York City on December 9, 1906. Her parents were Walter Fletcher Murray, an insurance broker, and Mary Campbell Van Horne Murray, the daughter of a New York City senior civil engineer. Hopper's church affiliation is Dutch Reformed; her political affiliation, Republican.

It is Wolfeboro, New Hampshire, that Hopper claims as her second hometown, inasmuch as she first traveled there in the summer of 1907 and spent many summers thereafter at the family summer home. In November 1983 Brewster Academy in Wolfeboro welcomed hundreds of guests to honor her, where the Grace Murray Hopper Center for Computer Learning was dedicated. New Hampshire's governor proclaimed November 7, 1983, Captain Grace Murray Hopper Day throughout the state.

Hopper considers herself fortunate that her father felt that his two daughters should be allowed the same educational opportunities as his son. She went to Vassar College (as did her younger sister) and received her B.A. in mathematics in 1928. In 1930 she married Vincent Foster Hopper, an educator whom she had met in Wolfeboro; this union was dissolved in 1945.

Following graduation from Vassar, Hopper received her M.A. (1930) and her Ph.D. (1934) from Yale, working under the algebraist Oystein Ore. During the years 1934–1937, Yale awarded only seven Ph.D.'s in mathematics, and that a woman received one of these was unusual for that day.

Hopper's distinguished career began with her return to Vassar as an assistant in mathematics in 1931; she eventually became associate professor. In 1941 she was awarded a Vassar Faculty Fellowship for a year's postdoctoral study at the Courant Institute of New York University.

Hopper's ancestry in the military service included a Minuteman from the Revolutionary War period and a great-grandfather who achieved the rank of rear admiral during the Civil War. Hence it is not surprising that in 1943, during

World War II, she took a leave of absence from Vassar and joined the military section of the Women Accepted for Voluntary Emergency Service (WAVES). After completion of training at the U.S. Naval Reserve Midshipman's School-W at Northampton, Massachusetts, she was commissioned lieutenant, junior-grade, and was assigned to the Bureau of Ordnance Computation Project at Harvard University. There Hopper's long-term professional association began with the computing pioneer Howard Aiken. He greatly influenced her later thinking on computer software and program documentation.

In 1946 Hopper left active navy duty and officially resigned from Vassar. Her subsequent career has had industrial, military, and academic components. A complete list of Hopper's professional activities, along with her numerous awards and honors, takes up seven pages (single-spaced) in her resume.

Continuing to work with Aiken, Hopper accepted a three-year research fellowship in engineering science and applied physics at the Computation Laboratory at Harvard. At the conclusion of her fellowship in 1949, Hopper joined the staff at Eckert-Mauchly Computer Corporation in Philadelphia. Despite corporate changes (i.e., it later became the Univac Corporation and eventually a division of Sperry-Rand Corporation), she continued this industrial affiliation in various capacities (senior mathematician, director of automatic programming development, staff scientist) until her official retirement in 1971.

Through the years she has maintained a close connection with the Naval Reserve; she was promoted to commander in 1957. The navy retired her on December 31, 1966, which she has called the saddest day of her life. On August 1, 1967, however, she was recalled to active duty. In 1973 she was too old for a regular promotion, but by a special act of Congress she was promoted to the rank of captain. By 1983 she was the oldest officer on active duty in the navy. On December 15, 1983, at a ceremony at the White House, President Ronald Reagan presented Hopper with a star that signified her promotion to commodore; the title of that grade was changed to rear admiral on November 8, 1985. She was on active duty with the Naval Data Automation Command. Her deactivation in the summer of 1986 marked forty-three years in military service.

Since 1959 Hopper has been a member of the adjunct faculty at the Moore School of Electrical Engineering, University of Pennsylvania. During the 1970s she also lectured at George Washington University.

Honors accrued have come from the navy, private industry, and academe. They include election to Phi Beta Kappa in 1928, to Sigma Xi in 1934, and to Fellow of the Institute of Electrical and Electronics Engineers in 1962; the Achievement Award by the Society of Women Engineers in 1964; and even the "Man-of-the-Year" Award of the Data Processing Management Association in 1969. Hopper holds honorary doctorates in engineering, law, science, and public service from at least ten universities in the United States and abroad.

Everywhere she has charmed audiences with her lectures. One anecdote she recounts involves her mother's dismay at finding seven of their alarm clocks dismantled. Hopper had taken one of them apart, and when she could not reassemble it, she had opened the next one to see where the parts should fit. This pattern of exploration had continued through the sequence of all seven clocks.

Her illustration of a nanosecond is famous: it is a wire 11.8 inches long, representing the distance that electricity travels in a billionth of a second. Following most lectures, the audience may "pick up a nanosecond" from a stack that she supplies.

One of her firm beliefs is that there is always room for improvement, and that things do not always have to be done in the same way. To prove her point, she keeps a clock that runs counterclockwise. Whenever someone in her office argues that something must be done in a traditional manner, she just points to her clock.

A portion of her life's principles can be shared in the following quotations:

I do have a maxim—I teach it to all youngsters: "A ship in port is safe, but that's not what ships are built for." I like the world of today much better than that a half-century ago. I am very sorry for the people who, at thirty, forty, or fifty, retire mentally and stop learning. Today, the challenges are greater. I like our young people; they know more, they question more, and they learn more. They are the greatest asset this country has. (Tropp 1984, 18)

She closes each of her public appearances with these words:

I've been grateful for all the help I've been given and all of the wonderful things that have happened to me. I've also received a large number of the honors that are given to anyone in the computer industry. But I've already received the highest award I will ever receive—no matter how long I live, no matter how many different jobs I may have— and that has been the privilege and honor of serving proudly in the United States Navy. (Tropp 1984, 18)

WORK

Hopper's achievements in the design of software for digital computers have spanned three computer generations. Initially she devoted her talents to the Mark I (also known as the Automatic Sequence Controlled Calculator); she was only the third person to work on this early large-scale digital computer. She devised computer solutions to war-related problems.

Hopper contributed to the development of the later Mark II and Mark III computers. In 1945 her computer team used the term "bug" to refer to a computer glitch. A two-inch moth was discovered in the circuitry of the malfunctioning Mark II. The computer operator carefully removed the dead moth with a pair of tweezers, put it in a logbook with plastic tape over it, and wrote: "The actual bug found." This first bug can still be seen in the Naval Surface Weapons Center in Dahlgren, Virginia.

At Eckert-Mauchly, Hopper coded for the Univac I, the first commercial large-scale electronic computer. She remains modest about her discoveries and work, which she says were just due to common sense and laziness. One day, while trying to find an error, she thought of the idea of letting the Univac manufacture its own programs. Hopper designed a piece of tape on which three letters were typed to represent each set of instructions. She completed a library of all the pieces of code for various functions and procedures and then gave each a name. When a programmer called on one of these names, the computer would locate the corresponding instructions from its memory store and copy the code and the address. Thus, the first compiler, the so-called A–O system, was developed and implemented in 1952 by Hopper and her staff. It was a single-pass compiler. Two years passed, however, before computer experts were convinced of the usefulness of this concept, which was actually a major breakthrough in automatic programming.

With her usual zeal to make knowledge more accessible, Hopper realized that most people were more conversant with a statement in English than with mathematical symbols. Thus, she explored means by which computer program commands could be written in English rather than in machine code. This was the basis for COBOL (Common Business Oriented Language), the high-level language developed in the 1960s, widely used in business today. She is sometimes called the "Mother of COBOL."

From 1946 to the present, Hopper has published over fifty papers and articles on software and programming languages. In addition, she is in great demand as a lecturer and advisor to private, public, and military institutions and organizations. In each of several recent years, she has logged over 100,000 miles and has given some 200 presentations.

BIBLIOGRAPHY

Works by Grace Brewster Murray Hopper

Mathematical Works

"New types of irreducibility criteria." Ph.D. diss., Yale University, 1934.

Computer Programming Works

(with Howard H. Aiken) "The automatic sequence controlled calculator. I, II, III." *Electrical Engineering* (=*Transactions of the American Institute of Electrical Engineers*) 65 (1946): 384–391, 449–454, 522–528. Russian translation in *Uspekhi Matematicheskikh Nauk* (N.S.) 3(4)(26) (1948): 119–142.

"The education of a computer." In *Proceedings of the Association for Computing Machinery* (meeting jointly sponsored by the Association for Computing Machinery and the Mellon Institute in Pittsburgh, Pa., May 2 and 3, 1952), 243–249. Pittsburgh: R. Rimbach, 1952.

"Compiling routines." *Computers and Automation* 2 (4) (May 1953): 1–5.

(with John W. Mauchly) "The influence of programming techniques on the design of computers." *Proceedings of the Institute of Radio Engineers* 41 (1953): 1250–1254.

"Automatic programming for computers." *Systems* 19 (5) (September–October 1955): 3–4.

"Automatic coding for digital computers." *Computers and Automation* 4 (9) (1955): 21–24.

"Programming business-data processors." *Control Engineering* 3 (10) (October 1956): 101–106.

"Automatic programming for computers." *Punched Card Annual* 5 (1956–1957): 197–198.

"Tomorrow—automatic programming." *Petroleum Refiner* 36 (2) (February 1957): 109–112.

"Computer programs 'in English.' " *Systems* 21 (5) (September–October 1957): 13–14.

"Automatic programming for business applications." In *Fourth Annual Electronics Conference Handbook*. New York: American Management Association, 1958.

"Automatic programming in business and industry." *Proceedings of Electronic Data Processing Conference*. University of Alabama, May 1958, 1–5.

"Automatic Programming: Present Status and Future Trends." In *Mechanisation of Thought Processes*. London, England: National Physics Laboratory Symposium (1958): 155–200.

"From programmer to computer." *Industrial and Engineering Chemistry* 50 (November 1958): 1661.

"Automatic programming language and programming aids." *Proceedings of Computers for Artillery Conference*. U.S. Army Artillery and Missile School, February 1959, 191–192.

"Conversion of electronic data-processing." *Proceedings of 10th National Conference*. American Institute of Industrial Engineers, May 1959, 157–159.

"Education can be 'Secondary.' " *Systems for Educators* 6 (2) (November–December 1959): 8.

"Progress in automatic coding for business data-handling." *Automation* 6 (5) (May 1959): 162–166.

"A data-processing compiler." *Proceedings of the National Machine Accountants Association, Data Processing 1959*, 69–76.

"The development of automatic programming." *Machine Accounting and Data Processing, The Punched Card Semi-Annual* 8 (1959): 28–32.

"Business data processing—a review." *Proceedings of the International Federation of Information Processing Congress* 1962, 35–39.

"Business data processing." *Tydschrift voor Efficientie in Docuentatie* 33 (6) (1962): 269–273.

"Automatic coding." *Proceedings of the National Office Management Association (NOMA) Conference*, Tokyo, Japan, June 1965.

"Computers and their people." *Proceedings of the NOMA Conference*, Kyoto, Japan, June 1965.

"Language standardization across manufacturers." *Proceedings of the Data Processing Management Association International Fall Conference*, Los Angeles, October 1966.

"A language of their own." *Financial Times* (London) (11 December 1967), Annual Computer Supplement.

"Standardization of high level languages." *American Federation of Information Processing Societies Conference Proceedings* 34 (1969): 608.

"Looking ahead to the '70s." *Proceedings of the UNIVAC Users Association* (September 1969): 1–9.

"Standardization of high level programming languages." *Data Processing* 14 (June 1969): 329–335.

"Standardization and the future of computers." *Data Management* 8 (4) (April 1970): 32–35.

"Possible futures and present actions." *Proceedings of the Fifth Australian Computer Conference,* Brisbane, 1972, 272–276.

"Dispersal of computer power." *Proceedings of Conference '73, Data Processing Institute,* Ottawa, 1973, 74–80.

"Technology: Future directions." *Proceedings of Conference '74, Data Processing Institute,* Ottawa, 1974, 251–256.

"David and Goliath." In *Computers in the Navy,* edited by Jan Prokop. Annapolis, Md.: Naval Institute Press, 1976.

(with Steven L. Mandell) *Understanding Computers.* West Publishing Company, 1984.

"Future possibilities: Data, hardware, software, and people." In *Naval Tactical Command and Control,* edited by Gordon R. Nagler. Washington, D.C.: Armed Forces Communication and Electronics Association International Press, 1985.

Works about Grace Brewster Murray Hopper

Blair, Marjorie. "Grace Hopper: Through the looking glass." *Electronic Education* (January 1984): 14–16, 24.

"Captain Grace M. Hopper honored at Brewster Academy in her hometown of Wolfeboro, New Hampshire." *Association for Women in Mathematics Newsletter* 14 (2) (March–April 1984): 5–6.

"Captain Grace Murray Hopper . . . still a maverick." *Concepts* (Wang Laboratories, Inc.) 6 (1) (1982): 2–7.

"Computer Sciences Man-of-Year Award." *Journal of Data Management* 7 (June 1969): 75.

Cushman, John H., Jr. "Admiral Hopper's farewell." *New York Times* (14 August 1986): B–6.

Evans, Christopher. Pioneers of Computing: An Oral History of Computing. Supported by the Science Museum and the National Physical Laboratory (England).
   Includes one-hour recorded interview with Hopper on audio cassette tape, available from the Science Museum.

Frank, Allan Dodds. "Older Than UNIVAC." *Forbes Magazine* (30 August 1982): 141.

Gilbert, Lynn, and Gaylen Moore. *Particular Passions: Talks with Women Who Have Shaped Our Times,* 58–63. New York: Crown, 1981.

"Grace Murray Hopper." *Association for Computing Machinery '71: A Quarter Century Review,* iii–iv. 1971.

Isgur, David. "Captain Hopper becomes commodore." *Granite State News* (9 November 1983).

Johnson, Steve, and Gary Miller. "Grace Hopper: A living legend." *All Hands* (788) (September 1982): 3–6.

Keerdoja, Eileen, with Paul Vercammen. "The grand old lady of software." *Newsweek* 101 (9 May 1983): 13–14.

Leopold, George. "Beacon for the Future." *Datamation* 32 (19) (1 October 1986): 109–110.

Mace, Scott. " 'Mother of COBOL'—still thinkin', still workin'." *Infoworld* 5 (18) (1983): 29–31.

Mason, John F. "Grand lady of software—Grace Hopper: It's rewarding trying to do things in a new way." *Electronic Design* 22 (25 October 1976): 82–86.

Pantages, Angeline. "Captain Grace Murray Hopper." *Data* (2 January 1985): 14–19.

Sammet, Jean E. *Programming Languages: History and Fundamentals,* 27. Englewood Cliffs, N.J.: Prentice-Hall, 1969.

Testorff, Ken. "The lady is a captain: She teaches computers how to talk." *All Hands* (700) (May 1975): 32–35.

Tropp, Henry S. "Grace Hopper: The youthful teacher of us all." *Abacus* 2 (1) (1984): 7–18.

Wexelblat, Richard, ed. *Proceedings, History of Programming Languages Conference.* New York: Academic, 1981.
  See "Introduction of Captain Grace Murray Hopper," by J. Sammet, 5–7; "Keynote Address," by G. Hopper, 7–24; and "COBOL," by J. Sammet, 199–278.

Zientara, Marguerite. "Capt. Grace M. Hopper and the genesis of programming languages." In *The History of Computing: A Biographical Portrait of the Visionaries Who Shaped the Destiny of the Computer Industry,* Part 11, 51–53. Framingham, Mass.: C. W. Communications, Inc. (375 Cochituate Rd., Box 880, Framingham, Mass. 01701), 1981.

HYPATIA (370?–415)

Ian Mueller

BIOGRAPHY

The one virtually certain date in the life of Hypatia is March 415, when she was murdered in Alexandria, Egypt. (The only reasonable alternative, March 416, is generally rejected.) Conventional wisdom places her birth at around 370, although several facts suggest that she may have been born at least twenty years earlier: the *Suidas Lexicon* says she reached her zenith in the reign of Arcadius (395–408); John Malalas calls her an old woman at the time of her death; and her most famous pupil, Synesius, is himself thought to have been born around 370. Hypatia was the daughter of Theon of Alexandria. As is frequently the case with famous figures of antiquity, we know nothing about her mother. Our one brief biography of her father (*Suidas Lexicon*, vol. 2, 702) indicates that he was "from the Museum," the famous Alexandrian institution of higher learning. Theon wrote commentaries on Ptolemy's *Almagest* and *Handy Tables;* he also published editions of Euclid's *Elements, Data,* and *Optics,* as well as of the *Catoptrics,* traditionally but quite certainly wrongly ascribed to Euclid. Theon's editions of Euclid almost entirely replaced earlier versions; in fact, until the early nineteenth century, his editions *were* Euclid.

The Museum was on its last legs in Theon's time; indeed, he is the last attested member. A contemporary (Epiphanios, *De Mensuris et Ponderibus* 9) describes the section of Alexandria in which the Museum was located as "desolate." Around 390, at a time of violent Christian-pagan confrontations, a large temple complex, housing the main library of the Museum, was destroyed by Christians; many intellectuals seem to have left Alexandria as a result of this turmoil (Sozomen, *Historia Ecclesiastica* VII 15; Socrates V 16).

Our knowledge of Hypatia suggests that, in an era in which the domains of intellect and politics were almost exclusively male, Theon was an unusually liberated person who taught an unusually gifted daughter and encouraged her to achieve things that, as far as we know, no woman before her did or perhaps even dreamed of doing. Socrates says that, after being educated by her father,

Hypatia came to surpass both contemporaries and later intellectuals in mathematical knowledge. Theon refers to Hypatia as his philosopher-daughter, and our sources also treat her as a philosopher. Although the word "philosopher" can have a general meaning approximated by our word "professor," there can be little doubt that Hypatia was a philosopher in our sense as well as a mathematician. She is said to have lectured on Plato, Aristotle, and "all the other philosophers," and to have attracted pupils "from all over the place." However, we do not know whether Hypatia had an official teaching position. The two passages that have been used to support the claim that she did are both problematic. In the *Suidas Lexicon*, her teaching is described with a word which ordinarily means "at public expense," but can mean "in public," a meaning which seems more appropriate to the context, in which Hypatia is said to have spoken on philosophy while walking through the middle of the city. Socrates says that she was head of the Platonic School in Alexandria; however, he also makes Plotinus a head of that school, which he certainly was not.

Hypatia's most famous pupil was Synesius of Cyrene, later bishop of Ptolemais, a provincial capital located on the coast of what is now Libya. His letters include seven to Hypatia and two in which she is mentioned in highly laudatory tones of a kind frequently found in pupils' descriptions of their teachers in this period. In one letter (16) he addresses her as "mother, sister, teacher, and benefactress"; and in another (136) he remarks that philosophy has left Athens for Egypt, which is nourished by the fecundity of Hypatia. The scientific side of Hypatia's teaching can be seen in his letter (15) requesting her to send him a hydrometer, the construction of which he describes roughly, and in a letter accompanying an astronomical instrument which he says he designed himself with "contributions" from Hypatia (*Address to Paeonius;* Synesius also sent a copy of this document to Hypatia [Letter 154]). The instrument is some form of planisphaerium, but Synesius' description is too vague to make a precise reconstruction possible.

Hypatia is described in the *Suidas Lexicon* as a beautiful and well-proportioned woman. It is generally believed that she never married. She dressed in the tattered cloak favored by many philosophers of antiquity; and, like them, she carried on discussions in the center of her city, feeling no reticence in the presence of males because of her intellectual gifts. Hypatia's listeners included many city officials. In one letter (81), Synesius praises her power and asks her to intercede on behalf of two young men with all those who honor her, both private citizens and officials. One of the officials closely associated with Hypatia toward the end of her life was Orestes, the Prefect of Alexandria, by then a part of the Christian Eastern Empire centered at Constantinople. In 412 Cyril became archbishop of Alexandria. Trouble between Orestes and Cyril began with Jewish-Christian antagonisms. Orestes, resentful of Cyril's growing power, arrested and publicly tortured one of Cyril's followers, accused by the Jews of being an agitator. Cyril demanded in a menacing way that the Jews stop harassing the Christians. When the Jews carried out a nighttime massacre of Christians, Cyril, apparently acting on his own authority, seized the synagogues and drove the Jews out of Alexandria. Both Cyril and Orestes appealed to the emperor, and Cyril appealed to Orestes in the name of Christianity. When Orestes was unmoved, Cyril enlisted the help of some 500 monks. They confronted Orestes and charged him with performing pagan rites, disregarding his protestations of having been baptized in Constantinople. One of them, Ammonius, bloodied Orestes's head with a stone, but Orestes was saved by the common people of Alexandria, who also turned Ammonius over to him for torture and execution.

The price for Ammonius's death appears to have been Hypatia's. She was thought by the Christians to be dissuading Orestes from friendship with Cyril. A group of them observed Hypatia on her way home. They threw her from her chariot and dragged her into the cathedral of Alexandria, where they stripped and killed her; they then cut her body into pieces, which they burned. It seems clear that Hypatia was the victim of the aggressive and fanatic policies of Cyril, whether or not he ordered her death. She would certainly not have been murdered if she had not been associated with Orestes, and she perhaps would not have been murdered if she had not been a woman. As an outstanding and unorthodox representative of pre-Christian Alexandrian traditions, she was a natural focus of resentment for those wanting to eradicate the old order. Her and Orestes's disapproval of Cyril's behavior may have been undergirded by a rational moderation transcending religious differences, but Cyril and his followers were unlikely to view it in this way. We hear no more of Orestes after Hypatia's death, which, as far as we know, was the last major event in the turmoils which brought it about. Her death was also the end of a woman who would stand out in any circumstances, but stands out especially in the ancient world.

WORK

The only extant trace of Hypatia's literary activity is her father's commentary on the *Almagest,* Book III of which is said (in words due to Theon himself) to be the version of Hypatia. However, no one has noticed any significant traits distinguishing the commentary on Book III from those on Books I and II, which are explicitly said to be Theon's own. (No indication of editorship is given for the other books.) According to the *Suidas Lexicon,* Hypatia "wrote a commentary on Diophantus, the Astronomical Table, and on Apollonius's *Conics* a commentary." Diophantus's *Arithmetic* and Apollonius's treatise on conic sections are two of the more important surviving Greek mathematical works, but we do not know what the "Astronomical Table" was. The scholarly consensus seems to be that the *Lexicon* is referring to another commentary analogous to Theon's commentaries on Ptolemy's *Handy Tables.* Judging from Theon's works, we can safely infer that Hypatia's writings were intended to help students deal with difficult mathematical classics. But, whatever the content of her writings, the fact of their existence is sufficient to establish her as the first woman known to have written on mathematical subjects.

BIBLIOGRAPHY ————————————————————————————

Works about Hypatia

Major Ancient Sources

John Malalas. *Chronographia*. In *Patrologia Graeca*. Edited by J. P. Migne. Vol. 97, XIV 359. Paris: J. P. Migne, 1865. English translation from the Slavonic version by Matthew Spinka and Glanville Downey in *Chronicle of John Malalas. Books VIII–XVIII*. Chicago: University of Chicago Press, 1940.
A church history written in the late sixth century, probably in Constantinople.

John of Nikiu. *Chronicle*, 84. Ethiopic text with French translation by M. H. Zotenberg, *Chronique de Jean, Évêque de Nikiou*. In *Notices et Extraits des Manuscrits de la Bibliothèque Nationale et autres Bibliothèques* 24 (1883): 127–608. English translation by R. H. Charles in *The Chronicle of John, Bishop of Nikiu*. London and Oxford: Williams and Norgate, 1916.
John was a late seventh-century bishop of Nikiu, south of Alexandria. His narrative of Hypatia's death largely agrees with Socrates's, but he is entirely favorable to Cyril. He describes Hypatia as a pagan magician who beguiled Orestes and other Alexandrians away from Christianity.

Philostorgius. *Historia Ecclesiastica*, VIII 9. Edited by Joseph Bidez, revised by Friedhelm Winkelmann. Berlin: Akademie Verlag, 1972. English translation by Edward Walford in *The Ecclesiastical History of Sozumen and the Ecclesiastical History of Philostorgius*. London: Henry G. Bohn, 1855.
Philostorgius, another church historian of the first half of the fifth century resident in Constantinople, ascribes the death of Hypatia to unnamed defenders of Arianism.

Socrates. *Historia Ecclesiastica*. In *Patrologia Graeca*. Edited by J. P. Migne. Vol. 67, VII 13–15. Paris: J. P. Migne, 1864. English translation by A. C. Zenos in *A Select Library of Nicene and Post-Nicene Fathers of the Christian Church*. 2nd series, vol. 2. New York: The Christian Literature Company, and Oxford and London: Parker and Company, 1890.
Socrates, often called Scholasticus, wrote his history of the church, which covers the years 405–439, in Constantinople in the first half of the fifth century. The account of Hypatia's death and the events surrounding it given above is derived from Socrates, who is also the source for the date of death.

Suidas Lexicon. Edited by Ada Adler. Part 4, 644–646. Leipzig: B. G. Teubner, 1935. This work, often called the *Suda*, is a late tenth-century encyclopedia. The Hypatia entry has two parts derived from two sources, both dating from about a century after her death. The first part of the entry makes Hypatia the wife of the Neoplatonist philosopher Isidor, a chronological impossibility; although it is brief, it is the only source for titles of her written works. The second and longer part includes the most personal details of any of the sources; it says that Hypatia died a virgin. (There is a German translation of the second part with notes by Rudolf Asmus in *Das Leben des Philosophen Isidoros von Damaskios aus Damaskos*, 31–33, 97–98; Leipzig: Verlag von Felix Meiner, 1911.)

Synesius. *Letters*. In *Synesii Cyrenensis Epistolae*. Edited by Antonius Garzya. Rome:

Istituto Poligrafico, 1979. English translation by Augustine Fitzgerald in *The Letters of Synesius of Cyrene*. Oxford: Oxford University Press, and London: Humphrey Milford, 1926.

The letters directed to Hypatia are 10, 15, 16, 33, 81, 124, 154; she is mentioned in 133, 136, and 137.

Modern Studies

Bregman, Jay. *Synesius of Cyrene*. Berkeley: The University of California Press, 1982.

The last chapter gives a useful summary, with references, of various accounts of Synesius's intellectual relationship to Christianity.

Évrard, Étienne. "A quel titre Hypatie enseigna-t-elle la philosphie?" *Revue des Études Grecques* 90 (1977): 69–74.

Argues against the view that Hypatia held an official position in Alexandria.

Hoche, Richard. "Hypatia, die Tochter Theons." *Philologus* 15 (1860): 435–474.

Although outmoded in certain respects, this article contains the arguments for some points (e.g., Hypatia's death date) that are taken for granted in subsequent work.

Lacombrade, Christian. *Synésios de Cyrène*, 38–71. Paris: Société d'édition "Les Belles Lettres," 1951.

The standard work on Synesius. Lacombrade attempts to reconstruct all aspects of the education given to Synesius by Hypatia, and argues that it included a version of speculative Neoplatonism.

Marrou, H. I. "La 'conversion' de Synésios." *Revue des Études Grecques* 65 (1952): 474–484.

———. "Synesius of Cyrene and Alexandrian Neoplatonism." In *The Conflict between Paganism and Christianity in the Fourth Century*, 128–150. Edited by A. Momigliano. Oxford: The Clarendon Press, 1963; reprinted with corrections, 1964.

Marrou's account of Synesius and Hypatia is in many ways quite close to the one suggested here. The volume edited by Momigliano provides a good introduction to the spiritual and intellectual climate in which Hypatia lived.

Praechter, Karl. "Hypatia." In *Paulys Real-Encyclopädie der Classischen Altertumswissenschaft*. Halbband 17, columns 242–249. Stuttgart: J. B. Metzler, 1914.

A standard account of Hypatia, still a good starting point for further study.

———. "Richtungen und Schulen in Neuplatonismus." In *Genethliakon. Carl Robert zum 8. März 1910*, 105–156. Berlin: Weidmannsche Buchhandlung, 1910.

A major contribution to the discussion of the contents of Hypatia's teaching, minimizing its speculative content. The discussion of Alexandrian Neoplatonism begins on p. 144.

Rist, John. "Hypatia." *Phoenix* 19 (1965): 214–225.

The most thorough recent treatment of Hypatia in English. Argues against the view that speculative Neoplatonism played a prominent role in Hypatia's teaching, and stresses the Cynic elements in the anecdotes about her.

Rome, A., ed. *Commentaires de Pappus et de Théon d'Alexandrie sur l'Almageste*. Vol. 3, cxvi–cxxi. Vatican City: Biblioteca Apostolica Vaticana, 1943.

The only detailed discussion of Hypatia's role in editing Theon's commentary on the *Almagest*. It is inconclusive.

Tannery, Paul. "L'article de Suidas sur Hypatie." *Annales de la Faculté des Lettres de*

Bordeaux et des Universités du Midi 2 (1880): 197–201. Reprinted in *Mémoires Scientifiques*. Vol. 1, 74–79. Toulouse: Édition Privat, 1912.

Makes a number of interesting suggestions about the Hypatia entry in the *Suidas Lexicon*.

Toomer, G. J. "Theon of Alexandria." In *Dictionary of Scientific Biography*. Edited by C. C. Gillispie. Vol. 13, 321–325. New York: Charles Scribner's Sons, 1976.

A reliable and informative account of Hypatia's father.

SOF'JA ALEKSANDROVNA JANOVSKAJA (1896–1966)

Irving H. Anellis

BIOGRAPHY

Sof'ja Aleksandrovna Janovskaja (née Neimark) was born on January 31, 1896. She was born in Pruzhany, at that time in Poland, now in Belorussia. Little is known about her family background or earliest childhood, although J. M. Bocheński (1973) speculates that the family was of Polish origin and may have belonged to the Polish gentry *(szlachta)*. By upbringing, education, language, and loyalty, Janovskaja was Soviet Russian, her family having moved to Odessa while she was still a young child.

In Odessa, Janovskaja received a classical education and also studied mathematics. She was greatly influenced by Ivan Jure'vich Timchenko, one of the most famous historians of mathematics in Russia at the turn of the century, under whom she studied in the Odessa gymnasium. In 1915 she entered the Higher School for Women in Odessa and there studied under S. O. Shatunovskii, who had also been a teacher of the founder of combinatory logic, Moses Schönfinkel.

Janovskaja's studies were interrupted by the revolution of 1917. While still in high school, she joined the underground Red Cross, helping political prisoners, and in November 1918 she became a member of the Bolshevik wing of the Russian Communist Party, at that time still illegal in Odessa. She remained an active political worker until 1923, serving as a political commissar in the Red Army in 1919, as editor of the party daily newspaper *Kommunist* in Odessa, and from 1920–1923 as a worker in the Odessa Regional Party. After 1923 she gave up active political work in favor of her scientific work.

In 1924 Janovskaja entered the Institute of Red Professors in Moscow, where she studied mathematics until her graduation in 1929, while also attending seminars in mathematics at Moscow State University. By 1925 she was already directing a seminar on methodology of mathematics at Moscow State University (MGU); she became an official faculty member in 1926. She received her doctorate from the Mechanical-Mathematical Faculty of MGU in 1935 without having to defend a thesis and was already a professor in 1931.

During the dark days of the "Great Patriotic War" (World War II), when Moscow was besieged by German forces, Janovskaja was evacuated for safety to Perm, on the western slope of the Urals; from 1941 to 1943, she taught at Perm University. On her return to Moscow in 1943, she became director of the seminar on mathematical logic at MGU, and in 1946 she began teaching mathematical logic in the philosophy faculty as well.

In 1951 Janovskaja received the prized Order of Lenin. On March 31, 1959, she became the first chairperson of the newly created department of mathematical logic at MGU, which came into existence primarily through her efforts. She died on October 24, 1966.

WORK

Janovskaja taught logic with dedication and zeal; she devoted her life to it. The influences of her teachers Timchenko and Shatunovskii remained profound. When in 1923 she gave up active political work and turned to academics, she did so with the conviction that it was her duty as a dedicated Marxist-Leninist to use the scientific arena in defense of the Bolshevik revolution. In her writings on philosophy of mathematics and philosophy of logic, she took the offensive against the idealist philosophy of the bourgeois West, represented in her mind by Gottlob Frege, and against the so-called Machism, that is, conventionalism, represented by Rudolf Carnap and his Principle of Tolerance, according to which in logic one is free to choose one's rules.

Unlike many of her contemporaries, however, Janovskaja strove to carefully distinguish philosophy of mathematics on the one hand from mathematical logic on the other. She waged a struggle to defend the integrity of her field: she fought to defend mathematical logic against the attacks of the dialecticians and from the misconceptions of those who confused mathematical logic with philosophy of mathematics. She did not, therefore, attempt to redefine logic to suit the needs and demands of overzealous dialecticians; instead, she sought to preserve the purity of mathematical logic by steering a path between the Scylla of the dialecticians and the Charybdis of the Western philosophers of mathematics. For her efforts she was often brought to task, and more than once was required to engage in "self-criticism" (e.g., (1959)). It was largely through her efforts, however, that in 1966, the year of her death, the philosopher I. S. Narskii (1966) was able finally to declare that traditional logic no longer existed, that now "formal logic *is* mathematical logic."

The change in attitude took place gradually and was sparked by Stalin's "Letter on Marxism and Linguistics" (1950). Stalin's "Letter" had wide impact; it stated that language is not class-dependent, as earlier Soviet linguistic theorists had said, but belongs to all of its native speakers. As a result, it became possible to separate logic from philosophy of logic and philosophy of mathematics, and thus to treat mathematical logic as a science rather than as something belonging exclusively to the bourgeoisie, as a methodology of idealist philosophy of mathematics. The mathematical logic defended by Janovskaja was not, then, to be mistaken for philosophical logic or for philosophy of mathematics. In reply to her critics, Janovskaja (1950) argued that mathematical "logic is not a special mathematical discipline, but logic," just as Stalin argued that language is a means of communication between its speakers, not a tool for class domination. Moreover, she noted that the classical logic that Soviet philosophers and dialecticians most reluctantly accepted was, after all, just a fragment of that part of mathematical logic known as the monadic predicate calculus.

In the decade that followed, Janovskaja helped to forge a strong program in mathematical logic. By the end of the decade she was no longer alone in her defense of mathematical logic. Even philosophers, under her guidance, came to be well trained in mathematical logic—much more so than is typical of philosophers in the West. Dialecticians at last came to accept a limited role for mathematical logic, thanks largely to her efforts.

According to Janovskaja—and as accepted today by all dialectical-materialist philosophers of mathematics—mathematics is rooted in material reality, and there are no Platonic entities such as "pure number": logical and mathematical concepts are abstracted from material reality. Moreover, the rules which govern logical method are strict and fully determined. These rules are themselves forged as algorithms that have been founded upon the collective experience of material existence. The ultimate test of mathematical truth is applicability in the material world.

Janovskaja was an omnivorous reader in mathematics and a vigorous teacher. She devoted her talent to the defense and dissemination of knowledge of mathematical logic. She read and took seriously every article on mathematical logic that came to her attention, including, as Bocheński (1973) recounts, a paper of his that he had intended as "a witty paper on the classical polemics against formal logic," published in 1954 in an obscure source. Janovskaja (1963) replied to Bochénski's tongue-in-cheek efforts with a serious thirty-two-page essay.

Her own writings were never original; they were intended as didactic expositions and exegetical examinations of the major issues in history and philosophy of mathematics and of important contemporary discoveries and results in mathematical logic. She was the editor and commentator of Russian translations of many of the most important works in mathematical logic of the period, including, for example, David Hilbert and Wilhelm Ackermann's *Grundzüge der theoretischen Logik,* Alfred Tarski's *Introduction to the Logic and Methodology of Deductive Sciences,* George Polya's *Mathematics and Plausible Reasoning,* Carnap's *Meaning and Necessity,* and Alan Turing's seminal paper "Can machines think?"

For Janovskaja, history of mathematical logic, and in particular of contemporary mathematical logic, was the center of attention. This did not at all preclude serious study of history of mathematics in general. She saw the history of mathematics, however, not as the history of the accumulation of mathematical knowledge, but as the history of the development of mathematical methodology. This view is reflected in the range of her publications and in her choice of topics. She wrote on Egyptian mathematics, on ancient methods of finding square roots, and on Zeno's paradoxes of the infinite. She wrote on Michel Rolle's criticisms of infinitesimals and on Descartes's geometry and methodology. She wrote on Marx's mathematical manuscripts and on Engels. She wrote on Nikolai Lobachevskii's development of non-Euclidean geometry, and even on N. G. Chernyshevskii, the nineteenth-century Russian philosopher who sought to reduce all of reality to the formula $2 \times 2 = 4$ and who attacked Lobachevskii for "attacking" Euclid.

Her articles for the *Big Soviet Encyclopedia* on such topics as formalism, logistics, and mathematical paradoxes did much to familiarize the general public with some of the most burning issues in mathematical logic and foundations of mathematics.

Above all, she wrote on history of logic, including the history of the axiomatic method, as well as on the history of mathematical logic in the USSR. Her most significant contributions, however, are her two monumental studies on the history of mathematical logic in the Soviet Union (1948, 1959).

These two surveys form a definitive history of the contributions by Soviet mathematicians to mathematical logic during the period 1917–1957. They present eloquent testimony for the defense of mathematical logic as a unique and valuable discipline. They belie the assertion by Alexander Philipov (1952) that *no* significant work at all had been done in logic in the USSR during the early Soviet period, and that none was likely ever to be done.

Janovskaja was also an influential teacher. Her two most notable students were Adol'f Pavlovich Jushkevich (1906–   ) and N. I. Stjazhkin (1932–   ). It was under the influence of Janovskaja, and with her advice and encouragement, that Jushkevich became interested in history of mathematics, and under her guidance that he turned his academic career in that direction. He is not only the dean of Soviet mathematics historians, but indeed one of the most influential historians of mathematics in the world today. Stjazhkin is the best known historian of logic in the Soviet Union today and has an international reputation as well.

Thanks to Janovskaja's work, Soviet mathematical logicians lost their defensive inhibitions and acquired renewed confidence in themselves and their work. The postwar period which Janovskaja described has been filled by a generation of giants in their field, people with deservedly proud international reputations. This is the heritage of S. A. Janovskaja. A small indication of the value of her contributions may be found in Ershov (1983), which borrows its title from Janovskaja (1959); in Jushkevich and Bogoljubov's (1983) history of mathematics in Russia and the Soviet Union; in the multivolume Russian *History of Native Mathematics* (Shtokalo et al. 1968); and above all, in the posthumous tribute edited by P. V. Tavanec (1970).

BIBLIOGRAPHY

Works by Sof ja Aleksandrova Janovskaja

Space does not permit a complete listing of the works of S. A. Janovskaja. A partial listing can be found in Bashmakova et al. (1966). Included below are works cited in the essay, together with other works not included in Bashmakova et al. (Note: Some publications index Janovskaja's works under ''Yanovskaya.'') All original titles and works are in Russian.

Mathematical and Mathematical Logic Works

''The contemporary crisis in the foundations of mathematics.'' *Estestvoznanie i Mark-sizma* 2 (1930).

''Paradoxes of mathematics.'' *Big Soviet Encylopedia* 44 (1939).

''Foundations of mathematics and mathematical logic.'' In *Matematika v SSSR za Tridcat Let 1917–1947,* 11–45. Moscow and Leningrad, 1948.

''Letter to the editor.'' *Voprosy Filosofii* (3) (1950): 339–342.

''Mathematical logic and foundations of mathematics.'' In *Matematika v SSSR za sorok let 1917–1957,* edited by A. G. Kurosh, 13–120. Moscow and Leningrad: Gos. izd.-vo fiziko-matematicheskoi lit-ry, 1959.

(editor) *Methodological Problems of Science.* Moscow: Institut Filosofii, Akad. Nauk SSSR, 1962.

''On the role of mathematical rigor in the history of the creative development of mathematics and particularly on the *Geometry* of Descartes.'' *Voprosy Filosofii* (3) (1963). Also included in (1962, 243–274). Reprinted in Tavanec 1970, 13–50. Reprinted in *Istoriko-Matematicheskie Issledovanija* 17 (1966): 151–183.

''Adol'f Pavlovich Jushkevich.'' *Uspekhi Matematicheskikh Nauk* 22 (1) (133) (1967): 187–194.

(editor) *The Mathematical Manuscripts of Karl Marx.* Moscow, 1932, 1968. English translation of Part I by C. Aronson and M. Meo. London: New Park Publications, 1983.

Works about Sof'ja Aleksandrova Janovskaja

Anellis, Irving H. ''History of philosophy of mathematics in the USSR, Janovskaja to Barabashev.'' In *Philosophic Sovietology,* edited by T. J. Blakeley and E. Swiderski. Sovietica vol. 50. Dordrecht: Reidel Publishing, 1987.

Bashmakova, I. G., et al. ''Sof'ja Aleksandrovna Janovskaja (on the occasion of her seventieth birthday)'' (in Russian). *Uspekhi Matematicheskikh Nauk* 21 (3) (1966): 239–247. Translation by Ann F. S. Mitchell in *Russian Mathematical Surveys* 21 (3) (1966): 213–221.

Portrait included in the Russian original.

Bocheński, Josef M. ''S. A. Janovskaja.'' *Studies in Soviet Thought* 13 (1973): 1–10.

―――. ''Sof'ja Aleksandrovna Janovskaja.'' *Studies in Soviet Thought* 7 (1967): 66–67.

Borodin, A. I., and A. S. Bugai. ''Sof'ja Aleksandrovna Janovskaja'' (in Russian). In *Biograficheskii Slovar' Dejatelei v oblasti Matematiki,* edited by A. I. Borodin and A. S. Bugai, 555–556. Kiev: Radjanska Shkola, 1977.

Gorskii, D. P. ''Sof'ja Aleksandrovna Janovskaja'' (in Russian). In Janovskaja 1962, 3–11. Reprinted in Tavanec 1970, 5–12.

Kline, George. Review of Janovskaja 1948. *Journal of Symbolic Logic* 16 (1951): 46–48.

''Sof'ja Aleksandrovna Janovskaja (On the occasion of her sixtieth birthday)'' (in Russian). *Uspekhi Matematicheskikh Nauk* 11 (3) (69) (1956): 219–222.

Portrait included.
"Sof'ja Aleksandrovna Janovskaja (1896–1966)." *Matematika v Shkole* (5) (1984): i.

Other References

Ershov, Jurii Leonidovich. "Mathematical logic and foundations of mathematics" (in Russian). In *Ocherki Razvitija Matematiki v SSSR*, 57–61, 686. Kiev: Naukova Dumka, 1983.

Jushkevich, Adol'f Pavlovich, and A. N. Bogoljubov. "Historico-mathematical studies" (in Russian). In *Ocherki Razvitija Matematiki v SSSR*, 514–535, 720–723. Kiev: Naukova Dumka, 1983.

Küng, G. "Bibliography of Soviet work in the field of mathematical logic and the foundations of mathematics, 1917–1957." *Notre Dame Journal of Formal Logic* 3 (1962): 1–40.
    Review: *Journal of Symbolic Logic* 28 (1963): 253–254.

Narskii, I. S. "On the situation in logic and its place in university education" (in Russian). *Filosofskie Nauk* 3 (1966): 101–110.

Philipov, Alexander. *Logic and Dialectic in the Soviet Union*. New York: Research Program on the USSR, 1952.

Shtokalo, I. Z., et al., eds. *History of Native Mathematics* (in Russian). 3 vols. Vol. 3, *1917–1967*. Kiev: Naukova Dumka, 1968.

Stalin, Iosef Vissarionevich. "Letter on Marxism and Linguistics" (in Russian). *Voprosy Filosofii* 4 (1) (1950): 3–6. Reprinted from *Pravda* (20 June 1950).

Tavanec, P. V., ed. *Studies in Systems of Logic* (in Russian). Moscow: "Nauka," 1970.

CAROL KARP (1926–1972)

Judy Green

BIOGRAPHY

Carol Karp was born Carol Ruth Vander Velde on August 10, 1926, in Forest Grove, Michigan. She was the daughter of Peter Nelson Vander Velde, office manager of a feed and grain store in Grand Rapids, and Janet Keizer Vander Velde. Both of her parents had strong family ties to the conservative and devout Dutch farming community centered around Holland, Michigan. Her brother, Wallace Earl Vander Velde, now a professor of aeronautics and astronautics at MIT, was born there in 1929. The Vander Velde children attended a school with a total of three rooms, each of which accommodated four or five grades.

When Karp was about eleven, her family moved to Alliance, Ohio, where her father became the manager of another feed and grain store. A second brother, Myron Dale Vander Velde, now the manager of a computer center for General Motors, was born in 1939. Even away from the Dutch community in Michigan, Karp's teenage activities were subject to the severe restrictions of the Dutch Reformed Church: dancing and movie-going were strictly forbidden, and card-playing was frowned upon. She did, however, learn to play the viola.

Her parents were not educated beyond high school, but they encouraged their children to pursue a college education. The summer after she graduated from high school, Karp's family moved from Alliance to Bremen, Indiana, and she attended Manchester College, a small college run by the Church of the Brethren, in nearby North Manchester. She graduated with distinction in 1948, just as her family resettled near Grand Rapids, in Ionia. Karp too returned to Michigan in 1948, enrolling in the mathematics graduate program at Michigan State College (now Michigan State University). Following receipt of a master's degree in 1950, Karp spent the summer as an instructor at Michigan State, and then for a time traveled around the country as a violist in an all-woman orchestra.

In 1951 Karp enrolled as a graduate student and teaching assistant in mathematics at the University of Southern California. At the end of the academic year, she married Arthur L. Karp and thereafter used the name Karp professionally.

Although she received her Ph.D. from Southern California in 1959, Karp spent most of the intervening period elsewhere. She was an instructor at the New Mexico College of Agricultural and Mechanical Arts (now New Mexico State University) during 1953–1954. From 1954 until 1956, she was a teaching assistant and graduate student at Berkeley, where her thesis advisor, Leon Henkin, had moved in 1953. In 1957 she moved to Japan with her husband, who was then with the Navy, and in 1958 returned to the United States to a position at the University of Maryland.

All of Karp's postdoctoral career was spent at the University of Maryland. She came as an instructor in 1958 and was promoted to assistant professor in 1960, a year after she received her degree. Although her initial promotion appears to have been delayed, later promotions came quickly: after three years to associate professor, and after another three to full professor.

In 1966 Karp was influential in bringing two younger logicians, James Owings and E. G. K. López-Escobar, to join her and the logician and number-theorist Sigekatu Kuroda at Maryland. Under her leadership the small group of Maryland logicians, later joined by Allen Bernstein, soon attracted a number of graduate students, four of whom wrote Ph.D. dissertations under Karp's direction: Robert Gauntt (1969), John Gregory (1969), Judy Green (1972), and Sister Ellen Cunningham (1974).

Karp continued her attempts to enlarge the logic group, and at the time of her death was trying to arrange for David Kueker to join the faculty; he did, in 1973. Karp was also the major influence in bringing to the Maryland Mathematics Colloquium and Logic Seminar many of the foremost logicians of the time. Her hospitality extended beyond the usual, since by 1963 she and her husband had a home with an extra apartment in which visiting logicians were frequently lodged.

Karp's intellectual standards were extremely high, and she was unfailingly honest in applying them. Although she showed an almost familial concern for her students and younger colleagues, she was consistently candid in appraising their mathematical contributions and promise. In particular, she advised working toward a doctorate only if one expected to make research the most important part of one's professional career, and she refused to allow her students to graduate until their results met her own high standards for publishability.

Karp's concerns about students were not only for her graduate students. She was deeply involved in the mathematics honors program at Maryland and for a number of years directed a National Science Foundation (NSF) sponsored Undergraduate Research Program.

Karp was a highly respected member of the international logic community, publishing regularly, participating in conferences, and giving frequent invited addresses throughout North America and Europe. She was supported by NSF grants throughout most of the 1960s. She served as the representative from the

Association for Symbolic Logic to the Division of Mathematical Sciences, National Academy of Sciences–National Research Council, from 1966 to 1969. From 1968 until her death Karp served as a consulting editor of the *Journal of Symbolic Logic*. Although her papers have not been collected, López-Escobar is in possession of what appears to be most of Karp's professional correspondence.

In 1969 Karp discovered that she had breast cancer, and by early 1971 it was clear that surgery had not been successful. She remained active, however, both in her own work and in advising her final two Ph.D. students, until weeks before her death on August 20, 1972. Volume 492 of the Springer Lecture Notes in Mathematics was published in her memory by her students and colleagues at the University of Maryland (Kueker 1975).

WORK

Karp begins the preface to her book, *Languages with Expressions of Infinite Length,* as follows:

My interest in infinitary logic dates back to a February day in 1956 when I remarked to my thesis supervisor, Professor Leon Henkin, that a particularly vexing problem would be so simple if only I could write a formula that would say $x = 0$ or $x = 1$ or $x = 2$ etc. To my surprise he replied, "Well, go ahead". The problem is now long-forgotten, but that reply has led to this monograph. (Karp 1964, v)

Karp's suggestion and Henkin's answer led to the development of infinitary logic, now a well-established area within mathematical logic, of which Karp's monograph was the first systematic exposition.

As early as the fall of 1956, there was a seminar at Berkeley on infinitary logic, organized by Henkin and Alfred Tarski, at which Karp, still a graduate student, reported on her results. There followed a period of intense research, centered at Berkeley, during which time Karp was first in Japan and later at the University of Maryland. The first published versions of Karp's work appear in papers by Dana Scott and Tarski (1958) and by Henkin (1961). Karp's monograph was based on her dissertation, finished in 1958; but as infinitary logic was developing rapidly, the monograph, which appeared several years later, has a different focus and includes others' results, too.

Infinitary logic is a modification of the first-order predicate calculus, whose formulas are formed from symbols representing variables, constants, functions, and relations, and logical symbols whose colloquial meanings are "implies" ($\rightarrow$), "not" ($\neg$), "and" ($\wedge$), "or" ($\vee$), "for all" ($\forall$), and "there exists" ($\exists$). Karp introduced four new symbols representing conjunction of infinite sets of formulas ($\bigwedge$), disjunction of infinite sets of formulas ($\bigvee$), universal quantification over infinite sets of variables ($\boldsymbol{\forall}$), and existential quantification over infinite sets of variables ($\boldsymbol{\exists}$).

Karp defined $L_{\alpha\beta}$ to be the language which permits conjunction and disjunction of any sequence of formulas of length less than α and quantification over any sequence of variables of length less than β. In this notation the first-order predicate calculus is $L_{\omega\omega}$, where ω is the first infinite ordinal. The first well-studied infinitary language was $L_{\omega_1\omega}$, where ω_1 is the first uncountable ordinal. In her dissertation Karp developed an axiom system which allowed her to prove a completeness theorem for $L_{\omega_1\omega}$, i.e., she showed, as Gödel had for $L_{\omega\omega}$, that the syntactical notion of provability and the model-theoretic notion of validity coincide for $L_{\omega_1\omega}$.

An early justification for the study of infinitary languages was their enhanced power of characterization. For example, well-ordering relations, simple groups, and Archimedean fields can be characterized by infinitary sentences but not by sentences of $L_{\omega\omega}$. Karp gave early applications of infinitary languages to the study of Boolean algebras, in her monograph and in abstracts presented to the American Mathematical Society in 1966. Her 1963 paper showed that well ordering cannot be expressed in an infinitary language that allows quantification over only finite sets of variables. This paper has as its main result an important theorem that describes when two models satisfy the same formulas in a finite-quantifier infinitary language. Since the late 1960s, a number of papers have used infinitary languages, mainly $L_{\omega_1\omega}$, to examine algebraic structures and properties. Although most of the model theory used by algebraic logicians is still the model theory of the first-order predicate calculus, the model theory of infinitary languages has proven to be an important tool.

G. Kreisel pointed out that the definition of languages by cardinality was not the most satisfactory one. He remarked that infinitary logic "becomes particularly neat if one uses languages with suitable infinitely long expressions, *provided one restricts the syntax not by simple-minded purely external conditions* (e.g. cardinality of the expressions), *but by conditions on* the satisfaction relation" (Kreisel 1965). In his 1967 dissertation, Jon Barwise, following Kreisel's suggestions, developed infinitary logic on sets for which, when a formula in a set is provable, it is provable in the set. Such sets are *admissible* sets or unions of admissible sets (Barwise 1969).

Karp was motivated by Kreisel's remark to embark on a research program which led to the development of primitive recursive functions on sets, in terms of which admissible sets could be characterized. This work was the subject of an influential joint paper with Ronald Jensen, who had come to the same basic development from the viewpoint of a set theorist (Karp and Jensen 1971). The paper, presented at the Set Theory Institute held at UCLA in 1967, grew out of conversations between Karp and Jensen at the Logic Colloquium at Leicester during the summer of 1965, where Karp had presented a talk on the beginning of her work. As a result of this work, Karp was invited to deliver a course on generalized recursion theory at the Summer School and Colloquium in Logic in Manchester, England, in August 1969. Unfortunately, her illness prevented her from writing up these lectures. Notes indicate that she intended to include them as the last and most important chapter of the monograph on which she was working at the time of her death (López-Escobar 1975, 3).

BIBLIOGRAPHY _____

Works by Carol Karp

Mathematical Logic Works

"Languages with expressions of infinite length." Ph.D. diss., University of Southern California, 1959.

"Independence proofs in predicate logic with infinitely long expressions." *Journal of Symbolic Logic* 27 (1962): 171–188.

"A note on the representation of α-complete boolean algebras." *Proceedings of the American Mathematical Society* 14 (1963): 705–707.

Languages with Expressions of Infinite Length. Amsterdam: North-Holland, 1964.

"Finite quantifier equivalence." In *The Theory of Models,* edited by J. W. Addison et al., 407–412. Amsterdam: North-Holland, 1965.

"A proof of the relative consistency of the continuum hypothesis." In *Sets, Models and Recursion Theory: Proceedings of the Summer School in Mathematical Logic and Tenth Logic Colloquium, Leicester, 1965,* edited by John N. Crossley, 1–32. Amsterdam: North-Holland, 1967.

"Nonaxiomatizability results for infinitary systems." *Journal of Symbolic Logic* 32 (1967): 367–384.

"An algebraic proof of the Barwise Compactness Theorem." In *The Syntax and Semantics of Infinitary Languages,* edited by Jon Barwise, 89–95. Berlin: Springer, 1968.

(with Ronald B. Jensen) "Primitive recursive set functions." In *Axiomatic Set Theory,* edited by Dana S. Scott, Part 1, 143–176. Proceedings of Symposia in Pure Mathematics, vol. 13. Providence, R.I.: American Mathematical Society, 1971.

"From countable to cofinality ω in infinitary logic." *Journal of Symbolic Logic* 37 (1972): 430–431.

"Infinite-quantifier languages and ω-chains of models." In *Tarski Symposium,* edited by Leon Henkin et al., 225–232. Proceedings of Symposia in Pure Mathematics, vol. 25. Providence, R.I.: American Mathematical Society, 1974.

Works about Carol Karp

López-Escobar, E.G.K. "Introduction." In *Infinitary Logic: In Memoriam Carol Karp,* edited by D. W. Kueker, 1–16. Springer Lecture Notes in Mathematics, vol. 492. New York: Springer-Verlag, 1975.
    A description of Karp's work by one of her colleagues at the University of Maryland.

Williams, Mary B. Obituary. *Association for Women in Mathematics Newsletter* 3 (1) (January–February 1973): 2–3.

Other References

Barwise, J. "Infinitary logic and admissible sets." *Journal of Symbolic Logic* 34 (1969): 226–252.

Henkin, Leon. "Some remarks on infinitely long formulas." In *Infinitistic Methods, Proceedings of the Symposium on Foundations of Mathematics, Warsaw, 2–9 September 1959,* 167–183. New York: Pergamon, 1961.

Kreisel, G. "Model-theoretic invariants: Applications to recursive and hyperarithmetic operations." In *The Theory of Models,* edited by J. W. Addison et al., 190–205. Amsterdam: North-Holland, 1965.

Scott, D., and A. Tarski. "The sentential calculus with infinitely long expressions." *Colloquium Mathematicum* 6 (1958): 165–170.

CLARIBEL KENDALL (1889–1965)

Ruth Rebekka Struik

BIOGRAPHY

Claribel Kendall was born on January 23, 1889, in Denver, the daughter of Charles M. Kendall and Emma Reily Kendall. She had a sister, Florence Kendall. According to the 1900 census, her parents had been born in Ohio, her father in February 1860 and her mother in June 1859. They had been married for thirteen years. Charles Kendall gave his occupation as a lawyer. The census also states that Emma was the mother of three children, two of whom were living: Claribel and Florence (1890–1971). Charles Kendall owned the home in which the family lived.

Kendall attended Denver public schools before going to the University of Colorado in 1907. She received B.A. and B.Ed. degrees in 1912 and the M.A. degree in 1914. Starting in 1913 she was an instructor in the mathematics department of the University of Colorado, where she continued teaching until her retirement in 1957. The summers of 1915 and 1918 were spent at the University of Chicago doing graduate work under Professors E. H. Moore, E. J. Wilczynski, L. E. Dickson, and G. A. Bliss. With the help of a leave of absence from the University of Colorado and a fellowship for 1920–1921, she completed her work for the Ph.D. degree. Nineteen doctorates were awarded in the United States in mathematics in the academic year 1921–1922, and Kendall was one of five women to receive one.

Kendall was an instructor from 1913 to 1921, when she was promoted to assistant professor. She became associate professor in 1928 and full professor in 1944. This career advance can be contrasted with that of George H. Light, who came to Colorado as an assistant professor in 1916 with a Yale Ph.D.; he was promoted to associate professor in 1918 and to full professor in 1920.

Kendall was active in the Christian Science Church, and left a substantial sum to the church when she died. She was secretary of the University of Colorado chapter of Phi Beta Kappa for over thirty years. She left $5,000 to the chapter in her will, and the Claribel Kendall Awards are still given by the University.

She was also active in the Colorado Mountain Club. Among her pastimes was driving a jeep on back trails in the mountains; she loved to go exploring. Music was a favorite activity; she would invite friends for dinner and then have a chamber music concert using records.

In the summer of 1928, Kendall traveled to Europe to represent the University of Colorado at the International Congress of Mathematicians held at Bologna, Italy.

After Kendall retired, she lived in Boulder with her sister until her death on April 17, 1965.

WORK

Kendall's master's thesis was entitled "Preassociative syzygies in linear algebra." In a linear algebra with generators $e_1, e_2, \ldots, e_n$ and multiplication table

$$e_i \, e_j = \sum_k \gamma_{ijk} e_k$$

she examined the differences $(e_i \, e_j) \, e_k - e_i \, (e_j \, e_k)$ for the case $n = 2$ and studied algebraic relations among the coefficients of e_1 and e_2 in these differences. The thesis itself consisted of six handwritten pages.

Her Ph.D. thesis, written under Wilczynski, was on "Congruences determined by a given surface." It studies a surface defined by a pair of differential equations.

For a while (1916–1917) she posed and solved problems that appeared in the problems section of the *American Mathematical Monthly*. Kendall was one of the founders of the Rocky Mountain Section of the Mathematical Association of America in 1917. She attended almost every meeting of the section and occasionally gave talks.

Kendall directed ten master's theses; eight were by women. No doubt she influenced the percentage of mathematics master's degrees received by women at the University of Colorado: it was close to 50% in her early years there but sank below 20% after World War II. During most of Kendall's teaching career, the mathematics department at the University of Colorado ranged from two to six members; Frances Stribic joined it in 1926, giving the department two females members.

Claribel Kendall was not a leading research mathematician, but she was a dedicated teacher who had an active life outside of mathematics, in her church, and in her community.

BIBLIOGRAPHY ─────────────────────────────────

Works by Claribel Kendall

Mathematical Works

"Preassociative syzygies in linear algebra." Master's thesis, University of Colorado, 1914. Abstract (with G. W. Smith): *American Mathematical Monthly* 30 (1923): 219.
"Congruences determined by a given surface." *American Journal of Mathematics* 45 (1923): 25–41.
    Doctoral thesis.

Works about Claribel Kendall

Jones, Burton W., and Wolfgang Thron. *A History of the Mathematics Departments of the University of Colorado*. Boulder, Colo.: 1979.

PELAGEYA YAKOVLEVNA POLUBARINOVA-KOCHINA (1899–   )

George W. Phillips

BIOGRAPHY

Pelageya Yakovlevna Polubarinova-Kochina is one of the most important women in mathematics in the Soviet Union and one of its leading scientists. Kochina's life spans the last two decades of tsarist Russia and the first seventy years of the Soviet Union. She was a gymnasium student in the last years of tsarist Russia, a student in Petrograd University during the years of the Russian revolutions of 1917 and the ensuing civil war, a leading mathematician in Stalin's Russia, and one of the leading Soviet scientists in Siberia after Stalin's death.

Kochina was born in Astrakhan in 1899. Her father, Yakov Stepanovich Polubarinov, was an accountant, educated and "bourgeois." He was deeply concerned about obtaining the best possible education for his children. Kochina entered a gymnasium in Astrakhan at age eight. According to Kochina's memoirs, her father moved the family to St. Petersburg so that his children could receive a better education. Kochina's mother, Anisiya Panteleimonovna, had three other children—Kochina's older brother Vasilii, a younger sister Ira, and a younger brother Alesha. In her memoirs Kochina reveals little about her parents' political views, which suggests that they may not have supported the Bolsheviks before 1917. Kochina attended the Pokrovskii Women's Gymnasium in St. Petersburg and noted that there was much more mathematics in this gymnasium than in her gymnasium in Astrakhan, where she had worked as a tutor.

Kochina's father died in 1918, and she went to work in the Main Physical (later Geophysical) Laboratory in Petrograd (St. Petersburg was renamed during World War I). At the same time she continued her studies at Petrograd University. One immediate result of the revolutions of 1917 had been the integration of the former "higher courses for women" into Petrograd University, thus ending the long pattern of discriminating against women in tsarist Russia by barring them from universities.

These were years of great hardship for Kochina. After her father's death, she had to support her mother, sister, and younger brother. Her sister died of tuberculosis, as did many other Russians during the civil war (1918–1921); Kochina's older brother was in the Red Army. Kochina also contracted tuberculosis, but still persisted in her university education. Among the lectures attended by Kochina during her first year at the University of Petrograd, those of V. I Smirnov (on complex variables and differential equations) and K. G. Vasilievich (on complex variables and the theory of elasticity) were probably the most closely related to her later work. Kochina wrote that Smirnov was one of the two university professors who most influenced her work, and referred to him as "the patriarch of Leningrad mathematicians in the 1920s" (Petrograd was renamed Leningrad after Lenin's death).

The other professor who had a profound influence on Kochina (and on her future husband) was A. A. Fridman, who lectured on hydrodynamics and theoretical meteorology. Kochina worked under his direction at the Main Geophysical Laboratory while she was still an undergraduate student. She returned there to work for Fridman after she graduated from Petrograd University in 1921.

When Kochina went back to work for Fridman, she worked in the Division of Theoretical Meteorology, doing "calculations" on Fridman's work. Kochina's future husband, Nikolai Evgrafovich Kochin, also worked there for Fridman and attended night courses at Petrograd University.

In her memoirs, Kochina makes clear that N. E. Kochin was the most important figure in her life. Kochin's work in mathematics—and their marriage—had an enormous impact on Kochina's life and her work. The most moving section of her memoirs is the tribute that she wrote to him, expressing the enormous sense of loss that she felt after his death in 1944. His extraordinary ability and political commitment, traits shared by Kochina, shaped their future after the Bolshevik victory.

In 1923 Kochin completed his course work at Petrograd University, graduated, and became a faculty member there. From 1922 to 1925 the young couple worked together and took vacations together; in 1925 they were married. Their relationship before 1925, and their marriage as well, reflected the new attitudes about courtship and marriage among many in the Soviet intelligentsia after the Russian revolution. Instead of a traditional "religious" wedding, they simply registered their marriage at a Leningrad office and took the witnesses to tea.

They had two daughters, Ira and Nina; Kochina left her job at the Main Geophysical Laboratory in order to raise the children. She also taught at a high school for workers, at the Institute of Transportation (1925–1931), and at the Institute of Civil Aviation Engineering (1931–1934). She was appointed professor at Leningrad University in 1934.

Kochina's teaching illustrated another profound change brought about by the revolution. The "workers' faculties" (rabfak) where she taught represented part of the immense increase in educational opportunities for Soviet workers—men and women—after the Communist victory. Admission standards were eased, and the democratization of Russian education that had started in the last two decades of Tsarist Russia was greatly accelerated.

Communist control of the universities and the Academy of Sciences steadily increased, particularly after Stalin gained power in 1928–1929. In this setting Kochin began a meteoric rise to become one of the leading mathematicians in Stalin's Russia. In 1935 he became the head of the division of mechanics in the Steklov Mathematics Institute, and Kochina and their daughters moved with him to Moscow.

Kochina's private life and professional work were closely connected with that of Kochin. In Moscow Kochina's career changed dramatically. She became a senior research associate in Kochin's division, concentrating on full-time research. In her memoirs, Kochina noted proudly that she was a "co-worker" with her husband in his division. In 1939 this division became part of the newly established Institute of Mechanics of the Academy of Sciences, and Kochin was named an "Academician" of the Academy of Sciences. Kochin's selection was part of "sovietization" of the Academy (Graham 1969, Chapter 3).

Kochin and Kochina moved into the "Stalinist" scientific elite because of several factors. Kochin was deeply committed to the Communist regime. He had been in the Red Army, in combat, at two of the most critical periods of the civil war. Both he and Kochina were well trained in pure mathematics but devoted much of their time and energy to the solution of practical problems. This was especially true of Kochina's work on the theory of filtration.

During the first part of World War II, Kochina and her daughters were evacuated from Moscow, to Kazan. After the Soviet military victories at Stalingrad and Kursk, they returned to Moscow. Kochin remained in Moscow, involved in military research, until his death on December 31, 1944, after a long illness. Immediately after his death, Kochina continued giving his course of lectures and helped with their publication.

Kochina continued teaching in Moscow, initially at the Hydrometeorological and Aircraft Building Institute, and then at the Aviation Industry Academy of the University of Moscow. In 1948 she became director of the division of hydromechanics, within the Institute of Mechanics. Her division concentrated on the problems of filtration. Kochina worked at the Institute of Mechanics until 1959, when she volunteered to leave Moscow for Siberia.

Kochina helped establish the Siberian branch of the Academy of Sciences at Novosibirsk and was a member of its Praesidium, directing its work from 1959 to 1970. She was director of the department of applied hydrodynamics at the Hydrodynamics Institute and was also head of the department of theoretical mechanics at the University of Novosibirsk. She was sixty when she went to Siberia, with all the hardships that entailed, remaining there until she was seventy. In 1970 she returned to Moscow, where she became director of the section for mathematical methods of mechanics at the Institute for Problems in Mechanics.

WORK

The degree conferred on Kochina in 1921 by Petrograd University was in pure mathematics. Nonetheless, her main contributions are applications to hydrodynamics of the theory of complex functions and the analytic theory of differential equations, in particular of Fuchsian differential equations.

Among the methods used in Kochina's work were those involving Green's function and the Schwarz-Christoffel transformations, which provide conformal mappings of arbitrary polygons onto the upper half plane and play a great role in solving partial differential equations.

Some applications of complex function theory had been made by mathematicians in prerevolutionary Russia—for example, by N. E. Zhukovskii and S. A. Chaplygin at Moscow University. Furthermore, in 1915 the Imperial Russian Academy of Sciences had taken the first step to encourage applications of theoretical results to economic and industrial problems. This occurred largely because Russia's entry into World War I had demonstrated the weakness of its industrial capacity and revealed the relative lack of governmental support for technological research (Graham 1969, 22–23).

The new Soviet government greatly accelerated these efforts in the 1920s by encouraging applications of basic mathematical techniques to a variety of technological and industrial problems. A major part of this effort involved the increased emphasis on such research at the Academy of Sciences. Kochina's research, and that of Kochin, fit in perfectly with the Soviet philosophy and the needs of the USSR.

Throughout her memoirs, Kochina repeatedly praises those scientists who are able to apply theoretical results to the solution of practical problems. This is not only an expression of her individual preference for applied mathematics, but also the reiteration of the Marxist ideological principle of "the unity of theory and practice." Its origins lie in Marx's and Engel's criticisms of speculative philosophy. Her restatement of the official Soviet position simultaneously demonstrates her political orthodoxy and also the reason why she so often was chosen as an official Soviet representative, inside and outside the Soviet Union.

In the first years after Kochina's marriage, much of her time and energy was devoted to teaching. In Moscow after 1934 she had far more time for research. Then she did the mathematical calculations for her doctoral dissertation and was drawn to the problems of filtration.

In 1940 Kochina completed and defended her doctoral dissertation on theoretical aspects of filtration, receiving the degree of doctor of physical and mathematical sciences. This was a new degree, established in 1935: Kochina was the third woman to receive it. (The first was N. K. Bari* [1935].)

The work for which Kochina is best known is in the theory of filtration of water in ground soil. She was drawn to the problem by an engineer, N. I. Anismov, who consulted her about the weakening of the foundations of a dam system by erosion caused by the uncontrolled, rapid movement of subsurface water. This very difficult problem had proved intractable to the methods of conformal transformations of the regions involved (Fil'chakov 1966–1970, 361).

Kochina's husband suggested the application of a method that had been discussed in a paper in a collection he had recently edited. Following the suggestion,

Kochina assumed a two-dimensional steady flow in a homogeneous subsoil. The problem was to determine two complex functions (of a complex variable) that represented, respectively, the coordinates of a point and the potential of filtration at that point. By making certain physical assumptions, Kochina demonstrated that the desired functions are linearly independent solutions of a second order Fuchsian differential equation (Aleksandrov et al. 1979, 193–194). The method later proved applicable to some cases of irregular (unsteady) flow (Fil'chakov 1966–1970, 361).

Kochina also did important research on the hydrodynamics of free-flowing currents and the theory of tides. She obtained results in the theory of tidal waves, showing that the characteristic oscillations of such waves are determined by the eigenvalues and eigenfunctions of an integral equation whose kernel may be expressed as a Green's function. The propagation of such waves in a large reservoir is described by a system of Laplacian equations. Kochina also worked on the theory of elasticity and in analytic mechanics.

Kochina's work on filtration illustrates how her mathematical work blended theory and practice. She helped solve urgent, practical problems. Her research was used in irrigation and hydroelectric projects in Soviet Central Asia and Azerbaijan, where there were often severe problems with drainage and the buildup of salt in the soil. Kochina made frequent trips to these areas to help solve their problems.

Kochina's research in these areas led to one of the most important decisions in her life. In 1958 M. A. Lavrent'iev invited Kochina to be considered for election to the highly prized position of Academician in the Academy of Sciences and to become the leading woman in the pioneering group of Soviet scientists and mathematicians moving to Novosibirsk in western Siberia. This group became the scientific elite of Siberia and Soviet Central Asia. The move was part of the broader, massive Soviet plan to develop Siberia's resources.

This bold decision by Kochina entailed enormous personal sacrifices. She gave up a comfortable life in Moscow for the crowded, primitive, poorly heated barracks in the harsh climate of Siberia, and had to leave her two daughters and grandchildren in Moscow.

From 1959 to 1970, Kochina headed the department of applied hydrodynamics, doing work on such topics as models of subsurface water in the conditions of the Siberian steppe. Her department also studied water and soil problems connected with hydroelectric and irrigation projects. It also used linear programming in some of the first Soviet studies on the cost-effectiveness of Siberian and Central Asian development projects.

In Moscow (from 1935 to 1958) and in Novosibirsk (from 1959 to 1970), Kochina's research was an important part of the hydroelectric and irrigation projects that were vital in the development of Siberia and Soviet Central Asia. This was one of the most profound changes taking place in the USSR, and Kochina was one of the leading scientists participating in it.

Kochina pioneered in another area, the history of mathematics and mechanics, and her studies in this area constitute a major part of her life work. She was the first person to write extensively on Sofia Kovalevskaia*, one of the greatest women in mathematics. Her studies of Kovalevskaia included several articles on her mathematical work, two volumes of her correspondence, and a detailed biography.

The second major mathematician studied by Kochina was her husband, N. E. Kochin. Kochin had made an immense contribution to Soviet science in dynamic meteorology, hydrodynamics, aerodynamics, and theoretical mechanics. Kochina worked for several years on a definitive study of him and his work, helped publish the two volumes of his collected works, and assisted in the publication of his lectures (Kochina 1950, 1979).

Finally, she did significant research on the work of Karl Weierstrass (1966) and A. A. Fridman.

Kochina was an important political activist. Her success reflects not only her obvious ability and industriousness, but also her dedication and loyalty to the Soviet Communist Party and the Soviet political system. In the grim years of Stalin's terror in the 1930s, Kochina and her husband rose to the top of the Academy of Sciences. At the same time, there were sweeping new forms of political and intellectual oppression. Since Kochina and Kochin were politically orthodox and highly talented, they escaped the purges and became part of the new elite.

During these years, Kochina was singled out by the Soviet Communist Party to be a deputy in the Leningrad (city) soviet in the late 1920s and early 1930s, a deputy in the Moscow (city) soviet after 1935, and a deputy in the Supreme Soviet of the Russian Republic. The members of these soviets are carefully chosen by the Communist Party. The selection is limited to high-ranking Party members and to non-Party individuals of outstanding achievement.

Kochina is an interesting example of a woman who took advantage of the vast new opportunities for talented, determined women in science in Stalin's Russia. After World War II, her prominence as one of the foremost scientists and one of the leading women in Soviet life was underscored by her selection as a Soviet representative at a series of international political and scientific conferences.

The Soviet Union has honored her achievements and work. Kochina was named a corresponding member of the Academy of Sciences of the USSR in 1946, and Academician of the Academy of Sciences—its highest rank—in 1958. She was also awarded the State Prize of the USSR in 1946. During her career she received four Orders of Lenin, the Order of the Red Banner of Labor, and various medals. In 1969, on her seventieth birthday, she became a Hero of Socialist Labor.

BIBLIOGRAPHY _____

Works by Pelageya Yakovlevna Polubarinova-Kochina

Space does not permit a full listing of Kochina's works; such a listing through 1969 can be found in "Pelageya Yakovlevna Kochina. . . . " (1969). Included below are works cited in the essay, together with other works not included in the list noted above. (Note: Some Western publications index Kochina's works under "Polubarinova-Kochina.") All original titles and works are in Russian.

Mathematical and Historical Works

N. E. Kochin: Life and Work. Moscow: Izdat Akad. Nauk. SSSR, 1950.
  Kochina wrote this biography of her husband in the last years of Stalin's life, and it reflects official political positions of that time. In 1970 she wrote a second biography that reflected post-Stalinist political positions: *Nikolai Evgrafovich Kochin, 1901–1944.* Moscow: "Nauka," 1979.
Life and Work of S. V. Kovalevskaya (On the Centenary of Her Birth). Moscow: Izdat. Akad. Nauk SSSR, 1950.
  This study was given two post-Stalinist reworkings: *Sofia Vasil' evna Kovalevskaya: Her Life and Work.* Moscow: Gosudarstv. Izdat. Tehn.-Teor. Lit., 1955. *Sofia Vasil' evna Kovalevskaya, 1850–1891.* Moscow: "Nauka," 1981. Translated by Michael Burov, under the title *Love and Mathematics: Sofya Kovalevskaya.* Moscow: Mir, 1985. The 1950 Russian work is 51 pages long; the others are, respectively, 100 and 312 pages.
The Theory of Ground Water Movement. Moscow: Gozudarstv. Izdat. Tehn.-Teor. Lit, 1952. 2nd ed. Moscow: "Nauka," 1977. English translation by J. M. Roger De Wiest. Princeton, N.J.: Princeton University Press, 1962.
"Karl Theodore Wilhelm Weierstrass (on the 150th anniversary of his birth)." *Uspekhi Matematicheskikh Nauk* 21 (3) (129) (1966): 213–224. Translated by R. O. Davies in *Russian Mathematical Surveys* 21 (3) (1966): 195–206.
(with V. G. Priazhinskaia and V. N. Emikh) *Mathematical Methods in the Theory of Irrigation.* Moscow: "Nauka," 1969.
"Nonlinear problems of the theory of nonstationary filtration." In *Certain Problems of Mathematics and Mechanics (on the Occasion of the Seventieth Birthday of M. A. Lavrent'ev)*, 223–232. Leningrad: "Nauka," 1970.
Memoirs. Moscow: "Nauka," 1974.
  An extremely limited, extraordinarily selective, and "official" autobiography: i.e., the book's contents reflect Soviet state policies, and there is no word of criticism of anything done by the Soviet state. (For example, Stalin is never mentioned.) A preordained political framework guided Kochina's selection of topics, as well as the way topics were presented. Also, the book has only short, superficial discussions of Kochina's mathematical work.
"A letter from H. A. Schwarz to S. V. Kovalevskaya." *Voprosy Istorii Estestvoznaniya i Tekhniki* (4) (1980): 105–111.
(with T. D. Dzuraev et al.) "Ivan Semenovich Arzhanyh." *Uspekhi Matematicheskikh Nauk* 36 (1) (217) (1981): 195–202.
"Circular polygons in filtration theory." In *Problems of Mathematics and Mechanics,* 166–177. Novosibirsk: "Nauka" Sibirsk. Otdel., 1983.
(with Roger L. Cooke) "An unknown letter of P. L. Chebyshev to S. V. Kovalevskaia." *Voprosy Istorii Estestvoznaniya i Tekhniki* (2) (1983): 162–166.
The Correspondence of S. V. Kovalevskaya and G. Mittag-Leffler. Edited by A. P. Yushkevich, with a commentary by P. Ya. Kochina. Nauchnoye Nacledstvo 7. Moscow: "Nauka," 1984.

Works about Pelageya Yakovlevna Polubarinova-Kochina

Aleksandrov, P. S., et al. "Pelageya Yakovlevna Kochina" (in Russian). *Uspekhi Matematicheskikh Nauk* 34 (4) (July–August 1979): 217–220. Translated by S. Rhodes in *Russian Mathematical Surveys* 34 (4): 193–197. Translation reprinted in *Association for Women in Mathematics Newsletter* 12 (1) (January–February 1982): 9–12.

> The citation in the footnote on the last page is to the wrong number of *Prikladnaia*. The correct reference is "Pelageya Yakovlevna Kochina. . . ." (1969) below.

Bogoliubov, A. N. "Mathematical methods in hydroaerodynamics" (in Russian). In Shtokalo et al. (1966–1970), Vol. 4, book 2, 290–303.

———. "Mathematics in the Academy of Sciences of the USSR, Leningrad and Moscow Institutions of Higher Education" (in Russian). In Shtokalo et al. (1966–1970), vol. 3, 61–74.

Cooke, Roger. *The Mathematics of Sonya Kovalevskaia*. New York: Springer-Verlag, 1984.

> Has a short bibliography of some of Kochina's work on Kovalevskaya on p. 217.

Fil'chakov, P. F. "Some applications of the theory of functions of complex variables." In Shtokalo et al. (1968–1970), Vol. 4, book 1, 355–367.

Koblitz, Ann Hibner. *A Convergence of Lives. Sofia Kovalevskaia: Scientist, Writer, Revolutionary*. Boston: Birkhäuser, 1983.

Pelageya Yakovlevna Kochina (in Russian). Bibliography of Soviet Scientists. Moscow, 1977.

"Pelageya Yakovlevna Kochina" (in Russian). *Dinamika Sploshnoi Sredy* 39 (1979): 5–8.

"Pelageya Yakovlevna Kochina (on the occasion of her eightieth birthday)" (in Russian). *Izvestiya Akademia Nauk SSSR Ser. Mekhanika Zhidkosti i Gaza* 3 (1979): 3.

"Pelageya Yakovlevna Kochina (on the occasion of her seventy-fifth birthday)" (in Russian). *Izvestiya Akademia Nauk SSSR Ser. Mekhanika Zhidkosti i Gaza* 3 (1974): 3–4.

"Pelageya Yakovlevna Kochina (on the seventieth anniversary of her birth)" (in Russian). *Prikladnaia Matematika i Mekhanika* 33(2) (1969): 193–211.

> Contains bibliography of Kochina's work.

Other References

Graham, Loren. *The Soviet Academy of Sciences and the Communist Party 1927–1932*. Princeton, N.J.: Princeton University Press, 1969.

Shtokalo, I. Z., et al. *Istoriia Otechestvennoi Matematiki*, 4 vols. Kiev: Naukova Dumka, 1966–1970.

SOFIA VASILEVNA KOVALEVSKAIA (1850–1891)

Ann Hibner Koblitz

BIOGRAPHY

Sofia Vasilevna Korvin-Krukovskaia (to be referred to as Kovalevskaia) was born on January 15, 1850, in Moscow. Her father, Vasilii Korvin-Krukovskii, was an officer in the Russian artillery; her mother, Elizaveta Shubert, came from a family of German scholars who had settled in Russia in the previous century. They had three children, of whom Kovalevskaia was the middle child. Kovalevskaia had a more or less typical gentry upbringing, but early in her youth she exhibited a decided preference for, and aptitude in, the natural sciences and mathematics. This bent was encouraged by her father, who allowed her to study algebra and geometry with a tutor, and eventually was even persuaded to hire a mathematician (A. N. Strannoliubskii) to teach her calculus.

Under the influence of her elder sister (Anna Korvin-Krukovskaia Jaclard, writer and participant in the Paris Commune of 1871), the mathematician Strannoliubskii, and others, Kovalevskaia soon became a staunch supporter of the political, social, and cultural radicalism of the 1860s. She found the philosophy of nihilism especially attractive, since it emphasized social revolution, equality of women, and faith in the natural sciences. Moreover, nihilism taught that it was the right and duty of every woman of the intelligentsia and nobility to free herself from "parental tyranny," obtain higher education, and embark on a career of usefulness to society.

Kovalevskaia determined to seek higher education abroad, since at that time Russian universities (like those in virtually all of Europe except Switzerland) were closed to women. She decided to contract a so-called fictitious marriage in order to facilitate going abroad, because she was afraid her father would not permit her to leave her family for purposes of obtaining a university degree. (Women in Russia could not leave the country, or live apart from their families within the country, without the written permission of father or husband.)

"Fictitious marriage" was somewhat in vogue among certain young radicals of the 1860s. Since nihilism taught that blind adherence to an archaic patriarchal family structure was wrong, some nihilists reasoned that any means of circumventing tyrannical parental authority was justified. The means advocated included running away from home, and marrying "fictitiously." That is, a woman legally married a nihilist man, but essentially left him (by mutual agreement) at the church door after he had officially given his permission for his "wife" to live apart from him.

Kovalevskaia married the future paleontologist Vladimir Kovalevskii (also a staunch nihilist) in 1868 with the above scenario in mind. Unfortunately, things did not turn out quite as she had planned. Kovalevskaia's fifteen-year marriage was a source of intermittent sorrow, exasperation, and tension. Kovalevskaia had a difficult character, and Kovalevskii's mild instability turned to more serious psychological abnormality with the passing years.

In 1869 Kovalevskaia traveled to Heidelberg to study mathematics and the natural sciences. The university administration agreed to allow her to attend courses, provided that she obtain the explicit permission of each of her professors. Kovalevskaia was persuasive, and most professors in the natural sciences were cooperative. She studied with the famous researchers Gustav Kirchhoff, Hermann von Helmholtz, Leo Königsberger, and Paul DuBois-Reymond, all of whom praised her and spread her fame among their colleagues. She even managed to convince the nihilist-hating misogynist R. Wilhelm Bunsen to allow her and her friend Iulia Lermontova (the first woman to obtain her doctoral degree in chemistry) to study chemistry in his laboratory.

After three semesters of successful study in Heidelberg, Kovalevskaia moved to Berlin to work with Königsberger's former teacher, the great analyst Karl Weierstrass. Weierstrass had to tutor her privately. Despite the combined efforts of himself and his eminent colleagues Emil DuBois-Reymond (Paul's brother), Rudolf Virchow, and Hermann von Helmholtz, the faculty senate refused to permit Kovalevskaia even to audit courses at the university.

Private tutoring strengthened the bonds between Kovalevskaia and Weierstrass; they developed a warm personal and professional relationship that lasted throughout her life. He called her the most talented of his disciples and watched out for her interests assiduously. She accorded him the affection of a daughter, propagandized his methods in her work, and always credited him as the source of her ideas.

Kovalevskaia worked steadily in Berlin for the next three years, her concentration broken only by a five-week stint as a medical aide in the Paris Commune of 1871 and by her frequent quarrels and misunderstandings with her husband. By the spring of 1874, Kovalevskaia had produced three doctoral dissertations. Each of these works was, in the opinion of Weierstrass, worthy of the doctoral degree; but he and Kovalevskaia had no wish to take chances. They realized that as the first woman to apply for her degree in mathematics, her case would have to be especially strong.

Thanks to the efforts of Weierstrass, DuBois-Reymond, Lazarus Fuchs, and others, Kovalevskaia was granted her degree, summa cum laude, from

Göttingen University in absentia in 1874. She was the first woman to be granted a doctorate in mathematics, and one of the first women in any field to receive this degree.

In the autumn of 1874, Kovalevskaia and her husband returned to Russia to seek positions in the academic world. For a combination of reasons, neither was able to obtain a university post. Russian academics were suspicious of the pair's politics and jealous of their German degrees and excellent letters of recommendation. In Kovalevskaia's case, of course, her sex was an added handicap.

Disillusioned with their lack of success, the pair turned to financial speculation and various commercial endeavors. Mathematics and paleontology were put aside, and Kovalevskaia concentrated on literary and social pursuits. Around this time Kovalevskaia and her husband inexplicably decided to consummate their six-year-old platonic union. In 1878 her only child, a daughter Sofia (nicknamed Fufa), was born. Kovalevskaia would later say that her daughter was the only good thing to have come out of her five-year hiatus in mathematical activity, the years of her "true" marriage with Vladimir.

From 1879 Kovalevskaia increasingly returned to her study of mathematics. She resumed her correspondence with Weierstrass, gave a talk at the Congress of Russian Naturalists and Physicians, and (unsuccessfully) petitioned for permission to take the Russian *magister* exam, which would have licensed her to teach higher mathematics. In late 1880 Kovalevskaia and her husband began to live apart again. Kovalevskaia took up a vagabond existence in straitened circumstances in furnished rooms in Paris and Berlin, and plunged into her studies. Her friend the Swedish mathematician Gösta Mittag-Leffler, a fellow student of Weierstrass, attempted to find a position for her at the university level, first in Helsinki and then in Stockholm.

Meanwhile, Kovalevskaia's husband was becoming increasingly unstable. He initiated a rash of financial dealings of dubious legality, refused to answer Kovalevskaia's and his brother's letters, and alternated between periods of deep depression and senseless euphoria. In April 1883, faced with possible prosecution in a stock swindle, and acutely aware of his failing mental powers, he committed suicide.

Shortly afterward, Mittag-Leffler was able to conquer opposition to Kovalevskaia at his university in Stockholm, and he offered her a position as *privat docent*. Kovalevskaia accepted and began her lectures in Stockholm in early 1884. In June of that year, she was appointed to a five-year "extraordinary professorship" (the equivalent, in modern American parlance, of a tenure-track assistant professorship); and in June 1889 she became the first woman since the physicist Laura Bassi and Maria Gaetana Agnesi* of mid-eighteenth century Bologna to hold a chair at a European university.

From the time of her appointment to Stockholm University until her death barely seven years later, Kovalevskaia was an integral member of the European mathematical community. Almost immediately she became an editor of the new journal *Acta Mathematica* and took over most responsibility as liaison with the mathematicians of Paris, Berlin, and her native Russia. She was consulted by her colleagues on hiring decisions, took part in the organization of international conferences, and was on cordial terms with the best mathematicians in the world (indeed, in her time, she was considered one of them). The eminent astronomer Hugo Gyldén referred ironically to the pentad of Charles Hermite, Kovalevskaia, Mittag-Leffler, Charles Émile Picard, and Weierstrass as the "mutual admiration society" of late nineteenth-century mathematics.

The French mathematical community thought so much of Kovalevskaia's work that in 1886 they announced the topic of the forthcoming Prix Bordin of the French Academy of Sciences to be a significant contribution to the problem of the study of the motion of a rigid body—a problem on which everyone knew Kovalevskaia was obtaining significant results. To the surprise of few people in the mathematical world, but to the blank astonishment of the European educated public as a whole, Kovalevskaia was awarded the Prix Bordin in December 1888. In recognition of the brilliance of her paper, the prize money was raised from 3,000 to 5,000 francs.

Kovalevskaia tried repeatedly to obtain a university position in her homeland, but was refused by the tsarist government. In 1889, however, on the initiative of Pafnuti Chebyshev and other mathematicians, Russian scientists honored Kovalevskaia by electing her a corresponding member of the Imperial Academy of Sciences. The rules of the organization had to be specifically changed to permit the election of a woman.

The years of Kovalevskaia's most creative mathematical activity were years of literary productivity as well. In the last years of her life, she wrote her lyrically beautiful childhood memoirs, two plays (in collaboration with the Swedish writer Anne Charlotte Leffler), a novella about the revolutionary movements of her youth, and several essays on political and social themes. She kept in contact with friends in revolutionary circles and helped them in small ways (smuggled letters for them, allowed "wanted" women to use her passport, etc.). Moreover, she belonged to several feminist discussion groups in Stockholm.

Kovalevskaia's varied interests and preoccupations brought her into contact with some of the best-known scientific, literary, and political figures of her day. As mentioned above, she was on good terms with most eminent European mathematicians of the time. In addition, she knew such intellectual luminaries as George Eliot, Henrik Ibsen, Fedor Dostoevskii, Anton Chekhov, Charles Darwin, T. H. Huxley, Peter Kropotkin, and others.

Kovalevskaia was a celebrity—a target for those who sought the vicarious excitement of attaching themselves to famous people. She had a voluminous correspondence and received her fair share of crank and hate mail. People wrote to her from all over the world, asking for advice, showing her their mathematical work, soliciting articles, and so on. In short, she had a visibility in the intellectual community not often achieved by mathematicians, male or female.

Kovalevskaia died of pneumonia in early 1891 at the age of forty-one. She was at the height of her mathematical powers and reputation.

WORK

Kovalevskaia published only ten mathematical papers, and of those, two are French and Swedish editions of the same work. The papers were written during two periods: from 1871 to 1874, when Kovalevskaia was studying with Weierstrass in Berlin and was more interested in theoretical analysis; and from 1881 to the end of her life ten years later, when she lived in various parts of Europe and was interested in mechanics and mathematical physics. The connection between the two periods is Kovalevskaia's constant use of function-theoretic techniques developed by Weierstrass and employed by her for the resolution of applied as well as theoretical problems.

Mathematicians and historians of science would agree that Kovalevskaia's most significant contributions were two: her proof of the theorem in partial differential equations now referred to as the Cauchy-Kovalevskaia Theorem, and her work on the revolution of a solid body about a fixed point. The former was one of the three papers she presented to Göttingen University as her doctoral dissertation in 1874. The latter was the research for which she won the Prix Bordin of the French Academy of Sciences in 1888.

Kovalevskaia's colleagues considered that her statement and proof of the Cauchy-Kovalevskaia Theorem was an important improvement over Cauchy's. Hermite called Kovalevskaia's paper "the last word" on the subject, and Henri Poincaré wrote that Kovalevskaia "significantly simplified Cauchy's method of proof, and gave the theorem its final form." Weierstrass was pleased with another aspect of Kovalevskaia's work. In a May 6, 1874, letter to her, he noted that her observation that an infinite series may formally satisfy a partial differential equation without converging for any system of values of its variables "was for me the starting point for interesting and illuminating research."

The other theme of Kovalevskaia's most important research concerns the classical problem of the revolution of a rigid body about a fixed point (the famous Kovalevskaia top). Two cases had been studied by Leonhard Euler, Joseph Louis Lagrange, Siméon Denis Poisson, and Carl Jacobi. Kovalevskaia analyzed the third, most difficult, classical case of this problem, and came up with a piece of work that astounded her contemporaries by its beauty and elegance. This work continues to have interest for mathematical physicists today. As Michael Tabor commented in a recent review article in *Nature* (1984), the top problem "is not a dessicated example of nineteenth century mathematics. More recently it has found useful applications in the theory of stationary flows of incompressible fluids." Kovalevskaia's asymptotic method for determining conditions of algebraic integrability, found in her classic Prix Bordin memoir, is cited increasingly today in literature on Korteweg-deVries equations, Kac-Moody Lie Algebras, etc.

Kovalevskaia's other works are of less importance than her memoirs on the Cauchy-Kovalevskaia Theorem and the Kovalevskaia top, but nevertheless they deserve mention here. The second of her three dissertation papers was on the reduction of abelian integrals to simpler elliptic integrals. This was a skillful series of manipulations which showed her complete command of Weierstrassian function theory.

Kovalevskaia's third dissertation, on the shape of Saturn's rings, was on a problem in classical astronomy. Operating on the theoretical assumption that the rings have a fluid layer, she improved upon Pierre Simon de Laplace's previous model of the shape of the rings. The power-series method she used in this paper was later applied to other problems by Poincaré.

On the subject of refraction of light in a crystalline medium, Kovalevskaia pointed out several mistakes which the physicist Gabriel Lamé had made in his presentation of the problem, and again used Weierstrassian function theory with great skill. Her argument was invalid, however; Vito Volterra found an error in the paper several months after Kovalevskaia's death.

Kovalevskaia's last published work was a short article of a theoretical character. In it she gave a simplified proof of a theorem of Heinrich Bruns in potential theory.

Kovalevskaia's works and their applications in modern mathematics and mathematical physics were discussed at length in a series of sessions at the American Mathematical Society (AMS) meeting in Amherst, Mass., and the Kovalevskaia Symposium in Cambridge Mass., both meetings held in October 1985. The proceedings of the sessions and symposium have been published under the auspices of the AMS (Keen 1987).

As significant as Kovalevskaia's published works were, they do not tell the whole story of her impact on mathematics. Kovalevskaia performed an important role as an intermediary between the mathematicians of Western Europe and her native Russia. She introduced Weierstrassian function theory to her suspicious compatriots (who did not like what they considered the abstract "analysis for analysis' sake" tendency of German analysis) by presenting her dissertation on abelian functions at the 1879 Congress of Russian Naturalists and Physicians. Kovalevskaia felt justly proud that after her talk Chebyshev no longer spoke slightingly of the Weierstrassian school.

Moreover, Kovalevskaia was a valuable resource for her colleagues, traveling as she did between the mathematical capitals of Europe with such frequency, and having so communicative a nature. Even such an eminent mathematician as Chebyshev, who had been publishing in French for forty years, would ask Kovalevskaia for help in sorting out the advances of Western mathematics. And mathematicians like Mittag-Leffler, Poincaré, Hermite, and others would often appeal to her for explanations of the more obscure points in Weierstrassian function theory. Kovalevskaia's service as a conduit of the newest theoretical ideas and approaches is less tangible than her own papers, but its importance should not be underestimated.

BIBLIOGRAPHY

Works by Sofia Vasilevna Kovalevskaia

Mathematical Works

"Zur Theorie der partiellen Differentialgleichungen." *Journal für die reine und angewandte Mathematik* 80 (1875): 1–32.
   First doctoral thesis.
"Über die Reduction einer bestimmten Klasse von Abel'scher Integrale 3-en Ranges auf elliptische Integrale." *Acta Mathematica* 4 (1884): 393–414.
   Second doctoral thesis.
"Sur la propagation de la lumière dans un milieu cristallisé." *Comptes rendus hebdomadaires de l'Académie des Sciences* 98 (1884): 356–357.
"Om ljusets fortplannting uti ett kristalliniskt medium." *Öfversigt Akademiens Forhandlinger* 41 (1884): 119–121.
   This and the previous paper are Swedish and French summaries of the results of the following work.
"Über die Brechung des Lichtes in cristallinischen Mitteln." *Acta Mathematica* 6 (1885): 249–304.
"Zusätze und Bemerkungen zu Laplace's Untersuchung über die Gestalt des Saturnringes." *Astronomische Nachrichten* 111 (1885): 37–48.
   Third doctoral thesis.
"Sur le problème de la rotation d'un corps solide autour d'un point fixe." *Acta Mathematica* 12 (1888–1889): 177–232.
"Sur une propriété du système d'équations différentielles qui définit la rotation d'un corps solide autour d'un point fixe." *Acta Mathematica* 14 (1890): 81–93.
"Mémoire sur un cas particulier du problème de la rotation d'un corps pesant autour d'un point fixe, où l'intégration s'effectue à l'aide de fonctions ultraelliptiques du temps." *Mémoires présentés par divers savants à l'Académie des Sciences de l'Institut national de France* 31 (1890): 1–62.
"Sur un théorème de M. Bruns." *Acta Mathematica* 15 (1891): 45–52.
Scientific Works. Moscow: Akademia Nauk SSSR, 1948.
   Contains all of Kovalevskaia's mathematical papers translated into Russian by P. Ia. Polubarinova-Kochina*.

Other Works

Kovalevskaia, Sofia Vasilevna. *Sonya Kovalevsky. Her Recollections of Childhood with a biography by Anna Carlotta Leffler, Duchess of Cajanello*. Translated by Isabel F. Hapgood and A. M. Clive Bayley. New York: The Century Company, 1895.
   Contains an idiosyncratic and often inaccurate biographical sketch by Mittag-Leffler's sister. Supplemented with some interesting quotations from correspondence, and the reminiscences of Kovalevskaia's best friend, Iulia Lermontova.

———. *Vera Barantzova*. Translated by Sergius Stepniak and William Westall. London: Ward & Downey, 1895.

This novella, alternately known under the titles *A Nihilist Girl* and *Vera Vorontsova*, contains Kovalevskaia's descriptions of the political trials of the 1870s in Russia, and other autobiographical fragments. This particular edition also has an interesting introduction by the Russian revolutionary S. Stepniak-Kravchinskii.

———. *Reminiscences and Letters* (in Russian). Edited by S. Ia. Shtraikh. Moscow: Akademia Nauk SSSR, 1951.

Contains a wide selection from Kovalevskaia's correspondence, letters about her, and many of her literary works, excellently annotated.

———. *Reminiscences: Literary Works* (in Russian). Edited by P. Ia. Polubarinova-Kochina. Moscow: "Nauka," 1974.

The most complete collection of Kovalevskaia's nonmathematical works.

———. *A Russian Childhood*. Translated and edited by Beatrice Stillman. New York: Springer-Verlag, 1978.

Successfully and lyrically translated version of Kovalevskaia's childhood memoirs. Also contains her short autobiographical sketch, an article on her mathematics by P. Ia. Polubarinova-Kochina, and some of Shtraikh's excellent notes from the 1951 *Reminiscences and Letters*.

Works about Sofia Vasilevna Kovalevskaia

Adelung, Sophie. "Jugenderinnerungen an Sophie Kovalewsky." *Deutsche Rundschau* 89 (1896): 394–425.

Letters from Kovalevskaia and her relatives.

Bell, Eric Temple. "Master and pupil: Weierstrass and Sonja Kowalewski." In *Men of Mathematics*, 423–429. New York: Simon and Schuster, 1937.

The standard account, on which many mathematicians base their knowledge of Kovalevskaia. Romanticized and inaccurate.

Bunsen, Marie von. "Sonja Kowalevsky. Eine biographische Skizze." *Illustrierte Deutsche Monatshefte* (82) (1897): 218–232.

Contains letters from Kovalevskaia to her friend the Berlin physicist Gustav Hansemann.

Cooke, Roger. *The Mathematics of Sonya Kovalevskaya*. New York: Springer-Verlag, 1984.

Excellent technical account of Kovalevskaia's mathematics.

Franklin, Fabian. " 'Masculine heads' and 'feminine hearts'. Apropos of Sonya Kovalevsky." *Century Magazine* 51 (1895–1896): 317–318.

Fascinating defense of Kovalevskaia by the mathematician husband of Christine Ladd-Franklin* against the disparaging biographical sketch of Isabel F. Hapgood (below).

Geronimus, J. L. *Sofja Wassiljevna Kowalewskaja*. Berlin: VEB Verlag Technik, 1954. Reasonably good biography.

Golubev, V. V. "The works of S. V. Kovalevskaia on the revolution of a rigid body about a fixed point" (in Russian). *Prikladnaia matematika i tekhnika* 14 (3) (1950): 236–244.

Hansson, Laura Marholm. "The learned woman: Sonia Kovalevsky." In *Six Modern Women: Psychological Sketches*, 3–58. Translated from German by Hermione Ramsden. Boston: Roberts Brothers, 1896.

Admiring but pitying psychological portrait. Hansson represents a conservative backlash against Kovalevskaia and other "new women."

Hapgood, Isabel F. "Notable women: Sonya Kovalevsky." *Century Magazine* 50 (1895): 536–539.

A belittling short sketch, which purports to prove that women's emotionalism and mathematics are a deadly combination.

Kannak, E. "S. Kovalevskaia and M. Kovalevskii" (in Russian). *Novyi zhurnal* (39) (1954): 194–211.

About Kovalevskaia's interactions with the Russian sociologist and jurist Maksim Kovalevskii (a distant relative of her husband), with whom she had a serious relationship in the last three years of her life.

Kennedy, Don H. *Little Sparrow*. Athens: Ohio University Press, 1983.

Review: *Historia Mathematica* 13 (1986): 74–77.

Key, Ellen. *Drei Frauenschicksale*. 2nd ed. Berlin: S. Fischer Verlag, 1908.

Sensitive, sometimes insightful memoirs by a Swedish feminist and pedagogue, the friend of Kovalevskaia in Stockholm.

Klein, Felix. *Vorlesungen über die Entwicklung der Mathematik im 19. Jahrhundert,* vol. 1, 293–295. Berlin: Springer, 1926.

Perhaps the most frequently cited disparaging opinion by a mathematician of Kovalevskaia's originality.

Koblitz, Ann Hibner. *A Convergence of Lives. Sofia Kovalevskaia: Scientist, Writer, Revolutionary*. Boston: Birkhäuser, 1983.

Emphasizes the social, political, and cultural circumstances that gave encouragement to Kovalevskaia in her search for a mathematical career. Reviews: *Physics Today* 37 (4) (1984): 79–81; *American Mathematical Monthly* 93 (1986): 139–144.

———. "Sofia Kovalevskaia and the mathematical community." *Mathematical Intelligencer* 6 (1) (1984): 20–29.

Archival information on Kovalevskaia's relations with her colleagues.

Korvin-Krukovskii, F. V. "Sofia Vasilevna Korvin-Krukovskaia" (in Russian). *Russkaia starina* 71 (9) (1891): 623–636.

Charming anecdotal reminiscences by Kovalevskaia's brother.

Kronecker, L. "Sophie von Kowalevsky." *Journal für die reine und angewandte Mathematik* 108 (1891): 88.

Eminently respectful obituary by the notoriously touchy Kronecker.

Litvinova, E. F. "From my student days. (Acquaintance with S. V. Kovalevskaia)" (in Russian). *Zhenskoe delo* (4) (1899): 34–63. (Under the pseudonym "E. El'.")

About Kovalevskaia in Zurich.

———. *S. V. Kovalevskaia (Woman-Mathematician): Her Life and Scientific Work* (in Russian). St. Petersburg: P. P. Soikin, 1894.

Sensitive, nontechnical, but mathematically aware account; contains some personal reminiscences.

Malevich, Iosif Ignatievich. "Sofia Vasilevna Kovalevskaia" (in Russian). *Russkaia starina* (12) (1890): 615–654.

Eccentric, self-laudatory reminiscences by Kovalevskaia's childhood tutor; interesting because they portray Kovalevskaia's youth as far happier than did Kovalevskaia herself in her memoirs.

Mendelson, Marie. "Briefe von Sophie Kowalewska." *Neue Deutsche Rundschau* (6) (1897): 589–614.
     Letters and some interesting biographical information on Kovalevskaia's Paris years, collected by her Polish revolutionary friend.
Mittag-Leffler, Gösta. "Une page de la vie de Weierstrass." *Compte rendu du deuxième congrès international des mathématiciens,* 131–153. Paris: Gauthier-Villars, 1902. About Weierstrass and Kovalevskaia.
———. "Sophie Kovalevsky, notice biographique." *Acta Mathematica* 16 (1893): 385–392.
     Includes her course lists.
———. "Weierstrass et Sonja Kowalewsky." *Acta Mathematica* 39 (1923): 133–198.
Oleinik, O. A. "Kovalevskaia's Theorem and its role in the modern theory of partial differential equations" (in Russian). *Matematika v shkole* (5) (1975): 5–9.
     A simplified explanation of the Cauchy-Kovalevskaia Theorem suitable for high school mathematics teachers and their brighter pupils.
Polubarinova-Kochina, P. Ia., ed. *Letters to Kovalevskaia from Foreign Correspondents* (in Russian). Preprint No. 121. Moscow: Institut problem mekhaniki Akademia Nauk SSSR, 1979.
     Translations into Russian of a number of letters preserved in the archives of the Institut Mittag-Leffler in Sweden.
———. *Memories of Sofia Kovalevskaia. A Collection of Articles* (in Russian). Moscow: Akademia Nauk SSSR, 1951.
     A centenary collection of reminiscences by Kovalevskaia's daughter and others, plus historical studies of Kovalevskaia's relations with Chebyshev, Strannoliub-skii, and others.
———. *Sofia Vasilevna Kovalevskaia 1850–1891* (in Russian). Moscow: "Nauka," 1981. Translated by Michael Burov, under the title *Love and Mathematics: Sofya Kovalevskaya.* Moscow: Mir, 1985.
     Detailed, well-documented scientific biography which supersedes the author's previous works. Contains as an appendix an expanded version of Kovalevskaia's daughter's reminiscences of her mother.
Rappaport, Karen D. "S. Kovalevsky: A mathematical lesson." *American Mathematical Monthly* 88 (1981): 564–574.
     A nice biographical sketch with relatively few errors of fact.
Shtraikh, S. Ia. *The Kovalevskii Family* (in Russian). Moscow: Sovetskii Pisatel', 1984.
     Combined biography of Kovalevskaia, her husband Vladimir the paleontologist, and his brother Alexander, an embryologist, in a sort of fictionalized format.
———. *The Sisters Korvin-Krukovskaia* (in Russian). Moscow: Mir, 1933.
     Joint biography of Kovalevskaia and her elder sister Anna. Useful because it often contains more complete letter quotations than even those in *Reminiscences and Letters* (1951).
Stillman, Beatrice. "Sofya Kovalevskaya: Growing up in the sixties." *Russian Literature Triquarterly* (9) (1974): 276–302.
     Sensitive biographical sketch, though slightly romanticized.
Tabor, Michael. "Modern dynamics and classical analysis." *Nature* 310 (26 July 1984): 277–282.
     Contains a clear description of how Kovalevskaia's classic Prix Bordin memoir relates to modern work.

Vorontsova, L. A. *Sofia Kovalevskaia* (in Russian). Moscow: Molodaia Gvardiia, 1957.
A popular biography written for young people, but nevertheless accurate and informative.

Weierstrass, Karl. *Briefe von Karl Weierstrass an Sofia Kowalewskaja*. Moscow: "Nauka," 1973.
Weierstrass's letters to Kovalevskaia are a fascinating chronicle of their professional and personal relations. In German, with Russian translation and annotation.

Yushkevich, A. P., ed. *The Correspondence of S. V. Kovalevskaya and G. Mittag-Leffler* (in Russian). Moscow: "Nauka," 1984.

EDNA ERNESTINE KRAMER LASSAR (1902–1984)

Sally Irene Lipsey

BIOGRAPHY

Edna Ernestine Kramer Lassar (to be referred to by her professional name, Kramer) was born in New York City in the borough of Manhattan. She was the eldest child of Joseph Kramer (1869–1949) and Sabine (Elowitch) Kramer (1879–1958), Jewish immigrants who had come from Rima-Sombad, Austria-Hungary (now in Czechoslovakia).

Joseph Kramer arrived in Manhattan at the age of fourteen, his future wife at age six. They grew up to be intellectual, ambitious adults but had to go to work at an early age and attended night school for their high school education. Joseph was interested in political science; Sabine was interested in music, especially opera. Excellent linguists who prided themselves on speaking and writing English beautifully, Joseph and Sabine retained a strong interest in their native German as well; the poems of Heinrich Heine played a role in Joseph's successful courtship of Sabine.

Joseph and Sabine were married in 1901, and Kramer was born on May 11, 1902. She was named after an uncle, Edward Elowitch, who had died shortly before her birth in his nineteenth year. Edward had shown a gift for mathematics and had been looking forward to becoming an engineer. Kramer later reminisced about her childhood desire to do well in mathematics in his honor (Robinson 1963). Kramer's father earned his living mostly as a salesman, heading a men's clothing department at Brooks Brothers. He had no academic affiliation but was proud to serve the New York City Board of Education as a local superintendent responsible for publicizing free lectures and submitting reports about them. Kramer's parents, who believed strongly in the importance of education, held all their children to high standards; and Kramer adopted the same attitude toward her sister, Martha (two years younger), and her brother, Herbert (1911–1983). All three were prize-winning students; all were elected to Phi Beta Kappa and became teachers.

Kramer was a precocious child who intrigued her relatives and was strongly affected by their interest in her. Especially influential were a young aunt, Therese Elowitch (later Drazin), who lived nearby and became a lawyer, and a cousin, Josephine Schwartz (later Treger), who lived with the Kramers as a child. They challenged Kramer to card games, such as Hearts, and to feats of memory, such as, at age five, Longfellow's poem "The Fiftieth Birthday of Agassiz." By the time she entered first grade in May 1908, she had already studied many higher-level elementary school assignments brought home by her cousin. Kramer was also impressed by the behavior of her mother and aunt as active suffragettes.

As a freshman at Wadleigh High School, Manhattan, in 1914, Kramer's initial enthusiasm for a career as a German teacher was dampened by the world war. In addition, her high school teacher, John A. Swenson, led her to see her future differently. Swenson, the chairman of the Wadleigh High School mathematics department, inspired her with a love of mathematics, befriended her, and guided her to a career as a mathematician. He remained an inspiration and a friend throughout his life.

In 1922 Kramer received a B.A. degree summa cum laude from Hunter College, where she had majored in mathematics and been elected to Pi Mu Epsilon honorary mathematics society and Phi Beta Kappa. Then, while teaching in high school, she studied at Columbia University, receiving an M.A. in mathematics in 1925 and a Ph.D. in mathematics (with a minor in physics) in 1930. In later years she returned to formal studies as a postgraduate student at the Courant Institute of New York University (1939–1940, 1965–1969) and at the University of Chicago (1941).

Kramer's first teaching positions were in DeWitt Clinton High School (Bronx, New York, 1922–1923) and Wadleigh High School (1923–1929), where Swenson arranged her program to fit with her classes at Columbia. In 1929 she rejected an offer of a position in the Education Department of Hunter College because she preferred to teach mathematics and was still hoping to do mathematical research. That year, with the help of a strong endorsement from Swenson, she became the first female instructor of mathematics at the New Jersey State Teachers College in Montclair; she was promoted to assistant professor in 1932. Colleagues John Stone and Virgil Mallory invited her to join them as a coauthor in writing high school texts; but she demurred because of her loyalty to Swenson's new teaching and curricular proposals (integration of mathematical topics and incorporation of advanced concepts) and her compunction against writing books that might compete with his. She did help Stone and Mallory with ideas, corrections, exercises, and applications, and gave them credit for influencing her to write a statistics textbook.

On July 2, 1935, Kramer married Benedict Taxier Lassar, a French teacher and guidance counselor at Abraham Lincoln High School (Brooklyn, New York), where her sister, Martha, also taught French. Lassar was a graduate of New York's City College (A.B., 1926) and of Columbia University (J.D., 1929) and a member of Phi Beta Kappa. Having been awarded a French government scholarship, he had also studied at the University of Grenoble (Certificat, 1930).

Subsequently, after military service (1943–1945) involving psychological tests of soldiers, Lassar obtained graduate degrees in psychology from Columbia (M.A., 1947) and New York University (Ph.D, 1956) and became a clinical psychologist. He retired from the New York City school system in 1962. After 1964, he was a psychologist on the staff of Bleuler Psychotherapy Center, Queens, New York. Lassar encouraged Kramer in her interests in teaching and writing and shared her pleasure in music and travel. In the course of a long marriage, they explored the United States, Canada, and the Near and Far East. Lassar played a role in the production of Kramer's major manuscripts—he helped with library searches and typing; her two major books were dedicated to him.

During the Depression of the 1930s, college positions were scarce, there was much anti-Semitism and discrimination against women (especially married women), and salaries were low. Planning to marry, and fearing the hostility of the prospective chairman of Montclair College, Kramer decided in 1934 to return to the New York City school system, accepting a teaching position at Thomas Jefferson High School (Brooklyn, New York); her salary doubled. She soon became acting chairman of the department. During this era, no appointments as chairman were being made; as soon as appointments became possible again, Kramer was promoted to chairman.

After school hours, Kramer was busy with her writing, consulting, and teaching college courses. From 1935 to 1938, she taught methods courses in the graduate division of Brooklyn College. During 1943–1945 her workdays were particularly long. She continued to teach at Jefferson High School, but after her early morning classes she worked at Columbia University as a statistical consultant to the university's Division of War Research, under the Office of Scientific Research and Development in Washington, D.C. Her work was concerned with probabilistic strategic tactics of the war in Japan, and with anti-aircraft fire control. Her group was directed by Allen Wallis, assisted by Jacob Wolfowitz and Abraham Wald. A long-lasting professional affiliation with the New York Polytechnic Institute (then called Brooklyn Polytechnic) began in 1948. Kramer started as an adjunct instructor and rose to adjunct professor in 1953.

Kramer retired from the New York City school system in 1956 and from New York Polytechnic Institute in 1965. During the course of her career, she held memberships in the American Mathematical Society, the Mathematical Association of America, the Société Mathématique de France, the Association for Women in Mathematics, the American Association for the Advancement of Science, the History of Science Society, and the New York Academy of Sciences. In retirement Kramer was active for many years, studying, publishing, and traveling. She attended classes at the Courant Institute from 1965 to 1969, and, in 1973, at Nanyang University in Singapore, gave an invited lecture, "The contributions of women, past and present, to the development of mathematics." Her greatest work, *The Nature and Growth of Modern Mathematics* (1970), took fourteen years to complete. Hunter College paid tribute to this distinguished alumna by electing her to its Hall of Fame in 1972. For the last ten years of her life Kramer suffered from Parkinson's disease; she died of pneumonia at her home in Manhattan on July 9, 1984.

WORK

Kramer's Ph.D. dissertation discussed geometric properties of polygenic functions, extending the work of Edward Kasner (her thesis advisor), Georg Scheffers, and Edmond Laguerre. Kasner had published a number of articles on "polygenic" functions (his coinage) of the ordinary complex variable z. In the first part of her thesis, Kramer developed an analogous theory of polygenic functions of the dual variable w. Similarities and differences between the two theories were found; no general principle of transference from one theory to the other appeared to exist. Other antecedents of Kramer's work are in the papers of Scheffers on monogenic functions of the dual variable w. The second part of Kramer's thesis was a treatment of the Laguerre group, a set of linear fractional polygenic transformations of the dual variable w, to which she gave a more extended analytic treatment than had been done previously.

While her dissertation reflects Kasner's influence, Kramer's earliest pedagogical publication reflects the influence of her mentor, John A. Swenson, and her job. She shows how prospective teachers can learn both content and method simultaneously, to the enrichment of both (Kramer 1931). One can see in this article the development of Kramer's ideas for her future books. She recommends bringing appropriate college-level mathematics to the high school level, and emphasizing concepts over mechanics, to avoid the common occurrence of "not being able to see the basic ideas through the haze of technique with which they are surrounded." Other pedagogical publications were concerned with applications of mathematics. *Mathematics Takes Wings* (1942) related aeronautics to many different topics in the high school mathematics curriculum; *The Integration of Trigonometry with Physical Science* (1948) showed how trigonometry could be taught with applications to electricity, sound, and light. Coauthor of *Experiences in Mathematical Discovery* (1966), she developed special materials for the student of general mathematics.

Kramer's knowledge of mathematical applications was increased by her statistical work during World War II. Her expertise in statistics had been demonstrated earlier at Montclair College, where she taught courses in educational statistics, culminating in the book *A First Course in Educational Statistics* (1935). This book (her only text) contained an exposition of modern mathematical statistics, written in such a way that it could be used by nonmathematicians. Illustrative tables and exercises used actual data drawn from journals of special interest to teachers. In addition to applications, Kramer was collecting all sorts of historical, cultural, and recreational materials to accompany each mathematical concept. She helped Kasner to prepare *Mathematics and the Imagination* and served as advisor to Richard Courant in the writing of *What Is Mathematics?*

By 1951 her extensive collection of applications and other enrichment materials had grown into a book, *The Main Stream of Mathematics*. It received many favorable reviews and was translated into Dutch, Italian, and Japanese. It is a combination of mathematical history and concepts up to the early part of the twentieth century, rounded out with applications to science, art, and music, and written with a lively flair. Thus it is enjoyable reading for the layman as well as the specialist, and a valuable reference for students and teachers. A voluminous expansion and sequel, *The Nature and Growth of Modern Mathematics,* was first published in 1970. It covers in a popular, but unusually comprehensive, fashion twentieth-century mathematics and the people responsible for creating it. In a long review, Carl Boyer (1971) praised the historical allusions and thorough mathematical content. "One cannot easily think," he wrote, "of a topic within a layman's comprehension which is not presented in considerable detail," including analysis, algebra, logic, and foundations. This book and *The Main Stream of Mathematics* use a spiral approach, emphasizing concepts over chronology. Kramer's purpose was to give the reader access to an understanding of the importance of mathematics and its relationship to other areas of scientific thought; to give "an all-round picture" with balance among computational, historical, recreational, and cultural points of view; and "to promote interest and diminish awe." In doing so, she provided much valuable background information for the specialist as well.

As a scientist with an interest in history, Kramer included in her books details about the lives of many of the mathematicians whose ideas and accomplishments she discussed. Women mathematicians, past and present, became a special interest. Her articles describing the lives of these women, as well as mathematical details of their achievements, appeared in *Scripta Mathematica* and the *Dictionary of Scientific Biography,* in addition to in her books. She traveled to Europe to interview some of the twentieth-century women mathematicians working at European universities and became friendly with Maria Pastori and her sister Giuseppina, and with Hanna Neumann* and her family.

In the first chapter of his "automathography," *I Want to Be a Mathematician,* Paul Halmos expresses the belief that mathematicians who "like words become famous and beloved for their clear explanations" (1985, 5). Kramer is an example of such a mathematician, gifted with respect to both mathematics and language. It happened that the onset of the Depression took place just at the time of her Ph.D., and she was unable to find a job conducive to the mathematical research she expected to do. The result was unusual productivity of another sort, utilizing her talent for writing and for clear explanations of very complicated ideas. She had the pleasure of exploring mathematics to an unusual breadth and depth, of writing about its most significant and profound aspects from a variety of perspectives, and then being well received by one of the biggest audiences a mathematical writer can hope to reach.

BIBLIOGRAPHY ————————————————————————————

Works by Edna Ernestine Kramer Lassar

Mathematical Works

"The mathematical theory of the top." Master's thesis, Columbia University, 1925.
"Polygenic functions of the dual variable $w = u + jv$." *American Journal of Mathematics*
    52 (1930): 370–376.
    Part I of Kramer's doctoral dissertation.
Polygenic Functions of the Dual Variable w and the Laguerre Group. Hamburg: Lütcke
    and Wulff, 1930.
    Part II of Kramer's doctoral dissertation, combined with a reprint of Part I (see
    above).
"Some methods in professionalized subject matter courses in mathematics for Teachers
    College." *Mathematics Teacher* 24 (1931): 429–435.
A First Course in Educational Statistics. New York: John Wiley and Sons, 1935.
Mathematics Takes Wings. New York: Barrie and Edwin, 1942.
    Aviation supplement to secondary mathematics.
"The integration of trigonometry with physical science." *Mathematics Teacher* 41 (1948):
    356–361.
The Main Stream of Mathematics. New York: Oxford University Press, 1951. Reprint.
    Greenwich, Conn.: Fawcett, 1961; Book Find Club ed., 1952. Translation. *A Che
    Serve La Matematica.* Milan: Feltrinelli, 1959. Translation. *Wiskunde.* Utrecht:
    Het Spectrum, 1964. Translation. Tokyo: Diamond, 1970.
"Six more female mathematicians." *Scripta Mathematica* 23 (1957): 83–95.
(with Oscar F. Schaaf et al.) *Experiences in Mathematical Discovery.* Washington, D.C.:
    National Council of Teachers of Mathematics, 1966.
The Nature and Growth of Modern Mathematics. New York: Hawthorn Books, 1970.
    Library of Science ed., 1970. Reprint, 2 vols. Greenwich, Conn.: Fawcett, 1974.
    Corrected reprint. Princeton, N.J.: Princeton University Press, 1982.
"The contributions of women to the development of mathematics." *Newsletter of the
    Southeast Asian Mathematics Society* 4 (July 1973): 4.1–4.3.
"Maria Gaetana Agnesi," "Sophie Germain," "Hypatia," "Sonia Kovalevsky,"
    "Amalie Emmy Noether," "Max Noether," "Duncan McLaren Young Som-
    merville." In *Dictionary of Scientific Biography,* edited by Charles Coulston
    Gillispie. New York: Scribners, 1972–1977.

Works about Edna Ernestine Kramer Lassar

Boyer, C. B. Review of *The Nature and Growth of Modern Mathematics. Mathematical
    Reviews* 42 (1971): 2911.
"Dr. Edna Kramer-Lassar, 82, ex-professor of mathematics." *New York Times* (25 July
    1984): D–23.
Hunter College Alumni Association. Papers. "Addendum." Hunter College, New York,
    1972.
    Brief account of her achievements in Kramer's handwriting.
Leef, A. "History of the influence of the Mathematics Department of Montclair State

College on Mathematics Education Between 1927 and 1972,'' 62–64. Ed.D. dissertation, Rutgers University, 1976.

Details of the genesis and development of Kramer's writing career.

Obituary. *Publishers Weekly* 226 (27 July 1984): 78.

Robinson, D. "Women in Math Count for More Today." *Eugene* (Oregon) *Register-Guard* (7 July 1963): sec. 5.

Interview with Kramer about her life and work.

Other References

Halmos, Paul R. *I Want to Be a Mathematician: An Automathography*. New York: Springer-Verlag, 1985.

CHRISTINE LADD-FRANKLIN (1847–1930)

Judy Green

BIOGRAPHY

Christine Ladd-Franklin was born on December 1, 1847, at Windsor, Connecticut, the daughter of Eliphalet Ladd and Augusta Niles Ladd. Her ancestors on her mother's side were prominent in Connecticut and included a great-uncle, John Milton Niles, who served as a United States Senator and as Postmaster General. Her ancestors on her father's side were prominent in New Hampshire and included a great-uncle, William Ladd, who founded the American Peace Society. She was brought up in New York City, where her father was a merchant until 1853; then in Windsor, Connecticut, in her maternal grandmother's home; and, after the death in 1860 of her mother, mostly in Portsmouth, New Hampshire, in the home of her paternal grandmother. She had two younger siblings, Henry Ladd (born 1850) and Jane Augusta Ladd McCordia (born 1854). Ladd-Franklin's father remarried in 1862; and from that marriage she had a half-sister, Katharine Ladd (born 1865), and a half-brother, George B. Ladd (born 1867), who died in an accident in 1881.

From the ages of twelve to sixteen, Ladd-Franklin attended school in Portsmouth. In August 1863 she read of the planned future opening of Vassar College and conceived the idea of attending it. She first attended the Wesleyan Academy in Wilbraham, Massachusetts, where she took classes which would prepare her for a higher education she dreamed of but had no reason to believe she would ever receive. Her studies included two years of Greek, a subject in which she was the only female student. She studied at Vassar in 1866–1867. Evidently, lack of funds prevented her return to Vassar the following year. Instead, she taught one semester in Utica, New York, practiced the piano, read in three or four languages, worked problems in trigonometry, collected about 150 botanical specimens, and published an English translation of Schiller's "Des Mädchens Klage" in the *Hartford Courant*. The generosity of an aunt enabled her to resume her studies at Vassar in the fall of 1868, and she graduated in 1869. While at Vassar, she studied languages, physics, and astronomy, but relatively little mathematics. However, by the time she graduated and returned to teaching, she was committed to learning higher mathematics. She explained much later that as women could not obtain "access to [physics] laboratory facilities . . . [she] took up, as the next best subject, mathematics, which could be carried on without any apparatus" (*Biographical Cyclopaedia of American Women* 1928, 3:136).

While teaching in Washington, Pennsylvania, in 1871, Ladd-Franklin came under the tutelage of George C. Vose of Washington and Jefferson College and began contributing to the Mathematical Questions section of the London-based *Educational Times*. She continued her study of mathematics at Harvard during the following year, under W. E. Byerly and James Mills Peirce. By 1878, when she applied to the graduate program offered at the newly opened Johns Hopkins University, her published work included several articles in the new American journal, *The Analyst,* as well as at least twenty mathematical questions or solutions to questions in the *Educational Times,* many of which were later abstracted in the *Jahrbuch über die Fortschritte der Mathematik.* Although the university was not open to women, Professor J. J. Sylvester, who was English and knew her contributions to the *Educational Times,* urged not only that she be admitted but also that she be granted a fellowship. During her four-year stay at Johns Hopkins, Ladd-Franklin continued her contributions to the *Educational Times* and *The Analyst,* contributed three papers to the newly founded *American Journal of Mathematics,* and became interested in Charles Sanders Peirce's work in symbolic logic. She wrote a dissertation in that subject, the content of which was presented to the Johns Hopkins Metaphysical Club, and which was published in *Studies in Logic by Members of the Johns Hopkins University* in 1883. However, as Johns Hopkins would not award degrees to women, she left in 1882 without the Ph.D. A few months later, on August 24, 1882, she married one of the members of the Johns Hopkins mathematics faculty, Fabian Franklin, who had received his Ph.D. from Johns Hopkins in 1880. One of the many anecdotes that she repeated concerns her contribution to the Johns Hopkins book and her marriage: "Peirce, giving, in the preface, an account of the contents of the book, spoke of the contribution on *The Algebra of Logic* as being by 'Christine Ladd (now Mrs. Fabian Franklin).' He told his class . . . that in a review of the book in a scientific journal in the Czech language the paper was referred to as having been written by 'Christine Ladd, now known to be the pen-name of Mr. Fabian Franklin' '' (*Biographical Cyclopaedia of American Women* 1928, 3:137).

Fabian Franklin remained on the mathematics faculty at Johns Hopkins until 1895, when he resigned his professorship to become editor of the *Baltimore News.* Fabian and Christine Ladd-Franklin had two children: a son who died in infancy in 1883, and a daughter, Margaret Ladd (born in 1884), who published an extensive bibliography on woman suffrage (Margaret Ladd Franklin 1913).

While continuing her work in symbolic logic, Ladd-Franklin began to work in the field of physiological optics; in 1887 she published her first of very many papers in that field. This paper, "A method for the experimental determination of the horopter," was a mathematical investigation of binocular vision. In 1891, while her husband was in Germany on a sabbatical leave, she began concentrating her research in optics on color vision, first in the Göttingen laboratory of Professor G. E. Müller, and then in the Berlin laboratory of Hermann von Helmholtz. She continued publishing on that subject during the next thirty-seven years; and her work in color vision culminated in 1929, when she was eighty-one years old, with the publication of her collected works on color vision, *Colour and Colour Theories*.

The theory of color vision that Ladd-Franklin constructed attempted to explain the way color is perceived both normally and by the color-blind. Her main thesis was that there is a development of color vision which proceeds in three stages: from achromatic (black and white alone), to dichromatic (yellow and blue), and finally to tetrachromatic (yellow, blue, red, and green). Her theory explained the observations that different colors are perceived in the three different zones of the retina (in the outer zone only black and white are seen, in the intermediate zone yellows and blues are seen, while in the central area all colors are seen) by postulating that the three zones develop to the three different stages. She explained partial color-blindness as occurring when the development stops at dichromatic vision (so that the central area of the retina also only perceives blue and yellow), while total color-blindness occurs when there is no development beyond the achromatic. She announced her theory at the International Congress of Psychology in London in 1892. She later reported that

although the paper was in flat opposition to the Helmholtz theory, Mr. Franklin happened to hear a remark made by the great physicist at one of the social gatherings of the Congress which gave him a thrill of pleasure. A little group of whom Helmholtz was one were discussing the two papers that had been read on color-vision, one by Mrs. Franklin and one by Professor Ebbinghaus. Helmholtz thought little of Ebbinghaus's paper, and someone asked him about Mrs. Franklin's. "Ach, Frau Franklin," he said, *"die* versteht die Sache. [Oh, Mrs. Franklin, *she* understands the subject.]" (*Biographical Cyclopaedia of American Women* 1928, 3:139–140)

Although her work in color theory was internationally recognized during her lifetime, it is a rare current text that mentions her theory when discussing the historical development of color theories. In fact, although her work was recognized, it was always controversial. In a review of her book, D. B. Judd, a physicist, wrote:

Some of the difficulty which has been encountered by Dr. Ladd-Franklin in achieving acceptance of her theory has doubtless been due to the reluctance of the physicist, on the one hand, and the psychologist, on the other, to admit that a mere logician, even so distinguished a logician as Dr. Ladd-Franklin, could possibly instruct them even slightly about their own fields of research. . . . Nevertheless, it must be admitted that both the physicist and psychologist, though they may not have entirely deserved all the harsh words showered upon them by this merciless and indomitable logician, have held views whose consistence was questionable and now stand in a position to benefit from the fruits

of the labors of a logician whose grasp of the phenomena of color vision is truly remarkable. (Judd 1929)

Christine Ladd-Franklin was also remarkable in other ways. She spent much
time, and some of her own money, helping women obtain graduate educations.
She was a lecturer in logic and psychology at the Johns Hopkins University
(1904–1909), and then, after her husband became associate editor of the *New
York Evening Post,* at Columbia University (1910–1930). In addition to publishing extensively on logic and on color theory (her bibliography in those subjects
alone comprised more than one hundred articles and reviews), she was associate
editor for logic and psychology and contributor for logic for Baldwin's 1902
Dictionary of Philosophy and Psychology; and she contributed many articles and
letters to various newspapers and news magazines, particularly on women's
issues, but also on such topics as the use of Esperanto, as well as on general
current events.

Although she had been awarded an LL.D. in 1887 by Vassar College, the
only honorary degree that college has ever bestowed, when she was offered a
doctorate from Johns Hopkins University at the age of seventy-eight, forty-four
years after the completion of her dissertation, she said, "Of course I've been a
doctor for a long time. I was given an LL.D. years ago. But I thought I'd like
to have my Ph.D. now. And I insisted that it should be given for the work I did
at Johns Hopkins, not what I've done since" ("Woman Ph.D. . . . " 1926).
Those attending the commemoration day ceremony on February 22, 1926, appreciated her long wait for her earned degree, and it was reported that "one of
the outstanding features of the day was an ovation accorded Mrs. Christine Ladd-
Franklin when the names of candidates for degrees were announced" ("To
Restore . . . " 1926). On March 5, 1930, four years after receiving her Ph.D.,
Christine Ladd-Franklin died at home of pneumonia at the age of eighty-two.

WORK

Symbolic logic is often said to have begun in 1847 with the publication of George
Boole's *The Mathematical Analysis of Logic, being an essay towards the Calculus
of Deductive Reasoning,* in which logical propositions are expressed symbolically
and algebraic operations on symbols are developed to represent the logical operations of conjunction, disjunction, and negation. By the end of the nineteenth
century, there were almost as many versions of the algebra of logic as there
were logicians. Common to almost all of them, however, was the use of a
symbolic system based on Boole's: i.e., using • for conjunction, + for disjunction, − for negation, and one or more symbols, called *copulae,* to denote
relationships between classes or qualities.

In 1889 Ladd-Franklin described the following requirements that she believed
any inventor of a system of logic had to meet:

1. He must take the multitudinous propositions which are handed in to him by common language and reduce them all to a limited number of forms of expression.
2. He must lay down the rules in accordance with which several of these statements are to be united into one, or one is to be broken up into several.
3. He must lay down rules in accordance with which information in regard to some of the terms is dropped while absolutely all the information which does not regard those terms is retained.

These three processes may be called, respectively, expression, combination and elimination. (Ladd-Franklin 1889, 549)

The third process, elimination, can be interpreted, in part, as one which would reduce reasoning of the syllogistic type to a purely mechanical operation.

Ladd-Franklin developed an algebra of logic which used two symmetric copulae. The symbolic representations basic to her logic were $x\bar{v}y$, denoting "no x is y," and xvy, denoting "some x is y." In this system "all x is y" is expressed by $x\bar{v}\bar{y}$. This contrasts with the more common use of a nonsymmetric copula by means of which "all x is y" can be expressed simply: e.g., $x<y$.

The most notable success of Ladd-Franklin's system was its extreme efficiency in providing a recognition principle for valid forms of syllogisms. Examples of valid syllogisms (there are fifteen), with their scholastic names, are:

Barbara: All M is P; all S is M; therefore all S is P.
Baroko: All P is M; some S is not M; therefore some S is not P.
Bokardo: Some M is not P; all M is S; therefore some S is not P.

In order to use Ladd-Franklin's recognition procedure for syllogisms, one must first convert both premises and the denial of the conclusion to symbolic form, using copulae. This can always be done, and it had long been known that the original syllogism is valid precisely if the resulting list of three symbolic statements forms an *antilogism,* or inconsistent triad, i.e., if the three statements cannot all hold at one time. Ladd-Franklin's contribution, described by Professor Josiah Royce of Harvard as "the crowning activity in a field worked over since the days of Aristotle" (*Biographical Cyclopaedia of American Women* 1928, 3:139), was to show that, if the only copulae used were $\bar{v}$ and v, there is an antilogism if and only if the following three conditions hold:

1. The three statements include exactly two formed with $\bar{v}$ and one with v,
2. Every pair of statements has one term in common, and
3. Only the term common to the two $\bar{v}$ statements appears in both the positive and negative forms.

The three forms of the syllogisms listed earlier are converted into the following antilogisms:

Barbara—$(M\bar{V}\bar{P})$ $(S\bar{V}\bar{M})$ $(SV\bar{P})$
Baroko—$(P\bar{V}\bar{M})$ $(SV\bar{M})$ $(S\bar{V}\bar{P})$
Bokardo—$(MV\bar{P})$ $(M\bar{V}\bar{S})$ $(S\bar{V}\bar{P})$

all of which satisfy Ladd-Franklin's "perfectly general rule . . . for testing the validity of any syllogism" (Ladd 1883, 41).

Ladd-Franklin's rule denied the validity of four forms of the syllogism that had been considered valid by scholastic logicians but not mathematical logicians. All of these rest on the assumption that every universal statement, "all x is y" or "no x is y," implies the corresponding particular statement, "some x is y" or "some x is not y." The modern view is that one cannot infer particular statements from universal statements, because if nothing at all has the property "x," "all x is y" and "no x is y" are both true while "some x is y" and "some x is not y" are both false.

In her later years, Ladd-Franklin often did not agree with the prevailing views on mathematical logic. She clearly failed to appreciate the power of the new ideas of Gottlob Frege, Giuseppe Peano, and Bertrand Russell, attacking the latter in particular in a number of abstracts and talks in 1918. She did understand, however, that symbolic logic was of use in common logic, and that philosophers' fears of symbols were keeping them from reaping the advantages of symbolic logic. She felt that mathematical logic had to become simpler, while common logic had to adopt some of the mathematical symbolism. Unfortunately, her desire to keep things simple made her reject some of the most fruitful developments in mathematical logic.

BIBLIOGRAPHY _____

Works by Christine Ladd-Franklin

Mathematical, Logical, and Related Works

"Crelle's Journal." *Analyst* 2 (1875):51–52 (as Christine Ladd).

"Determination of the locus of *O*." *Analyst* 4 (1877):47–48 (as Christine Ladd).

"Quaternions." *Analyst* 4 (1877): 172–174 (as Christine Ladd).

"On some properties of four circles inscribed in one and circumscribed about another." *Analyst* 5 (1878): 116–117 (as Christine Ladd).

"The polynomial theorem." *Analyst* 5 (1878): 145–147 (as Christine Ladd).

"The Pascal hexagram." *American Journal of Mathematics* 2 (1879): 1–12 (as Christine Ladd).

"The nine-line conic." *Analyst* 7 (1880): 147–149 (as Christine Ladd).

"On De Morgan's extension of the algebraic processes." *American Journal of Mathematics* 3 (1880): 210–225. Errata to page 224, 3 (1880): v (as Christine Ladd).

"On segments made on lines by curves." *American Journal of Mathematics* 4 (1881): 272 (as Christine Ladd).

"On the algebra of logic." *Studies in Logic by Members of the Johns Hopkins University*, 17–71 (as Christine Ladd). Edited by C. S. Peirce. Boston: Little and Co., 1883.

Accepted as Ladd-Franklin's Ph.D. dissertation in 1926.

"On the so-called d'Alembert-Carnot geometrical paradox." *Messenger of Mathematics* 15 (1885–1886): 36–37.

"On some characteristics of symbolic logic." *American Journal of Psychology* 2 (3) (1889): 543–567.

"Some proposed reforms in common logic." *Mind* 15 (January 1890): 75–88.

"Dr. Hillebrand's syllogistic scheme." *Mind* n.s. 1 (1892): 527–530.

"Sophie Germain, an unknown mathematician." *Century* 48 (1894): 946–949. Reprinted in *Association for Women in Mathematics Newsletter* 11 (3) (May–June 1981): 7–11. "Postscript." *Century* 49 (1894): 157.

"The reduction to absurdity of the ordinary treatment of the syllogism." *Science* n.s. 13 (328) (12 April 1901): 574–576.

"Some points in minor logic." *Journal of Philosophy, Psychology and Scientific Methods* 1 (1904): 13–15.

"Minor logic." *Journal of Philosophy, Psychology and Scientific Methods* 1 (1904): 494–496.

Answer to note by editor of *Science* on above in vol. 1, no. 2.

(with Edward V. Huntington) "Symbolic logic." In *The Encyclopedia Americana,* vol. 9. New York: 1905. Reprinted. *The Encyclopedia Americana,* vol. 17, 568–573. New York and Chicago: 1934, 1941, and 1952.

"The foundations of philosophy: Explicit primitives." *Journal of Philosophy, Psychology and Scientific Methods* 8 (1911): 708–713.

"Implication and existence in logic." *Philosophical Review* 21 (6) (1912): 641–665.

"Explicit primitives again: A reply to Professor Fite." *Journal of Philosophy, Psychology and Scientific Methods* 9 (1912): 580–585.

Reply to Warner Fite, "Explicit primitives: A reply to Mrs. Franklin," in 9 (1912): 155–158.

"The antilogism—an emendation." *Journal of Philosophy, Psychology and Scientific Methods* 10 (1913): 49–50.

"Charles S. Peirce at The Johns Hopkins." *Journal of Philosophy, Psychology and Scientific Methods* 13 (1916): 715–722.

"Symbol logic and Bertrand Russell." *Philosophical Review* 27 (2) (March 1918): 177–178.

"Bertrand Russell and symbol logic." *Bulletin of the American Mathematical Society* 25 (November 1918): 59–60.

"A logic poem." *Science* n.s. 64 (1658) (8 October 1926): 358.

"The antilogism." *Psyche* (1927): 100–103.

"The antilogism." *Mind* n.s. 37 (1928): 532–534.

"Some questions in logic." *Journal of Philosophy* 25 (1928): 700.

During the years 1873 to 1883, Ladd-Franklin (as Ladd) also published more than fifty solutions of questions from the *Educational Times* and another two solutions of questions from the *Analyst*. Fourteen of these items were abstracted in *Jahrbuch über die Fortschritte der Mathematik* and one other was listed in Alonzo Church's "Bibliography of Symbolic Logic (1666–1935)," *Journal of Symbolic Logic* 1 (4) (1936): 121–218.

Cited Works on Physiological Optics by Christine Ladd-Franklin

"A method for the experimental determination of the horopter." *American Journal of Psychology* 1 (1) (1887): 99–111.

Colour and Colour Theories. International Library of Psychology, Philosophy, and Scientific Method. New York: Harcourt, Brace and Co., 1929. London: Kegan Paul, Trench, Trubner and Co., 1929. Reprint. Classics in Psychology. New York: Arno Press, 1973.

Works about Christine Ladd-Franklin

Bushaw, D. "Mathematical Portraits—II. Christine Ladd-Franklin." *Mathematical Notes from Washington State University* 20 (February 1977): 2–3.
"Christine Ladd-Franklin." In *Biographical Cyclopaedia of American Women*, vol. 3, 135–141. New York: Halvord Publishing Co., 1928.
    Biography prepared from typescripts submitted by Christine Ladd-Franklin in 1926.
Hurvich, Dorothea Jameson. "Christine Ladd-Franklin." In *Notable American Women 1607–1950*, vol. 2, 354–356. Cambridge, Mass.: Harvard University Press, 1971.
    Biography and discussion of Ladd-Franklin theory of color vision by color theorist.
Reyes y Prosper, Ventura. "Christina Ladd Franklin, matemática americana y su influencia en la lógica simbólica." *El Progreso matemático* 1 (1891): 297–300.
    Discussion of Ladd-Franklin's contributions to logic.
Shen, Eugene. "The Ladd-Franklin formula in logic: The antilogism." *Mind* n.s. 36 (1927): 54–60.
    Discussion of Ladd-Franklin's solution to the problem of the syllogism, by a former student.
"To restore ideal at Johns Hopkins." *New York Times* (23 February 1926): 12.
"Woman Ph.D. at 78 tells life story." *New York World* (28 February 1926): 9.

Other References

Franklin, Margaret Ladd. *The Case for Woman Suffrage: A Bibliography*. New York: National College Equal Suffrage League, 1913.
Judd, D. B. "Review of *Colour and Colour Theories*." *Journal of the Optical Society of America* 19 (2) (August 1929): 104.
Ladd, Warren. *The Ladd Family*. New Bedford, Mass.: E. Anthony & Sons, 1890.
    Genealogy on p. 130.
Ladd-Franklin, Christine. Diaries (ages twelve to twenty-five). Vassar College Library, Department of Special Collections. Poughkeepsie, New York.
Ladd-Franklin, Christine. Papers. Columbia University Rare Book and Manuscript Library, New York.

ELIZAVETA FEDOROVNA LITVINOVA (1845–1919?)

Ann Hibner Koblitz

BIOGRAPHY

Elizaveta Fedorovna Ivashkina (to be referred to as Litvinova) was born in 1845 to a landowning family in the Tula region of Russia. Little is known about her childhood and family background. She went to one of the few women's gymnasiums in Russia—the Marinskaia in St. Petersburg. These institutions were on a far lower level than boys' gymnasiums, but at least they provided some education other than sewing and deportment.

In St. Petersburg, Litvinova fell under the influence of the cultural movements of the 1860s, specifically the social philosophy known as nihilism. The early nihilists (not to be confused with later, more extremist groups with the same name) taught that the natural sciences were by their nature progressive: the sciences improved people's lives and contributed to the fight against backwardness and superstition. The early nihilists believed that intensive study of the natural sciences would not only help the lot of the Russian peasant masses, but also hasten along the day of (peaceful) social revolution, which they were convinced was not far off.

The nihilists were also staunch advocates of the equality of women. They felt that women of the educated classes and the nobility had a right, and even a duty, to develop their minds and strive toward a career in the natural sciences or medicine.

Litvinova found the nihilist philosophy attractive. She became involved in discussion circles of revolutionary young people, wrote radical poetry, and decided to pursue advanced studies. She encountered many obstacles to her desire: the strenuous objections of relatives, the poorness of her scholastic preparation, the difficulty of obtaining the certificate of competency necessary for entrance into the university. She was not alone; the informal yet organized nihilist women's education network helped and supported her.

Universities in Russia, as in all of Europe, were closed to women as officially enrolled students. But from the early 1860s, Russian women had hopes that their universities would soon allow them to matriculate, and prepared themselves for university study as if this hope were a certainty. They enlisted the aid of sympathetic professors and held preparatory classes in the homes of wealthy supporters.

By the mid-1860s some women decided that they could not wait and resolved to try their luck abroad. This generation of Russian women pioneered higher education for women in continental Europe; Russian women were among the first official students in Zurich, Geneva, Bern, Heidelberg, and Paris. They were particularly successful in Zurich, which became the mecca for Russian women interested in higher education.

Litvinova was eager to join the women's colony in Zurich, but for several years she was prevented by circumstances. In 1866 she had married a Dr. Litvinov. Apparently he was willing for her to continue her studies in St. Petersburg, but, unlike some husbands of the 1860s (including that of the famous mathematician Sofia Kovalevskaia*), he refused to permit Litvinova to study abroad. (Russian women at this time could not obtain passports for international travel without the written permission of either father or husband.)

Litvinova marked time by studying mathematics privately with A. N. Strannoliubskii. He was a typical "man of the 'sixties,'" as the early nihilists sometimes called themselves. He sacrificed much of his spare time to prepare young women for the university, and he established free schools for workers in St. Petersburg. Moreover, he used the story of his most successful pupil, Sofia Kovalevskaia, to encourage his women students.

By 1870 or so, Litvinova was sufficiently well-prepared to enter a university, and she had acquired a certificate of competency. Her marriage stood in her way, though. Indeed, judging by her memoirs, she seems to have viewed her marriage solely as an obstacle to her further education. At this point, as she declares with deliberate vagueness in her memoirs, "fate itself" freed her from her marital duties and made it possible for her to leave for Zurich in 1872.

Life in Zurich was extremely difficult for Litvinova. She encountered the usual hardships that most of the Russian students faced: relative poverty, the ridicule of Swiss male students, the distrust and scorn of most Swiss citizens. But she had added problems, because she chose to study at the Polytechnic Institute rather than the university, where there were far more women students. In many of the lectures, Litvinova was the only woman in a class of 150, and she was afraid to raise her eyes or look in anyone's direction too long for fear someone would get the wrong impression of her.

Fortunately, Litvinova's instructors were helpful and friendly. She studied under Professor Mequet and the well-known analyst Hermann Schwarz. Schwarz gave her occasional tutoring sessions at his home and sometimes invited her to tea or for the evening with his family. One summer he even repeated for her individually a course of lectures he had given before she arrived in Zurich.

Litvinova looked forward to completing her studies within four years. But the tsarist government was becoming uneasy about the Zurich student colony. The government considered it a hotbed of revolutionary ideas and felt that the women were contributing more than their share to the political climate. In June 1873 the Russian authorities issued a decree stating that all Russian women studying in Zurich had to return to Russia by the first of the following year, whether or not they had completed their training. The penalties for disobedience were severe (though hypothetical): loss of admission rights at any Russian educational institution that might open its doors to women in the future, and disbarment from any licensing examinations and civil service posts that might at some time be made available to women.

For many of the Russian women, this decree marked the end of their plans for a scientific career. They were afraid to disobey the ban and took hope from the promise of women's higher education implied in the document. Litvinova and several others, however, could not bear to have their studies interrupted. With the encouragement of her professors, Litvinova remained in Zurich until she received her baccalaureate degree in 1876. Then she stayed in Switzerland two more years, to complete graduate work under L. Schläfli at Bern. In 1878 Litvinova received her doctoral degree summa cum laude from Bern University, with a dissertation in function theory. This work was to be her only published paper in higher mathematics.

Litvinova returned to Russia with a baccalaureate, a doctorate, and a Swiss certificate qualifying her to teach in all grades of boys' gymnasiums. But these degrees, even with the warm recommendations of her professors, were not enough to persuade the tsarist government to make an exception to its proscriptions against women. She was not allowed to take the licensing examinations for teachers in the higher grades of the gymnasium or to be hired as a full-time instructor in any state-licensed institution. Litvinova (along with Kovalevskaia) was also forbidden to take the examination for the Russian *magister* degree, which would have entitled her to teach at the university level.

The Higher Women's Courses that opened in St. Petersburg in 1878 hired several women baccalaureates and doctorates from Zurich as laboratory instructors and classroom supervisors, although none were given professorships. Litvinova repeatedly was passed over even for these relatively undistinguished appointments, apparently because she had disobeyed the tsarist government's decree summoning women students back from Zurich.

Litvinova was forced to accept a post as a teacher in the lower classes of a women's academy. She was paid by the hour and did not have the the rights to pension and vacations of a licensed teacher. Nine years later, after repeated pleas by her and her superiors, she became the first woman in Russia permitted by the Ministry of Education to teach mathematics in the upper division of the gymnasium (though she still was not granted the rights and privileges of male teachers of her rank).

Litvinova eked out the meager living she made from teaching by writing popular biographies of mathematicians and philosophers. Among these were works on Kovalevskaia, Aristotle, D'Alembert, Lobachevskii, Laplace, and Euler, and a series of essays comparing and contrasting "rulers" and "thinkers" from various historical epochs.

In addition to her teaching and literary activities, Litvinova participated in the European women's movement. In the 1890s and 1900s, the feminist *Bulletin de l'Union universelle des Femmes* carried articles with her initials. Since the pieces deal with Russian affairs, and one of them is an obituary of Kovalevskaia, it is safe to assume that they were written by Litvinova. We know for certain that Litvinova was one of the four Russian delegates to the 1897 International Women's Congress in Brussels.

Litvinova did not pursue her research after she returned to Russia. Indeed, as a teacher paid by the hour who had to use most time left over to write for pay, she had neither the time nor the intellectual atmosphere to continue original mathematical work. Moreover, teaching began to interest her as a fascinating task in its own right. In her thirty-five years of teaching, she published over seventy articles on the philosophy and practice of teaching mathematics, and was respected as one of the foremost pedagogues in Russia.

Not much is known about Litvinova's life after she retired from teaching. Apparently she lived with her sister in the country during the turmoil of the Russian Revolution. Even the date of her death is unknown. Probably she died in 1919 during the famine, but it is possible that she survived until 1921 or 1922.

WORK

Litvinova's dissertation, on function theory, was the only original mathematical paper she wrote. It was enthusiastically received by her advisor and had the honor of being published by the Russian Imperial Academy of Sciences. But it was an accomplished rather than a brilliant piece of work, and Litvinova had the added disadvantage (besides her sex) of being unfavorably compared to her more talented countrywoman Sofia Kovalevskaia. There was, apparently, room for only one Russian woman mathematician at a time, and Kovalevskaia was the woman of choice. Litvinova did not have the right combination of talent and luck (and financial independence) to enable her to succeed against the incredible obstacles in her way, so she left research mathematics.

Litvinova's contributions to mathematical pedagogy were considerable, however, especially considering how little time she had to devote to her pedagogical writings. Her methods were surprisingly modern: she emphasized alternative approaches to proofs and the use of word problems to stimulate clear thinking. The revolutionary activist and pedagogue Nadezhda Krupskaia (wife of Lenin), who was Litvinova's student at the A. A. Obolenskaia gymnasium, recalled with pride that Litvinova not only taught her students the usual mathematical rules and theorems. She also used mathematics to teach her pupils how to think logically, how to make generalizations, how to extract principles and laws from

a series of individual cases. These concerns are reflected in Litvinova's pedagogical writing.

Litvinova was a constant source of inspiration and encouragement to her
women students, several of whom went on to become scientists in their own
right. The crystallographer and applied mathematician Varvara Tarnovskaia, for
example, remembered with gratitude the training and support she received from
Litvinova. Krupskaia traced her own interest in mathematics and pedagogy to
the influence of Litvinova and cited the latter in her own pedagogical articles.

Perhaps Litvinova's most enduring contribution was contained in her popular
science writings and biographical sketches. Like many people of her generation—
the generation of the nihilists and "children of the 'sixties'"—she believed that
she had the duty to inform the Russian peasantry and working classes about
social, cultural, and political issues. The media often used for this were popular
science and biography, since one ran less risk of falling afoul of the tsarist
censors than if one wrote overtly political essays or tracts. Litvinova expertly
wove egalitarian themes into her works, and mostly managed to avoid offending
the authorities (though approximately seventy pages of her *Rulers and Thinkers*
were struck from the published edition by the tsarist censors).

BIBLIOGRAPHY

Works by Elizaveta Fedorovna Litvinova

Except where noted, all works are in Russian. All book volume numbers are
of the Pavlenkov series "Lives of Remarkable People."

Mathematical Works

Lösung einer Abbildungsaufgabe. St. Petersburg: Buchdruckerei der Kaiserlichen Akademie der Wissenschaften, 1879.
    Doctoral thesis.

Other Works

"Sophie Kowalewska" (in French). *Bulletin de l'Union universelle des Femmes* (14) (15
February 1891): 1–4. (Signed "E.L.")
D'Alembert: His Life and Scientific Activity. St. Petersburg: Iu. N. Erlikh, 1891. Vol.
52.
F. Bacon: His Life, Scientific Works, and Social Activism. St. Petersburg: Obshchest-
vennaia Pol'za, 1891. Vol. 12.
Laplace and Euler: Their Lives and Scientific Work. St. Petersburg: Obshchestvennaia
Pol'za, 1892. Vol. 97.
John Locke: His Life and Philosophical Work. St. Petersburg: Iu. N. Erlikh, 1892. Vol.
109.
Aristotle: His Life, Scientific and Philosophical Work. St. Petersburg: I. G. Salov, 1892.
Vol. 7.
V. Ia. Struve: His Life and Scientific Work. St. Petersburg: Iu. N. Erlikh, 1893. Vol.
172.

S. V. Kovalevskaia (Woman-Mathematician): Her Life and Scientific Work. St. Petersburg: P. P. Soikin, 1894. Vol. 83.

Condorcet: His Life and Scientific and Political Work. St. Petersburg: Obshchestvennaia Pol'za, 1894. Vol. 86.

N. I. Lobachevskii: His Life and Scientific Work. St. Petersburg: P. P. Soikin, 1895. Vol. 107.

Rulers and Thinkers: Biographical Essays. St. Petersburg: S. N. Khudekov, 1897.

"From my student days. (Acquaintance with S. V. Kovalevskaia)." *Zhenskoe delo* (4) (1899): 34–63. (Under the pseudonym "E. El' ".)

" 'Little One' (From the life of the Zurich women students)." *Pervyi Zhenskii Kalendar' na 1912* (1912): 112–116.

P. Laplace. Petrograd: Sotrudnichestvo, 1919.

In addition, see the journal *Zhenskoe obrazovanie* (Women's education) and its successor *Obrazovanie* for Litvinova's numerous pedagogical writings.

Works about Elizaveta Fedorovna Litvinova

Gratsianskaia, L. N. "Elizaveta Fedorovna Litvinova" (in Russian). *Matematika v shkole* (4) (1953): 64–67.

Koblitz, Ann Hibner. "Elizaveta Fedorovna Litvinova (1845–1919)—Russian mathematician and pedagogue." *Association for Women in Mathematics Newsletter* 14 (1) (January–February 1984): 13–17.

Also, Litvinova's works on Kovalevskaia and the *Zhenskoe delo* and *Pervyi Zhenskii Kalendar'* articles cited above contain some autobiographical information.

AUGUSTA ADA LOVELACE (1815–1852)

Karen D. Rappaport

BIOGRAPHY

Augusta Ada Byron Lovelace was the only child of the short, tempestuous marriage of Anna Isabella (Annabella) Millbanke and the poet George Gordon, the sixth Lord Byron. They were married in January 1815, and their daughter, Ada, was born in London on December 10, 1815. Only thirty-six days after Lovelace's birth, Lord Byron left England, never to see his wife and child again. However, less than a year after leaving England, Byron wrote about his daughter in the opening line of Canto Three of his epic *Childe Harold's Pilgrimage*. Byron was exiled in Greece for the next eight years, until his death in 1824. He frequently wrote to his wife and sister for news of his daughter, and on his deathbed his last words were about her.

Lovelace was raised by her mother, who encouraged her mathematical aptitude. Lady Byron herself had been known for her mathematical ability, and early in their courtship, Lord Byron had called her his "Princess of Parallelograms." It was not surprising, then, that the young Lovelace received more than the usual mathematical education given to young girls of her class during the 1800s.

Lovelace never attended any school or university. Her education was provided by governesses, tutors, and self study. Her mathematics education was received primarily from William Frend. Family friends, such as Mary Somerville* and Augustus De Morgan, often consulted and gave advice to Lovelace about mathematical questions.

In May 1833 Lovelace was presented at court and attended numerous balls, where she met many famous people. However, the party which significantly affected her career took place in June 1833. There she met Charles Babbage, who was to be a major influence in her life. Other social acquaintances present at this party included Augustus De Morgan and Mary Somerville. All of these mathematicians advised and encouraged Lovelace in her mathematical career, but it was Babbage whom she turned to for scientific training and whose disciple she became.

Lovelace often attended parties at the Babbage home, and in 1835 Babbage first began corresponding to Lovelace about these parties. It was at one of them that Lovelace first developed her interest in Babbage's Difference Engine. She attended lectures on it given by Dionysius Lardner at the Mechanic's Institute. The Difference Engine, never completed by Babbage, was to be an automatic machine for calculating and printing mathematical and astronomical tables. The construction of this calculating machine drew inspiration from the Jacquard loom and led to Babbage's design of a program-controlled computer called the Analytical Engine.

In 1835, when she was nineteen, Lovelace married William, Lord King, who was thirty. William was named the first Earl of Lovelace three years after their marriage. Although the earldom was ostensibly given for his work in the foreign service, it was assumed that the Byron family connections were really responsible (the prime minister was Lady Byron's first cousin).

Lovelace had two sons and a daughter: Byron Noel (1836), Anne Isabella (1837), and Ralph Gordon (1839). Lovelace had never been physically strong, and giving birth to three children in three years further weakened her.

Shortly after the birth of her last child, Lovelace asked Babbage to find a mathematics tutor for her. Eventually, in 1840, Augustus De Morgan agreed to tutor Lovelace. In the same year Lord Lovelace was made a Fellow of the Royal Society. Through him Lovelace now had access to numerous books and papers. At this point Lovelace became totally immersed in mathematics, and, in addition to her studies, offered to work with Babbage on his Analytical Engine, the general-purpose calculating machine to operate from punched cards. She left her children's upbringing to her husband, her mother, and servants, a practice not uncommon for the English upper classes. The major career difficulty encountered by Lovelace was the social pressure against using her name in connection with her scientific endeavors. When her major work was published, initials were used instead of her name.

It is believed by some that in her later years Lovelace attempted to use the Analytical Engine to develop a system for gambling on the horse races. Although there were financial losses and familial difficulties in Lovelace's later years, there is no concrete evidence to support this claim.

Lovelace's health, weakened since her childbearing years, continued to deteriorate, until in the later years of her life she was forced to stay in London to be near doctors. Her condition was eventually diagnosed as cancer, and she died, after months of suffering, in 1852, at the age of thirty-six. At her request Lovelace was buried next to her father, in the Byron family vault in Hucknall Torkard Church in Nottinghamshire.

WORK

Lovelace's major work was the translation and notes on a paper by L. F. Menabrea about the Analytical Engine. Menabrea was an Italian mathematician who heard Babbage speak on the Analytical Engine in Turin. In 1842 Menabrea's paper was published in French in the *Bibliothèque Universelle de Genève*. Lovelace, who was fluent in French, proposed to translate the paper into English. Babbage suggested that she write her own paper or else notes to the Menabrea paper. She did the latter, providing also the illustrations and the solution to algebraic problems as applications of the Analytical Engine. The notes developed the subject of programming in great detail, and the resulting work was significantly longer than the original paper. According to Babbage, the Menabrea and Lovelace articles together indicated that the sequencing of arithmetic operations could be done by machinery.

There was a significant mathematical, as well as personal, correspondence between Babbage and Lovelace during the period when she was working on the article. The development of the mathematical analyses can be seen in this correspondence, especially the program she developed with Babbage to compute Bernoulli numbers.

Lovelace compared the Difference Engine and the Analytical Engine. She demonstrated the superiority of the Analytical Engine by showing that rather than computing the result of only one particular function, it could develop and compute results for any function. She described the use of cards to determine the mathematical operations to be used, and introduced variable cards and operation cards. Each operation card defined one of the four arithmetic operations (addition, subtraction, multiplication, division), and any calculation could be represented as a sequence of operation cards. The variable cards indicated the operands of each operation. Each arithmetic operation has three operands; for example, addition has two summands and a sum. Thus each operation card had three variable cards. As examples, Lovelace derived the operation cards needed to solve specific algebraic and trigonometric equations. She described two important programming techniques, known today as looping and recursion, and how they could be accomplished on the Analytical Engine. She also alluded to another programming technique now known as selection: "The engine is capable, under certain circumstances, of feeling about to discover which of two or more possible contingencies has occurred, and then of shaping its future course accordingly" ([1843] 1982, 10, footnote). She explained how the Analytical Engine could use looping to solve a set of nine simultaneous linear equations, and actually wrote out a program to calculate the Bernoulli numbers recursively.

The paper and the notes were published using the initials A.A.L. There was much speculation over the identity of the author. However, those who knew Lovelace offered their congratulations on the value of the notes. Both De Morgan and Somerville praised the work highly. De Morgan further wrote to Lady Byron about his high estimation of her daughter's abilities. Babbage himself felt that the notes were the most comprehensive analysis of the power of his Analytical Engine. To acknowledge Lovelace's contribution to the development of the field of programming and the documentation of Babbage's work, the 1980s programming language Ada was named after her.

BIBLIOGRAPHY

Works by Augusta Ada Lovelace

Mathematical Works

"Sketch of the Analytical Engine invented by Charles Babbage, Esq., by L. F. Menabrea
of Turin, officer of the Military Engineers." Translation with extensive notes.
[Taylor's] Scientific Memoirs, Art. 29 (1843): 666–731. Reprinted in *Charles
Babbage and His Calculating Engines*, edited by Philip Morrison and Emily
Morrison: 225–297. New York: Dover, 1961. Also reprinted in *Babbage's Cal-
culating Engines*, by Henry Prevost Babbage. London: Spon & Co., 1889. Reprint.
Los Angeles and San Francisco: Tomash Publishers, 1982.
Contains the first set of computer programs designed to instruct a machine to solve
mathematical problems.

Works about Augusta Ada Lovelace

Angluin, Dana. "Lady Lovelace and the Analytical Engine." *Association for Women in
Mathematics Newsletter* 6 (1) (January 1976): 5–10; 6 (2) (February 1976): 6–8.
Baum, Joan. *The Calculating Passion of Ada Byron*. Hamden, Conn.: Archon Books/
The Shoe String Press, 1986.
Review: *New York Times Book Review* (5 October 1986): 44.
Bowden, B. V., ed. *Faster Than Thought*. London: Pitman and Sons, 1953.
Describes the Difference Engine and the Analytical Engine, and Lovelace's con-
tribution to their history.
Hollingdale, S. H. "Charles Babbage and Lady Lovelace—two 19th century mathe-
maticians." *Bulletin of the Institute of Mathematical Applications* 2 (1966): 2–
15.
Traces the history of the Difference Engine and the Analytical Engine. Describes
how to use the machine to solve numerous mathematical problems. Special attention is given to Lovelace's applications.
Huskey, Velma R., and Harry D. Huskey. "Lady Lovelace and Charles Babbage."
Annals of the History of Computing 2 (4) (1980): 299–329.
Reproduction with commentary of correspondence between Lovelace and Babbage, from the Lovelace-Byron papers at Oxford University, the Babbage Correspondence in the British Library, and the letters of the Somerville Collection at
Oxford. Most of the letters are from the period when Lady Lovelace wrote her
work on the Analytical Engine, and the article emphasizes her mathematical
research and her mathematical background.
Kean, David W. "The countess and the computer." *Datamation* 19 (May 1973): 60–
63.
Summary of Lovelace's life, with focus on her work as a programmer.
Moore, Doris L. *Ada, Countess of Lovelace: Byron's Legitimate Daughter*. New York:
Harper and Row, 1977.
Based on information in the Lovelace-Byron papers.
Moseley, Maboth. *Irascible Genius: A Life of Charles Babbage, Inventor*. London:
Hutchinson and Co., 1964.

Chapter 3 refers extensively to Lovelace.

Neumann, B. H. "Byron's daughter." *Mathematical Gazette* 57 (400) (1973): 94–97.
Short but informative paper on the Lovelace family. Discusses the mathematical ability of both Lovelace and her children.

Petrenko, A. K., and O. L. Petrenko. "The Babbage machine and the origins of programming" (in Russian). *Istoriko-Matematicheskie Issledovaniia* (24) (1979): 340–360.
Analysis of the Lovelace and Menabrea papers. The programs have been rewritten in Fortran.

Stein, Dorothy. *Ada, A Life and a Legacy.* Cambridge, Mass.: MIT Press, 1985.
Controversial new biography claiming that Lovelace had no mathematical talent and was not an important figure. Reviews: *New York Times Book Review* (29 December 1985): 6–7; *New Scientist* (23 January 1986): 56; *Abacus* 4 (1) (Fall 1986): 46–53, 56.

Tee, G. J. "The pioneering woman mathematicians." *Mathematical Chronicle* 10 (1–2) (1981): 31–56.
Gives a brief summary of the lives of six women mathematicians, including Ada Lovelace. Includes general biographical information and a short bibliography.

SHEILA SCOTT MACINTYRE (1910–1960)

Florence D. Fasanelli

BIOGRAPHY

Sheila Scott Macintyre was the only child of Helen Myers Meldrum, of the town of Kilmuir Easter, County Ross, and James Alexander Scott, M.A., of Banchory. Macintyre was born in Edinburgh on April 23, 1910, and attended Trinity Academy, where her father was rector from 1925 to 1942.

Macintyre also attended Edinburgh Ladies' College (now the Mary Erskine School) from 1926. In 1928 she was joint Dux (top student) and Dux in mathematics. She then continued her achievements at the University of Edinburgh, where she again gained distinction, including the Newton Bursary (faculty award), the Spence Bursary, and the Bruce of Grangehill Mathematical Scholarship. Her M.A. was granted in 1932 with first class honors in mathematics and natural philosophy. The staff at Edinburgh recommended that she go on to Cambridge. At that time and later, it was quite usual for first class honors graduates at a Scottish university to take a second "first" degree at Oxford or Cambridge. The Scottish school and university education was much wider and less specialized than in England and so did not go as far in each individual subject. In 1934, after two years at Girton College, she was a Wrangler (First Class Honors) in the Mathematical Tripos and received a B.A. degree. She then went on to do a year's research under the supervision of Mary Cartwright (now Dame Mary Cartwright, known for her research in the theory of integral functions and nonlinear oscillations), which resulted in the publication (at age twenty-five) of her first paper (1935).

Meanwhile, after trying research for one year, she appears to have decided that she did not wish to continue. She qualified as a teacher in Scotland and took a succession of teaching jobs between 1934 and 1939.

She was introduced to Archibald James Macintyre by Professor Edmund Whittaker. A. J. Macintyre (1908–1967) had earned a Ph.D. at Cambridge in 1933 and was a lecturer at Aberdeen. He and Macintyre were married on December 27, 1940.

Macintyre was appointed assistant in the same department as her husband in March 1941. She began teaching special War Office and Air Ministry courses and to take on other duties of staff who were absent on war service. Macintyre held this position until October 1943, when she was five months pregnant. Her first child, Alister William, was born in February 1944. In October Macintyre began teaching again.

Macintyre was appointed assistant lecturer, on a permanent basis, in October 1945. She also began thesis research from a short paper of Professor (now Sir) Edward M. Wright, the department chairman at Aberdeen (later principal and vice-chancellor). Macintyre's husband delivered a draft of a chapter of her thesis to Wright with the comment, "Sheila finished this yesterday just before I took her to the nursing home; she had a baby early this morning." Her second son, Douglas Scott, was born in August 1946; he died suddenly of enteritis in March 1949. Her last child, Susan Elizabeth, was born in March 1950. During the next five years, Macintyre continued her teaching duties and cared for her two small children.

In 1957 A. J. Macintyre was urged to apply for a position as visiting research professor at the University of Cincinnati. He accepted the position in 1958; Macintyre and the family, including her father, moved to Cincinnati a year later. In her final year at Aberdeen, she published her last paper and was elected a Fellow of the Royal Society of Edinburgh. She became a visiting professor at Cincinnati. She taught there until she succumbed to cancer on March 21, 1960, at the age of fifty.

WORK

Macintyre is known for her work on the Whittaker constant and interpolation series of various kinds for integral functions. According to R. C. Buck, "In her chosen area of analysis, she introduced powerful refinements of techniques, and what is much harder, new and original problems for investigation" (Cartwright 1961, 255). Her chief interest was the theory of functions of a complex variable.

Wright (1947) gave proofs of theorems about inequality conditions on a function and some of its derivatives to ensure that $f(x) \leq \sin x$ for $x \in (0, \pi/2)$. In his introductory paragraph, Wright stated, "Mrs. S. Macintyre will prove a set of similar, but not equivalent, theorems by the use of the 2-point Taylor series." According to Wright, "She extended and transformed this problem considerably and all the ideas in the thesis were wholly hers." In her thesis, published in 1948, Macintyre went on to prove two theorems, one of which has some of the inequalities in the hypotheses reversed and others omitted. Wright was her supervisor and internal examiner. He believed that "good as her research was there would have been more of it had she not had a family to look after."

In 1947 Macintyre published her second paper. In 1949 she was elected to a lectureship and also published another paper. She published six more papers before 1956, including one jointly with her husband (Macintyre and Macintyre

1952). With a member of the German department, Macintyre published a German-English mathematical dictionary (Macintyre and Witte 1955).

Macintyre was a superb teacher, noted for her clarity as well as shrewd assessment of her students. She was active in the Mathematical Association and the Edinburgh Mathematical Society.

BIBLIOGRAPHY

Works by Sheila Scott Macintyre

Mathematical Works

"On the asymptotic periods of integral functions." *Proceedings of the Cambridge Philosophical Society* 31 (1935): 543–554. Published under the name Sheila Scott.

"An upper bound for the Whittaker constant *W.*" *Journal of the London Mathematical Society* 22 (1947): 305–311.

"A functional inequality." *Journal of the London Mathematical Society* 23 (1948): 202–209.

"On the zeros of successive derivatives of integral functions." *Transactions of the American Mathematical Society* 67 (1949): 241–251.

"Some problems in interpolatory function theory." Ph.D. diss., Aberdeen University, 1949.

"Overconvergence properties of some interpolation series." *Quarterly Journal of Mathematics* (Oxford Series) 2 (2) (1951): 109–120.

"Some generalizations of two-point expansions." *Proceedings of the Cambridge Philosophical Society* 48 (1952): 583–586.

(with A. J. Macintyre) "Theorems on the convergence and asymptotic validity of Abel's series." *Proceedings of the Royal Society of Edinburgh* A 63 (1952): 222–231.

"An interpolation series for integral functions." *Proceedings of the Edinburgh Mathematical Society* (2) 9 (1953): 1–6.

"Transform theory and Newton's interpolation series." *Proceedings of the London Mathematical Society* (3) 4 (1954): 385–401.

"On a problem of Ramanujan." *Journal of the London Mathematical Society* 30 (1955): 310–314.

"μ-transforms and interpolation series: Abel's series." *Proceedings of the London Mathematical Society* (3) 8 (1958): 481–492.

Other Works

(with Edith Witte) *Mathematical Vocabulary (German-English)*. Edinburgh, 1955. 2nd ed. New York: Wiley, 1966.

Works about Sheila Scott Macintyre

Bowen, N. A. "Archibald James Macintyre." *Bulletin of the London Mathematical Society* 1 (1969): 368–381.

A discussion of the paper Macintyre and Macintyre 1952 is included in this obituary by a long-term colleague.

Cartwright, Mary L. "Sheila Scott Macintyre." *Journal of the London Mathematical Society* 36 (1961): 254–256.
Obituary by her former tutor and brief analysis (by R. C. Buck) of Macintyre's work.
Cossar, J. "Sheila Scott Macintyre." *Edinburgh Mathematical Notes* 43 (1960): 19. In *Proceedings of the Edinburgh Mathematical Society* (2) 12 (1960–1961): 112.
Wright, E. M. "Sheila Scott Macintyre." *Year Book of the Royal Society of Edinburgh* (1961): 21–23.

Other References

Wright, E. M. "Functional inequalities." *Journal of the London Mathematical Society* 22 (1947): 205–210.

ADA ISABEL MADDISON (1869–1950)

Betsey S. Whitman

BIOGRAPHY

Ada Isabel Maddison was born in Cumberland, England on April 13, 1869, the daughter of John and Mary Maddison. She studied for two years at Miss Tallies School in Cardiff, South Wales, before going to the University of South Wales from 1885 until 1889. Then she went to Girton College, Cambridge, staying there for three years. During that time, she knew Grace Chisholm (later Grace Chisholm Young*). When they were both first-year students at Girton, their tutor suggested they attend a lecture of Arthur Cayley. The women persuaded their headmistress to allow them to go, and apparently they enjoyed the lecture. In 1892 Maddison passed the examination of the Honour School at Oxford University; that same year, she passed the Cambridge Mathematical Tripos Examination, first class, equal to the twenty-seventh Wrangler, but was not allowed to receive a degree.

During 1892–1893 she was at Bryn Mawr and attended lectures in graduate mathematics by Charlotte Scott*. During part of the year, she read papers by James Sylvester and Arthur Cayley on modern algebra; during the rest of the year, she pursued an investigation relating to the singular solutions of differential equations. Scott wrote that "Miss Maddison has a powerful mind and excellent training."

In 1893 the University of London conferred on Maddison the degree of Bachelor of Science with Honours. During the 1893–1894 year, she was awarded the resident mathematics fellowship at Bryn Mawr; the following year, she was the first student to win the Mary E. Garrett Fellowship from Bryn Mawr for study abroad.

She studied at the University of Göttingen and attended lectures of Felix Klein, David Hilbert, and others. She once again met Grace C. Young, and she knew Mary Winston Newson* during that year.

Maddison returned to Bryn Mawr in the fall of 1895 to complete her work for the Ph.D., which she received in 1896. She also served as the assistant secretary to the president of the college that year; after her degree was awarded, she was made secretary to the president and reader in mathematics. She continued in these roles until 1904, when she was appointed both associate professor and assistant to the president.

The University of Dublin, the first university in the British Isles to grant degrees to women, conferred the B.A. degree on Maddison in 1905. She had not studied at Dublin, but her work at Girton College was considered.

By 1910 her duties were entirely administrative, as recording dean and assistant to the president. She continued in these capacities until she retired in 1926.

Maddison was very efficient in her administrative duties, but she was always a shy person. In 1913, while President M. Carey Thomas was in the hospital recovering from a minor operation, she wrote to Maddison: "At the doctors examination under the new plan Dr. Frank had better preside. Do remember to speak distinctly. When you get embarrassed your voice gets lower and lower. I am sure the Faculty thinks it is shyness as it is. You must conquer it."

Maddison retired from Bryn Mawr in 1926 and went to live in England. However, she later returned to Pennsylvania and died there on October 22, 1950. In her will, she left $10,000 in memory of President M. Carey Thomas, directing that it be used as a pension fund for nonfaculty members of the college staff.

WORK

Maddison published her dissertation in 1896, in the area of differential equations. She also published a translation of Felix Klein's 1895 address before the Royal Academy of Science at Göttingen, "The arithmetizing of mathematics." She also reviewed several textbooks during the late 1890s. However, her administrative duties at the college evidently kept her from much mathematical study or research after the turn of the century. She wrote in a letter in 1937, "I confess to feeling ashamed of having deserted mathematics for a less rarified atmosphere of work among people and things," although she admitted to still having "my old allegiance to the most perfect of the sciences" (Appendix C, Owens).

Maddison compiled a *Handbook of Courses Open to Women in British, Continental and Canadian Universities*. She also helped to compile a statistical study of women college graduates (AAUW 1917). In 1897 she was elected to membership in the American Mathematical Society. She joined the London Mathematical Society that same year as a life member. She was also a member of the Daughters of the British Empire.

BIBLIOGRAPHY

Works by Ada Isabel Maddison

Mathematical Works

"On certain factors of c- and p- discriminants and their relation to fixed points on the family of curves." *Quarterly Journal of Pure and Applied Mathematics* 26 (1893): 307–321.

"On singular solutions of differential equations of the first order in two variables and the geometric properties of certain invariants and covariants of their complete primitives." *Quarterly Journal of Pure and Applied Mathematics* 28 (1896): 311–374.

Doctoral thesis.

"The arithmetizing of mathematics" by Felix Klein. Translation. *Bulletin of the American Mathematical Society* 2 (1896): 241–248.

"Note on the history of the map coloring problem." *Bulletin of the American Mathematical Society* 3 (1897): 257.

Other Works

Handbook of Courses Open to Women in British, Continental and Canadian Universities. New York: Macmillan, 1896. Supplement, 1897; 2nd ed. 1899. Supplement to 2nd ed. 1901.

American Association of University Women (AAUW). *A Preliminary Statistical Study of Certain Women College Graduates, Dealing with the Health, Marriage, Children, Occupations of Women Graduating between 1869 and 1898 and Their Sisters and Brothers;* compiled from information collected for the Association (AAUW) in 1900 by their Publication Committee. Bryn Mawr: Printed privately, 1917.

"Charlotte Angas Scott: An appreciation." *Bryn Mawr Alumnae Bulletin* (January 1932): 9–11.

Works about Ada Isabel Maddison

Obituary. *New York Times* (24 October 1950): 29.

Whitman, Betsey S. "Women in the American Mathematical Society before 1900." *Association for Women in Mathematics Newsletter* 13 (5) (September–October 1983): 7–9.

Discusses the twenty-two women who joined the AMS between its founding in 1888 and 1900, including Maddison.

Williams, Mary. "Ada Isabel Maddison." Handwritten manuscript. 5 pp., n.d. In the Mary Williams Collection, Schlesinger Library, Radcliffe College, Cambridge, Mass.

HELEN ABBOT MERRILL (1864–1949)

Claudia Henrion

BIOGRAPHY

Helen Abbot Merrill was in many respects a pioneer. She was in one of the earliest graduating classes at Wellesley College and later received her Ph.D. in mathematics when there were no more than twenty female doctorates in mathematics in the entire United States. She chose a profession and lifestyle that were far from traditional and found in them a life and community that made her extremely happy.

Merrill was born on March 30, 1864, in Llewellyn Park, Orange, New Jersey, but spent most of her early life in Newburyport, Massachusetts (Young 1932). She was a descendant of the early Massachusetts settlers.

Merrill's mother was Emily Abbot; her father, George Dodge Merrill, was an importer, insurance auditor, and inventor. Religion was important to the Merrill family; two of Merrill's brothers, Robert Dodge Merrill and William Pierson Merrill, became pastors of Presbyterian churches (*Wellesley College News* 1949). Merrill had at least one sister, Emily Dodge Merrill, but it is not clear how many other siblings she had.

Merrill started formal schooling at age twelve at Newburyport High School. She started at Wellesley College in 1882. She planned to study Latin and Greek, but after taking a mathematics course in her freshman year, she changed her mind.

Merrill's undergraduate years at Wellesley were an important and formative period of her life. She found in Wellesley a place that respected intellectual attributes at least as much as domestic attributes. It was a community that honored lifestyles other than the traditional one of becoming a wife and mother. Merrill thrived at Wellesley, with the close bonds she formed with her classmates, the personal freedom she felt, and the inspiration of her teachers. All of the teachers in the mathematics department at Wellesley were women for the fifty years she was there (with the exception of a part-timer for two years) (1944, 61).

In an alumnae biographical questionnaire, Merrill was asked, "In the light of your experience since leaving college, how do you wish your course had been shaped?'' To which she responded, ''I am chiefly thankful that so little effort was made to shape my course'' (Wellesley College Biographical Record 1935).

Because Wellesley was still so young when Merrill entered in 1882 (the first students began in 1875), there was a bonding among classmates based on being in a highly unusual and experimental situation, with intense class spirit and loyalty. The group spirit is evident in a long booklet handwritten by Merrill, ''Peeps into the past,'' a history of the class of 1886. ''The plan of this work is most comprehensive. It embraces in its scope the origin, development and culmination of the class of '86. It is essentially a history of modern times. . . . '' Although this was said in a humorous manner, it is undoubtedly how Merrill and her classmates felt. They were at the forefront of a radically new enterprise: the higher education of women, and their training for professions previously occupied exclusively by men.

The playfulness and humor that were an integral part of Helen Merrill's experience at Wellesley continued for the rest of her life. For example, she describes the footwear of Ellen Hayes* thus: ''Her shoes, however, even in the early '80's, were so thicksoled that some declared that when they met her coming up over a hilltop the soles of her shoes were the first thing visible'' (1944).

After graduating in 1886, Merrill went to work as an instructor at the Classical School for Girls in New York City, where she taught history, Latin, and mathematics until 1889. Next she worked at the Dutch Reformed Church in New Brunswick, New Jersey, where she taught a class of mill girls from 1889 to 1891. From 1891 to 1893, she taught mathematics and Latin at the Walnut Lane School in Germantown, Philadelphia, Pennsylvania (Wellesley College Biographical Record 1942).

At this point Helen Shafer of Wellesley College wrote to Merrill, offering her a job as instructor in the mathematics department. The salary was $300 per year plus housing. Shafer asked Merrill to come to teach at Wellesley ''in order to lead the freshmen in flowery, not thorny paths'' (Young 1932). Merrill accepted the job and remained at Wellesley until she retired in 1932.

Merrill served as instructor (1893–1901), associate professor (1902–1915), and full professor (1915–1932), and was named Professor Emerita upon her retirement (Wellesley College Biographical Record 1942).

Merrill took time off to complete her Ph.D. During the year 1896–1897, she went to the University of Chicago and studied the theory of functions with Heinrich Maschke. From 1901 to 1903 she continued her graduate work at Göttingen and Yale. At Göttingen Merrill studied descriptive geometry with G. F. Schilling; at Yale she studied the theory of functions with James Pierpont. When Merrill returned to Wellesley, she introduced courses in both of these subjects (Young 1932). Yale awarded Merrill a Ph.D. in 1903.

There seems to be no indication that Merrill struggled with questions about career versus marriage. Graduates of Wellesley were expected to lead useful, productive lives in a professional field and simultaneously lead fulfilling domestic lives, that is, marry, have children, and care for the home. However, in most cases it was impossible to do both.

Merrill's enthusiasm for mathematics and her desire to pursue it left her with few options. At the time, the job possibilities for women in mathematics were extremely few. And far fewer were available for married women. Had she been married, she surely would not have been offered the job at Wellesley. In Margaret Rossiter's book *Women Scientists in America,* we read: "It also went without saying that according to the mores of the time, all candidates had to be of good Christian character and not only single but in no danger of marrying. Married women were not even considered for employment at the early women's colleges, even, it seems, when they were clearly the best candidates available." She goes on to say that "resignation upon marriage was a matter of course." The situation for men was quite different; in fact, many schools were prejudiced against men who were not married. Even in 1921 fewer than 12% of women mathematicians were married (Rossiter 1982, 15, 140).

One of the attitudes that was carried down to Helen Merrill from her teachers was to see her work as a mission. This sense of mission had two components. The first was that mathematics was one of the finest fields one could study; the second was that women were just as capable of doing mathematics as men.

Merrill's postgraduate life and education were not limited to Wellesley. She traveled through Europe, Canada, and the United States. Later in life she continued to take courses during the summer at Berkeley in music and in languages (Wellesley College Reunion Questionnaire 1925). Merrill died in her sleep on May 1, 1949, at her home in Wellesley.

WORK

Merrill's field of specialization was analysis, though one would be hard pressed to pin her down to any single discipline. Her research was primarily in the theory of functions. In 1903 she published her thesis, in which she studied differential equations satisfying "Sturmian" properties.

Merrill wrote several textbooks. Two were coauthored with Clara E. Smith, also at Wellesley: *A First Course in Higher Algebra,* and *Selected Topics in Higher Algebra.* A year after her retirement, she published an entertaining book for the general reader called *Mathematical Excursions* (1933).

Merrill was passionately dedicated to teaching. Mabel Young, a colleague in the mathematics department, wrote:

Miss Merrill was deeply interested in mathematics, but rather as a teacher than as a research worker. She was preeminently a teacher. To share with her students subjects which she enjoyed in graduate work, she planned introductory courses in Theory of Functions and Descriptive Geometry, work rarely open to undergraduates at that time. The girls responded and not a few went on in later years to explore these fields for themselves. She had the enviable power of suggesting to students that the subject in hand led up and on. She could detect promise in unskilled performance and led many a girl to discover unexpected abilities in herself. The high standard set became not a barrier but a challenge. (Young 1949)

Maintaining "high standards" was an important issue throughout the history of the mathematics department at Wellesley, in part to prove that an education at a women's college was not inferior. If anything, standards may have been too severe. Merrill wrote:

During eleven years a strong department was built up; the teachers were of unusual excellence, and the standards of work were high. Many of the texts used would be thought of as unduly difficult today. . . . It is a matter of record that in 1880 the Trustees warned the departments of Greek, Latin and mathematics that the examinations which they were setting were altogether too difficult. (1944)

In addition to her work as a teacher and author of several books, Merrill held many administrative positions. She was the chair of the mathematics department from 1916 until her retirement. In 1920 she served as vice-president of the Mathematical Association of America, and she was on its board of trustees from 1917 to 1919 (Wellesley College Biographical Record 1935).

Her interests extended beyond mathematics. She was elected to the executive committee of the National Historical Society, was the first president of the New York Wellesley Club, and served as class representative and historian (Wellesley College Biographical Record 1942).

She was a member of numerous other organizations and societies, including the American Association for the Advancement of Science, American Association of University Women, American Mathematical Society, Mathematical Association of America, Deutsche Mathematiker Vereinigung, Phi Beta Kappa, Sigma Xi, and "several others, membership in which means merely paying dues" (Wellesley College Biographical Record 1935).

BIBLIOGRAPHY

Works by Helen Abbot Merrill

Mathematical Works

"On solutions of differential equations which possess an oscillatoin [sic] theorem." *Transactions of the American Mathematical Society* 4 (1903): 423–433. Reprint. Lancaster, Pa.: New Era Printing Co., 1903. Doctoral thesis.

(with Clara E. Smith) *Selected Topics in College Algebra.* Norwood, Mass.: Norwood Press, 1914.

———. *A First Course in Higher Algebra.* New York: Macmillan, 1917.

"Why students fail in mathematics." *Mathematics Teacher* 11 (1918): 45–56.

Higher Analysis. Privately planographed, 1924. 2nd ed., 1929. 3rd ed., 1939.
    Used as a course text at Wellesley.
"3 mathematical songs." *Mathematics Teacher* 25 (1932): 36–37.
Mathematical Excursions: Side Trips along Paths Not Generally Traveled in Elementary Courses in Mathematics. Norwood, Mass.: Norwood Press, 1933. Reprinted. Boston: Bruce Humphries, 1934. Reprinted. New York: Dover, 1957.

Other Works

"Peeps into the past." Handwritten document in Wellesley College Archives, 1887.
"The religious life at Wellesley." *Our Town* (Wellesley Catalogue) (1) (January 1902): 3–4.
"A history of the Mathematics Department, Wellesley College, from the opening of the College in 1875." Unpublished document in Wellesley College Archives, 1944.

Works about Helen Abbot Merrill

Obituary. *New York Times* (3 May 1949): 25.
Obituary. *School and Society* 69 (14 May 1949): 351.
Williams, Mary. "Hellen Abbott [sic] Merrill." Typed, 4 pp., n.d. In Mary Williams Collection, Schlesinger Library, Radcliffe College.
Young, Mabel. "Helen Abbot Merrill." *Wellesley Magazine* (June 1932): 405–406.
Young, Mabel, Marion Stark, and Helen Russell. "Helen A. Merrill, '86." *Wellesley Magazine* (July 1949): 353–354.

Other References

Rossiter, Margaret. *Women Scientists in America*. Baltimore: Johns Hopkins University Press, 1982.
Wellesley College Biographical Record 1935, 1942.
Wellesley College News (5 May 1949).
Wellesley College Reunion Questionnaire 1925.

CATHLEEN SYNGE MORAWETZ (1923–)

James D. Patterson

BIOGRAPHY

Cathleen Morawetz was born on May 5, 1923, in Toronto, Canada. Her father was the mathematician John Synge, known for his work in tensor analysis, and her mother was Eleanor Mabel (Allen) Synge. She obtained a scholarship in mathematics to the University of Toronto and obtained her B.A. degree in 1943. She then spent 1943–1944 as technical assistant for inspection of the Board of the United Kingdom and Canada. She obtained a master's degree from the Massachusetts Institute of Technology in 1946. She married Herbert Morawetz, a chemist, on October 28, 1945. They had four children: Pegeen Ann, John Synge, Lida Joan, and Nancy Babette.

After MIT Morawetz moved to New York with her husband. Originally she considered finding a job rather than immediately pursuing the Ph.D., but apparently she was not encouraged when she talked to people at Bell Laboratories about employment.

Fortunately, her father was acquainted with Richard Courant of New York University, and at least partly because of this connection, Morawetz ended up with the job of editing a book by Courant and Kurt Friedrichs called *Supersonic Flow and Shock Waves*. This undertaking led to taking graduate courses and writing a Ph.D. thesis under the direction of Friedrichs. The thesis was on imploding shock waves, and she received her Ph.D. in 1951. She became a naturalized U.S. citizen in 1950.

After receiving the Ph.D. she returned to MIT as research associate (1951–1952), but then she came back to NYU as research associate, supported by various Navy contracts (1952–1957). She has spent her whole career since then at NYU, becoming assistant professor in 1957, associate professor in 1960, and professor in 1965. She was made associate director of the Courant Institute of Mathematical Sciences in 1978, deputy director in 1981, and director in 1984—the first woman in the United States to head a mathematics institute.

She also served as chairman of the department of mathematics from 1981 to 1984.

Morawetz has had numerous honors during her career. She has been a Guggenheim Fellow on two occasions (1966–1967 and 1978–1979). She received the Lester R. Ford Award of the Mathematical Association of America in 1980 for her 1979 article on nonlinear conservation equations. She has received honorary degrees from Eastern Michigan University (1980), Smith College (1982), and Brown University (1982). She is a Fellow of the American Association for the Advancement of Science and of the American Academy of Arts and Sciences.

Morawetz has been a trustee for Princeton University, the American Mathematical Society, and the Alfred P. Sloan Foundation. She has been a director of NCR Corporation since 1978, a member of the Advisory Committee for the Mathematical Sciences for the National Science Foundation, and a member of the Mathematical Advisory Committee to the National Bureau of Standards.

WORK

Morawetz's work has been in applications of partial differential equations. In earlier years she did much work on the mathematical analysis of transonic flow, and in later years she has concentrated on the mathematics associated with the scattering of waves. In the 1960s she showed that shock waves always accompany the motion of any sufficiently swiftly moving airplane wing. This, of course, does not mean that one cannot minimize the effect of these shocks.

One of the problems that has attracted her attention in the scattering of waves is the inverse problem. That is, by looking at how waves are scattered, how does one decide what they are scattered from? This inverse problem is of considerable current interest in imaging problems in medicine as well as in seismic searching for oil. Of particular interest is how to deal with the scattering of lower-frequency waves. Morawetz in the last several years has succeeded in solving (with Walter A. Strauss) two important wave problems. The first problem had applications to elementary particle physics, and the second had to do with trapping of light reflected from special mirrors. Her work has been supported by the Air Force Office of Scientific Research and the Office of Naval Research.

She is an editor of the *Journal of Mathematical Analysis and Applications*, of *Communications in Partial Differential Equations*, and of *Advances in Applied Mathematics*.

BIBLIOGRAPHY

Works by Cathleen Synge Morawetz

Space does not permit the listing of the complete works of Cathleen Synge Morawetz. The Author Cumulative Index volumes for *Mathematical Reviews* (for 1940–1959, 1960–1964, 1965–1972, and 1973–1979) list more than thirty books and papers by her. Listed below are works not listed there, including more recent works, plus works cited in the essay.

Mathematical Works

"Contracting spherical shocks treated by a perturbation method." Ph.D. diss., New York University, 1951.

"Asymptotic solutions of the stability equations of a compressible fluid." *Journal of Mathematical Physics* 33 (1954): 1–26.

"Hydromagnetic shock waves in high temperature plasmas." In *Proceedings of the First United Nations International Conference on the Peaceful Uses of Atomic Energy,* vol. 16, *Nuclear Data and Reactor Theory,* September 1958.

"Modification for magneto-hydrodynamic shock structure without collisions." *Physics of Fluids* 5 (1962): 1447–1450.

"Collisionless shocks and solitary waves." *Proceedings of the 11th International Congress of Applied Mechanics* (1964): 980–983.

"Transonic flow and mixed equations." *Rendiconti del Seminario Matematico dell'Universita del Politecnico di Torino* 25 (1965/66): 73–74.

"Appendix 3: Energy decay for star-shaped obstacles." In *Scattering Theory,* by P. D. Lax and R. S. Phillips, 261–264. New York: Academic, 1967.

"A regularization for a simple model of transonic flow." *Communications in Partial Differential Equations* 4 (1979): 79–111.

"Nonlinear conservation equations." *American Mathematical Monthly* 86 (1979): 284–287.

(with G. A. Kriegsmann) "Numerical methods for solving the wave equations with variable index of refraction." In *Boundary and Interior Layers—Computational and Asymptotic Methods,* edited by J.J.H. Miller, 118–123. Dún Laoghaire, Ireland: Boole, 1980.

(with G. A. Kriegsmann) "Solving the Helmholtz equation for exterior problems with variable index of refraction: I." *SIAM Journal of Scientific and Statistical Computing* 1 (1980): 371–385.

"A formulation for higher-dimensional inverse problems for the wave equation." *Computers and Mathematics with Applications* 7 (1981): 319–331.

Lectures on Nonlinear Waves and Shocks. Bombay: Tata Institute of Fundamental Research, 1981.

(with G. A. Kriegsmann) "Computations with the nonlinear Helmholtz equation." *Journal of the Optical Society of America* 71 (1981): 1015–1019.

"The mathematical approach to the sonic barrier." *Bulletin of the American Mathematical Society* 6 (1982): 127–145.

(with A. Bayliss and G. A. Kriegsmann) "Strange boundary layer effects on the edge of a nonlinear plasma." In *Computational and Asymptotic Methods for Boundary and Interior Layers,* edited by J.J.H. Miller, 3–12. Dún Laoghaire, Ireland: Boole, 1982.

(with A. Bayliss and G. A. Kriegsmann) "The nonlinear interaction of a laser beam with a plasma pellet." *Communications on Pure and Applied Mathematics* 36 (1983): 399–414.

(with G. A. Kriegsmann) "The calculations of an inverse potential problem." *SIAM Journal of Applied Mathematics* 43 (1983): 844–854.

Works about Cathleen Synge Morawetz

"Cathleen Morawetz, first woman to head a mathematics institute." *SIAM News* 17 (4) (1984): 5. Reprinted in *Association for Women in Mathematics Newsletter* 15 (1) (January–February 1985): 7–8.

Kolata, Gina Bari. "Cathleen Morawetz: The mathematics of waves." *Science* 206 (1979): 206–207.

HANNA NEUMANN (1914–1971)

M. F. Newman

BIOGRAPHY

Hanna Neumann was born in Berlin on February 12, 1914, the youngest of three children of Hermann and Katharina von Caemmerer. Her father was the only male descendant of a family of Prussian officer tradition; he broke the tradition to become a historian. He was well on the way to establishing himself as an archivist and academic historian when he was killed in the first days of World War I. Her mother was descended from a Huguenot family that settled in Prussia in the second half of the eighteenth century. The older children were Ernst (1908) and Dora (1910). Neumann's brother became professor of law at Freiburg; he was for a time Rektor (vice-chancellor). Her sister (who also received a doctorate) worked in Berlin in the retraining of social workers.

As a result of her father's death, the family lived impecuniously on a war pension. Already at age thirteen, Neumann contributed to the family income by tutoring younger school children; by the time she reached the final years at school, she was tutoring up to fifteen periods a week.

After two years in a private school, she entered the Augusta-Victoria-Schule, a girls' grammar school *(Realgymnasium)*, in 1922. She graduated in 1932.

Her early hobby was botany. She collected plant specimens and built up voluminous herbaria for about four years, until at about the age of fourteen this interest was superseded by mathematics.

Neumann entered the University of Berlin at Easter, 1932. Three of her teachers that year, Ludwig Bieberbach, Erhard Schmidt, and Issai Schur, were to have strong mathematical and personal influences on her life. Bieberbach was to her an inspiring mathematician, in spite of disorganized lecturing. He nearly turned her into a geometer. Schmidt and Schur were responsible for her introduction to analysis and algebra, respectively.

Neumann soon found herself in a coffee-break group with more senior students, including Werner Fenchel and his future wife Käte*, and, in particular, her own future husband, Bernhard H. Neumann.

In August 1933 Bernhard left for Cambridge. At Easter 1934, Neumann visited Bernhard in London, and they became secretly engaged; already the climate in Germany, and soon the law, was against "mixed" marriages.

As a result of her work in her first year, Neumann got a part-time job in the library of the Mathematical Institute. This meant not only a lighter tutoring load, but also, very importantly, an earlier than usual introduction to a wider range of mathematical books and journals.

During Neumann's first year at university, the Nazis came to power, and Neumann was outspokenly critical of them. The Nazis tried to stop the lectures by Jewish staff members by organizing protests and violence during them. In her second year, Neumann was active in a group of students who tried in vain to protect the Jewish lecturers by ensuring that only genuine students attended their lectures. Neumann lost her job in the Mathematical Institute, presumably as a result of her activities.

There was also a direct effect on her studies. Neumann had by now set her sights directly on a doctorate. However, in her fourth year she was warned that in the oral examination, one particular mathematician would personally examine her on "political knowledge," which was by now compulsory. She was advised to switch quickly to the *Staatsexamen,* for which—though it had similar requirements—the oral might be arranged with a different examiner. She could then go on and do a doctorate at another university.

The *Staatsexamen,* a necessary prerequisite for entry into public service, including teaching, placed more emphasis on breadth of knowledge than the doctorate. Neumann chose to be examined in mathematics, physics, and philosophy.

During all this time, Hanna and Bernhard kept in contact by correspondence, conducted anonymously through various friendly channels. They met only once during this period: in Denmark, for a couple of weeks in 1936, when Bernhard was traveling from the International Congress of Mathematicians in Oslo.

With the *Staatsexamen* completed, Neumann was accepted as a research student by Helmut Hasse at Göttingen. Göttingen was very active, though it was no longer the outstanding center that it had been before the advent of the Nazis. Hasse believed in teamwork: he assigned each of his students some task toward a common goal. At that time it was the Riemann conjecture in algebraic function fields of characteristic p. Seminars were used to ensure that everyone obtained an overall picture of the project.

In Göttingen Neumann found time for some chess and some gliding. She also found time to attend a course on Czech—this because a friend wanted to learn the language and the minimum class size was two.

Early 1938 saw the annexation of Austria, and summer brought the Czechoslovakian crisis. Neumann decided that it would be impossible to complete her course without risking a prolonged delay in her marriage plans. So, after three semesters, she gave up her course of study and in July 1938 went to Britain.

The first years in Britain were far from easy, yet they saw the beginning of her family and the beginning of productive research. Bernhard was a temporary assistant lecturer in Cardiff. Late in 1938 Hanna and Bernhard were married. In 1939 their first child, Irene, was born. During this time in Cardiff, Hanna's earlier interest in botany was turned to practical use. The family diet included wild plants such as sorrel.

Both Hanna and Bernhard were classified as "least restricted" aliens. However, after Dunkirk, a larger part of the coast was barred to all aliens, and they were required to leave Cardiff. They moved to Oxford because it was a university town. Within a week Bernhard was interned; a few months later, he was released into the British army. Meanwhile, Hanna, expecting a second child, made arrangements to complete a doctorate (D.Phil.). Just after Christmas, the second child, Peter, was born (he later became a mathematics don at Oxford).

Her thesis was largely written by candlelight in a rented trailer, to which the difficulties of finding housing had forced the family to move. The typing was done on a card table by a haystack when the weather permitted. The thesis was submitted in mid-1943. Soon after, restrictions on aliens were eased, and she was able to return to Cardiff. In November of that year, the third child, Barbara, was born (she too went on to teach mathematics).

After the war, Bernhard resumed his university career with a temporary lectureship at Hull. At the same time, their fourth child, Walter, was born (also to become a mathematician). For the next academic year, Bernhard was a lecturer and Hanna was offered a temporary assistant lectureship; thus began her formal teaching career.

Neumann took an active interest in her students at Hull. She was a strong supporter of the student mathematical society and gave lectures to it on a number of occasions. She participated in the model-building group, making paper models of regular and other solids. An outstanding feature, though, was her coffee evening. She often invited staff and students to meet at her house over coffee. This turned into a regular weekly open house at which her students were always welcome. As one of her colleagues of those times said, "Many benefited greatly from being able to drop in for company, discussion and often help with personal affairs" (Newman and Wall 1974, 9). She was very interested in people and in seeing that they made the most of their abilities. Neumann's fifth child, Daniel, was born in 1951 (he completed a university course in mathematics and Greek and became a professional musician).

Neumann prepared two papers based on her thesis and published them in the *American Journal of Mathematics*. Bernhard shared an office with Graham Higman, and this proximity fostered a joint paper with Neumann in 1949 that has led to certain groups being called HNN-groups. Neumann's own research and her joint research with Bernhard both progressed well and resulted in a number of papers. In 1955 her published work was submitted to Oxford and judged worthy of a D.Sc. degree. In 1958 she took a position at the University of Manchester.

During 1961–1962 Hanna and Bernhard had a joint study leave at the Courant Institute of Mathematical Sciences in New York. Before they went to New York, an offer came to Bernhard to set up a research department of mathematics at the Australian National University. Hanna was offered a post as reader. They accepted, with Bernhard to take up his appointment after the year in New York and Hanna to come a year later, after discharging her obligations to her research students in Manchester.

Neumann believed in making herself available: as far as formal commitments allowed, she was always in her office with the door open. She encouraged students to seek help with their difficulties, and she was often to be seen explaining a point at her blackboard. She also found herself helping students with nonmathematical problems. Her impact in Australia is best summed up by the following extract from a letter by two students, published in the local paper just after her death:

We will remember her not only as a mathematician; she was a friend who always had a sympathetic ear for any student, and was never too busy.

We will always miss her tremendous dedication and sincerity, and the friendliness of her presence. (Newman and Wall 1974, 15)

Of course, the price was paid in much midnight oil.

At the end of October 1971, Hanna set off on a Canadian lecture tour. She arrived at Carleton University, Ottawa, on November 8. On the evening of November 12 she felt ill, admitted herself to the hospital, and quickly went into a coma. She died on November 14 without regaining consciousness.

WORK

Neumann's first paper was on a problem suggested by her husband, on a mathematical equivalent of a rule for breaking ties in team chess matches. She did her work on it after joining him in England.

It was also then that she started working on finite plane geometries, an interest that she retained throughout her life. This too was sparked by Bernhard, when he reported to her on a lecture he had heard.

On leaving Germany she had abandoned her research on the problem of algebraic function fields, feeling that it would not be fruitful to continue outside Hasse's team. After the war she learned that Andre Weil had solved it in 1940.

For her D.Phil. thesis, she chose a problem in combinatorial group theory (that of determining the subgroups of free products of groups with an amalgamated subgroup). The topic was suggested to her by reading work of A. G. Kurosh; her thesis supervisor was Olga Taussky-Todd*.

During her twelve years at Hull, she directed two master's theses and one doctorate. At Manchester and in Australia, she had several more doctoral students.

In 1952 she was inspired by a lecture by Heinz Hopf, a very distinguished topologist, to work on a group-theoretic problem of his related to the structure of certain surfaces. She investigated what are now called Hopf groups.

She eventually came to work on what are known by the technical term *varieties* of groups, on which she became a leading figure. She published a monograph on the subject in 1967, which was translated into Russian.

In Australia Neumann became involved with helping teachers in secondary schools prepare to teach new syllabi. She lectured to parents on the ideas behind the new syllabi in order to enlist their cooperation. She believed that the community had to be educated to create a more favorable climate—one in which mathematics is not feared—for the learning of mathematics, especially among girls. When the Australian Association of Mathematics Teachers was founded in 1966, she was elected one of its vice-presidents. She later became president of the Canberra Mathematical Association.

Her other impact in Australia was to build up a keen and active department of pure mathematics. She put into operation her own ideas about teaching (such as take-home examinations). Her committee work involved her in wider university affairs, and in 1968–1969 she held the position of Dean of Students for almost two years.

BIBLIOGRAPHY

Works by Hanna Neumann

Newman and Wall give a complete list of Neumann's publications (1974, 26–27). Because of space limitations, we do not reproduce it here.

Works about Hanna Neumann

Higman, G. "Hanna Neumann." *Bulletin of the London Mathematical Society* 6 (1974): 99–100.
Newman, M. F. "Hanna Neumann." *Australian Mathematics Teacher* 29 (1973): 1–22.
    Includes a photograph.
Newman, M. F., and G. E. Wall. "Hanna Neumann." *Journal of the Australian Mathematical Society* 17 (1974): 1–28.
    Includes a different photograph.

MARY FRANCES WINSTON NEWSON (1869–1959)

Betsey S. Whitman

BIOGRAPHY

One hundred outstanding women were honored in 1940 by the Women's Centennial Congress because they held positions that were not open to women one hundred years earlier. One of them was Mary Frances Winston Newson, known to family and friends as May, the first American woman to receive a Ph.D. in mathematics from a European university. She did not attend the banquet honoring her and the other ninety-nine women, though; it fell on the first day of a new term at Eureka College where she taught, and she felt that she had to teach her classes. She did not even mention the invitation to her friends or colleagues. The headline in the local newspaper read, "Gets national honor and tells nobody."

Newson was born August 7, 1869, in Forreston, Illinois. She was the fourth child of Thomas and Caroline (Mumford) Winston. Four more children were born after her, and three of them lived. Consequently, she grew up as the middle child in a family of seven.

Newson's mother, Caroline Winston, tutored all the children at home during the 1870s. Occasionally, when she became too burdened with mothering a new baby, she had to send some of the older children to public school for a semester; but she was always dissatisfied with the instruction they received. She taught herself Latin and Greek to prepare her children for college.

When Newson was fifteen and her next older brother was seventeen, they set off by train from Chicago to Madison, Wisconsin, to enroll at the University of Wisconsin. Her brother passed the exam to be admitted as a sophomore, and Newson was enrolled as a freshman. Although she had to stay out of school and teach high school for one year, she graduated with a classical degree with honors in mathematics in 1889.

She taught for a year at Downer College in Fox Lake, Wisconsin, and applied for a mathematics fellowship at Bryn Mawr in 1890. Professor Charlotte Scott* told her that she was almost chosen for the grant but another student's credentials were just a little better. However, Scott urged her to apply again. So she taught for another year and reapplied. This time she was chosen and studied during 1891–1892 at Bryn Mawr. Scott wrote that Newson "has shown herself to be a most diligent student; her abilities are not striking but she has a decided grasp of her subject and is a thoroughly good worker and all that reflects on the subjects presented to her mind" (Graduate Book, Bryn Mawr Archives). During the year she studied modern analytical geometry, differential equations, theory of functions, linear differential equations, Chrystal's algebra, elements of the Jacobi theory of elliptic functions, and theory of substitutions.

Although she was urged to stay at Bryn Mawr for further study, Newson returned home to Chicago to study at the new University of Chicago during 1892–1893. During the summer of 1893, she met Felix Klein of the University of Göttingen at the International Mathematical Congress at the World's Columbian Exposition, held in Evanston, Illinois. He urged her to come to Göttingen to study, although he could not assure her that she would be admitted. She applied for a fellowship from the Association of Collegiate Alumnae (later the American Association of University Women) but did not receive it.

Then a letter came from Christine Ladd-Franklin*, offering $500 for study abroad. Ladd-Franklin had met Newson at the exposition and felt that she was a student worthy of support. The very next day, a letter arrived from Vassar offering Newson a teaching position. She said later she was so glad the letters arrived in the order they did.

Newson, Margaret Maltby (a physics major from Ohio), and Grace Chisholm (later Grace Chisholm Young*) (from England) all arrived in Germany about two weeks before Klein returned home from the United States. However, Klein's wife helped them get settled, and when classes began for the fall term, Klein asked the women to come into his office each day between classes, so that the male students could not complain that the hallways were cluttered with females!

Newson stayed at Göttingen for three years. During her last year, 1895–1896, she was awarded a European Fellowship from the Association of Collegiate Alumnae. She finished her dissertation and passed her examinations magna cum laude in 1896. However, her dissertation was not yet published, so she brought it home with her to find a publisher. She could not find a printer in the United States who could print the German symbols. Her degree was actually granted in 1897, after the dissertation was printed in Germany. Meanwhile, she had to settle for a high school teaching job in Missouri for that year. Finding a college position was difficult because she had been away three years.

Newson then became the head (and sole member) of the mathematics department at Kansas State Agricultural College in Manhattan. She stayed there for three years, and then in 1900 she gave up the position and married Henry Byron Newson, acting head of the mathematics department at the University of Kansas.

A daughter, Caroline, was born in 1901. A second daughter, Josephine, was born in 1903, and a son, Henry Winston, in 1909.

In the meantime Newson's country doctor father and her mother moved just two doors away. Fortunately for her, they were there when her husband died of a heart attack in 1910 at age forty-nine. Newson had no job, no pension, no life insurance benefits, and three small children. Within a month, she and the children moved to her parents' home.

It was not easy to find a job. It was not until 1913 that she got an offer from Washburn College in Topeka, Kansas, twenty-five miles away. She left the children at home and rented an apartment at Washburn, where she stayed during the week. Eventually, the children moved there too.

One of the first cases of academic freedom investigated by the American Association of University Professors was on the Washburn campus near the end of World War I. Newson was one of eight faculty members to sign a petition to support a political science professor who had been dismissed for talking too freely about his political views with his students. Within a year or two, all eight had found other positions. Newson became department head at Eureka College in Illinois, where she stayed until she retired in 1942.

When she grew older and her sister came to live with her for a while, they started a chapter of the American Association of University Women in Eureka. The subject of international relations was her hobby, and she served as chairperson of the international relations roundtable of the local chapter for many years.

She finally retired when she was seventy-three years old. She died on December 5, 1959, at age ninety.

WORK

Newson studied the field of differential equations at Göttingen. In October 1894, when she had been there about one year, she wrote her first paper, on hypergeometric functions, which was published in 1895. Her subsequent dissertation was also on differential equations. After returning to the United States, however, she published only one more article: the translation into English of the famous lecture delivered by David Hilbert before the Second International Congress of Mathematicians in Paris in 1900.

In his lecture Hilbert tried to unveil the future of mathematics by posing twenty-three major unsolved problems that he expected to be taken up in the twentieth century. These problems, now known as the Hilbert Problems, have indeed played an important role in mathematical thought and research in the years since.

In a letter written in 1937, Newson indicated that she was "very humble about my claims as an early research student as I know how completely I have neglected that type of work these many years" (Appendix C, Owens).

Newson was one of the twenty-two women who became members of the American Mathematical Society before 1900; she joined in 1896 after she returned from Germany. She was also a member of the Mathematical Association of America and attended many of its regional meetings. She served a term as president of the Kansas Association of Teachers of Mathematics and was an alumna member of the Phi Beta Kappa chapter at the University of Wisconsin.

An annual lecture at Eureka College is the Mary Winston Newson Memorial Lecture on International Relations. The fund to support the series was started by her three children, and the lectures began in 1970.

BIBLIOGRAPHY

Works by Mary Frances Winston Newson

Mathematical Works

"Eine Bemerkung zur Theorie der hypergeometrischen Function." *Mathematische Annalen* 46 (1895): 159–160.
"Über den Hermite'schen Fall der Lamé'schen Differentialgleichungen." Ph.D. diss., Göttingen University. Hanover, Germany, 1897.
"Mathematical problems." Translation of lecture delivered before the International Congress of Mathematicians in Paris in 1900 by Professor David Hilbert. *Bulletin of the American Mathematical Society* 8 (1901/1902): 437–479.

Works about Mary Frances Winston Newson

"Miss Mary F. Winston." *The Industrialist* (Manhattan, Kansas) 22 (40) (15 July 1897): 166.
        Describes Newson's accomplishments before her appointment as chair of the mathematics department in 1897.
Obituary. *Washington Post* (6 December 1959).
Whitman, Betsey S. "Mary Frances Winston Newson: The first American woman to receive a Ph.D. in mathematics from a European university." *Mathematics Teacher* 76 (1983): 576–577.
———. "Three nineteenth century women mathematicians." *American Mathematical Association of Two-Year Colleges Review* 3 (2) (1982): 27–31.
        Brief account of the lives of Newson and two other early women Ph.D.'s in mathematics.
———. "Women in the American Mathematical Society before 1900." *Association for Women in Mathematics Newsletter* 13 (6) (November–December 1983): 9–12.
        Newson is discussed on p. 10.

Other References

Archives. College of Agriculture and Applied Sciences, Kansas State University, Manhattan, Kansas.
Archives. Eureka College, Eureka, Ill.
Beshers, Caroline Newson. Interview with author, December 14, 1981.
Graduate Book. Archives, Bryn Mawr College, Bryn Mawr, Pa.
        Book in which professors wrote commendations and evaluations of graduating students' work.

EMMY NOETHER (1882–1935)

Gottfried E. Noether

BIOGRAPHY

Amalie Emmy Noether, known to mathematicians throughout the world as Emmy Noether, was the daughter of the mathematician Max Noether and his wife Ida, born Kaufmann. The Noether ancestors came from the Black Forest area of Germany; they were well-to-do Jewish tradesmen. Max Noether was the first family member to choose an academic career. Although handicapped by an attack of polio at age fourteen, he earned a Ph.D. in mathematics from Heidelberg in 1868. After five years teaching at Heidelberg, he moved to a chair in mathematics at Erlangen. On her mother's side, Emmy Noether's ancestors were wealthy Jewish merchants and property owners from the Cologne area.

Emmy Noether, born in Erlangen on March 23, 1882, was the oldest of four children. There were three younger brothers: Alfred (1883–1918); Fritz (1884–194?), who also became a mathematician; and Gustav Robert (1889–1928).

Noether had the typical upbringing of a daughter of the German upper middle class: finishing school from age seven to fifteen, some involvement in managing the Noether household, piano lessons, and attendance at dances for the children of family friends and university colleagues. After finishing school, she pursued further study of French and English, and at age eighteen passed the official examinations of the State of Bavaria for teachers of English and French at schools for girls. But rather than pursue a career as a language teacher, she began to think of a university education in mathematics.

Around 1900 German universities admitted women students only as auditors, and only with special permission of the lecturer, which was not always granted. An additional obstacle often faced by women was inadequate school preparation. From 1900 to 1902, Noether audited mathematics courses at Erlangen while she prepared for the *Absolutorium* (high school certification), which she passed in 1903. During the winter semester 1903–1904, she enrolled as an auditor at Göttingen, attending lectures by the mathematicians Otto Blumenthal, David Hilbert, Felix Klein, and Hermann Minkowski. But after only one semester she returned to Erlangen, where it had become possible for women to matriculate as regular students. In October 1904 she was the only enrolled woman student in mathematics among forty-six male colleagues, attending lectures given by her father and by Paul Gordan, the other holder of a mathematics chair at Erlangen. In December 1907 she passed the final examination for the Ph.D. in mathematics, summa cum laude.

For the next eight years, Noether continued to live in the family home at Erlangen. Without any formal appointment, she worked at the Mathematical Institute of the university. In addition to doing research, she began to substitute for her father, who was increasingly handicapped by his physical disability. In this Erlangen period she also played a major advisory role for two doctoral students.

In 1909 she joined the Deutsche Mathematiker-Vereinigung (German Mathematical Association) and gave her first public talk at the annual meeting in Salzburg. By 1915 she had established herself sufficiently as a mathematician to be invited by Hilbert and Klein to Göttingen. She stayed there until her dismissal by the Nazi regime in 1933, without ever being appointed to a regular chair in mathematics. Her attempt to obtain the *Habilitation* (permission to lecture) in 1915 was derailed, officially for legal reasons, in reality because of objections by philologists and historians to having a woman become a potential member of the university senate. Not until 1919 were women legally admitted to the *Habilitation*. For the years 1915–1919, Hilbert solved the problem by having Noether's lectures announced under his own name.

In 1919 Noether was appointed a *Privatdozent* and was now able to lecture under her own name. But the title carried no salary. In 1922, at the recommendation of the mathematics department, her title was changed to *nichtbeamteter ausserordentlicher Professor* (associate professor without tenure), and her position was supplemented by a lecturership in algebra, which assured her a small regular salary.

There was no change in her position during the remaining eleven years she was to spend in Göttingen. Even though several vacancies occurred during these years, she was never offered a mathematics chair. The most likely reason was that she was a woman. Unquestionably, she had the mathematical ability to compete with the best. Even though the legal position of women had changed under the German Republic, old prejudices continued to persist. That there was prejudice against women in academic circles was clearly demonstrated by the fact that Noether was denied election to the Göttingen Gesellschaft der Wissenschaften (Göttingen Academy of Sciences), an honor bestowed on several of her male colleagues. But additional reasons quite likely played a role too. She was a Jew; during the early 1920s, she was a member of the Social Democratic Party in Germany; she was a lifelong pacifist.

During the winter semester of 1928–1929, Noether accepted the invitation of P. S. Alexandrov to spend some time at the University of Moscow.

In 1932, the year before the Nazi takeover in Germany, Emmy Noether received long-delayed recognition. Together with Emil Artin, she was awarded the Alfred Ackermann-Teubner Memorial Prize for the Advancement of the Mathematical Sciences. In honor of her fiftieth birthday, Helmut Hasse dedicated to her an important paper in the *Mathematische Annalen*. In September of the same year, at the International Mathematical Congress in Zurich, she was the only woman mathematician invited to give a plenary lecture.

In April 1933, less than three months after the seizure of power by the Nazis in Germany, Noether was informed by the Ministry of Education that her permission to teach had been withdrawn. Efforts by mathematicians throughout Germany to have the decision reversed remained unsuccessful.

In August 1933 Noether accepted the offer of a guest professorship at Bryn Mawr College. In addition to conducting a seminar in algebra for a few advanced graduate and postgraduate students at Bryn Mawr, in early 1934 she started to give weekly lectures at the Institute for Advanced Study in Princeton. The guest professorship at Bryn Mawr was extended for a second year, and efforts were under way to find a more permanent position for her, when she died suddenly, on April 14, after an operation for removal of a tumor. The urn with Noether's ashes rests in the Cloister of Bryn Mawr College. A simple stone marker with the initials E. N. was dedicated in 1982 on the occasion of the hundredth anniversary of her birth.

Among the tributes to Emmy Noether, three stand out: Hermann Weyl's beautiful memorial address delivered at Bryn Mawr (1935); Alexandrov's address at the memorial session of the Moscow Mathematical Society (1935); and B. L. van der Waerden's obituary (1935).

In 1960 the city administration of Erlangen decided to name a street in a new part of town the Noetherstrasse to honor both Max and Emmy Noether. At the Mathematical Institute in Erlangen, a tablet commemorates both father and daughter. In 1982, on the hundredth anniversary of Emmy Noether's birth, the successor of the school which she attended as a girl—now a full-fledged high school that emphasizes mathematics, the sciences, and modern languages—was named the Emmy Noether School.

In 1983 Springer-Verlag published Emmy Noether's *Collected Papers*. A review by the French mathematician Jean Dieudonné begins with the words: "The publication of Emmy Noether's collected papers has long been overdue, since she was by far the best woman mathematician of all time, and one of the greatest mathematicians (male or female) of the XXth century."

WORK

Noether's development as the initiator of new mathematical ideas was slow compared to that of most mathematicians of her standing. Hermann Weyl refers to the period from the receipt of her Ph.D. in 1907 until about 1919 as a period of relative dependence on the ideas of others.

Gordan, under whom she studied in Erlangen, had solved the finiteness problem of invariants for two variables by purely formal and constructive methods. In her Ph.D. thesis, Noether extended Gordan's approach to ternary biquadratic forms, producing a system of 331 explicitly stated covariant forms. In later years she used to speak rather disdainfully of this effort.

Already in 1888 Hilbert had produced a solution to the finiteness problem involving n variables. But in contrast to Gordan's constructionist approach, Hilbert gave an existence proof, which to Gordan's thinking seemed more like theology than mathematics. Under the influence of Ernst Fischer, who succeeded to Gordan's chair in Erlangen in 1911, Noether's work on invariants turned increasingly toward Hilbert's abstract way of thinking.

Her mastery of the subject and her innovative ideas, which put Hilbert's methods in an algebraic setting, induced Hilbert and Klein to invite her to Göttingen in 1915 to assist them with certain problems arising out of their interest in the general theory of relativity. Noether's contribution, known to physicists as Noether's theorem, is basic for the general theory of relativity and for elementary particle physics. In a letter to Hilbert in 1918, Albert Einstein expressed his great appreciation of Emmy Noether's penetrating mathematical thinking.

While her work on invariants would have guaranteed Noether a place among the leading mathematicians of her time, her real claim to fame is based on her work in algebra, dating from about 1919. The change becomes evident in what many mathematicians consider to be her most important paper, "Idealtheorie in Ringbereichen" (Theory of ideals in rings), published in 1921.

This is how B. L. van der Waerden (1935) characterizes her new way of thinking: "For Emmy Noether, relationships among numbers, functions, and operations become transparent, amenable to generalization, and productive only after they have been disassociated from any particular objects and have been reduced to general conceptual relationships." Terms like addition and multiplication become simply names for two kinds of operations which are to be performed, subject to certain axioms, on elements called numbers, but which in reality are completely undefined. In everyday operations with numbers, multiplication is commutative. But in a more general interpretation of multiplication as the successive performance of a certain operation, such as a linear transformation (matrix multiplication), the order in which successive operations are performed becomes relevant, giving rise to so-called noncommutative operations. Much of Emmy Noether's later efforts concentrated on the study of noncommutative systems. Such systems had been studied before Noether, but she used her conceptual approach to unify the study of so-called noncommutative algebras.

Slowly, Noether succeeded in converting other mathematicians. Over the years she attracted a following of outstanding students who became the exponents of her way of thinking. Other algebraists, among them Artin, Hasse, van der Waerden, and, to a lesser extent, Richard Brauer, followed her example. In particular, van der Waerden's masterful two-volume exposition *Moderne Algebra*, first published in 1931, did more than any other work to change the face of algebra and mathematics in general.

Göttingen's reputation as a world center of mathematics and its attraction to foreign visitors owed much to Emmy Noether's presence there. In particular, the Russian topologist P. S. Alexandrov, who was a frequent visitor to Göttingen, freely acknowledged his debt to Noether's influence on his work in topology. At her suggestion, Alexandrov, together with Heinz Hopf, introduced group theory into combinatorial topology and thus started its transformation into algebraic topology.

During her stay in Göttingen, Noether acted as Ph.D. advisor for ten students, practically all of whom made a name for themselves in the mathematical world. One of them, Max Deuring, achieved what had been denied to Noether, a chair at the University of Göttingen and membership in several academies. During her short stay in Bryn Mawr, Noether sponsored one more mathematics Ph.D., that of Ruth Stauffer McKee.

For many years, Emmy Noether was an ardent and conscientious collaborator of the *Mathematische Annalen*. When reading a manuscript, she did not spare criticism. But she was equally ready to give valuable advice and provide direction.

Between 1930 and 1932, together with Robert Fricke and Oystein Ore, she edited Richard Dedekind's *Collected Works*, and with Jean Cavaillès she edited the correspondence between Georg Cantor and Dedekind.

BIBLIOGRAPHY

Works by Emmy Noether

Mathematical Works

Gesammelte Abhandlungen—Collected Papers. Edited by N. Jacobson. New York: Springer-Verlag, 1983.
    Review: J. Dieudonné, *Mathematical Reviews* 1984k:01069.

Works about Emmy Noether

Alexandrov, P. S. "In memory of Emmy Noether" (in Russian). *Uspekhi Matematicheskikh Nauk* 2 (1936): 254–266. English translations in Dick 1981, Brewer and Smith 1981, and *Gesammelte Abhandlungen* (1983).
    Address at the memorial session of the Moscow Mathematical Society on September 14, 1935. Commemorates Emmy Noether both as a mathematician and as a human being.
Brewer, J. W., and Martha K. Smith, eds. *Emmy Noether: A Tribute to Her Life and Work*. New York: Dekker, 1981.
    Commemorates the hundredth anniversary of Noether's birth.
Dick, A. *Emmy Noether, 1882–1935*. Basel: Birkhäuser, 1970. English translation by H. I. Blocher. Boston: Birkhäuser, 1981.
    Most thorough study of Emmy Noether's life. The author spent many years researching available documents and talked to many persons who had known and

worked with Emmy Noether. Lists all of her publications and the thirteen students who obtained Ph.D.'s under her direction. Complete list of obituaries.

Kimberling, C. "Emmy Noether." *American Mathematical Monthly* 79 (1972): 136–149.

Earlier version of biography in Brewer and Smith 1981.

Srinivasan, B., and J. Sally, eds. *Emmy Noether in Bryn Mawr: Proceedings of a Symposium Sponsored by the Association for Women in Mathematics in Honor of Emmy Noether's 100th Birthday.* New York: Springer-Verlag, 1983.

Contains eight scientific and four biographical and historical contributions, including reminiscences of students and colleagues during the Bryn Mawr period, plus a complete bibliography of Emmy Noether's writings.

van der Waerden, B. L. "Nachruf auf Emmy Noether." *Mathematische Annalen* 111 (1935): 469–476. English translations in Dick 1981 and in Brewer and Smith 1981.

Weyl, H. "Emmy Noether." *Scripta Mathematica* 3 (1935): 201–220. Reproduced in Dick 1981.

Published version of Hermann Weyl's beautiful eulogy delivered at Bryn Mawr College on April 26, 1935.

Other References

Dedekind, R. *Gesammelte mathematische Werke.* Edited by R. Fricke, E. Noether, and O. Ore. 3 vols. Braunschweig: Vieweg Verlag, 1930–1932.

Noether, E., and J. Cavaillès, eds. *Briefwechsel Cantor-Dedekind.* Actualités Scientifiques et Industrielles. Paris: Hermann, 1937.

van der Waerden, B. L. *Moderne Algebra.* 2 vols. Berlin: Springer, 1931.

RÓZSA PÉTER (1905–1977)

Hajnal Andréka

BIOGRAPHY

Rózsa Péter was born in Budapest on February 17, 1905. Her father, Dr. Gusztav Politzer, was a lawyer, and her mother, Irma Klein, worked at home as a homemaker. Péter had one elder and one younger brother. She did not marry or have children, but around 1930 she changed her name from Politzer to Péter.

Péter went to elementary and secondary schools in Budapest. In 1922 she enrolled at Eötvös Loránd University in Budapest to study chemistry. She chose chemistry because her father wanted his elder son to study medicine and his daughter chemistry so that the two siblings could cooperate later. However, at the university it soon became clear to her that what she was really interested in was mathematics.

Péter graduated in 1927, having had world-famous teachers in mathematics, such as Lipót Fejér and József Kürschák. Also, here began her friendship with László Kalmár, another famous Hungarian pioneer mathematician, whom she always considered to be her master in mathematics. They maintained a very close professional friendship all their lives. It was Kalmár who called her attention to the new subject of recursive functions.

After graduating she was practically unemployed for eighteen years. More precisely, she lived on occasional and provisional jobs, she gave private lessons, and so on. She got her first permanent appointment only in 1945. But in this period she began to do research in mathematical logic, which was in its formative stages at the time.

In the 1930s she was already a world-famous logician. In 1932 she lectured on recursive functions at the International Congress of Mathematicians in Zurich. In 1935 she defended her Ph.D. dissertation summa cum laude. At the next congress, in 1936, she gave talks on "higher-order" recursion. She was invited to join the editorial boards of several leading international mathematical journals, including, in 1937, the *Journal of Symbolic Logic*, which has been the leading journal in logic since its founding in 1936.

From 1945 till 1955 she worked at a teachers' college (Pedagógiai Förskola) in Budapest. This was a place she really loved; she created a very good atmosphere there around herself. She was given a department in which to realize her ideas; it was a happy and creative place, and very successful.

It was in this period that she wrote her first book on recursive functions, the first monograph on the subject (1951). One can say with justice that Péter was the mother of recursive function theory. It is true that other researchers had proved results on recursive functions already, but it was Péter who recognized first that the subject should be investigated as a separate whole in its own right. In 1951 she received the Kossuth Award (of the state of Hungary) for the monograph.

Péter also wrote mathematical textbooks and elaborated reforms for teaching mathematics. In 1952 she defended her dissertation for the higher "doctoral degree with the Academy." In 1953 she received the Manó Beke Award of the János Bolyai Mathematical Society for popularizing mathematics, and also became a member of the editorial board of the journal *Zeitschrift für Mathematische Logik und Grundlagen der Mathematik*.

In 1955 her favorite teachers' college was closed down, and Péter became a professor at Eötvös Loránd University. She was always unhappy about this change, because she had enjoyed the very close contact with her students at the teachers' college.

Péter very much enjoyed richness of colors, of life, of culture, of everything. She wrote film reviews and translated poems by Rainer Maria Rilke into Hungarian; cooking was her hobby, and she liked intelligent humor very much. She was a real humanist, a renaissance woman scientist. In her eyes, the presence of women in science serves to enhance richness and wholeness in science, too. She cared about the careers of women in science (not just in Hungary); in particular, she cared about her female students. She was rather successful in this, and several of her former students are doing well in academic life today.

Péter became a corresponding member of the Hungarian Academy of Sciences in 1973. In 1975 she retired from the university, and afterward she was interested mostly in educational reforms in teaching mathematics. She died of cancer in 1977.

WORK

Rózsa Péter was a world renowned pioneer in mathematical logic and one of the creators of the branch called recursive function theory. All told, she wrote two books and more than fifty papers in the area. Partly as a result of her work, mathematical logic is today a fully developed field of mathematics. Her work culminated in the mid-1970s in a book on the connections between recursive function theory and computer programming languages (1976).

More so than most mathematicians, Péter devoted herself to trying to convey the spirit of mathematics to the public. She considered mathematics an integral part of science and science an indispensable part of human culture. She stressed the unity of this culture and strongly opposed any tendency to treat mathematics in isolation. She fought hard against "aristocratism" and the so-called cult of geniuses, and also against any tendency for mathematics to degenerate into a mere intellectual sport, like chess or a kind of IQ test.

She considered this fight of hers to be one of the specific tasks of the female scientist. She felt that the inclination of males to be highly competitive and their tendency to care too much for their reputations together contain the danger of distorting the evolution of science into sidetracks, dead ends, or overspecialization. The presence of female scientists can balance these tendencies and help science flourish.

Her major effort at popularizing mathematics was her book *Playing with Infinity: Mathematical Explorations and Excursions* (1945). The original subtitle was "Mathematics for Outsiders." The book evolved from her correspondence with the Hungarian writer Marcell Benedek; it has been translated into fourteen languages and printed in many editions. While being entertaining reading, the book still conveys such a tremendous amount of insight that even professional mathematicians learn from it. Péter wrote the book to show that mathematics is a part of science. She tried to bridge the gaps between the hard sciences and the soft sciences, between the "two cultures" of the sciences and the humanities, and between mathematicians and the rest of the world. She managed to do this on a very high level, and to communicate deep and new results and problems of mathematics in such a way that any intelligent person can understand and enjoy them.

Péter was concerned about the roots of the average citizen's alienation from science and mathematics, which she traced to ages seven to eleven. She urged leading scientists and mathematicians to visit primary schools and try very hard to communicate to children the enjoyment, adventure, fun, and joy of scientific work.

BIBLIOGRAPHY ───────────────────────────────────

Works by Rózsa Péter

Space does not permit a full listing here of the works of Rózsa Péter. Such a list can be found in the article by Ruzsa and Urbán (1975). Listed below are the works cited in the essay.

Mathematical Works

"Rekursive Funktionen." *Proceedings of the International Congress of Mathematicians*, Zurich, 1932, vol. 2, 336–337.
"Über rekursive Funktionen der zweiten Stufe." *Proceedings of the International Congress of Mathematicians*, Oslo, 1936, vol. 2, 267.
Playing with Infinity: Mathematical Explorations and Excursions (in Hungarian). Bu-

dapest: Dante Könyvkiadó, 1945. 5th ed. Budapest: Tankönyvkiadó. English
translation by Z. P. Dienes. London: Bell, 1961. New York: Simon and Schuster,
1962. New York: Dover, 1976. Also translated into Rumanian, Slovak, Czech,
Polish, Russian, Dutch, Swedish, Italian, and other languages.

Rekursive Funktionen. Budapest: Akadémai Kiadó, 1951. 2nd ed., 1957. 3rd ed., translated by Istvan Földes as *Recursive Functions.* Budapest: Akadémai Kiadó, 1967;
New York: Academic, 1967. Also translated into Russian and Chinese.

Rekursive Funktionen in der Komputer-Theorie. Budapest: Akadémai Kiadó, 1976. English translation as *Recursive Functions in Computer Theory.* New York: Halsted,
1981.

Works about Rózsa Péter

Andrásfai, B. "Rózsa Péter" (in Hungarian). *Magyar Tudomány* 92 (1985): 601–605.

Császár, A. "Rózsa Péter: February 17, 1905–February 16, 1977" (in Hungarian).
Matematikai Lapok 25 (1974): 257–258 (1977).

Dömölki, B., et al. "The work of Rózsa Péter" (in Hungarian). *Matematikai Lapok* 16
(1965): 171–184.

Filep, L. "Great female figures of Hungarian mathematics in the 19th–20th centuries"
(in Hungarian). In *Proceedings of the Conference on the Role of Women in the
History of Science, Technology and Medicine in the 19th and 20th Centuries* (in
Hungarian), 56–63. Veszprém, Hungary, 1983.

Genewein, Ferenc. "Interview with Rózsa Péter" (in Hungarian). In *Face to Face with
Scientists,* edited by I. Kardos, 181–195. Budapest: MRT Minerva, 1974.

Hajnal, András. "Rózsa Péter" (in Hungarian). *Magyar Tudomány* 84 (1977): 477–478.

"Rózsa Péter (1905–1977)." *Annales Universitatis Scientiarum Budapestinensis de Ro-
lando Eötvös nominatae, Sectio Mathematica* 20 (1977): 3.

Ruzsa, I., and J. Urbán. "In memoriam Rózsa Péter" (in Hungarian). *Matematikai Lapok*
26 (1975): 125–137 (1978).

MINA REES (1902–   )

Phyllis Fox

BIOGRAPHY

The maternal grandfather of Mina Rees was a union leader in the Midland coal mines in England. After being blacklisted, he and his wife sought a new life in the United States, arriving in 1882 with their sons and their daughter, Alice Louise Stackhouse, who would become Mina Rees's mother.

Moses Rees was an insurance salesman. He met Alice in Lebanon, Pennsylvania, and they were married there in 1892. Their eldest daughter, Elsie, was born in 1893; a son, Albert (still living in 1985), in 1894; and two more sons, Clyde and Clarence, in 1896 and 1898. Mina Rees, the last child, was born in Cleveland on August 2, 1902.

Life was not easy for the Rees family, especially since Moses had a tendency to give money away to friends and relatives who sought his help. When Mina Rees was two, the family moved to the Bronx in New York City. She attended elementary school there, getting straight A's on her report cards, which made them so beautiful to her father that he had them framed. When she was in eighth grade, her teacher told her that she should take the entrance examination for Hunter High School. Though she had never heard of the school, she took the test and was admitted.

Hunter High School was an administrative unit of Hunter College and was the publicly supported high school in New York City designed to educate bright girls. It recruited its faculty nationwide and had superb teachers. Mathematics was strong at Hunter, but in those days that did not include going as far as trigonometry in high school. Rees had always liked mathematics and had, in fact, figured out the "rule of nine" on her own when quite young. She was valedictorian of her class and went on to Hunter College.

Fortunately, considering her family circumstances, Hunter College was tuition-free. Even better, at the end of her freshman year, the Hunter mathematics department asked Rees if she would like to teach, the following year, the course called "transit." This mysterious offering provided the "laboratory" in trigonometry. So she took a summer course at Teachers College, Columbia in surveying, accepted the part-time teaching job, and for the next three years got half the beginning salary of a regular instructor. Rees graduated summa cum laude in 1923. She made Phi Beta Kappa, was president of the student body, and served as yearbook editor.

The mathematics department asked her to stay on to teach, but Rees felt that she "did not know enough to really teach in a college," so she took a job teaching in Hunter High School while she worked on a master's degree at Columbia. In 1925 the degree was achieved; in 1926 she went to teach at Hunter College. The mathematics faculty at the college was strong at the time—Tomlinson Fort was head of the department and had brought in people with Ph.D.'s from Harvard and elsewhere. The job emphasis was still entirely on teaching, but there were opportunities to keep up with new mathematics, via faculty-organized seminars and attendance at meetings of the American Mathematical Society, often held conveniently at Columbia University.

In 1929 Rees secured a sabbatical (the high school teaching counted toward it) and went to the University of Chicago for a doctorate in mathematics. Her doctoral dissertation (1932) was in the field of division algebras and was done under L. E. Dickson. She then returned to Hunter.

At a party in 1936, Mina Rees met Leopold Brahdy, a physician. As they got to chatting, he said that he was about to go to Russia with a group, to study various aspects of life in that country under the current regime. He suggested she join the group, and since she was planning to go to the Mathematical Congress in Oslo anyhow, she went along. Rees and Brahdy were eventually married, in 1955.

In 1943 Mina Rees took a leave from Hunter College to become technical aide and executive assistant to Warren Weaver, chief of the newly established Applied Mathematics Panel, Office of Scientific Research and Development. Rees's contribution to the successful application of mathematics to wartime problems won her the President's Certificate of Merit and the (British) King's Medal for Service in the Cause of Freedom.

Following the war, the Office of Naval Research (ONR) played an important part in supporting scientific research. Mina Rees established its program in mathematics (1946–1952) and finally became ONR's deputy science director (1952–1953). F. J. Weyl called Rees "the architect of the first large-scale, comprehensively planned program of support for mathematical research; she pioneered its style, scale and scope." He went on to say that the program she built there and the policies she set had a strong influence on the National Science Foundation, founded in 1950 (Weyl 1970).

To various fronts of mathematical science—linear programming, operations research, computer development and application, the rediscovered field of numerical analysis—Mina Rees in her role at ONR brought wisdom, guidance, and support. In 1962 she received the first Award for Distinguished Service to Mathematics of the Mathematical Association of America.

In 1953 Mina Rees returned to Hunter College as professor of mathematics and dean of the faculty. She continued to play an important role on the national front by strong participation in various policy-setting committees, including the Advisory Committee on Mathematics of the National Bureau of Standards (member, 1954–1958; chairman, 1954–1957), the Advisory Panel for Mathematics of the National Science Foundation (1955–1958), the General Sciences Advisory Panel of the Department of Defense (1958–1961), and the Advisory Board of the Computation and Exterior Ballistics Laboratory, U.S. Naval Proving Ground, Dahlgren (1958–1961). Rees was also involved simultaneously in various councils and advisory groups in education, as a member and then vice-chairman of the Conference Board of the Mathematical Sciences, and as a member of the Executive Committee of the Mathematics Division of the National Research Council.

In 1961 Rees was invited to become the first dean of graduate studies in the newly created City University of New York. She worked to create a graduate school based on a consortium of the colleges of the university, with an independent graduate center. Rees became provost in 1968 and then, from 1969 to 1972, president of the Graduate School and University Center. In these new activities, she generalized her interests to include graduate education on a national level, becoming a member and later chair of the Council of Graduate Schools in the United States (1967–1971).

Rees's interest in the directions of scientific research continued. She was a member of the National Science Board (1964–1970) and was active in the American Association for the Advancement of Science (AAAS) as vice-president and chairman of Section A (1954), member of the board of directors (1957–1960, 1966–1972), president-elect (1970), president (1971), and chairman of the board (1972).

There was a considerable brouhaha in the press when a woman became president of the AAAS. The *New York Times* printed an article of congratulation (December 31, 1969) that included the sentence, "The modern breed of women militants will no doubt take it for granted that male chauvinism was primarily responsible for denying members of their sex earlier occupancy of the AAAS presidency," but went on to end with a plea to encourage potential women scientists in their graduate work and research.

In November 1985 the City University of New York dedicated the Mina Rees Library of its Graduate School and University Center.

WORK

The work of the Applied Mathematics Panel, Office of Scientific Research and Development, which Rees joined in 1943, is described in (Rees 1980), but that document does not comment adequately on the extent of Rees's contribution in getting together mathematicians from many disciplines across the country to work on problems of crucial importance to the war effort. The obstacles were numerous. Except for Richard Courant's group at New York University and William Prager's program at Brown University, applied mathematics was not a popular research area in the United States. Moreover, there had been little notable cooperation between mathematicians and the armed services. The important thing was to detect for what problems there was hope of a useful solution and which mathematicians might have the best chance of solving them. The members of the panel's Committee Advisory to the Scientific Officer, a group of experienced and distinguished mathematicians, had the needed understanding; and Mina Rees, as her performance showed, had what might be called the perceptive taste to provide support for the combinations that emerged.

Her abilities in this direction were of equal value in the various positions Rees held with ONR. In two excellent summaries (Rees 1977, 1982), she describes the work of this office and looks at the general role played by mathematics in the government in the postwar years. The support of mathematical research by ONR in the universities was a delicate balance between the desires of the navy for applicable results and the desire of the academics for free-form, open-ended investigation. One remarkable example of her powers of persuasion was that she was able to extend ONR funding to support not only applied but also pure research, by convincing the navy of the long-range benefits of such an investment.

Fairly early in her tenure at ONR, Mina Rees learned of the work done by George Dantzig in developing the simplex method for solving the linear programming problem. Understanding the boon such research could be to the severe logistical problems of the navy, she arranged for Dantzig and an air force colleague to describe to a meeting of navy personnel the new approach to solving logistics problems. At this key meeting, which resulted in the establishment of an entire new program in logistics at ONR, Rees, as usual, was the only woman in the room, and she subsequently remarked, with some amusement, that the only discrimination she felt was from a civilian.

The simplex method needed computers, but there had been delays on all fronts in getting them built. In order to test out his method, Dantzig arranged for hand computation of the simplex solution of a minimax problem that previously resisted solution. The solution required nearly 17,000 multiplications and divisions, which "were carried out by five statistical clerks using desk computers in 21 working days" (Rees 1982).

Development of computers needed lots of money. The ONR-funded Whirlwind computer at MIT was a heinous offender in regard to budget overruns and made Rees' job particularly difficult (Redmond and Smith 1980). In many ways, Rees was the link between Whirlwind's pioneer designers and navy funding.

Rees was convinced that, in the long run, the manufacture of computers would have to be done by commercial firms, not government and academia, and it distressed her (Rees 1982) that some of the directors of leading companies felt that there would never be a need for more than a few machines in the entire country.

A couple more examples illustrate Rees's ability to detect the directions research and development should take. In the 1950s a classic battle was going on between the promoters of analog machines (based on physically representable quantities such as electric circuits, shaft motion, or even hydraulic circuits) and the believers in digital machines. Rees attended a meeting where an analog machine for doing crystallography calculations was being displayed to a rapt audience. The graphical displays presented by the machine were apparently excellent, but Rees suggested that a digital machine with the same display equipment would be more efficient and involve less knob twiddling. Rees also suggested that it would be worthwhile to investigate possible uses of semiconductor devices, such as transistors, to replace vacuum tubes (Rees 1950). And so it has turned out.

In a pattern somewhat different from that of most mathematicians, what Rees accomplished in her roles as administrator and head of many organizations has been her life and her contribution. Her intelligence and her decisive grasp of the directions mathematical and computer research could take influenced the scientific world from the 1940s through the mid-1980s. Her ideas have had tremendous impact.

BIBLIOGRAPHY

Works by Mina Rees

Mathematical and Related Works

"Division algebras associated with an equation whose group has four generators." *American Journal of Mathematics* 54 (1932): 51–65.
   Doctoral thesis.
Applied Mathematics Panel, NDRC, Summary Technical Report, 3 vols. New York: McGraw-Hill, 1947.
   Rees was chairman of the board of editors.
"The mathematics program of the Office of Naval Research." *Bulletin of the American Mathematical Society* 54 (1948): 1–5.
"Applied Mathematics in Western Europe." *Monthly Research Report* (Office of Naval Research) (1 December 1948).
"The federal computing machine program." *Science* 112 (22 December 1950): 731–736.
   Reprinted, with added introductory material, in *Annals of the History of Computing* 7 (1985): 156–163.
(with H. W. Brinkman, Z. I. Mosesson, S. A. Schelkunoff, and S. S. Wilks) "Professional opportunities in mathematics: A report for undergraduate students in mathematics." *American Mathematical Monthly* 58 (1951): 1–24.
"Digital computers—their nature and use." *American Scientist* 40 (1952): 328–335.
(with R. Courant and E. Isaacson) "On the solution of non-linear hyperbolic differential equations by finite differences." *Communications on Pure and Applied Mathematics* 5 (1952): 243–255.
"Modern mathematics and the gifted student." *Mathematics Teacher* 46 (1953): 401–406.

"The mathematician in government establishments." In *Proceedings of a Conference on Training in Applied Mathematics*. Providence, R. I.: American Mathematical Society, 1953.

"Mathematics and federal support." *Science* 119 (21 May 1954): 3A.

"Computers: 1954." *Scientific Monthly* 79 (August 1954): 118–124.

"Digital computers." *American Mathematical Monthly* 62 (1955): 414–423.

"New frontiers for mathematicians." *Pi Mu Epsilon Journal* 1 (1955): 122–127.

"The impact of the computer." *Mathematics Teacher* 51 (1958): 162–168.

"Mathematicians in the market place." *American Mathematical Monthly* 65 (1958): 332–343.

"Modern algebra." *Encyclopedia Americana*, 1958.

"Support of higher education by the federal government." *American Mathematical Monthly* 68 (1961): 371–377.

"The nature of mathematics." *Science* 138 (5 October 1962): 9–12; also in *Mathematics Teacher* 55 (1962): 434–440.

"How can the undergraduate college best meet curricular pressures from graduate and professional schools and from new developments in secondary education?" In *Undergraduate Education*, edited by G. Kerry Smith et al. Current Issues in Higher Education, 1964. Washington, D.C.: Association for Higher Education, NEA, 1964.

"Efforts of the mathematical community to improve the mathematics curriculum." In *Emerging Patterns in American Higher Education*. Washington, D.C.: American Council on Education, 1965.

"Graduate Education in the decade of the seventies." Chairman's Address. In *Proceedings of the Tenth Annual Meeting of the Council of Graduate Schools*, 1970.

"Changing patterns of graduate education—perspectives." In *Report of a Conference of the Western Association of Graduate Schools*. Seattle, Washington, March 1970.

"A humane approach to population problems." *Science* 173 (30 July 1971): 381.

"Graduate education—a long look." In *Graduate Education Today & Tomorrow*, edited by L. J. Kent and G. P. Springer, 139–151. Albuquerque: University of New Mexico Press, 1972.

"The saga of American universities: The role of science." *Science* 179 (5 January 1973): 19–23.

"The graduate education of women." In *Women in Higher Education*, edited by W. Todd Furniss and Patricia Albjerg Graham, 178–187. Washington, D.C.: American Council on Education, 1974.

"The scientist in society: Inspiration and obligation." *American Scientist* 63 (1975): 144–149.

"The ivory tower and the marketplace." In *On the Meaning of the University*, edited by Stirling M. McMurrin, 81–101. Salt Lake City: University of Utah Press, 1976.

"Mathematics and the government: The post-war years as augury of the future." In *The Bicentennial Tribute to American Mathematics, 1776–1976*, edited by Dalton Tarwater, 101–116. Washington, D.C.: Mathematical Association of America, 1977.

"The mathematical sciences and World War II." *American Mathematical Monthly* 87 (1980): 607–621.

"The computing program of the Office of Naval Research, 1946–1953." *Annals of the History of Computing* 4 (1982): 102–120.

Works about Mina Rees

"Academy of Sciences cites Mina Rees." *SIAM News* 16 (4) (July 1983): 1, 9.

"Creative mathematician—Mina Spiegel Rees." *New York Times* (10 July 1961): 23.

Dana, Rosamond, and Peter J. Hilton, interviewers. "Mina Rees." In *Mathematical People*, edited by Donald J. Albers and G. L. Alexanderson, 256–267. Boston: Birkhäuser, 1985.

"Dynamic scientist." *New York Times* (31 December 1969): 10.

Fritchey, Clayton. "Women & politics" (column). *New York Post* (9 January 1970): 43.

Redmond, Kent C., and Thomas M. Smith. *Project Whirlwind*. Billerica, Massachusetts: Digital Press, 1980.

Rees, Mina. Interview by Phyllis Fox, in New York, N.Y., March 4, 1985.

Rees, Mina. Transcript of panel address. In "Women mathematicians before 1950," *Association for Women in Mathematics Newsletter* 9 (4) (July-August 1979): 15–18.

"Rees awarded medal." *Association for Women in Mathematics Newsletter* 13 (3) (May-June 1983): 9–10.

Taylor, Mildred E. "Mina Spiegel Rees." *Pi Mu Epsilon Journal* (1954): 395–399.

Weyl, F. Joachim. "Mina Rees, President-Elect 1970 (AAAS)." *Science* 167 (20 February 1970): 1149–1151.

JULIA BOWMAN ROBINSON (1919–1985)

Constance Reid with Raphael M. Robinson

BIOGRAPHY

Julia Bowman Robinson was the first woman mathematician to be elected to the National Academy of Sciences and the first woman to be president of the American Mathematical Society (AMS). Her mathematical work was most often centered on the border between logic and number theory.

"I think that I have always had a basic liking for the natural numbers," she once said, recalling that her earliest memory was of arranging pebbles in the shadow of a giant saguaro on the Arizona desert, where she lived as a small child. "We can conceive of a chemistry which is different from ours, or a biology, but we cannot conceive of a different mathematics of numbers. What is proved about numbers will be a fact in any universe."

She was born Julia Bowman on December 8, 1919, in St. Louis, Missouri, the second daughter of Ralph Bowers Bowman and Helen Hall Bowman. Shortly after her second birthday, her mother died. Her father found that he had lost interest in his machine tool and equipment business, and a year later, when he remarried, he decided to retire. The family lived first in Arizona and then in San Diego.

When Julia was nine years old, she contracted scarlet fever, which was followed by rheumatic fever. After several relapses she was forced to spend a year in bed at the home of a practical nurse. She had been in the fifth grade when she fell ill, and by the time she recovered she had missed two additional years of school. After a year of tutoring, she returned as a ninth grader.

She now knew that mathematics was the school subject which she liked above all others, and she persisted with it at San Diego High School in spite of the fact that by her junior year all the other girls had dropped the subject. When she graduated in 1936, she was awarded the honors in mathematics and the other sciences which she had elected to take, as well as the Bausch-Lomb medal for all-around excellence in science.

At the age of sixteen, she entered San Diego State College, now San Diego

State University. It had recently been a teachers' college and, before that, a normal school. Emphasis was still largely on preparing teachers. By this time the savings that her father had counted on to support his family in his retirement had been almost completely wiped out in the Depression of the 1930s. At the beginning of Julia's sophomore year, he took his own life. In spite of the family's straitened circumstances, she was able to continue her education, tuition at that time being only $12 a semester. When her older sister was hired as a teacher in the San Diego school system, money became available for Julia to transfer to the University of California at Berkeley for her senior year.

"I was very happy, really blissfully happy, at Berkeley," she later recalled.

In San Diego there had been no one at all like me. If, as Bruno Bettelheim has said, everyone has his or her own fairy story, mine is the story of the ugly duckling. Suddenly, at Berkeley, I found that I was really a swan. There were lots of people, students as well as faculty members, just as excited as I was about mathematics. I was elected to the honorary mathematics fraternity, and there was quite a bit of departmental social activity in which I was included. Then there was Raphael.

"Raphael" was assistant professor R. M. Robinson, who taught the number theory course which she took during her first year at Berkeley. In the second semester there were only four students in the class—she was again the only woman—and he began to invite her to go on walks with him. In the course of these he told her about various interesting things in modern mathematics, including Kurt Gödel's results: "I was very impressed and excited by the fact that things about numbers could be proved by symbolic logic. Without question what had the greatest mathematical impact on me at Berkeley was the one-to-one teaching that I received from Raphael."

At the end of the first semester of her second graduate year at Berkeley, a few weeks after Pearl Harbor, she and Raphael Robinson were married. There was a rule at Berkeley that members of the same family could not teach in the same department. Since Julia already had a mathematics department teaching assistantship—she was teaching statistics for Jerzy Neyman—this rule did not immediately apply. Later, the prohibition did not concern her, since, now that she was married, she expected and very much wanted to have a family. In the meantime, while the United States was engaged in World War II, she and other mathematics faculty wives worked for Neyman in the Berkeley Statistical Laboratory on secret projects for the military.

When Julia finally learned that she was pregnant, she was delighted—and very disappointed when, after a few months, she lost the baby. She was then advised that because of the buildup of scar tissue in her heart (a result of the rheumatic fever), she should under no circumstances become pregnant again.

For a long time she was very depressed because she could not have children, but during the year 1946–1947, when she and Raphael were in Princeton, she took up mathematics again at his suggestion. The following year, back in Berkeley, she began to work toward a Ph.D. with Alfred Tarski, the noted Polish-born logician, who had joined the Berkeley faculty during the war. Her thesis, "Definability and decision problems in arithmetic," was accepted in June 1948.

The same year that she received her Ph.D., she began to work on the Tenth Problem on David Hilbert's famous list: to find an effective method for determining if a given Diophantine equation is solvable in integers. The problem was to occupy the largest portion of her professional career. As in the case of her thesis problem, the initial impetus came indirectly from Tarski, who had discussed casually with Raphael the problem whether, possibly using induction, one could show that the powers of 2 cannot be put in the form of a solution of a Diophantine equation. Not realizing, initially, the connection with the Tenth Problem, which she said later would have frightened her off, she began to work on solving Tarski's problem. When she found that she could not do so, she turned to related problems of existential definability.

During 1949–1950, when Raphael had a sabbatical, she worked at the RAND Corporation in Santa Monica. It was there that she solved the widely discussed "fictitious play" problem (see below). She did not, however, stop working on problems of existential definability relevant to Hilbert's Tenth Problem, and in 1950 she presented her results in a ten-minute talk at the International Congress of Mathematicians in Cambridge, Mass.

Following a frustrating and unsuccessful experience with a problem in hydrodynamics for the Office of Naval Research, she threw herself into Adlai Stevenson's presidential campaigns (1952 and 1956) and Democratic party politics for the next half dozen years.

In the summer of 1959, Martin Davis and Hilary Putnam proved a theorem which turned out to be an important lemma in the ultimate solution of the Tenth Problem. They sent a copy of their work to Julia, some of whose methods they had utilized.

"Her first move, almost by return mail, was to show how to avoid the messy analysis," Davis recalls. "A few weeks later she showed how to replace the unproved hypothesis about primes in arithmetic progression by the prime number theorem for arithmetic progressions. . . . [She] then greatly simplified the proof, which had become quite intricate. In the published version, the proof was elementary and elegant."

By the time that the Davis-Putnam-Robinson paper appeared in 1961, she was forced by the deterioration of her heart to undergo surgery for the removal of the buildup of scar tissue in the mitral valve. After the operation her health improved dramatically. During the years that followed, she was able to enjoy many outdoor activities, particularly bicycling, which she had had to forego since childhood. She still found, however, that teaching one graduate course a quarter at Berkeley, as she did on occasion, was about all she could manage.

With Yuri Matijasevič's unexpected solution of Hilbert's Tenth Problem at the beginning of 1970 and the recognition of the crucial importance of Julia's work in the solution, many honors began to come to her. In 1975 she became the first woman mathematician to be elected to the National Academy of Sciences and, somewhat tardily, a full professor at Berkeley (with the duty of teaching just one-fourth time). In 1978 she became the first woman officer of the AMS and in 1982 its first woman president. She was also elected president of the Association of Presidents of Scientific Societies, a position she later had to decline because of ill health. In 1979 she was awarded an honorary degree by Smith College, and the following year she was asked to deliver the Colloquium Lectures of the AMS. It was only the second time a woman had been so honored (Anna Pell Wheeler* was the first, in 1927). In 1983 she was awarded a MacArthur Fellowship of $60,000 a year for five years in recognition of her contributions to mathematics. In 1984 she was elected to the American Academy of Arts and Sciences.

Even after Matijasevič's solution, Hilbert's Tenth Problem continued to pose interesting questions. She collaborated on two papers with Matijasevič, whom she had come to know personally on a 1971 trip to Leningrad. For the Symposium on Hilbert's Problems at De Kalb, Illinois, in May 1974, she also collaborated with Davis and Matijasevič on a paper concerning the positive aspects of the negative solution to the problem. It was her last published paper, the business of the AMS occupying most of her time and energy during the next decade. She was also frequently active during this period with problems of human rights.

At the 1984 summer meeting of the AMS in Eugene, Oregon, over which she was presiding, she learned that she was suffering from leukemia. After a remission of several months in the spring of the following year, she died on July 30, 1985.

WORK

Julia Robinson's dissertation was written under the direction of Alfred Tarski. He characteristically suggested many problems in class and in conversation, and she pursued those that particularly interested her. Her dissertation contained several results, the most interesting of which will be discussed here.

It follows from the work of Gödel that there can be no algorithm for deciding which sentences of the arithmetic of natural numbers are true. The sentences referred to in this context are those using the concepts of elementary logic, variables, and the operations of addition and multiplication. Since the theorem of Lagrange that every natural number is the sum of four squares can be used as a definition of natural numbers in the ring of all integers, it follows that the arithmetic of integers is also undecidable. On the other hand, Tarski had previously shown that the arithmetic of real numbers is decidable. In all three of these cases the same sentences are used; only the range of the variables is different.

The question raised by Tarski was whether the arithmetic of the rational numbers is decidable or undecidable. If an arithmetical definition of the integers in the field of rational numbers could be given, the undecidability would be proved. Such a definition was given in Julia Robinson's thesis (1949).

The first breakthrough was the observation that if M is a rational number, expressed as a fraction in lowest terms, then the denominator of M is odd if and only if $7M^2 + 2$ can be expressed as a sum of three squares of rational numbers. This follows easily from the classical result that a natural number is the sum of three squares of integers if and only if it does not have the form $4^a (8b + 7)$.

This result led her to study the theory of quadratic forms. If one quadratic form could be used to eliminate the prime 2 from the denominator, perhaps other forms could be used to eliminate other prime factors. (If all prime factors could be eliminated from the denominator, the rational number would be an integer.) Other ternary quadratic forms were located which served this purpose. In the end the prime 2 was handled in a different way, in combination with other primes, so that the original observation does not appear in the dissertation.

There remained the problem of combining all the required conditions in one formula. It was impossible, in the language used, to describe the various quadratic forms which were needed. She resolved this difficulty by using a larger class of forms which could be described but which would not eliminate any integers.

In this way she used the theory of ternary quadratic forms in a successful attack on a problem of logic. In a later paper, she extended the result to fields of finite degree over the rationals ("The undecidability . . . '' 1959).

Her dissertation exemplifies the fact that her main field of interest lay on the borderline between logic and number theory; however, she wrote two papers completely outside of this field. One was a small paper on statistics (1948), written before her dissertation when she was working in the Berkeley Statistical Laboratory. The other was an important paper on game theory (1951), written when she was working at the RAND Corporation. This latter paper solved one of a list of problems for which RAND had offered monetary prizes (although as an employee she was not eligible for the prize).

George W. Brown had proposed a method of finding the value of a finite two-person zero-sum game, sometimes called the method of fictitious play. Two players are imagined as playing an infinite sequence of games, using in each game the pure strategy which would yield the optimal payoff against the accumulated mixed strategy of the opponent. Brown noted that the value of the game lay between these optimal payoffs for the two players and conjectured that they would converge to the value of the game as the number of plays increased. Julia's paper, "An iterative method of solving a game," verified Brown's conjecture. It is still considered a basic result in game theory.

Several of her papers played an essential role in the negative solution of Hilbert's Tenth Problem, which asked for an algorithm to decide whether a Diophantine equation has a solution. The first of these was "Existential definability in arithmetic" (1952). The problem studied was whether various sets are existentially definable in the arithmetic of natural numbers. The set of composite numbers is existentially definable, but at the time it was not known whether the set of primes is, as was later established. In this paper she proved that binomial coefficients, factorials, and the set of primes are existentially definable in terms of exponentiation, and that exponentiation in turn is existentially definable in terms of any function of roughly exponential growth.

At the time these results seemed somewhat fragmentary, but they took on added importance after the publication of a joint paper with Davis and Putnam (1961). In this paper it is proved that every recursively enumerable set is existentially definable in terms of exponentiation. It follows that there is no algorithm for deciding whether an exponential Diophantine equation (that is, a Diophantine equation in which exponentiation as well as addition and multiplication is allowed) has a solution in natural numbers. In view of her earlier proof that exponentiation is existentially definable in terms of any function of roughly exponential growth, the negative solution of Hilbert's Tenth Problem was reduced to finding an existential definition of such a function. That was finally done by Matijasevič at the beginning of 1970.

Later she collaborated with Matijasevič (1975) in proving that there is no algorithm for deciding whether a Diophantine equation in thirteen variables has a solution in natural numbers. (Matijasevič has since reduced the number of variables to nine.)

Among her other works are two papers dealing with general recursive functions (1950, 1968), as well as one on primitive recursive functions (1955) and one on recursively enumerable sets (1968). The 1950 paper on general recursive functions was her first paper after the dissertation. In it she starts from the characterization of general recursive functions as those obtained by adjoining the μ-rule to the rules used to obtain primitive recursive functions, and then asks what restrictions can be placed on the defining schemes. One result is the proof that all general recursive functions of one variable can be obtained from two special primitive recursive functions (one of which is rather complicated) by composition and inversion. In the later paper, she showed that this same class of functions can be obtained from the zero and successor functions by composition and a new scheme which she calls general recursion.

Other papers include one giving an expository treatment of the class of hyperarithmetical functions (1967) and one giving a finite set of axioms for number-theoretic functions from which the Peano axioms can be derived (1973).

Her Colloquium Lectures, delivered in 1980, have not been published. The first, which was introductory, discussed Gödel's work and the concept of computability. The second dealt with work related to Hilbert's Tenth Problem and included a new proof, due to Matijasevič, of the undecidability of exponential Diophantine equations. The third treated the decision problem for various rings and fields; and the fourth, nonstandard models of arithmetic.

BIBLIOGRAPHY

Works by Julia Bowman Robinson

Mathematical Works

"A note on exact sequential analysis." *University of California Publications in Mathematics* (N.S.) 1 (1948): 241–246.

"Definability and decision problems in arithmetic." *Journal of Symbolic Logic* 14 (1949): 98–114.

Doctoral Thesis.

"General recursive functions." *Proceedings of the American Mathematical Society* 1 (1950): 703–718.

"An iterative method of solving a game." *Annals of Mathematics* 54 (1951): 296–301.

"Existential definability in arithmetic." *Transactions of the American Mathematical Society* 72 (1952): 437–449.

"A note on primitive recursive functions." *Proceedings of the American Mathematical Society* 6 (1955): 667–670.

"The undecidability of algebraic rings and fields." *Proceedings of the American Mathematical Society* 10 (1959): 950–957.

"Problems of number theory arising in metamathematics." *Report of the Institute in the Theory of Numbers*, 303–306. Boulder, Colo.: 1959.

(with Martin Davis and Hilary Putnam) "The decision problem for exponential Diophantine equations." *Annals of Mathematics* 74 (1961): 425–436.

"On the decision problem for algebraic rings." In *Studies in Mathematical Analysis and Related Topics: Essays in Honor of George Polya*, edited by Gabor Szegö et al., 297–304. Stanford, Calif.: Stanford University Press, 1962.

"The undecidability of exponential Diophantine equations." In *Logic, Methodology, and Philosophy of Science: Proceedings of the 1960 International Congress*, edited by E. Nagel, P. Suppes, and A. Tarski, 12–13. New York: North-Holland, 1963.

"Definability and decision problems in rings and fields." In *The Theory of Models*, edited by J. W. Addison et al., 299–311. New York: North-Holland, 1965.

"An introduction to hyperarithmetical functions." *Journal of Symbolic Logic* 32 (1967): 325–342.

"Recursive functions of one variable." *Proceedings of the American Mathematical Society* 19 (1968): 815–820.

"Finite generation of recursively enumerable sets." *Proceedings of the American Mathematical Society* 19 (1968): 1480–1486.

"Diophantine decision problems." In *Studies in Number Theory*, MAA Studies in Mathematics, vol. 6 (1969), pp. 76–116.

"Finitely generated classes of sets of natural numbers." *Proceedings of the American Mathematical Society* 21 (1969): 608–614.

"Unsolvable Diophantine problems." *Proceedings of the American Mathematical Society* 22 (1969): 534–538.

"Hilbert's Tenth Problem." In *Proceedings of the 1969 Summer Institute on Number Theory . . .*, edited by Donald J. Lewis, 191–194. Proceedings of Symposium in Pure Mathematics, vol. 20. Providence, R.I.: American Mathematical Society, 1971.

"Solving Diophantine equations." *Proceedings of the Fourth International Congress for Logic, Methodology and Philosophy of Science*, edited by Patrick Suppes et al., 63–67. New York: North-Holland, 1973.

"Axioms for number theoretic functions." In *Selected Questions of Algebra and Logic*, edited by A. I. Shirshov et al., 253–263. Novosibirsk: Izdat. "Nauka" Sibirsk. Otdel., 1973.

(with Yuri Matijasevič) "Two universal three-quantifier representations of enumerable sets" (in Russian). *Theory of Algorithms, and Mathematical Logic* (in Russian), edited by B. A. Kushner and N. M. Nagornyi, 112–123, 216. Moscow: Vychisl. Centr Akad. Nauk SSSR, 1974.

(with Yuri Matijasevič) "Reduction of an arbitrary Diophantine equation to one in 13 unknowns." *Acta Arithmetica* 27 (1975): 521–553.

(with Martin Davis and Yuri Matijasevič) "Hilbert's 10th Problem. Diophantine equations: Positive aspects of a negative solution." In *Mathematical Developments Arising from Hilbert Problems*, edited by Felix F. Browder, 323–378 + loose erratum. Proceedings of Symposia in Pure Mathematics, vol. 28. Providence, R. I.: American Mathematical Society, 1976.

Works about Julia Bowman Robinson

Gaal, Lisl. "Julia Robinson's thesis." *Association for Women in Mathematics Newsletter* 16 (3) (May-June 1986): 6–8.

"Julia Bowman Robinson: 1919–1985." *Notices of the American Mathematical Society* 32 (1985): 739–742.

Obituary. *New York Times* (2 August 1985): D–15.

Reid, Constance. "The autobiography of Julia Robinson." *College Mathematics Journal* 17 (1986): 2–21.

Smoryński, C. "Julia Robinson, *In Memoriam*." *The Mathematical Intelligencer* 8 (2) (1986): 77–79.

MARY ELLEN RUDIN (1924–   )

Rosemary McCroskey Karr, Jaleh Rezaie,
and Joel E. Wilson

BIOGRAPHY

Mary Ellen (Estill) Rudin was born on December 7, 1924, in Hillsboro, Texas, the daughter of Joe Jefferson Estill and Irene (Shook) Estill. Rudin's father was born in Tennessee and grew up in a middle-class Presbyterian family. Her mother was born in Texas, likewise growing up in a middle-class family. Joe Estill pursued a career as a civil engineer, having earned a C.E. degree. Irene Estill, with a B.A. degree, became a high school English teacher. Rudin's single sibling, Joe Jefferson Estill, Jr., is ten years younger than she.

Upon completing her elementary and secondary education in the school system of a small Texas town, Rudin enrolled as a student at the University of Texas, where her interest in mathematics flourished. She has attributed the development of her career in mathematics to "a most unusual teacher" at the University of Texas, R. L. Moore, a research mathematician/teacher well known for his "Moore method" of teaching students to do research on their own. Rudin received a B.A. degree in 1944 and a Ph.D. in 1949, both from Texas. She then taught at Duke University until 1953.

Rudin married Walter Rudin, also a mathematician, on August 19, 1953. They are the parents of four children: Catherine (born 1954), Eleanor (1955), Robert Jefferson (1961), and Charles Michael (1964).

Rudin was a visiting assistant professor at the University of Rochester from 1953 to 1958. In 1959 she became a lecturer at the University of Wisconsin and held this position until 1971, when she was given professorial rank. Both she and her husband currently teach there.

Rudin has been a visitor at Yale University (1958), at the University of California at San Diego (1969), and at the University of Hawaii (1983).

WORK

Rudin has written about seventy research papers in topology, particularly in the construction of counterexamples. She is a respected authority on set-theoretic topology and published a book on the subject in 1975.

Rudin has displayed outstanding dedication and service to the profession as an educator and a mathematician. From 1969 to 1983, she supervised eleven Ph.D. students. She has held three research grants from the National Science Foundation. She has been affiliated with the Mathematical Association of America since 1950 as well as an active and influential member of the American Mathematical Society (AMS) since 1948, and belonged to the Association for Women in Mathematics and the Association for Symbolic Logic. She was vice-president of the AMS in 1980–1981.

Rudin has been a member of various national boards, including the Committee of the National Academy of Science for Eastern Europe, 1980–1983; National Committee for Mathematics of the Board of Mathematical Science of the National Research Council since 1983; and the editorial board of *Topology and Its Applications* since 1976.

In accordance with her expertise in set-theoretic topology, she has presented fourteen invited addresses at annual topology conferences, including being the principal lecturer at Colloquia Mathematica Topology in Hungary in 1972, and the Emmy Noether* Lecturer at the joint U.S. winter mathematics meeting in 1984.

Rudin has received two major awards: in 1963 the Prize of Nieuw Archief voor Wiskunde (Mathematical Society of the Netherlands); and in 1981 the Grace Chisholm Young* Professorship, which she still holds.

BIBLIOGRAPHY

Works by Mary Ellen Rudin

Space does not permit the listing of the complete works of Mary Ellen Rudin. The Author Cumulative Index volumes for *Mathematical Reviews* for 1940–1959, 1960–1964, 1965–1972, and 1973–1979 list more than fifty books and papers by her. Those below are works not listed there, including more recent ones, plus works cited in the essay.

Mathematical Works

"Concerning abstract spaces." Ph.D. diss., University of Texas at Austin, 1949.
Lectures on Set Theoretic Topology. Providence, R.I.: American Mathematical Society, 1975.
(with S. Shelah) "Unordered types of ultrafilters." *Topological Proceedings* 3 (1978): 199–204.
"Hereditary normality and Souslin lines." *General Topology and Its Applications* 10 (1979): 103–105.
"The undecidability of the existence of a perfectly normal nonmetrizable manifold." *Houston Journal of Mathematics* 5 (1979): 249–252.
"S & L spaces." In *Surveys in General Topology*, edited by George M. Reed, 431–444. New York: Academic, 1980.

"Directed sets which converge." In *General Topology and Modern Analysis*, edited by L. F. McAuley and M. M. Rao, 305–307. New York: Academic, 1981.

"A normal screenable nonparacompact space." *General Topology and Its Applications* 15 (1983): 313–322.

"The shrinking property." *Canadian Mathematical Bulletin* 26 (1983): 385–388.

"Collectionwise normality in screenable spaces." *Proceedings of the American Mathematical Society* 87 (1983): 347–350.

"Dowker's set theory question." *Questions and Answers in General Topology* 1 (1983): 75–76.

"Yasui's questions." *Questions and Answers in General Topology* 1 (1983): 122–127.

(with S. Watson) "Countable products of scattered paracompact spaces." *Proceedings of the American Mathematical Society* 89 (1983): 551–552.

"Dowker spaces." In *Handbook of Set-Theoretic Topology*, edited by K. Kunen and J. Vaughan, 761–780. New York: North Holland, 1984.

"Two problems of Dowker." *Proceedings of the American Mathematical Society* 91 (1984): 155–158.

"κ-Dowker spaces." In *Aspects of Topology, In Memory of Hugh Dowker (1912–1982)*, edited by I. M. James and E. H. Kronheimer, 175–193. New York: Cambridge University Press, 1985.

(with A. Beslagic) "Set-theoretic constructions of non-shrinking open covers." *Topology and Its Applications* 20 (1985): 167–177.

(with P. J. Collins et al.) "A lattice of conditions on topological spaces." *Proceedings of the American Mathematical Society* 94 (1985): 487–496.

(with K. Chiba and T. C. Przymusiniski) "Normality of products and Marita's conjectures." *Topology and Its Applications* 22 (1986): 19–32.

Other References

Rudin, M. E. Letter to authors (11 March 1985).

CHARLOTTE ANGAS SCOTT (1858–1931)

Patricia Clark Kenschaft

BIOGRAPHY

Charlotte Angas Scott was born on June 8, 1858, in Lincoln, England, the second of seven children of Caleb (1831–1919) and Eliza Exley Scott. The only extant information about her mother is references in her father's obituaries. They report that the marriage was "a source of profound happiness" to him and that she died in 1899 when he was on his way home from the United States, where he had attended the International Congregational Council and visited his "eldest daughter at Bryn Mawr" ("Ministers Deceased" 1919).

However, a great deal is known about Caleb and his father, Walter Scott (1779–1858), because they were both ministers of the Congregational Church and presidents of colleges training such ministers. Walter Scott was a hard-driving man who struggled for education of the working classes and against slavery and alcohol consumption. His eighth offspring, Caleb, had had three successful years in business and had obtained two degrees by the age of twenty-three. Since their religion was "Non-conformist," and Cambridge and Oxford Universities required a vow of loyalty to the Church of England, Walter and Caleb developed alternative sources of education for young men of their religion.

Since there were no colleges in England open to women while Charlotte Scott was growing up, and almost no secondary schools either, the support of her family and church was indispensable to her education. In a speech to newly elected deacons, Caleb admonished their wives, "Let the innocent tastes and tendencies of youth not be all repressed and stifled in the iron mould of any conventionalism" (Scott 1865). This was a man who encouraged his family to think and to enjoy life, and Scott's later writing indicates that mathematical games were part of their home entertainment. In 1865 Caleb became principal of the Lancashire Independent College (now called the Congregational College) and thus was able to provide good tutors for an ambitious daughter.

In 1876, at the age of eighteen, she won a scholarship on the basis of home tutoring to the recently opened Girton College. Most of her classmates had never attended a secondary school either. However, secondary schools for girls were springing up in England, so educated women suddenly had career opportunities as teachers. Thus there were eleven students, an unprecedented number, in Scott's entering class at Girton College, the first college in England for women. Life was austere. "When retiring for study after an extremely simple 'tea' in the Commons, they would pick up three things en route to their rooms . . . two candles, a bucket of coals, and a chamber pot" (Silver 1981).

Girton College had opened in 1869 with five students at a different location and in 1873 had moved to a modest three miles from Cambridge University, thereby enabling its students to attend the lectures of the twenty-two (out of thirty-four) Cambridge professors who were willing to let women listen to them. Such women had to be carefully chaperoned, because until 1894 Cambridge University maintained the "Spinning House," a special prison for prostitutes and "suspected prostitutes," where any unescorted woman would be summarily sent, her entire future thereby ruined. One student of the 1890s told her son-in-law that women attending lectures sat in the back behind a screen, obviously posing special problems to mathematics students (Silver 1981).

Any further instruction was from idealistic, or at least flexible, young tutors. Since the male Cambridge undergraduates received bachelor's degrees with honors by taking the Tripos examinations, the women wanted to pass these examinations too. Three of the first five students had done so in 1872, and songs in the memory of these "Girton Pioneers" were sung during the long dark winter evenings of Scott's student days.

Women would not receive degrees at Cambridge until 1948, but every year after 1872 women applied to take the Tripos exams, and some were given special permission to do so. On nine bitterly cold days in January 1880, Charlotte Scott spent over fifty hours taking the mathematics Tripos. When word leaked out that she had done as well as the eighth man in the entire university, the news permeated England that a woman had succeeded in a "man's" subject.

Because she was female, she could not be present at the award ceremony, nor could her name be officially mentioned. However, a contemporary report says, "The man read out the names and when he came to 'eighth,' before he could say the name, all the undergraduates called out 'Scott of Girton,' and cheered tremendously, shouting her name over and over again with tremendous cheers and waving of hats." The young men of Cambridge gave honor where it was due, even though their elders followed the established rules. At Girton College there were cheers and clapping at dinner, and a special evening ceremony where she was led up an "avenue of students" while they sang "See the Conquering Hero Comes." She stood on "a sort of dais" while an ode written by a staff member was read to her, and then she was crowned with laurels, "while we clapped and applauded with all our might" (Megson and Lindsay 1961, 31).

In 1922 James Harkness, who was only a schoolboy in 1880, remembered that Scott's achievement impressed even him at the time, its widespread impact marking "the turning point in England from the theoretical feminism of Mill and others to the practical education and political advances of the present time" (Putnam 1922). The publicity resulted in pressure on Cambridge University to admit its resident female students to university examinations as a matter of policy, not just special privilege, and to post their names with those of the male students, an important step toward qualifying for jobs. After a year of controversy, this resolution was passed on February 24, 1881. Its national implications are reflected by the fact that at the newly opened college for women at Oxford, the news was proclaimed loudly in the dining room, "We have won! We have won!" (Bradbrook 1969, 55).

Arthur Cayley, a renowned algebraist, was one of those leading the effort for this recognition of women's education, and for the rest of his life, Scott was the recipient of "his kindness" (Scott 1895). She attended his lectures, did her graduate research under him, and obtained her first and only position outside Girton College on the basis of his recommendation. Meanwhile, she was hired as a resident lecturer by Girton College and taught there until receiving her doctorate in 1885.

Although by Scott's time Cambridge University no longer required an oath of allegiance to the Church of England, it would not grant her a degree, because of her sex. Fortunately, the University of London began granting "external" degrees to women in 1876, so Scott took two entirely different sets of examinations from two universities, one to place her with her peers, and the other to obtain degrees. She thus received a B.Sc. in 1882 and a D.Sc. in 1885 from the University of London, both "First Class," the highest possible rank.

Bryn Mawr College, which opened in Pennsylvania in 1885, was dedicated to providing both undergraduate and graduate education of the highest level to women. Since comparable positions for women were virtually nonexistent in Europe, Scott went to Bryn Mawr, becoming its first mathematics department head and the only mathematician on its founding faculty of eight. There was one other woman, a biologist. There were no better options in the world for a woman mathematician during the next forty years, so Scott remained there.

Occasionally her father or brother Walter visited her at Bryn Mawr. Her older sister, with whom she had grown up, died the spring before Scott left for Girton College, and her youngest sister died as an infant; so in her adulthood she was the oldest of five siblings, with two younger brothers and two younger sisters. Her will also mentions her "beloved" sister-in-law, Walter's widow. Walter, who was in the machinery business, died suddenly in Scott's home on August 7, 1918, a great blow to her. One of her sisters worked for a while in an orphanage and then married. The other remained home and cared for her father, Caleb, in his old age. The family was a close and loving one; surviving relatives remember with affection "Auntie Charley [pronounced 'Sharly']."

The early Girton College community had strictly observed the social mores of the time. The existence of the Spinning House left little margin for experimentation, and the prevailing opinion was that personal conservatism was required to promote women's educational and political equality. Charlotte Scott maintained this view throughout her life, disapproving of smoking and makeup, but her disapproval extended equally to both sexes. She bobbed her hair before arriving at Bryn Mawr in 1885, although short hair for women was still controversial in the 1920s. She had at least one close male friend outside her family, Frank Morley, whose time studying mathematics at Cambridge University overlapped hers. He told his son that the social conventions made it more acceptable for her to visit him and his family in Baltimore than for him to visit her, and she did so often.

Scott's relationship with M. Carey Thomas, the first dean of Bryn Mawr College and its president from 1894 to 1922, was always formal, despite the fact that Scott was only one year younger. Thomas had become the first American woman to earn a doctorate in any field (linguistics), in 1882 at the University of Zurich, and had visited Girton College on her way home. A biographer of Thomas says that Scott was hurt by her initial coldness after Scott's lonely trip across the ocean (Finch 1947, 194). Thomas had the impatience of many dynamic reformers, and her correspondence with Scott also includes a confession that mathematics had always been her most difficult subject, suggesting a special tension because of this. In 1906 Scott wrote a letter apparently in response to Thomas's desire to know when a certain student would finish her Ph.D. Patiently she explained, "If it were simply a matter of surveying the field, collating papers and stating the contents clearly, she could do the thesis before June certainly; but to produce an original piece of work is quite another matter . . . '' (Scott Papers). Thomas's lack of knowledge about mathematics is also reflected in much earlier correspondence about the necessity of mathematics journals for the library; Scott was always fighting for her discipline on her home turf.

During Scott's first three years at Bryn Mawr, there was a total of only four serious mathematics students—three undergraduates and one ''graduate'' student who had studied nothing higher than differential equations before she came. Scott worked intensely, writing her lecture notes ''*after*, not before, the lecture . . . at the end of a busy day . . . word perfect . . . knowing that at nine a.m. tomorrow [she would give another lecture]. . . . But the next delivery showed no lack of spontaneity for changes and improvement were made until the notes could be, and as a matter of fact were, used as text-book material'' (Maddison and Lehr 1932). Gradually her classes grew larger, and by her ninth year there were six new mathematics students, two undergraduates and four graduates, including her first two successful doctoral candidates. Indeed, three of the nine American women to earn doctorates in mathematics in the nineteenth century studied with her. Her professional correspondence shows her intense involvement with each student, arguing against the doctoral candidacy of one who demonstrated ''everything except that one essential, capacity'' for doctoral work, and for one who has been discovered to have tuberculosis but has already published good work. She pleads on behalf of a student who inadvertently left a notebook in an examination room, and against those sitting on a fire escape to eavesdrop on a faculty meeting. Former students remembered her kindness and her ability to help them solve their problems.

Her Girton propriety and calm exterior slipped on January 12, 1898, when she wrote to President Thomas:

I am most disturbed and disappointed at present to find you taking the position that intellectual pursuits must be "watered down" to make them suitable for women, and that a lower standard must be adopted in a woman's college than in a man's. I do not expect any of the other members of the faculty to feel this way about it; they, like (nearly) all men that I have known, doubtless take an attitude of toleration, half amused and half kindly, on the whole question; for even where men are willing to help in women's education, it is with an inward reserve of condescension. (Scott Papers)

The word "nearly" is inserted in small lettering above the handwritten letter. It is indeed unfortunate that Scott's entire correspondence with her family has apparently been lost.

Thomas wrote to her niece in 1932 that "in my generation marriage and an academic career was impossible" (Dobkin 1979, xv), and this fact was basic to Scott's life too. She wanted to build her own house but was unable to find a suitable plot, so in 1894 she moved from a small apartment on the Bryn Mawr campus to a house rented from the college. Her cousin Eliza Nevins joined her to become her companion and housekeeper until Nevins's death in 1928. Others, including an early doctoral student, lived with them occasionally. Scott was a leader among the tenants in campaigning for such mundane matters as access to direct paths and more effective heating of the homes. On February 27, 1901, her own house caught fire; the house was saved, but Scott could not live in it for months afterward.

An even more serious disruption occurred in the spring of 1906, when she developed an acute case of rheumatoid arthritis. After that her ill health and her increasing deafness, which was apparent even in her Girton College days and was complete by the time anyone now living knew her, marred her life significantly. Her publications ceased for two decades, and the doctor recommended outside exercise. Gardening was compatible with her academic duties; and her garden was "brought, year after year, unbelievably, to greater beauty" (Maddison and Lehr 1932). She developed a new strain of chrysanthemum. Her correspondence reveals the zest with which she continued to live. "I am not a Vandal, as you know; but this tree is not good, it simply encourages visitors of objectionable kinds, beginning with scab and continuing accordingly, and any miserable little apples that it does produce are infected with maggots. My wish is to cut it down and dig it up, and then plant a less troublesome tree a few feet away, so as not to spoil the appearance of the slope" (Scott Papers).

Scott maintained her church membership in England for at least a decade after she came to the United States. American mathematicians joked about her leaving for Europe every spring as soon as exams were marked, but this was not literally true. Still, she crossed the Atlantic Ocean often, at a time when each voyage involved at least a week of discomfort and danger. She thus provided an invaluable link between the fledgling mathematical community of the United States and the established centers in Europe.

Scott officially retired in 1924 but remained an extra year at Bryn Mawr to help her seventh and last doctoral graduate complete her dissertation. Then she moved to a large house on the bus line halfway between Girton College and the center of Cambridge University. Her complete deafness made social interactions difficult, even with her next door neighbor, who also happened to be a retired mathematician. Her primary diversion was betting on horses, an activity to which she applied mathematical statistics. Her doctor, who had introduced her to his own bookie, Mr. Cook, believed that she neither gained nor lost much money. However, he was amused how her Victorian outlook affected her view of Cook. One Christmas when he visited her home, she was extremely agitated. "Dr. Nourse, I am very worried. Do you see that umbrella in the corner? That has been sent to me by Mr. Cook. Of course I couldn't accept it!" The doctor explained that the bookie sent umbrellas to all his women clients and purses to the men and would feel hurt if the presents were returned. "Do you really think I can keep it?" Scott replied, obviously relieved that the umbrella was not an indication of moral turpitude.

On November 10, 1931, she died quietly in Cambridge. She was buried with Miss Nevins in St. Peter's part of the St. Giles's Churchyard in Cambridge near the northwest corner of the chapel. The inscription on a small stone gives only her date of death and age and no indication of her place in the history of mathematics.

Although she seems almost forgotten today, Scott received many honors in her lifetime. Rebière, writing in Paris in 1897, called Scott "one of the best living mathematicians" with no apparent need to justify its claim. She was the only woman starred in the first edition of *American Men of Science* (i.e. considered prominent in mathematics by her contemporaries) and the only mathematician included in *Notable American Women, 1607–1950*.

Her honors at Cambridge in 1880 were informal because she was female, but they had a lasting impact on women everywhere. Later honors by academic institutions were official. She was the chief examiner in mathematics of the College Entrance Examination Board in 1902 and 1903. In 1909 the alumnae of Bryn Mawr honored her with the college's first endowed chair. When she retired, the board of directors of Bryn Mawr College cited her contribution to the college in its first forty years as "second only to that of President Thomas."

On April 18, 1922, the American Mathematical Society met at Bryn Mawr, and about 200 people gathered in her honor. Alfred North Whitehead gave the featured talk on "Some principles of physical science." Although it was his first trip across the Atlantic Ocean, he refused invitations from Harvard and Columbia universities because he did not want competing attractions in Scott's "neighborhood." At the end of his talk Whitehead observed, "A friendship of peoples is the outcome of personal relations. A life's work such as that of Professor Charlotte Angas Scott is worth more to the world than many anxious efforts of diplomatists. She is a great example of the universal brotherhood of civilizations" (Putnam 1922).

WORK

When the New York Mathematical Society opened its membership to people outside New York, Scott immediately responded, and she was one of the major organizers who developed the group into the American Mathematical Society (AMS) in 1891. She served on its council from 1891 to 1894 and again from 1899 to 1902, and was its vice-president in 1905–1906. When Thomas Fiske gave an anniversary talk in 1938 reviewing the first fifty years of the society, he cited the work of about thirty people, of whom Scott was the only woman.

She brought experience as a member of established European societies, including the London Mathematical Society, the Edinburgh Mathematical Society, the Deutsche Mathematiker-Vereinigung, the Circolo Matematico di Palermo, and as an "honorary member" of the Amsterdam Mathematical Society. She was one of only seventeen Americans who attended the World Congress of Mathematicians in 1900, and she wrote an extensive report of it for the *Bulletin* of the AMS. Since Scott's field (algebraic geometry) was the same as that of both the father and the future dissertation advisor of Emmy Noether*, both of whom attended the congress and must have conferred with Scott there, perhaps it is not coincidence that Emmy Noether switched fields that summer from languages (more common for young women) to mathematics (still largely male-dominated).

In 1899 Scott became coeditor of the eminent *American Journal of Mathematics*, an influential position she held for twenty-seven years. Her own papers were published not only in American journals, but also in the more competitive European publications, where American mathematicians appeared extremely rarely.

Her book, *An Introductory Account of Certain Modern Ideas and Methods in Plane Analytical Geometry*, was published in 1894 and reprinted, essentially without change, thirty years later. Although its title includes the word "introductory," and it was indeed used by many beginners, it took its readers to the edges of research. It was used widely. Cole's review (1896) praised its inclusion of such recent concepts as groups, subgroups, invariants, and covariants. However, even more far-reaching than its subject matter was its obvious "distinction between a general principle and a particular example." Scott was one of the first textbook writers, especially those writing in English, to be "perfectly aware" of this distinction and to teach it to the next generations of college mathematics students. Her other book, a "school" book about plane geometry, was not well received, because she based her development on lines instead of points, an innovation that was not widely adopted.

F. S. Macaulay's obituary of her summarized, "Miss Scott was a geometer who whenever possible brought to analytical geometry the full resources of pure geometrical reasoning" (1932, 232). Her published research, like most mathematical writing of her time, consisted of discussions of various specific mathematical phenomena. Her specialty was the geometric interpretations of algebraic expressions in two variables of degree greater than two, that is, of plane curves neither linear nor quadratic. However, she had a keener sense of the difference between example and proof than most of her contemporaries, playing an important role in the transition to the twentieth-century custom of presenting mathematics via abstract proofs. Her most notable paper may be her 1899 "geometric" proof of a theorem of Max Noether, Emmy Noether's father. Unfortunately for Scott's fame, her particular field fell out of fashion in the twentieth century.

She was hired by Bryn Mawr College to be department head, to teach ten or eleven hours a week of both graduate and undergraduate courses, and to supervise graduate research. Although her written offer in 1884 said that her hours of teaching would be diminished as her other duties grew, they were still at their original level thirty years later. Committees also absorbed much time. "She would . . . sit through a long meeting . . . and at just the right moment make a brief, incisive speech which—such was the respect with which her opinion was regarded—often turned the vote from the direction in which it was tending to the side which she supported."

Her impact on mathematics education in the United States was enormous. Although Harvard University had dropped its requirements that all freshmen take a course in addition, subtraction, and multiplication only fifty years earlier, her initial requirements for students entering Bryn Mawr College included passing examinations in arithmetic, plane geometry, and algebra through quadratic equations and geometric progressions. Students who did not pass admission examinations in solid geometry and trigonometry had to pass courses in these subjects before graduation. Mathematics majors were required to take one semester of algebra and the theory of equations, a year of differential and integral calculus, and a semester of differential equations and elements of finite differences. Early Bryn Mawr students took another sequence concurrently in "analytical geometry," one year in two dimensions and another in three.

During her early years at Bryn Mawr, she was distressed at the amount of time she spent writing and grading entrance examinations, so she worked for a nationwide testing service. The College Entrance Examination Board began in 1901, and she was its chief examiner in mathematics in 1902 and 1903, setting standards that have changed little in over eighty years, although, ironically, the name of their promulgator is rarely mentioned.

Scott was a special inspiration to women, who received three times the percentage of American Ph.D.'s in mathematics before 1940 that they did in the 1950s. She herself was the dissertation advisor of seven women, and Bryn Mawr conferred two other Ph.D.'s in mathematics while she was department head. During this time Bryn Mawr College was third only to the University of Chicago and Cornell University, both much larger institutions, in the number of doctorates in mathematics granted to women in mathematics. When she had delivered her talk to the AMS in 1905, nine of the forty-five listeners were women, only two of whom were from Bryn Mawr. It is difficult to measure influence by numbers, but her visibility, her conversations, and her preparation of many women to teach younger women clearly had a major impact on the academic and economic position of women in America.

BIBLIOGRAPHY

Works by Charlotte Angas Scott

Mathematical Works

"The binomial equation $x^p - 1 = 0$." *American Journal of Mathematics* 8 (1886): 261–264.

"On the higher singularities of plane curves." *American Journal of Mathematics* 14 (1892): 301–325.

"The nature and effect of singularities of plane algebraic curves." *American Journal of Mathematics* 15 (1893): 221–243.

"On plane cubics." *Philosophical Transactions of the Royal Society of London* 185(A) (1894): 247–277.

An Introductory Account of Certain Modern Ideas and Methods in Plane Analytical Geometry. London and New York: Macmillan, 1894. 2nd ed. New York: G. E. Stechert, 1924. 3rd ed. under the title *Projective Methods in Plane Analytical Geometry.* New York: Chelsea, 1961.
    Review: F. N. Cole. *Bulletin of the American Mathematical Society* 2 (1896): 265–269.

"Arthur Cayley." *Bulletin of the American Mathematical Society* 1 (1895): 133–141.

"Note on adjoint curves." *Quarterly Journal of Pure and Applied Mathematics* 28 (1896): 377–381.

"Note on equianharmonic cubics." *Messenger of Mathematics* 25 (1896): 180–185.

"Sur la transformation des courbes planes." *Comptes rendus de l'Association Française, pour l'Avancement des Sciences (Congrès de St. Étienne)* (26) (1897): 50–59.

"On Cayley's theory of the absolute." *Bulletin of the American Mathematical Society* 3 (1897): 235–246.

"Studies in the transformation of plane algebraic curves." Parts I, II. *Quarterly Journal of Pure and Applied Mathematics* 29 (1898): 329–381; 32 (1901): 209–239.

"Note on linear systems of curves." *Nieuw Archief voor Wiskunde* (2) 3 (1898): 243–252.

"On the intersections of plane curves." *Bulletin of the American Mathematical Society* 4 (1898): 260–273.

"A proof of Noether's fundamental theorem." *Mathematische Annalen* 52 (1899): 592–597.

"The status of imaginaries in pure geometry." *Bulletin of the American Mathematical Society* 6 (1900): 163–168.

"On von Staudt's Geometrie der Lage." *Mathematical Gazette* 1 (1900): 307–314, 323–331, 363–370.

"On a memoir by Riccardo de Paolis." *Bulletin of the American Mathematical Society* 7 (1900): 24–38.

"Report on the International Congress of Mathematicians in Paris." *Bulletin of the American Mathematical Society* 7 (1900): 57–79. Excerpts printed in *The Mathematical Intelligencer* 7 (4) (1985): 75–78.

"Note on the geometrical treatment of conics." *Annals of Mathematics* (2) 2 (1901): 64–72.

"On a recent method for dealing with the intersections of plane curves." *Transactions of the American Mathematical Society* 3 (1902): 216–263. Reprinted as a Bryn Mawr College Monograph, vol. 4, no. 2.

"On the circuits of plane curves." *Transactions of the American Mathematical Society* 3 (1902): 388–398. Reprinted as a Bryn Mawr College Monograph, vol. 4, no. 3.

"Note on the real inflexions of plane curves." *Transactions of the American Mathematical Society* 3 (1902): 399–400. Reprinted as a Bryn Mawr College Monograph, vol. 4, no. 4.

"Elementary treatment of conics by means of the regulus." *Bulletin of the American Mathematical Society* 12 (1905): 1–7. Reprinted as a Bryn Mawr Monograph, vol. 8, no. 3.

"Note on regular polygons." *Annals of Mathematics* 8 (1906): 127–134. Reprinted as a Bryn Mawr College Monograph, vol. 8, no. 8.

Cartesian Plane Geometry. Part I: Analytical Conics. London: J. M. Dent and Company, 1907.

"Higher singularities of plane algebraic curves." *Proceedings of the Cambridge Philosophical Society* 23 (1926): 206–232.

Scott's name appears in the list of contributors to problem-solving in the *Educational Times* until 1892.

Works about Charlotte Angas Scott

Bradbrook, M. C. *"That Infidel Place": A Short History of Girton College, 1869–1969.* London: Chatto & Windus, 1969.

Dobkin, Marjorie Housepain. *The Making of a Feminist; Early Journals and Letters of M. Carey Thomas.* Kent, Ohio: Kent State University Press, 1979.

Finch, Edith. *Carey Thomas of Bryn Mawr.* New York: Harper, 1947.

Jones, E. E. Constance. *Girton College.* London: Adam and Charles Black, 1913.

Katz, Kaila, and Patricia Kenschaft. "Sylvester and Scott." *The Mathematics Teacher* 75 (1982): 490–494.

Kenschaft, Patricia C. "Charlotte Angus [*sic*] Scott 1858–1931." *Association for Women in Mathematics Newsletter* 7 (6) (November-December 1977): 9–10; 8 (1) (April 1978): 11–12.

———. "The students of Charlotte Angas Scott." *Mathematics in College* (Fall 1982): 16–20.

Biographies of four of Scott's outstanding students.

————. "Women in mathematics around 1900." *Signs* 7 (4) (Summer 1982): 906–909.
Compares the participation of women in the United States research mathematical community in the era of Charlotte Scott to that of recent years and indicates that the modern feminist movement has just barely regained the position that women had at the turn of this century.

Lehr, Marguerite. "Charlotte Angas Scott." *Notable American Women, 1607–1950*, vol. 3, 249–250. Cambridge, Mass.: Belknap Press of Harvard University Press, 1971.

Macaulay, F. S. "Dr. Charlotte Angas Scott." *Journal of the London Mathematical Society* 7 (1932): 230–240.
Summary of Scott's research achievements written by a contemporary in her field.

Maddison, Isabel, and Marguerite Lehr. "Charlotte Angas Scott: An Appreciation." *Bryn Mawr Alumni Bulletin* 12 (1932): 9–12.
This article in two parts (one by each author) is probably the most personal published piece written by people who knew Scott. Maddison was one of her doctoral graduates who spent her career on the Bryn Mawr campus and lived with Scott for a while. Lehr was her last doctoral graduate, who also taught at Bryn Mawr for forty years.

Megson, Barbara, and Jean Olivia Lindsay. *Girton College, 1869–1959, An Informal History*. London: W. Heffer, 1961.

"Ministers Deceased: Dr. Caleb Scott." *Manchester Guardian* (23 July 1919).

Putnam, Emily James. "Celebration in honor of Professor Scott." *Bryn Mawr Bulletin* 2 (1922): 12–14.

Rebière, A. *Les Femmes dans la Science*. 2nd ed. Paris: Nony, 1897.

Scott, Caleb. "An Address to the newly elected deacons." Delivered March 15, 1865.
Unpublished records in the Lincoln Public Library, Lincoln, England.

Scott, Charlotte A. Papers. Bryn Mawr College Archives, Bryn Mawr, Pa.

Silver, John. Letter to author, March 29, 1981.

Thomas, M. Carey. Papers. Bryn Mawr College Archives, Bryn Mawr, Pa.

MARY EMILY SINCLAIR (1878–1955)

Laurel G. Sherman

BIOGRAPHY

Mary Emily Sinclair was the daughter of John Elbridge Sinclair and Marietta S. Fletcher Sinclair; she was born in Worcester, Massachusetts, where her father was professor of mathematics at Worcester Polytechnic Institute. It appears that her family encouraged scholarship, as each of the three daughters, Mary Emily and her two sisters, Helen and Alice, attended college. Helen graduated from Mount Holyoke in 1902, having attended Oberlin College in 1899–1900. Alice graduated from Oberlin in 1899, one year before Sinclair.

Sinclair, the middle daughter, attended the Worcester public schools until she left for Oberlin College in 1896. She graduated from Oberlin in 1900, a member of Phi Beta Kappa and of Sigma Xi. She then went to the University of Chicago, where she completed the M.A. degree in 1903 and the Ph.D. in 1908. It was in Chicago that her interest in the calculus of variations developed, under the influence of Oscar Bolza.

Her years of graduate study were punctuated by periods of teaching. She taught mathematics at Woodside Seminary in Hartford, Connecticut, 1900–1901, and taught in Painesville, Ohio, in the spring of 1903. For three years (1904–1907), she was an instructor in the department of mathematics at the University of Nebraska at Lincoln while she worked on her Ph.D. dissertation.

She became instructor of mathematics at Oberlin College in 1907 and was promoted to associate professor once her dissertation was completed in 1908. Her first courses at Oberlin included geometry (solid and spherical), plane analytic geometry, college algebra, trigonometry, theory of equations, history of mathematics, geometry of position, and projective geometry.

The young, single teacher did a rather startling thing in 1914. She adopted an infant daughter, Margaret Emily. The next year she adopted a son, naming him Richard Elbridge. One of her students, Gertrude Jacobs, remembers how astonished she was to meet the family of "*Miss* Sinclair." Sinclair cared for these children by herself.

Sinclair was promoted to full professor in 1925 and was made head of the mathematics department in 1939, a position she held until her retirement in 1944. She was appointed Clark Professor of Mathematics in 1941.

Her terms at Oberlin were separated by periods away. Many of her summers were spent in New England, frequently in Worcester. Her first sabbatical leave came in 1914–1915, a year that coincided with her adoptions, and she studied at Columbia and Johns Hopkins.

In 1922–1923 Sinclair was the recipient of a Julia C. G. Piatt Fellowship from the American Association of University Women. She traveled with her young family to the University of Chicago and to Cornell University. It was a very productive year, with papers presented at meetings of the American Mathematical Society. "I look back on the year I held my AAUW Fellowship as the best period of creative scholarship in my life" (Sinclair 1956).

In 1925–1926 she used her sabbatical leave from Oberlin to study at the University of Rome and at the Sorbonne. The 1927–1928 year was spent teaching at the University of Miami, a leave from Oberlin taken for the sake of the health of twelve-year-old Margaret. Her next leave was at the Institute for Advanced Study in the spring of 1935.

The 1930s were a difficult time at many colleges and universities; and her faculty file shows that from 1932, when her salary was $5,000, to 1936, all faculty salaries were reduced by 11–18%.

Her teaching at Oberlin included a great deal of hospitality and good advice. She was particularly interested in encouraging women mathematicians; in 1927 she endowed a vocational loan fund of $1,000, in memory of her father, for the use of Oberlin alumnae.

Her last sabbatical leave was in the spring of 1942. After her retirement, she taught part-time at Berea College in Kentucky. She returned to Oberlin in 1947 and remained there with frequent visits to her daughter in Brackenridge, Pennsylvania. In a letter written at this time concerning her will, she remarks that $5,000 is to go to Oberlin College and the rest to be divided between her daughter and the college.

One violent event marked the last years of her life. In May 1950 she drove a young black man home from town. Newspaper accounts differ as to whether she offered the man a ride or whether he forced her to drive him. Giving her a fictitious address, he waited until she was on a deserted lane, beat the seventy-two-year-old woman until she was unconscious, and dragged her from the car. The seventeen-year-old youth, Charles Smith, took her car and drove to a dance in a town thirty-five miles away. He also took her pocketbook.

She was discovered by a neighbor and taken to the local hospital to be treated for a fractured skull, compound nose fracture, broken bones in her right hand, and cuts and bruises to the head and arms. Sinclair slipped into a coma in the hospital and was thought to be so close to death that Oberlin College sent her biography to the *Cleveland Plain Dealer*.

It was alleged that the young man had asked her to lend him her car so that he could attend the out-of-town dance. When she refused, he decided to simply take the car. He was apprehended the next day and eventually sentenced to ten to twenty years in prison.

In 1953 she finally left Oberlin, buying a house with her daughter-in-law Myrtle, and settling in Belfast, Maine, where she died two years later.

WORK

The calculus of variations has roots in the partial solution of the problem of the curve of quickest descent, the brachistochrone, devised by Johann Bernoulli in the seventeenth century. Advances on a general theory were made by Joseph Louis Lagrange and Leonhard Euler in the eighteenth century and by Carl Gustav Jacob Jacobi and others in the nineteenth century. But it was Karl Weierstrass in the late nineteenth century who first noticed that the whole class of problems, of which the brachistochrone is a special case, still contained a flaw. His general theory eliminated the flaw and put the calculus of variations on a firm footing.

Sinclair's work came soon after Weierstrass and was influenced by the interest in these problems at the University of Chicago in the first decade of the twentieth century. All of her published work concerned curves that would generate the surface of revolution of minimum area.

In her thesis she deals with a special aspect of the surface of revolution of minimum area that the general theory of Weierstrass did not cover. She proceeded to fill a gap in the general theory, thus covering her special case. She pointed out that a surface of revolution of minimum area would result if the two endpoints were not too far apart. However, in some cases, when the points were too far apart, there was no smooth curve solution to the problem; and the minimum became, instead, the sum of the areas of the two circles formed by rotating each point around the axis. This is the Goldschmidt discontinuous solution.

Her work on catenaries extended through her papers of the 1920s. She discusses the surface of revolution of minimum area for curves defined by two points, by a fixed point and some point on a generalized curve, by two fixed points and some point on a line perpendicular to the x-axis, and by endpoints variable on curves in a plane.

Always interested in the physical applications of her work, she refers to the work of Joseph Plateau, who used liquid films to demonstrate minimum surfaces. She also conducted and described experiments of her own to show the minimum stable surface formed by a film suspended between two concentric rings at various separations and of varying diameters.

BIBLIOGRAPHY

Works by Mary Emily Sinclair

Mathematical Works

"Minimum surface of revolution in the case of one variable end point." *Annals of Mathematics* 8 (1906/1907): 177–188.

"Absolute minimum in the problem of the surface of revolution of minimum area."
Annals of Mathematics 9 (1907/1908): 151–155.

"Concerning a compound discontinuous solution in the problem of the surface of revolution of minimum area." *Annals of Mathematics* 10 (1908/1909): 55–80.
Doctoral thesis.

"The discriminantal surface for the quintic in the normal form, $u^5 + 10\,xu^3 + 5yu + \leq\ = 0$." Halle, Germany: Martin Schilling, n.d.
Master's thesis

Works about Mary Emily Sinclair

Maltby, Margaret. "Mary Emily Sinclair." In *History of the Fellowships Awarded by the American Association of University Women: 1888–1929*, 65–66. Washington, D.C.: AAUW, 1930.

"Mary Emily Sinclair." *Oberlin Alumni Magazine* 28 (May 1932): 239.
Short notice and photo.

"Mary Emily Sinclair." *Oberlin Alumni Magazine* 51 (October 1955): 21.
Obituary notice.

Parmenter, Ella C. "Oberlinian of the month." *Oberlin Alumni Magazine* 40 (June 1944): 4–5.

Sinclair, Mary Emily. "If the good luck had not come to me . . . " *Journal of the American Association of University Women* (March 1956): back cover.
A brief reminiscence of her year as an AAUW fellow, 1922–1923.

MARY FAIRFAX GREIG SOMERVILLE (1780–1872)

Elizabeth Chambers Patterson

BIOGRAPHY

Mary Fairfax Greig Somerville was born on December 26, 1780, at the manse in Jedburgh (Roxburghshire), Scotland, the home of a maternal aunt who later became her mother-in-law as well. Her mother, Margaret Charters Fairfax, was returning to Edinburgh from London when she went into labor at Jedburgh; she had gone south to bid farewell to her husband, Lt. William George Fairfax of the Royal Navy, before he departed for a long tour of sea duty.

The family lived frugally in Burntisland. The father was frequently absent at sea, and the mother—a conventional, easy-going woman—reared the children simply and lovingly. Three of the seven Fairfax children died in infancy. Samuel (1777–1798) died in India; Margaret (1787–1805) was killed in a carriage accident; and Henry (1790–1860) became an army officer and was created baronet in 1836.

Among well-born Scots of the period, it was customary to give sons good educations to fit them for the kirk, law, medicine, or service in the East India Company; while daughters had a minimum of book learning, just enough to read the Bible, write social notes, and keep household accounts. Female tuition emphasized domestic skills and social graces. Fairfax, returning home from sea when young Mary was around nine, was shocked, she later reported, to find her "such a savage," reading very badly, unable to write, and knowing nothing of arithmetic. Despite his strong Tory distaste for girls' boarding schools, he sent her, at age ten, to an expensive and exclusive academy, Miss Primrose's at Musselburgh.

There she remained for a year, badly and tediously taught, and often miserably unhappy, but acquiring the first principles of writing, rudiments of French and English grammar, and a taste for learning. This stay was her only full-time formal schooling.

On her return to Burntisland, she resumed her active outdoor life, wandering freely over links, hills, and seashore, closely observing fauna and flora. She learned plain needlework at the village school and had lessons on the celestial and terrestrial globes from the village schoolmaster. Her mother did not prevent her reading Shakespeare and the few other available books, although some of her female relations disapproved.

When she was about thirteen, the Fairfax family began to rent an apartment in Edinburgh for the winter months. In the Scottish capital, young Mary attended a writing school (where she also did arithmetic), took lessons on the pianoforte and in fine cookery, went to dancing school, and learned to draw and paint skillfully. At Burntisland she taught herself enough Latin to read Caesar's *Commentaries* and enough Greek to read Xenophon and parts of Herodotus.

One day she chanced to see some strange symbols in a ladies' fashion monthly. At the time, riddles, puzzles, and simple mathematical problems were popular features in such publications. The symbols aroused her curiosity, but no one in her acquaintance could tell her more than that they were a kind of arithmetic called "algebra." Since a young lady of her station could not properly ask for a mathematical volume in an Edinburgh bookshop, she persuaded her younger brother's tutor to buy her copies of Bonnycastle's *Algebra* and Euclid's *Elements*, books used in the schools of the day. When her father discovered her reading them, he instantly forbade it, fearing the bad effects of such abstruse study on the delicate female frame. His view was widely and long held; Mary Somerville herself years later suggested that her own encouragement of her eldest daughter's intellectual precocity had been a factor in the child's early death, at age nine.

Despite her father's strictures, however, young Mary secretly and intermittently continued reading mathematics. Her days were filled with the activities of an Edinburgh belle—balls, parties, concerts, the opera, the theatre, and visits. The Scottish capital at the turn of the century was at a high point of its cultural, intellectual, and social history. She thoroughly enjoyed her life there and was a popular member of its younger society.

In 1804 she married a cousin, Captain Samuel Greig of the Russian navy. After their marriage Greig took his bride to London, where he was stationed as Russian consul and commissioner of the Russian navy. She knew few people in the metropolis and found her new life strange and lonely. Her husband had little sympathy with female learning but did not interfere when she began French lessons and resumed her mathematical studies. Two sons were born: Woronzow (1805–1865) and William George (1806–1814). Greig died in 1807, and his widow and her two infants returned to Scotland.

With the new independence conferred by widowhood and a modestly comfortable inheritance, she began openly to study mathematics. She read Newton's *Principia* and began to investigate physical astronomy and higher mathematics. Several of her relatives—especially female relatives—and acquaintances loudly disapproved, but she found encouragement among Edinburgh intellectuals. The mathematician and geologist John Playfair (1748–1819) gave her useful hints on her studies. A group of young Whigs in her social circle supported her efforts, seeing her as charming evidence of female capacity and of the need for female higher education, two points urged in their new journal, the *Edinburgh Review*.

One of her most helpful mentors was the self-educated Scotsman William Wallace (1768–1843), one of Playfair's protégés. Wallace, who later became professor of mathematics at the University of Edinburgh, was at the time mathematics master at a military college and a contributor to the popular and respected *Mathematical Repository* and to the *Ladies' Diary*. A feature of both of these magazines was prizes offered for solutions to set problems. She and Wallace began a mathematical correspondence about these contests, an exchange particularly useful to her, as he was an excellent teacher by post. It was Wallace who suggested that she engage his brother John, also a mathematician, to read Pierre Simon de Laplace's new *Mécanique céleste* with her and help with physical astronomy and higher mathematics. In 1811 one of her solutions to a prize problem won a silver medal from the *Mathematical Repository*.

Another champion of her unusual studies was a cousin, Dr. William Somerville (1777–1860), who returned to Scotland late in 1811 after nearly fifteen years abroad in the army medical department. The two cousins had seldom met, but they were drawn together by the similarity of their views on politics, religion, social reform, and many other questions. In 1812, with the approval of both families, they were married; they settled in Edinburgh when William Somerville became head of army hospitals in Scotland. In the five years following, four children were born to them: Margaret Farquhar (1813–1822), Thomas (1814–1815), Martha Charters (1815–1880), and Mary Charlotte (1817–1875).

With her husband's active encouragement, Mary Somerville continued her studies. Advised by Wallace, she acquired a choice library of mathematical books, most of them recent French works. She thus became familiar with the new French analysis long before most English mathematicians were aware of its significance.

Late in 1815 William Somerville was ordered to London. Frequently accompanied by her husband, Mary Somerville attended the popular scientific lectures given at the Royal Institution, including those by Sir Humphry Davy (1778–1829). Introduced by other Scottish friends to the chemist Alexander Marcet (1770–1822) and his writer wife Jane (1769–1858), the Somervilles soon made places for themselves in a distinguished scientific circle that gathered around this Anglo-Swiss couple. These scientists and their wives were charmed by Mary Somerville's intelligence, grace, and obvious interest in science and mathematics, and also found her husband a congenial and obliging companion.

When William Somerville's post was abolished, the couple decided to go abroad for a time. They had met with visiting French scientists in London, and through them were now introduced into the best French scientific circles. During a fortnight in Paris, the Somervilles visited museums, observatories, and laboratories, attended a *séance* of the Académie des Sciences and one of the Institut de France, and were hospitably received by French scientists, including Laplace,

Siméon Denis Poisson, Louis Poinsot, and Émile Léonard Mathieu. The travelers received a similar reception in Geneva. The friendships formed on this trip were of lasting value to Mary Somerville.

On returning home the couple took a house in Hanover Square, convenient to the residences of many of their scientific friends and to the headquarters of various scientific societies and dining clubs valued by William Somerville. Their life was a full one, for they were part of the best scientific, literary, and political society at a time of great ferment and change in Britain. Their sympathies were unabashedly Whiggish, and they took an active interest in reform, especially reform in the Royal Society; yet they stayed on good terms with persons of all persuasions.

Mary Somerville's interest in science steadily deepened and expanded. In this period no English university offered systematic training in the modern sciences; the informal apprenticeship she served to master scientists was similar to that given males and represented the best instruction to be had. From 1826, when her first publication appeared, her fame grew steadily. Any criticism of her "unwomanly" studies—and an occasional voice was raised in the early years of her career—came from ill-educated, narrow, and ungenerous persons; they were promptly and firmly refuted by her scientific admirers.

In the 1820s a number of talented younger men became part of the Somerville scientific circle, including the astronomer John F. W. Herschel (1792–1871) and the mathematicians Charles Babbage (1792–1871), William Whewell (1794–1866), and George Peacock (1791–1858). Through the years, they and other scientists gave Mary Somerville the same unstinting assistance, regard, and esteem that their elders had bestowed on her. For half a century, she could claim outstanding scientists as her consultants. Her own skill as an expositor of science, coupled with her ready access to authoritative information and opinion on current scientific work, made her mathematical and scientific writings unique and highly useful.

Mary Somerville was persuaded to authorship by an old Edinburgh friend, Henry Brougham. Through William Somerville he solicited from her a translation of Laplace's *Mécanique céleste*. A "rendition," rather than a mere translation, proved necessary, for much of the French mathematics had to be explained to English readers. *The Mechanism of the Heavens* (1831) won approbation on both sides of the Channel. Not only did it bring important mathematical and astronomical work to a wider audience, but it was also seen by a number of British scientists as refutation of recent charges that British science was in decline. Admirers in the Royal Society commissioned a portrait bust of Mary Somerville, now in the headquarters of the society in London.

In 1832–1833 Mary Somerville and her two surviving daughters spent eleven delightful and rewarding months on the Continent, chiefly in Paris. During these months she resumed her ties with leaders of French science and largely completed her second book, an account of the connections among the physical sciences. Its publication in 1834 brought her praise and new distinctions. With Caroline

Herschel, she was elected (1835) to the Royal Astronomical Society, the first women so honored. The Société de Physique et d'Histoire Naturelle de Genève (1834), the Royal Irish Academy (1834), and the Bristol Philosophical and Literary Society (1835) bestowed honorary memberships on her. Her publisher John Murray commissioned her portrait (now in the National Portrait Gallery of Scotland) from the artist Thomas Phillips. Queen Adelaide, to whom the book was dedicated, received her at a Royal Drawing-Room; she also had a private audience with Princess Victoria. An extraordinary evidence of approval was the award to her of an annual civil pension of £200 (increased to £300 in 1837) for her "eminence in science and literature."

During the 1830s Mary Somerville continued to be a prominent figure in London intellectual circles. Visitors sought her out as a celebrity. Her help and opinions were solicited on a variety of subjects, including the education of women showing interest in mathematics and science. Thus it was to her that a neighbor in nearby Esher, Lady Byron, widow of the poet, turned early in the decade for advice on the education of Ada Byron, the future Lady Lovelace*, who already displayed a gift for mathematics. Mary Somerville became the girl's instructor and lifelong friend; it was Mary Somerville who introduced her to Charles Babbage and his calculating engine.

In 1838 William Somerville's health failed, and the family migrated to the warmer climate of Italy, where Mary Somerville passed her last thirty-six years. William Somerville died there in 1860.

Far from the centers of science, Mary Somerville nevertheless kept up with much current work through reading, correspondence, and visits from scientific friends. In these years three more books came from her pen: on physical geography (1848); on molecular and microscopic science (1869); and her autobiography, published after her death in a heavily edited form (1873).

She also continued to be widely honored. Between 1840 and 1857, she was made an honorary member of eleven Italian scientific societies. In 1857 she was elected to the American Geographical and Statistical Society, and in 1869 to the American Philosophical Society. In 1870 the Royal Geographical Society presented her with its Victoria Gold Medal, and she became a member of the Italian Geographical Society.

Although deaf and frail in her later years, she retained to the last her mental alertness and her interest in life. At the time of her death in Naples almost ninety-two (November 29, 1872), she was revising a paper on quaternions. She is buried in the English cemetery there.

Mary Somerville was a staunch but never shrill supporter of women's education and women's emancipation and, in her last years, of the antivivisection movement. At John Stuart Mill's request, she was the first to sign his great petition to Parliament for women's suffrage. After her death much of her library was given to the new Ladies' College at Hitchin (now Girton College, Cambridge). Somerville College (1879), one of the first two women's colleges at Oxford, is named after her.

WORK

Mary Somerville was fortunate in beginning her systematic study of mathematics in Scotland and in having the advice of Wallace. At that date in England, Newton was still dominant, and only a handful of English mathematicians—among them Babbage, Herschel, and Peacock—were aware of the new French mathematics and of how far English mathematics lagged behind it. Scotland, with its long history of friendly association with France, was more open to French ideas. It is said that as a lad Wallace was aided in his mathematical self-education by French internees held in Edinburgh, a number of them educated at the new French military academies and competent in the new French mathematics.

The mathematical library that Somerville bought in 1813 included at least fifteen significant French books published between 1795 and 1813. These works were important in forming her mathematical style and account in part for her mastery of French mathematics.

Mary Somerville's scientific investigations began in the summer of 1825, when she carried out experiments on magnetism. She began to look for connections between light and magnetism. Taking advantage of magnificent weather, she carried out simple trials in her garden. She focused the sun's rays on a long steel sewing needle; after sufficient exposure the needle appeared to be magnetized by the violet rays of the solar spectrum. This demonstration was the subject of her first experimental paper, communicated to the Royal Society by William Somerville (Somerville 1826). It attracted immediate and favorable notice, Herschel calling it the most interesting piece of experimentation done in 1825. Researchers in Vienna successfully repeated the work, which was accepted as valid for a number of years, until other investigators showed that the effect was not due to the sun's violet rays.

Mary Somerville's paper placed her among scientific practitioners at a time when sharp distinction was being made between those actively engaged in scientific work and those who were merely friends and patrons of science. Aside from the astronomical observations of Caroline Herschel, her paper was the first by a woman that was read to the Royal Society and published in its *Philosophical Transactions*.

Ten years later Mary Somerville sought to determine whether the "chemical" rays of the sun (which were known to blacken silver and fade vegetable and flower colors) displayed activity analogous to light rays and "calorific" rays passing through various solid media. Using paper coated with silver chloride and prepared with Michael Faraday's advice, she placed on it various solids and exposed them all to the sun. She demonstrated that rock salt transmitted the greatest number of chemical rays, violet- and blue-colored materials the fewest. When she wrote D.F.J. Arago of these results, he read extracts of her letter to a meeting of the Académie des Sciences (Somerville

1836). Neither she nor Arago sensed that her method was a kind of primitive photography.

In Italy in 1845 she carried out a series of investigations on the action of the rays of the sun on vegetable juices and sent her results and a description of her methods to Herschel, who immediately asked permission to publish parts of her letter (Somerville 1845).

Mary Somerville's only work in a popular journal was a long essay on comets (Somerville 1835). Halley's comet returned in that year, and interest in the subject was high. She prepared a similar piece on meteors, but it was never published.

Her most important works were her four books. *The Mechanism of the Heavens* (1831) was a "rendition," with mathematical explanations and illustrative figures, of the first four books of Laplace's *Mécanique céleste*. The Somerville account, handsomely printed and liberally illustrated, was far superior to the previous attempts (mere translations of only the first book) to bring the work to English readers. The 750 copies that were printed sold within a year. Widely mentioned in the weekly journals of the day, the book was also favorably reviewed. At Cambridge, Whewell and Peacock made it a classbook for students of higher mathematics. Its long introductory essay was printed separately (1832) and promptly pirated in America.

Mary Somerville's second book, *On the Connexion of the Physical Sciences* (1834), met with even greater success. While preparing her first book, she had been struck by the mutual dependence of the sciences and set out in her second to demonstrate their connections. Through her choice of material, she greatly influenced the very definition of "physical sciences," restricting them to the "group of sciences, treating of matter and energy." American publishers immediately pirated the work; later it was translated into French, Italian, and Swedish. Forty years after its first publication, J. C. Maxwell described it as a seminal work because of its insistence at an early date on viewing physical science as a whole. The discoverer of Neptune, J. C. Adams (1819–1892), attributed his first notions about the new planet to a passage he read in the book.

In 1848, at age sixty-eight, Mary Somerville published her third and most successful book, *Physical Geography*, warmly praised by Alexander Humboldt (1769–1859). It was widely used in schools and universities for the next fifty years.

Mary Somerville's last scientific book, *On Molecular and Microscopic Science*, appeared when she was eighty-eight. It dealt with the molecular constitution of matter and the microscopic structure of plants. At the time its science was considered old-fashioned; it was received kindly but more as a curiosity than a significant work.

In 1869 Mary Somerville completed a lively account of much of her life and many of the personages she had known. After her death her daughter Martha published parts of the manuscript (Somerville 1873).

BIBLIOGRAPHY _____

Works by Mary Fairfax Greig Somerville

Mathematical and Scientific Works

"On the magnetizing power of the more refrangible solar rays." *Philosophical Transactions of the Royal Society of London* 116 (1826) Part I: 132–139.
The Mechanism of the Heavens. London: John Murray, 1831.
A Preliminary Dissertation to the "Mechanism of the Heavens" by Mary Somerville. London: W. Clowes, 1832.
On the Connexion of the Physical Sciences. London: John Murray, 1834.
"Art. VII.–1. Ueber den Halleyschen Cometen. Von Littrow. Wien, 1835. 2. Ueber den Halleyschen Cometen. Von Professor von Encke. Berliner Jarbuch [*sic*], 1835 &c. &c. &c." *Quarterly Review* 55 (1835): 195–233.
"Experiments on the transmission of chemical rays of the solar spectrum across different areas. Excerpt from a letter of Mrs. Sommerville's [*sic*] to Mr. Arago." *Comptes rendus hebdomadaires des séances de l'Académie des Sciences* 3 (1836): 473–476.
" 'On the action of the rays of the spectrum on vegetable juices,' . . . " *Abstracts of the Papers Communicated to the Royal Society of London from 1843 to 1850, Inclusive* 5 (1845): 569.
Physical Geography. London: John Murray, 1848. 7th ed., 1877.
On Molecular and Microscopic Science. London: John Murray, 1869.

Other Works

Personal Recollections from Early Life to Old Age of Mary Somerville, with Selections from Her Correspondence. Edited by Martha Somerville. London: John Murray, 1873.

Works about Mary Fairfax Greig Somerville

Baker, J.N.L. "Mary Somerville and geography in England." *The Geographical Journal* 111 (1948): 207–222.
Oughton, Marguerita. "Mary Somerville. 1780–1872." In *Geographers: Bibliographical Studies*, vol. 2, 109–111. London: Mansell, 1978.
Patterson, Elizabeth C. "The case of Mary Somerville: An aspect of nineteenth-century science." *Proceedings of the American Philosophical Society* 118 (1974): 269–275.
———. "Mary Somerville." *British Journal for the History of Science* 4 (4) (1969): 311–339.
    A sketch of Mrs. Somerville's career and an introduction to her personal papers in the Somerville Collection at the Bodleian Library, Oxford.
———. *Mary Somerville 1780–1872*. New York: Oxford, 1979.
    Describes Somerville's life and explores her interest in female education and other social issues.
———. *Mary Somerville and the Cultivation of Science 1815–1840*. Dordrecht: Martinus Nijhoff Publishers, 1983.

A detailed account of the development of Somerville's mathematical and scientific career and of its course during the quarter century that encompassed her London life.

———. "A Scotswoman abroad: Mary Somerville's 1817 visit to France." In *The Light of Nature*, edited by J. D. North and J. J. Roche, 321–362. Dordrecht: Martinus Nijhoff Publishers, 1985.

Transcription, with commentary, of her travel diary.

PAULINE SPERRY (1885–1967)

Florence D. Fasanelli

BIOGRAPHY

Pauline Sperry was born on March 5, 1885, in Peabody, Massachusetts. Her parents were Henrietta Leoroyd and Willard G. Sperry, a Congregational minister from York Beach, Maine.

In 1906, at age twenty-one, Sperry received a B.A. from Smith College and was elected to Phi Beta Kappa. She had sung in the chapel choir and been a member of the mathematics club. After graduation Sperry taught for one year at Hamilton Institute, a private school in New York City. In 1907 she returned to Smith as a fellow to do graduate work in mathematics and music; she received an M.A. in music in 1908. Sperry remained at the college as an assistant in mathematics until 1911, when she was promoted to instructor. She taught plane and solid geometry, plane and spherical trigonometry, as well as analytic geometry. She was granted a traveling fellowship from Smith for 1912–1913.

Sperry matriculated at the University of Chicago in 1913 and received an M.S. in mathematics in 1914. For the academic year 1915–1916 she held a teaching fellowship at Chicago and wrote her Ph.D. thesis. Also, she was elected to the honor society Sigma Xi.

Sperry was one of many students under the guidance of Ernest Julius Wilczynski (1876–1932), who created a new school of geometers known as the American school of projective differential geometers. He was the first to develop completely integrable systems of linear homogeneous differential equations for projective differential geometry. One of his most important activities was directing thesis work. Twenty-five students wrote Ph.D.'s under his supervision. Sperry's dissertation utilized five memoirs in which Wilczynski had established the theory of non-developable curved surfaces. She read her paper at a meeting of the American Mathematical Society in Chicago in April 1916, a few months before receiving her doctorate in mathematics and astronomy.

Sperry returned to Smith as assistant professor for one year (1916–1917) and then moved to the University of California at Berkeley for the remainder of her academic career. Originally hired as instructor, in 1923 she became the first woman to be promoted to assistant professor in the mathematics department at Berkeley. In 1932 she was promoted to associate professor, remaining in that position until her dismissal in 1950. Known as a great educator, she even taught navigation to the Reserve Officers Training Corps in 1949. She also helped organize the Women's Faculty Club.

In 1950, with a small group of other faculty members, Sperry refused on principle to sign a special loyalty oath required by the Regents of the University of California. She placed her career on the line to defend academic freedom at a time when national and state authorities were systematically firing and black-listing opponents of Cold War hysteria. She was restrained from teaching and received no salary. In 1952 Provost Monroe E. Deutsch paid homage to the retiring professors, including Pauline Sperry, as one of "two who are not present today but have served their University for long years. Though technically not retiring they have reached the age of retirement. Through holding out for a principle they forfeited their University posts." On October 17, 1952, the California Supreme Court declared the loyalty oath unconstitutional and ordered reinstatement of eighteen of those faculty members who had refused to sign the oath. Sperry's reinstatement gave her the title of emeritus associate professor. In May 1956 her back salary was paid.

In her retirement, Sperry continued to be politically active from her home in Carmel, California, through her membership in the Monterey Peninsula Friends Meeting. She petitioned to ban testing of nuclear weapons. She was involved with the American Civil Liberties Union and the League of Women Voters. Her influence and reputation as a humanitarian spread after her eightieth birthday, when an article was published describing how she gave away money to help those with special needs (Sperry 1965). She continued to publish poetry in *Modern Maturity* and *The Friends Journal* from a home for retired men and women in Pacific Grove, California, until her quiet death on September 24, 1967.

WORK

Pauline Sperry published no research after her doctoral dissertation (Sperry 1918). She did write two trigonometry textbooks (Sperry 1926, 1928).

Her last publication was a bibliography of projective differential geometry (Sperry 1931). Sperry had been associated with this field almost since its inception in 1906, when Wilczynski had published the first treatise on partial differential geometry.

Pauline Sperry is honored for her struggle against the loyalty oath at Berkeley. She was also an active member of the American Mathematical Society, the Mathematical Association of America, and the Society of Friends. Her responsibilities as a Quaker included serving on the executive council of the Friends Committee on Legislation of Northern California, the Fellowship of Reconciliation, the American Friends Service Committee, and the Committee for a Sane Nuclear Policy. She also founded and maintained the Step-by-Step school in Port-au-Prince, Haiti, to feed and teach starving children.

BIBLIOGRAPHY

Works by Pauline Sperry

Mathematical Works

"On the theory of a one-to-one and one-to-two correspondence with geometric illustrations." Master's thesis, University of Chicago, 1914. 38 pp.
"Properties of a certain projectively defined two-parameter family of curves on a general surface." *American Journal of Mathematics* 40 (1918): 213–224. Doctoral thesis.
(with H. E. Buchanan) *Plane Trigonometry and Tables*. Richmond: Johnson Publishing Company, 1926.
Short Course in Spherical Trigonometry. Richmond: Johnson Publishing Company, 1928.
"Bibliography of projective differential geometry." *University of California Publications in Mathematics* 2 (1931): 119–127.

Works about Pauline Sperry

Rodenmayer, Robert. *How Many Miles to Babylon*. New York: Seabury Press, 1966.
A chapter is devoted to Pauline Sperry and the resilience of the human heart.
Sperry, Pauline. "Formula for happiness at eighty." *Smith Alumnae Quarterly* (Spring 1965): 154–155.

ALICIA BOOLE STOTT (1860–1940)

H.S.M. Coxeter

BIOGRAPHY

Alicia Boole Stott (known to her family and friends as Alice) was the third of the five daughters of George Boole (1815–1864) and Mary Everest Boole, niece of Sir George Everest, after whom the mountain was named.

George Boole was professor of mathematics at the newly founded Queen's College in Cork, Ireland. In 1842, when he was twenty-eight, the Royal Society awarded him their handsome Royal Medal, kindly including a silver replica so that the gold one could be sold. His strong sense of duty led to his untimely death, for he got soaked on his way to a lecture and died from fever in 1864. His widow, though left with very little money, sold the gold medal and bought a harmonium with the proceeds.

Their five daughters (all born in Cork, Ireland) were Mary, Margaret, Alice, Lucy, and Ethel. The last was born a few months after Boole's death in 1864; and the youngest three saw almost nothing of their mother, who took a post in London as matron of Queen's College, Harley Street. Mrs. Boole's mother and uncle wished to keep one of the five children with them in Cork. Alice, born in December 1860, was the one they liked best, so she had to live there, repressed and unhappy. Her great-uncle was fond of her, and the Irish maids were kind, but his sister was so selfish and conventional that Alice suffered much from loneliness and boredom.

At age ten or eleven, Alice returned home to London, where she lived for seven years with her invalid mother and four sisters in a poor, dark, dirty, uncomfortable lodging in Marylebone. At first all five girls slept in one sunless and dismal bedroom. No privacy was possible; even cleanliness was difficult. They had no education; everyone's nerves were on edge; and Mrs. Boole's friendship with James Hinton (1822–1875), author of *The Mystery of Pain* (Hinton 1866), brought into the house a continual stream of cranks. In their one sitting room, they talked endlessly about subjects that Alice, Lucy, and Ethel were too young to understand but not too young to brood over.

At about sixteen years of age, Alice was sent back to Ireland to be a probationer in a children's hospital in Cork. Later she returned to London, where some intellectual stimulus was provided at home by James Hinton's son Howard, who was a teacher at Uppingham School and author of *Scientific Romances* (Hinton 1980). He brought a lot of little wooden cubes and piled them up into shapes in his attempt to elucidate the four-dimensional hypercube, or *tesseract*. He set the three youngest girls the task of memorizing the arbitrary list of Latin words (*Decus*, *Pulvis*, etc.) by which he had named the little cubes. Lucy, being a child with a strong sense of duty, worked hard. Ethel found the whole project a meaningless bore and dropped out as soon as she was allowed to do so. But for Alice, age seventeen or eighteen, it was an inspiration, the mainspring of all her research. Despite this intellectual bond, it was not Alice but her eldest sister Mary whom Howard eventually married.

Alice's second sister Margaret married an artist, Edward Ingram Taylor. Their son was the well-known applied mathematician Sir Geoffrey Taylor, F.R.S., who eventually introduced this author to his mother and to his aunts Alice and Ethel (Taylor 1956).

In 1889 Alice was living alone in lodgings near Liverpool, doing secretarial work for Howard's friend, John Falk. In 1890 she married Walter Stott, an actuary, and for some years she led a drudging life rearing her two babies, Mary and Leonard, on a regular but very small income.

Being fond of animals, she joined the London Zoological Society. In winter she used to put out food for birds and watch them through the window. She was struck by the ingenious way the squirrels stole the food, even when it was hung on wires. She admired the English naturalist who called himself "Grey Owl" and lived among the Canadian Indians, studying and befriending wild beavers. Another of her interests was music.

In 1938 she wrote: "Walter and I have had a rather trying time for over a year—illness, a general running down of energy; but only what is inevitable as one grows older. The trouble is that as one grows old only *once* in a lifetime, one has no experience on which to base one's adaptations to new conditions!"

During World War II, she was further troubled by air raid precautions. In a letter of 1940, telling of her death on December 17, her son wrote: "The hard old arteries were hopelessly inadequate for the violent fluctuations in pressure which ensued, and she was found one day with a medullary thrombosis. She spent the last few weeks of her life in a Catholic Nursing Home of such pleasing aspect that it formed a happy setting for the fantasy of disintegration" (L. Stott 1940).

WORK

Howard Hinton, who had aroused Alice Stott's interest in regular and semi-regular polytopes, described his own work on the subject in *The Fourth Dimension* (Hinton 1904). Most of this is too confused to have any lasting value, but it does contain one highly original discovery: a semi-regular four-dimensional polytope whose facets (or cells) consist of ten truncated octahedra and twenty hexagonal prisms. He saw also that replicas of this hypersolid can be fitted together, like tiles or bricks, to form an infinite "honeycomb" filling the four-dimensional space. Alice, disregarding his rather wild speculations, gradually began to surpass him in her ability to imagine what happens in hyperspace. For each of the six convex regular four-dimensional polytopes, analogous to the five Platonic solids, she constructed the solid sections by a sequence of three-spaces parallel to the three-space that contains one facet (Stott 1900). (For something analogous in ordinary space, think of the hexagonal section of the octahedron by the plane midway between two opposite triangular faces.)

Meanwhile, in the Netherlands, Professor Pieter Hendrik Schoute of the University of Groningen was describing the central sections of the same polytopes. About 1895 Walter Stott drew his wife's attention to Schoute's work (Schoute 1893); so she sent Schoute photographs of her whole sequence of parallel sections including, for each polytope, the middle section, which agreed with his result. In an enthusiastic reply, he asked when he might come over to England and work with her. This led to a friendly and fruitful collaboration that continued for some twenty years. Her power of geometric visualization supplemented Schoute's more orthodox methods of using coordinates, so they were an ideal team. Her mother's cousin Ethel Everest invited them to her house at Hever, Kent, for some months during each summer vacation.

Schoute arranged for the publication of Alice's two papers (Stott 1900; 1910). The latter describes her ingenious processes of "expansion" and "contraction" (Coxeter 1978, 125). In three dimensions these processes enable the Archimedean solids to be derived from the Platonic solids in a more satisfactory manner than that of Kepler. For instance, when the expanding operator e_1 or e_2 is applied to the cube C, the edges or faces (respectively) are detached from their neighbors and translated away from the center until the new positions of each vertex can be joined by new edges of the same length as the original edges. Thus e_1C is Kepler's *truncated cube*, e_2C is his *rhombicuboctahedron*, and the two processes can be combined to yield his *truncated cuboctahedron* e_1e_2C. The contracting operator c is applied after the expansion to bring closer to the center those faces which arise from the original vertices. Thus ce_1C is the *cuboctahedron*, ce_2C is the *octahedron*, and ce_1e_2C is the *truncated octahedron*. The essential justification for these procedures is that they can be applied in spaces of any number of dimensions. For instance, Hinton's four-dimensional polytope is $e_1 e_2 e_3 S$, a triple expansion of the regular five-cell or simplex S.

Another of her discoveries was the notion of the Cartesian product of any two polytopes (Stott 1919, 4, footnote). For instance, a p-gonal prism is the product of a p-gon and a line segment (or "1-dimensional polytope"), and the product of two triangles is a four-dimensional polytope with nine vertices whose facets consist of six triangular prisms (Coxeter 1974, 108, Figure 11.5A).

Schoute was eighteen years older than Alice. After his death in 1913, she attended the tercentenary celebrations of his University of Groningen, which conferred upon her an honorary degree and exhibited her models. The way she combined her two roles of amateur mathematician and housewife is well illustrated by her remark to her husband when showing him the degree document in its cardboard cylinder: "This will be a good place to keep sticks of macaroni!" She then abandoned the former role for about seventeen years.

In 1930, when this author was introduced to her, her old enthusiasm for polytopes was rekindled. We had many exciting discussions over the next several years.

This author made a complete enumeration of kaleidoscopes (Coxeter 1968, 42), and demonstrated the three-dimensional instances by sets of three triangular mirrors inclined to one another at angles that are submultiples of 180°. When informed that the display was ready, she wrote: "I can't tell you how thrilled I am at the thought of seeing your magic mirrors. It seems too wonderful for words and I am longing for next week to come. *How* you will wake up the stuffy mathematicians on Saturday!!"

The kaleidoscopes led to "graphical" symbols for many of the uniform polytopes (Coxeter 1968, 43), including all the Archimedean solids except the snub cube and the snub dodecahedron. She thought of a charmingly simple way to bring those two chiral polyhedra into the same scheme (Coxeter 1974, 18). They have a four-dimensional analogue: the "snub 24-cell," whose facets consist of 120 tetrahedra and 24 icosahedra (Coxeter 1968, 52). Alice discovered two new constructions for it. Its 96 vertices lie on the 96 edges of the regular 24-cell, dividing them according to the "golden section" (just as the 12 vertices of the icosahedron lie on the 12 edges of the octahedron); and these same 96 points occur among the 120 vertices of the regular 600-cell. She made cardboard models of a sequence of sections, which can still be seen in Cambridge.

We were disappointed to learn that the same polytope had been discovered before 1900 by Thorold Gosset (1869–1962) in the course of his enumeration of all uniform polytopes whose facets are regular (Gosset 1900). Gosset never knew Hinton or Schoute, and they never thought of the snub 24-cell. Gosset's complete work on semi-regular polytopes was not accepted for publication, and this rejection disappointed him so cruelly that, a few years later, he abandoned mathematics and became a lawyer.

BIBLIOGRAPHY

Works by Alicia Boole Stott

Mathematical Works

"On certain sections of the regular four-dimensional hypersolids." *Verhandelingen der Koninklijke Akademie van Wetenschappen* (Amsterdam) (1. sectie) 7 (3) (1900): 1–21 with 5 plates.
"Geometrical deduction of semiregular from regular polytopes and space fillings." *Ver-*

handelingen der Koninklijke Akademie van Wetenschappen (Amsterdam) (1. sectie) 11 (1) (1910): 1–24 with 3 plates.

Other References

Coxeter, H.S.M. "Polytopes in the Netherlands." *Nieuw Archief voor Wiskunde* (3) 26 (1978): 116–141.
———. *Regular Complex Polytopes*. Cambridge, England: Cambridge University Press, 1974.
———. *Twelve Geometric Essays*. Carbondale, Ill.: Southern Illinois University Press, 1968.
Gosset, Thorold. "On the regular and semi-regular figures in space of *n* dimensions." *Messenger of Mathematics* 29 (1900): 43–48.
Hinton, C. Howard. *The Fourth Dimension*. London: 1904.
———. *Speculations on the Fourth Dimension. Selected Writings*. Edited by R. von B. Rucker. New York: Dover, 1980.
Hinton, James H. *The Mystery of Pain*. London: Smith, Elder, 1866.
Schoute, P. H. "Regelmässige Schnitte und Projektionen des Hundertzwanzigzelles und Sechshundertzelles in vierdimensionalen Räume (I)." *Verhandelingen der Koninklijke Akademie van Wetenschappen* (Amsterdam) (1. sectie) 2 (7) (1894): 1–26 with plates.
Stott, Leonard. Letter to H.S.M. Coxeter, December 1940.
Taylor, Sir Geoffrey. "George Boole, F.R.S." *Notes and Records of the Royal Society of London* 12 (1) (1956): 44–52.

OLGA TAUSSKY-TODD (1906–   )

Edith H. Luchins

BIOGRAPHY

Olga Taussky was born on August 30, 1906, in Olmütz, then in the Austro-Hungarian Empire (now Olomouc in Czechoslovakia). She was three years younger than her sister Ilona and three years older than her sister Herta. Her father, Julius David Taussky, was an industrial chemist as well as a journalist who wrote for newspapers. Her mother, Ida (Pollach) Taussky, was a country girl, not educated but intelligent and practical. She had a mind of her own, and her daughters took after her. She managed the household effectively during her husband's many absences and made a comfortable home. It was a loving, harmonious marriage; Taussky recalls evenings when she could not fall asleep and how good it felt to hear her parents' relaxed tones as they made a late supper for themselves in the kitchen.

There was great respect for education, as in many European homes. It was expected that the girls would get a good education, would work hard, and would do well in school. Her mother "was rather bewildered about our studies and compared herself to a mother hen who had been made to hatch duck eggs and then felt terrified on seeing her offspring swimming in a pool" ("Olga Taussky-Todd," 1985, 311). Yet in some ways she was less old-fashioned than her husband, for the idea of the girls later using their education to earn a living seemed all right to her, but not to him. He preferred that his daughters seek careers in the arts, but they all took to the sciences. Taussky's older sister has worked as an industrial chemist and consultant. Her younger sister (deceased) got a degree in pharmacy and later held a research position at Cornell Medical School.

In 1909 the family moved to Vienna. In elementary school Taussky's best subjects were grammar and essay-writing. She was not a straight A student like her older sister.

In the middle of World War I, the family moved to Linz, a small town in upper Austria where her father was director of a vinegar factory. Apparently recognizing her growing mathematical ability, he assigned her mathematically related chores. One of them was to figure out how much water to add to mixtures of various vinegars to achieve the acidity level required by law. Her solution in positive integers of the resulting Diophantine equation was posted in the factory: a real-life use for a mixture problem! But she kept her primary interest in grammar and writing essays, as well as in composing music and poems, which she still does today.

At the age of fourteen, Taussky transferred to the *Mittelschule* and a year later entered its gymnasium. While initially proud that she studied Latin for eight hours a week, later she wished that she had spent the time studying science or mathematics.

Her father died in the middle of her last year in the gymnasium. The grieving family was devastated emotionally as well as financially, for while there were savings, there was no income whatsoever. It was necessary for the girls to earn money. Taussky increased her tutoring load and took on a contract with the vinegar factory. Now the top pupil in her class and faced with the final exams— the *Matura*—she worried about whether she should continue the routine work in the factory. It gave her confidence when an essay she wrote on Pascal pyramids, "From the binomial to the polynomial theorem," was well received by her teachers. Worried about finances, "I did not dare to ask my family to share my faith" (1986). With her family's approval, in 1925 she began studies in mathematics at the University of Vienna, with a major in chemistry ("a truly wonderful subject" ("Olga Taussky-Todd," 1985, 315)), which she later dropped.

In her first year she took courses in mathematics, chemistry, astronomy, and philosophy of mathematics. She attended a course and seminars conducted by the philosopher Moritz Schlick, as well as meetings of his Vienna Circle, a mini-association which frequently discussed the work of Ludwig Wittgenstein. Among those who attended the same seminars was Kurt Gödel, a student of Schlick. Her mathematics teachers included Hans Hahn (of Hahn-Banach theorem fame), Karl Menger (who wrote a book on dimension theory and did research on metric geometry), E. Helly, W. Mayer, and Philip Furtwängler, a German number-theoretician, who was her major professor.

The first year, she took his course in number theory, and the second year, his seminar on algebraic number theory. He had proved some, and disproved others, of David Hilbert's conjectures in class field theory. It was this research area that he suggested when Taussky asked to work with him on a thesis in number theory.

The subject matter was difficult and not made any easier by her advisor. Not only did he then have a physical disability which impeded his availability, but he was also quite secretive. While she was struggling to learn about the area, an ingenious technique was developed by Emil Artin to translate a problem concerning principal ideals into one about finite groups. Furtwängler was able to make good use of this technique (of which he gave tantalizing glimpses to his advisee). Taussky was to generalize what Furtwängler had done for $p = 2$ to odd primes.

However, the technique was not applicable, and the theorems seemed to be of a chaotic nature. Taussky was able to establish results for $p = 3$ and to show that the case was different for every prime p. In 1930 she received her doctoral degree.

The thesis research led to an invitation from Richard Courant (whom she had met through Hahn) to come to Göttingen to edit David Hilbert's work in number theory, a rather prestigious post for a new Ph.D. Her coeditors were Wilhelm Magnus and Helmut Ulm. They found errors in Hilbert's work, and they discovered that some of his conjectures were false. While it has been rumored that Hilbert found the care that Taussky took somewhat excessive (Reid 1970, 201), he was very pleased with her work, as is evident in his introduction to the volumes.

Taussky also edited Emil Artin's 1932 lectures in class field theory, since translated into English (1978). Furthermore, Courant asked her to be the assistant in his differential equation course and she agreed, even though it required a great deal of effort. Her duties were so excessive that she had little time to profit from the talent at Göttingen: Hilbert, Edmund Landau, Hermann Weyl, and Emmy Noether*, to name but a few, as well as a host of brilliant students. Noether ran a seminar in class field theory precisely because Taussky was visiting there, and gave her opportunities to lecture.

In 1932, with the growing political tension at Göttingen making it inadvisable to stay there (Pinl and Furtmüller 1973, 180), she returned to Vienna, first doing tutoring and then getting a small salary as an assistant to Hahn and Menger. She supervised a thesis on multiple monotonic sequences, ''learning functional analysis in this way'' (''Olga Taussky Todd,'' 1977, xxxvi), and developed an interest in ''sums of squares'' and in topological algebra. The latter interest came about via L. S. Pontryagin's work in topological fields and some problems posed by B. L. van der Waerden, who had been a disciple of Emmy Noether.

An announcement in the newsletter of the International Federation of University Women led Taussky to apply for a science fellowship in Girton College at Cambridge. She was awarded a three-year fellowship, shortly after accepting a scholarship from Bryn Mawr. Actually, Bryn Mawr had invited Taussky for 1933–1934 but had to cancel the invitation because of financial losses during the Depression; the college was able to renew the invitation for 1934–1935. Because Emmy Noether had just come there, in a visit arranged by the Rockefeller Foundation, it was agreed that Taussky could spend the first year of the fellowship in Bryn Mawr. The invitation had come about because Oswald Veblen, whom Taussky had met in Göttingen, mentioned her to Anna Pell Wheeler*, chairman of the mathematics department at Bryn Mawr. Taussky took a few lessons in English and purposely took a boat from London to Liverpool to be with English-speaking passengers.

At Bryn Mawr Taussky found that Noether could be critical. ''She felt close enough to me to criticize a great many personal things about me, and, on the other hand, to scold me for being weak if I yielded to her criticism'' (Taussky-

Todd, "My personal recollections . . . " 1981, 87). Noether did not care for Taussky's Austrian accent or for her green felt hat, chided her for having worn an "expensive" gown to Hilbert's seventieth birthday party, and even brought up others' criticisms of the work by Hilbert that Taussky had helped edit. Noether's moodiness may have been occasioned by concerns about her professional situation (she did not want to teach undergraduates and had no position for the next year), about the political situation in Germany, and about her health. She underwent surgery and died unexpectedly in 1935.)

But there were also happy times, especially when Taussky accompanied Noether to the lectures that Noether gave every Tuesday at Princeton. Taussky went as often as she could afford the train fare. There she was introduced to Albert Einstein and met the other illustrious scholars at the Institute for Advanced Study. They included Morgan Ward, who later played a role in her appointment as the first woman in the mathematics department at the California Institute of Technology; Frederic H. Bohnenblust, chairman of the mathematics department at the time of her appointment; and Howard Percy Robertson, who became professor of mathematical physics there.

For Taussky, Princeton was a dream come true. She was fascinated by the work going on there in topological algebra. She did some joint work with Magnus, her former coeditor at Göttingen, and with Nathan Jacobson, later an eminent algebraist at Yale.

In June 1935 Taussky left the United States for Girton College, Cambridge, England, where she was a so-called don. Unfortunately, no one there shared her particular interests in topological algebra or algebraic number theory (although work was going on in elementary and analytic number theory). There were colleagues who wanted to work with her but not on the subjects she knew. The distinguished mathematician Godfrey Harold Hardy and the well-known group-theorist Philip Hall "seemed on different planes. . . . If my mind had not been so deeply anxious to continue on topological algebra, I might have been able to attach myself to one of the research groups that existed there" ("Olga Taussky Todd," 1985, 325).

The second year in England she spent much time in supervising students—partly to gain experience in teaching in English—and in looking for a position. Jobs were very scarce, especially for foreigners. Thanks to Hardy and the head of Girton College, she succeeded in 1937 in obtaining a junior-level teaching position at Westfield College, one of the women's colleges in the University of London. The duties were arduous, with nine courses to teach every week, each for one or two hours, and homework to grade. The students were kind about her language difficulties, but some of the faculty regarded her as a foreigner and were not very friendly. Despite the workload, she got some research done and had time to participate in intercollegiate seminars. At one of these seminars she met John (Jack) Todd, who worked in analysis and was employed in a position similar to hers. Their scientific contacts led them to confer frequently. They were married in 1938.

Less than a year later, war broke out. Life became very difficult, with anxiety about air raids, food shortages, and homelessness; the couple moved eighteen times during the war. Todd was given leave from his college to take a scientific war job. It did not materialize for a year; in the interim, they moved to Belfast, his family's home. He taught at his school, Queen's University. She supervised a young theologian, E. Best, who was also interested in mathematics, and they did research together on finite groups. She also worked on two subjects that still form a large part of her program: generalization of matrix commutativity and matrices with integer entries.

The next year Todd was assigned to London. Taussky returned to teach in her college, which had moved to Oxford to be safer from air raids. Her teaching duties became heavier but no more interesting.

In 1943 she obtained a research position in aerodynamics with the Ministry of Aircraft Production, working with the so-called Flutter Group at the National Physical Laboratory. Flutter concerns the self-excited oscillations of part of an airplane, e.g., the wings. A corresponding mathematical problem involves the stability of a certain matrix. The Flutter Group was under the direction of Robert A. Frazer, coauthor of a book on applied matrix theory. There Taussky became fully interested in matrix theory, especially in problems of stability. "It was impossible not to come under the spell of matrix theory in that group" ("Olga Taussky-Todd," 1977, xxxvii). Actually the work assigned to her was not in matrix theory but on a boundary value problem for a hyperbolic differential equation arising from flutter at supersonic speed. "For the first time I realized the beauty of research on differential equations" ("Olga Taussky–Todd," 1985, 326).

Taussky left the Civil Service in 1946, quite exhausted. In 1947 her husband accepted an invitation to come to the United States for a year to work at the National Bureau of Standards' (NBS) field station, the Institute for Numerical Analysis, at UCLA; Taussky was also invited to join the Bureau staff.

Taussky wrote half a dozen papers and lectured at Caltech, as well as in Vancouver and in Wisconsin. Although John M. Curtiss, their boss, repeatedly urged them to stay on after the year, they felt compelled to return to London. But life in England was still harsh; and when Curtiss invited them back, they accepted, this time working at the NBS headquarters in Washington, D.C., for ten years.

Taussky writes in her memoirs:

Life for me became very busy. My title was consultant in mathematics and this I truly was, because everybody dumped on me all sorts of impossible jobs, from refereeing every paper that was written by a member or visitor to the group, to answering letters from people who claimed to have "squared the circle" to helping people on their research. ("Olga Taussky-Todd," 1985, 329).

She provided meaningful research problems for visitors; worked with young postdoctoral employees, one of whom, Karl Goldberg, had written a thesis under her direction while at the NBS; started a fellowship postdoctoral program; and worked with bright high school students and other trainees during the summer. The director of the National Bureau of Standards, Edward U. Condon, started the now well-known *Handbook of Physics*, to which Taussky contributed three chapters, on algebra, operator theory, and ordinary differential equations. She helped organize in 1951 the first symposium on numerical aspects of matrix theory, forerunner of a chain of such symposia known as the Gatlinburg meetings. She provided suitable problems in number theory for the NBS's high-speed computers.

Yet despite its interests, the jobs at the NBS were not quite right. When in 1957 an offer came to join Caltech, the Todds were ready to accept. With the move it seemed to Taussky that a twenty-year odyssey had ended since her leaving Cambridge in 1937.

However, the change from a civil service job to academic life was almost as great as the change in the opposite direction years before. Taussky was given a research position with permission to teach. This created a difficult situation for her, particularly since the department was understaffed. "It is not entirely pleasant not to teach when everybody else is, and besides, I simply love to teach and feel I have a good bit of natural talent for it" ("Olga Taussky-Todd," 1985, 331). Characteristically, she took on more teaching than she had anticipated. She taught graduate courses only, although undergraduates also attended and were excellent students. Taussky has had fourteen Ph.D. thesis students at Caltech. She has also worked with many postdoctorals, helping them take those difficult steps from thesis research to independent research. In 1971 she became professor emeritus, when "I was 'retired,' a phrase I absolutely abhor. Nobody, absolutely nobody, ought to be burdened with it, unless by fate or by oneself" ("Olga Taussky-Todd," 1985, 336).

WORK

Circumstances have not always allowed Taussky to concentrate on number theory. A case in point is her thesis, which turned out to be more in group theory than in number theory. Another example is her war work in aerodynamics, which focused her attention on differential equations and stability of matrices.

Yet she also has an inner desire for variety:

I developed rather early a great desire to see the links between the various branches of mathematics. This struck me with great force when I drifted, on my own, into topological algebra, a subject where one studies mathematical structures from an algebraic and a geometric point of view simultaneously. From this subject I developed a liking for a sum of squares, a subject where one observes strange links between number theory, geometry, topology, partial differential equations, Galois theory, and algebras. ("Olga Taussky-Todd," 1985, 331)

The following description of her overall interests in matrix theory is a composite of two accounts she wrote for this article (1986).

Matrix theory has emerged as my major subject. My interests in it fall into three categories. (1) analytic, (2) algebraic, (3) arithmetical.

(1) *Analytic*. This interest is related to my training in aerodynamics and the flutter problem. I value very much the work on the signs of the real parts of the eigenvalues of a matrix via the Lyapunov theorem (matrix stability criterion). This was closely connected with a result to which I gave the name Stein theorem that deals with matrices whose powers tend to zero. Stein was a very creative man from South Africa who had little patience for writing up his papers. Hence, I helped him a good bit. Earlier he co-authored a paper with a man named Rosenberg who probably wrote the joint paper. It came to me for refereeing via Mordell and I rescued the paper. In those days there was so little knowledge and training in theoretical matrix theory that it would have been rejected. However, it became a classic (Rosenberg & Stein 1948).

I became one of the first in this country to work on the Lyapunov theorem. Then there is the Gershgorin theorem where one shows that a matrix with dominant main diagonal is nonsingular. This follows from a result I called the "recurrent theorem." Further, there is my work on the Hilbert matrix.

(2) *Algebraic*. Here I am interested in commutativity, generalized commutativity, and commutators, additive and multiplicative ones. My work, done initially together with T. S. Motzkin, concerns a concept suggested to me by Mark Kac which I named the L-property: A pair of matrices A, B, with entries from an algebraically closed field F and with eigenvalues $\{\alpha_i\}$, $\{\beta_i\}$, have property L if the pencil of matrices $\lambda A + \mu B$, for all λ and μ in F, has $\{\lambda\alpha_i + \mu\beta_i\}$ for eigenvalues. The main result Motzkin and I achieved states that if $\lambda A + \mu B$ is diagonable for all values of λ and μ, then $AB = BA$ (1955).

(3) *Arithmetical*. This is my favorite subject because it brings me back readily to number theory, including algebraic number theory, and introduces new methods, mainly non-commutative tools. Integral matrices (which are also linked up with the integral group ring) have been my main interests for some time now. I became interested in the subject, maybe for the first time, due to a theorem of Latimer and MacDuffee which gives a 1–1 correspondence between certain classes of integral matrices and ideal classes in an algebraic number field. In 1939, while waiting with a heavy heart for the outbreak of war, John Todd and I wrote a joint paper on integral matrices of finite period (1941). Of the papers I have published on integral matrices, my favorite, and my main success so far, is 'Composition of binary integral quadratic forms . . . ' (1981).

Her honors include a Ford Prize for her paper "Sums of squares" (1970). She was proclaimed "Woman of the Year" by the *Los Angeles Times* in 1964, which pleased her insofar as it delighted her husband and none of her colleagues (all male) could be jealous. In 1976–1977 numerous honors came her way. A symposium at Caltech brought many mathematicians to honor her. Two journals, *Linear Algebra and Its Applications* and *Linear and Multilinear Algebra*, published issues dedicated to her. The University of Vienna renewed her doctorate fifty years later by awarding her a Golden Doctorate in 1980 with appreciation of her achievements in research and in teaching. She carries the Golden Cross of Honor First Class of the Austrian Republic and is a corresponding member of the Austrian Academy of Sciences. In 1985 she was elected to the Bavarian Academy of Sciences. In 1986–1987 she served as a vice-president of the American Mathematical Society (AMS), having served six years on its council.

At present she is an editor for four journals: *Linear Algebra and Its Applications* (a founding editor), *Linear and Multilinear Algebra, Journal of Number Theory*, and *Advances in Mathematics*. She writes reviews for *Mathematical Reviews* and referees for other journals.

Does she think that she was treated differently professionally because she was a woman? Was being a woman a factor in not attaining a full professorship until recent years? She does not want to emphasize complaints. It may be significant that she disagreed with the view expressed by Emmy Noether in 1934. "She [Noether] saw women as being protected by their families and even admitted to me that she gave young men preference in her recommendations for jobs so they could start a family. She asked me to understand this, but, of course, I did not" (Taussky-Todd, "My personal recollections . . . ," 1981, 91).

Yet there is some objection after all: "It seems that some men do not want to cite my published work in their work; if they work on a problem suggested by myself, they put the credit into the middle of their publication, hoping it will not be noticed. (Wonderful exceptions, e.g., Conner and Perlis 1984, Kato 1966)" (Taussky-Todd 1986).

Two important mathematical items which would never have reached the mathematical community without Taussky pointing them out are (1) the theorem of Latimer and MacDuffee (Estes and Guralnick 1984); and (2) the work of Arnold Scholz (Taussky-Todd 1952).

She also mentioned a theorem by K. Shoda, "one of my favorite results," which she brought to the attention of others through a paper she wrote using the theorem (Shoda 1936; Taussky 1954). Shoda attempted to characterize commutator matrices by their trace of 0 (sum of diagonal values) and their determinant of 1. He succeeded for many fields, and the case of determinant 1 was fully settled by the thesis of her student, R. C. Thompson (1959).

BIBLIOGRAPHY

Works by Olga Taussky-Todd

Over 165 publications can be found in the "Bibliography of Olga Taussky-Todd" in Zassenhaus (1977). The present list picks up where that bibliography left off. (Note: Taussky-Todd is variously indexed under "Taussky" and "Taussky-Todd.")

Mathematical Works

"Über eine Verschärfung des Hauptidealsatzes." Ph.D. diss., University of Vienna, 1930.
"A recurring theorem on determinants." *American Mathematical Monthly* 56 (1949): 672–676. Reprinted in Montgomery et al. (1977): 308–312.

"Arnold Scholz zum Gedächtnis." *Mathematische Nachrichten* 7 (1952): 379–386.

"Generalized commutators of matrices." In *Studies in Mathematics and Mechanics Presented to R. von Mises*, 67–68. New York: Academic, 1954.

(with T. S. Motzkin) "Pairs of matrices with property ≤ (II)." *Transactions of the American Mathematical Society* 82 (1955): 387–401.

"Commutativity in finite matrices." *American Mathematical Monthly* 64 (1957): 229–235. Reprinted in Montgomery et al. (1977): 435–442.

"Sums of squares." *American Mathematical Monthly* 77 (1970): 805–830. Reprinted in Montgomery et al. (1977): 487–513.

"A matrix version of the principal genus in quadratic fields." *Proceedings of a Conference on Quadratic Forms—1976*, edited by Grace Orzech, 632–633. Kingston, Ontario: Queen's University, 1977.

"Norms from quadratic fields and their relation to non-commuting 2×2 matrices. III. A link between the 4–rank of the ideal class groups in $Q(\sqrt{m})$ and in $Q(\sqrt{-m})$." *Mathematische Zeitschrift* 154 (1977): 91–95.

"Connections between algebraic number theory and integral matrices." Appendix in Cohn (1978).

"From cyclic algebras of quadratic fields to central polynomials." *Journal of the Australian Mathematical Society* 25 (1978): 503–506.

"Some comments concerning G. B. Price's note on 'Determinants with dominant principal diagonal: A personal historical note.' " *Linear and Multilinear Algebra* 6 (1978): 251.

(editor) "Artin's 1932 Göttingen Lectures on class field theory." Appendix in Cohn (1978).

"Some remarks concerning matrices of the form $A - A'$, $A^{-1}A'$." *Zeitschrift für angewandte Mathematik und Physik* 30 (1979): 370–373.

"A Diophantine problem arising out of similarity classes of integral matrices." *Journal of Number Theory* 11 (1979): 472–475.

"Results concerning composition of sums of three squares." *Linear and Multilinear Algebra* 8 (1979): 231–233.

(with R. Guralnick) "A remark concerning unipotent matrix groups." *Linear and Multilinear Algebra* 7 (1979): 87–89.

"Sets of complex matrices which can be transformed to triangular forms." In *Numerical Methods*, edited by Pál Rózsa, 579–590. New York: North-Holland, 1980.

"More on norms from algebraic number fields, commutators and matrices which transform a rational matrix into its transpose." *Linear Algebra and Its Applications* 29 (1980): 459–464.

"Some facts concerning integral representations of the ideals in an algebraic number field." *Linear Algebra and Its Applications* 31 (1980): 245–248.

"Pairs of sums of three squares of integers whose product has the same property." In *General Inequalities 2*, edited by E. F. Beckenbach, 29–36. Boston: Birkhäuser, 1980.

(with H. Shapiro) "Alternative proofs of a theorem of Moyls and Marcus on the numerical range of a square matrix." *Linear and Multilinear Algebra* 8 (1980): 337–340.

"My personal recollections of Emmy Noether." In *Emmy Noether: A Tribute to Her Life and Work*, edited by James W. Brewer and Martha K. Smith, 79–92. New York: Dekker, 1981.

"Some facts concerning integral representations of ideals in an algebraic number field."

In *Integral Representations and Applications*, edited by K. W. Roggenkamp, 145–158. New York: Springer-Verlag, 1981.

"Composition of binary integral quadratic forms via integral 2 × 2 matrices and matrix theory composition of matrix classes." *Linear and Multilinear Algebra* 10 (1981): 309–318.

"History of sums of squares in algebra." In *American Mathematical Heritage: Algebra and Applied Mathematics*, edited by D. Tarwater et al., 73–90. Lubbock, Tex.: Texas Tech University, 1981.

(with D. R. Estes) "Remarks concerning sums of three squares and quaternion commutator identities." *Linear Algebra and Its Applications* 35 (1981): 279–285.

"The many aspects of the Pythagorean triangles." *Linear Algebra and Its Applications* 43 (1982): 285–295.

(editor) *Ternary Quadratic Forms and Norms*. New York: Dekker, 1982.

"Some non-commutative methods in algebraic number theory." In Srinivasan and Sally (1983): 47–57.

"On the congruence transformation of a pencil of real symmetric matrices to a pencil with identical characteristic polynomial." *Linear Algebra and Its Applications* 52/53 (1983): 687–691.

(with Grace S. Quinn et al.) "Emmy Noether in Bryn Mawr." In Srinivasan and Sally (1983): 145–146.

"The semigroup of non-left zero divisors in an algebra, infinite powers of matrices and related matters." *Rocky Mountain Journal of Mathematics* 14 (1984): 925–926.

"Ideal matrices. III." *Pacific Journal of Mathematics* 118 (1985): 599–601.

"Remarks concerning possible connections between Fermat's Last Theorem and integral $p \times p$ circulants." *Linear Algebra and Its Applications* 71 (1985): 295–297.

"A factorization of an integral 2 × 2 matrix via a rational method." *Monatshefte für Mathematik* 102 (1986): 79–83.

"Simultaneous similarities of two integral symmetric matrices." *Rocky Mountain Journal of Mathematics*. In press.

Other Works

"Olga Taussky-Todd." In Zassenhaus (1977), xxxiv–xlvi.

"Olga Taussky-Todd: An autobiographical essay." In *Mathematical People*, edited by D. J. Albers and G. L. Alexanderson, 310–336. Boston: Birkhäuser, 1985.

Personal memoirs written at the request of the Oral History Project of the Caltech Archives, and delivered to the archives in 1980.

Personal communications to the author. February–April 1986.

Works about Olga Taussky-Todd's Work

Carlson, D. H., and R. S. Varga (eds.). *Linear Algebra and Its Applications* 13 (1976). Dedicated to Olga Taussky-Todd.

Conner, P. E., and R. Perlis. *A Survey of Trace Forms of Algebraic Number Fields*. New York: Springer-Verlag, 1966. Dedicated to Olga Taussky-Todd.

Estes, D. "Determinants of Galois automorphisms of maximal commutative rings of 2 × 2 matrices." *Linear Algebra and Its Applications* 27 (1979): 225–227.

Estes, D., and R. Guralnick. "Representations under ring extensions: Latimer and MacDuffee and Taussky correspondences." *Advances in Mathematics* 54 (1984): 302–313.

Marcus, M., and N. Khan. "On a commutator result of Taussky-Todd and Zassenhaus." *Pacific Journal of Mathematics* 10 (1960): 1327–1346.

Newman, M. "On a problem suggested by Olga Taussky-Todd." *Illinois Journal of Mathematics* 24 (1980): 156–158.

Pinl, M., and L. Furtmüller. "Mathematicians under Hitler." In *Leo Baeck Yearbook XVIII*, 129–182. London: Secker and Warburg, 1973.

Redheffer, R. "Remarks on a paper by Taussky." *Journal of Algebra* 2 (1966): 42–47.

Schneider, H. "On Olga Taussky's influence on matrix theory and matrix theorists: A discursive personal tribute." *Linear and Multilinear Algebra* 5 (1977–1978): 197–224.

Serre, J. "Sur un problème d'Olga Taussky." *Journal of Number Theory* 2 (1970): 235–236.

Thompson, R. C., and M. Marcus (eds.). *Linear and Multilinear Algebra* 3 (1975–1976). Dedicated to Olga Taussky-Todd.

Varga, R. S., and B. W. Levinger. "On a problem by Olga Taussky-Todd." *Pacific Journal of Mathematics* 19 (1966): 473–487.

Zassenhaus, Hans (ed.). *Number Theory and Algebra*. New York: Academic, 1977. Dedicated to Henry Mann, Arnold E. Ross, and Olga Taussky-Todd.
Contains Taussky's own technical survey of some of her work and her bibliography up to that point (pp. xxxiv–xlvi).

Other References

Cohn, Harvey. *A Classical Introduction to Algebraic Numbers and Class Fields*. New York: Springer-Verlag, 1978.

Kato, T. *Perturbation Theory for Linear Operators*. New York: Springer-Verlag, 1966.

Montgomery, Susan, et al. (eds.). *Selected Papers on Algebra*. The Raymond W. Brink Selected Mathematical Papers, vol. 3. Washington, D.C.: Mathematical Association of America, 1977.

Reid, Constance. *Hilbert*. New York: Springer-Verlag, 1970.

Rosenberg, R. L., and P. Stein. "On the solution of linear simultaneous equations by iteration." *Journal of the London Mathematical Society* 23 (1948): 111–118.

Shoda, K. "Einige Sätze über Matrizen." *Japan Journal of Mathematics* 13 (1936): 361–365.

Srinivasan, B., and J. D. Sally (eds.). *Emmy Noether in Bryn Mawr*. New York: Springer-Verlag, 1983.

Thompson, R. C. "On matrix commutators." *Notices of the American Mathematical Society* 6 (1959): 164.

MARY CATHERINE BISHOP WEISS (1930–1966)

Guido Weiss

BIOGRAPHY

Mary Weiss was born in Wichita, Kansas, on December 11, 1930. Her father, Albert Bishop, was a West Point graduate who, after his retirement from the army, turned to a career in mathematics and university teaching. He and his wife Helen had two children, Errett and Mary. Albert died when Errett was four and Mary not quite two. After his death, Helen moved to Florence, Kansas, where most of her family lived. The various mathematics books that were left by Albert caught his son's attention and motivated the latter to go to the University of Chicago (after his sophomore year in high school!) in order to begin a career as a mathematician. Errett became a distinguished mathematician who made important contributions to mathematical analysis and to the foundations of mathematics; his untimely death in 1983 stopped a most influential career.

The family moved to Chicago with Errett. Mary Weiss's education also took place at the University of Chicago, starting at the Laboratory School (at the high school level) and continuing to the university. There she met and married Guido Weiss when both were undergraduates. Much influenced by Errett, both entered the graduate department of mathematics, where they obtained their Ph.D. degrees as students of Antoni Zygmund.

From the very beginning of her graduate studies, Mary Weiss exhibited unusual strength and intuition in the theory of real variables and the connections of Fourier analysis with probability theory. Her Ph.D. thesis dealt with lacunary trigonometric series. The properties of these series are very similar to those of series of independent random variables. The principal result in her thesis was to show, as is the case in probability theory, that these lacunary series have a "law of the iterated logarithm."

Mary Weiss was a "natural mathematician." She could spend long hours—even days—completely absorbed in a mathematical problem. Yet she was a very complete human being. An accurate description of her must include some of her other traits. She was an avid reader; Jane Austen was her favorite author. She had a deep appreciation of painting and other art forms. Mary Weiss was also very involved in many causes: she supported many civil liberties organizations, participated actively in the protest movement against the Vietnam War, and wanted to help minimize suffering and injustice in the world. All who knew her were also struck by her modesty as a mathematician and indifference to her considerable physical beauty.

Mary Weiss was an exceptionally good teacher. She took her teaching duties very seriously and spent much energy and time in preparing her lectures and working individually with students. During her career, she held faculty positions at De Paul University, Washington University, the University of Chicago, and Stanford University. She spent the 1965–1966 academic year as a National Science Foundation senior postdoctoral fellow at Cambridge University in England. During that year, she accepted a position at the University of Illinois in Chicago. She died on October 8, 1966, three weeks after assuming her duties there.

WORK

Mary and Guido Weiss worked in the same general area of mathematics. They shared many interests; however, they agreed to collaborate in research only when this collaboration came naturally. Each pursued his or her own direction in research, often in collaboration with others. In particular, Mary continued her study of lacunary series during a period of about three years after obtaining her doctoral degree. She extended the law of the iterated logarithm to uniformly bounded orthonormal systems of functions. She also turned her attention to the study of a class of power series that were shown by Godfrey Harold Hardy and John E. Littlewood to have certain connections with lacunary trigonometric series. Using the results obtained in her thesis, she obtained some very deep and precise estimates for the behavior of the partial sums of these power series. She also gave a proof of a theorem of Raymond E.A.C. Paley, which had been stated but never proved by him. The theorem states that a certain class of lacunary power series, restricted to the real line, consists of series that converge to each complex number in the extended plane. While still a student, she resolved a problem posed by Littlewood when he gave a series of lectures at the University of Chicago. She did this by showing that trigonometric series whose partial sums have uniformly bounded $L(1)$ norm need not be a Fourier series.

Mary Weiss did return to the topic of lacunary series. In the academic year 1960–1961, however, while on a sabbatical leave in Buenos Aires and Paris, she and Guido Weiss started a collaboration that began in an area that her husband was working in, the theory of Hardy spaces. The first result of this collaboration was the establishment of a new approach to the classical theory of these spaces (which later on proved to be very appropriate for the extension of these spaces to domains in the complex plane that are multiply connected). The second direction of this joint work was in lacunary series. They showed that a lacunary

power series (with sufficiently large gaps) which converges in the interior of the
unit disk, but whose coefficients form an absolutely divergent series, assumes
each complex value infinitely often. This result led to a natural problem of
finding the "best" condition on the size of the gaps that allowed the conclusion
to hold. This problem attracted the attention of several mathematicians until it
was solved some twenty years later. Later on during this sabbatical leave, this
collaboration joined with J. P. Kahane to extend the result of Paley to more
general lacunary power series.

After her return from this sabbatical year, Mary Weiss turned her attention to
problems in two different areas: differentiability of functions and singular integrals. Her results in these fields are very technical. They involve very powerful
methods that are still far from being assimilated and exploited. These are results
in n-dimensional Euclidean space and are basic for the understanding of harmonic
analysis in higher dimensions. The differentiability results involve the study of
the existence and properties of differentials of order k. Mary Weiss showed that
the behavior of these differentials for functions in certain Lebesgue spaces is
different in the two-dimensional case than it is in higher dimensions. An important
class of operators was introduced in the early 1950s by A. P. Calderón and A.
Zygmund; these operators are now known as the "Calderón-Zygmund singular
integral operators." Mary wrote three papers on this subject, the last one in
collaboration with Calderón and Zygmund. It is often a difficult problem to show
that some of these operators are well-defined on certain important classes of
functions; one usually makes some assumptions on the kernels that define these
operators. The problem of determining whether these assumptions are necessary
is a natural and important one. In one of these papers, Mary Weiss showed the
necessity of these hypotheses; in the other two, she showed the existence of
certain classes of these operators.

Mary Weiss's strong geometric insight and analytical power were the principal
force in one more collaboration with her husband. The latter, together with
E. M. Stein, introduced several extensions of the theory of Hardy spaces to
higher dimensions. One of these extensions involved functions of several complex variables defined on "tube domains." A tube domain is a Cartesian product
of Euclidean n-space with a convex subset. The convex set is called the *base*
of the tube domain. The Hardy spaces associated with a tube domain have features
that are intimately connected with the geometry of the base. In a paper with
E. M. Stein and Guido Weiss, Mary Weiss gave a very complete description,
in the two-dimensional case, of this connection. In an unpublished manuscript,
she extended most of these notions to the three-dimensional case.

Six months after Mary Weiss's death, a conference was held in her honor on
the campus of Southern Illinois University at Edwardsville. This conference was
attended by the leading harmonic analysts of that time. At the beginning of the
proceedings volume Antoni Zygmund wrote a more technical description of the
results of Mary Weiss than is presented above. Moreover, a previously unpublished part of Mary Weiss's Ph.D. thesis was prepared for inclusion in that

volume by Zygmund. The conference and its proceedings volume gave testimony of the brilliant career of Mary Weiss that was abruptly ended by her untimely death.

BIBLIOGRAPHY

Works by Mary Catherine Bishop Weiss

Mathematical Works

"The law of the iterated logarithm for lacunary series and its application to the Hardy-Littlewood series." Ph.D. diss., University of Chicago, 1957.

"The law of the iterated logarithm for lacunary trigonometric series." *Transactions of the American Mathematical Society* 91 (1959): 444–469.

"On a problem of Littlewood." *Journal of the London Mathematical Society* 34 (1959): 217–221.

"On the law of the iterated logarithm for uniformly bounded orthonormal systems." *Transactions of the American Mathematical Society* 92 (1959): 531–553.

"Concerning a theorem of Paley on lacunary power series." *Acta Mathematica* 102 (1959): 225–238.

"On the law of the iterated logarithm." *Journal of Mathematics and Mechanics* 8 (1959): 121–132.

"On Hardy-Littlewood series." *Transactions of the American Mathematical Society* 91 (1959): 470–479.

(with A. Zygmund) "A note on smooth functions." *Indagationes Mathematicae* 21 (1959): 52–58.

(with A. Zygmund) "On the existence of conjugate functions of higher order." *Fundamenta Mathematica* 48 (1959/1960): 175–187.

(with Guido Weiss) "A derivation of the main results of the theory of H^p spaces." *Revista de la Unión Matemática Argentina* 22 (1960): 63–71.

(with Guido Weiss) "On the Picard property of lacunary power series." *Studia Mathematica* 22 (1962/1963): 221–245.

(with J.-P. Kahane and G. Weiss) "Lacunary power series." *Arkiv för Matematik* 5 (1963): 1–26.

(with E. M. Stein and G. Weiss) "H^p classes of holomorphic functions in tube domains." *Proceedings of the National Academy of Sciences of the U.S.A.* 52 (1964): 1035–1039.

"On symmetric derivatives in L^p." *Studia Mathematica* 24 (1964/1965): 89–100.

"Total and partial differentiability in L^p." *Studia Mathematica* 25 (1964/1965): 103–109.

(with A. Zygmund) "An example in the theory of singular integrals." *Studia Mathematica* 26 (1965): 101–111.

"Strong differentials in L^p." *Studia Mathematica* 27 (1966): 49–72.

(with A. P. Calderón and A. Zygmund) "On the existence of singular integrals." In *Singular Integrals*, edited by Alberto P. Calderón, 56–73. Proceedings of Symposia in Pure Mathematics, vol. 10. Providence, R.I.: American Mathematical Society, 1967.

"A theorem on lacunary trigonometric series." In *Orthogonal Expansions and Their*

Continuous Analogues, edited by D. T. Haimo, 227–230. Carbondale, Ill.: Southern Illinois University Press, 1968.

(with A. Zygmund) ''On multipliers preserving convergence of trigonometric series almost everywhere.'' *Studia Mathematica* 30 (1968): 111–120.

Works about Mary Catherine Bishop Weiss

Zygmund, A. ''Mary Weiss: December 11, 1930–October 8, 1966.'' In *Orthogonal Expansions and Their Continuous Analogues*, edited by D. T. Haimo, xi–xviii. Carbondale, Ill.: Southern Illinois University Press, 1968.

ANNA JOHNSON PELL WHEELER (1883–1966)

Louise S. Grinstein and Paul J. Campbell

BIOGRAPHY

Anna Johnson Pell Wheeler was the daughter of Swedish immigrants, Andrew Gustav and Amelia (Friberg) Johnson, who came to the United States in 1872 from the same Swedish parish—Lyrestad in Skaraborglän, Wästergotland. Settling originally at Union Creek in Dakota Territory, they lived in a dugout hollowed from the side of a small hill, and the father tried to eke out a living as a farmer. In 1882 he moved his ever-growing family to the nearby town of Calliope (now Hawarden), Iowa, where Wheeler was born on May 5, 1883, the youngest of three surviving children. Her sister Esther, to whom she was very close, was four years older, and her brother Elmer was two years older. Around 1891 the Johnsons moved to Akron, Iowa, where her father became a furniture dealer and undertaker.

The earliest extant records indicate that Wheeler was sent to the Akron public school. Though there appears to have been no tradition of academic achievement in the family, in the fall of 1899 Wheeler enrolled at the University of South Dakota, where her sister had already been studying for a year. After one year as a "sub-freshman" making up entrance requirements, she fulfilled the degree requirements in three years. Her main interest—mathematics—was evinced early in her college career. One of her mathematics professors at South Dakota, Alexander Pell, recognized her talent for mathematics and actively coached her into a mathematical career.

Obtaining an A. B. degree from South Dakota in 1903, Wheeler won a scholarship to the University of Iowa. She completed a master's degree the following year, taking five mathematics courses and a philosophy course. Simultaneously, she taught a freshman mathematics course and wrote her master's thesis, "The extension of the Galois theory to linear differential equations." The quality of her work was high, and she was elected to the Iowa chapter of the scientific society Sigma Xi. Winning a scholarship to Radcliffe, she earned a second master's degree in 1905. She stayed at Radcliffe an additional year on scholarship, enrolling in courses with such noted mathematicians as Maxime Bôcher, Charles Bouton, and William Osgood.

In 1906 she applied for and won the Alice Freeman Palmer Fellowship offered by Wellesley College to a woman graduate of an American college. A stipulation of the fellowship was that she agree to remain unmarried throughout the fellowship year. Wheeler used the funds to finance a year's study at Göttingen University, then the worldwide center of intense mathematical activity. While at Göttingen, Wheeler attended lectures given by the mathematicians David Hilbert, Felix Klein, Hermann Minkowski, and Gustav Herglotz, and the astronomer Karl Schwarzschild. Of these professors, she was most influenced by Hilbert and his work.

Throughout Wheeler's years of graduate study at Iowa, Radcliffe, and Göttingen, her former teacher, Alexander Pell, kept in touch with her. He was very proud of her progress and achievements. His first wife having died in the interim, he and Wheeler finally decided to marry, despite her family's objections to the twenty-five-year age differential. In July 1907, when her fellowship expired, they were married in Göttingen. They then returned to South Dakota, where Pell had been promoted to the position of first dean of the College of Engineering. During the fall term of 1907–1908, the young wife taught two courses at South Dakota—theory of functions and differential equations. Still, she wanted the Ph.D.; and in the spring of 1908, she decided to return to Göttingen alone to complete her doctoral work.

By the late fall of 1908, Wheeler had almost completed the requirements. The final examination for the Ph.D. was imminent. Evidently, some conflict of unknown origin arose between her and Hilbert, and she returned to America in December 1908 with a thesis (written independently of Hilbert) but no degree. She rejoined her husband in Chicago, where he had moved after academic policy disagreements forced his resignation from the University of South Dakota. His new position involved teaching at the Armour Institute of Technology.

Undeterred by the turn of events in Göttingen, Wheeler enrolled immediately at the University of Chicago. After a year's residency, during which she studied under the mathematician E. H. Moore, the astronomer Forest Moulton, and the astronomer/mathematician William Macmillan, she received a Ph.D. magna cum laude. The thesis accepted by her advisor, Professor Moore, was the one she had written initially for the Göttingen degree.

After receiving the Ph.D., she sought a full-time teaching position. Unfortunately, the large midwestern universities were reluctant to hire women. In the fall of 1910, she taught part-time at the University of Chicago. When Pell suffered a paralytic stroke in the spring of 1911, she substituted for him at the Armour Institute of Technology, another institution that did not want to hire women on a full-time basis.

In the fall of 1911, a vacancy opened at Mount Holyoke College. She applied for it and was accepted. Hired initially as an instructor, she was promoted to associate professor in 1914. However, Wheeler's years at Mount Holyoke (1911–1918) were not easy ones. Teaching loads were heavy. She felt compelled at all costs to continue her research work, and she had to take care of her husband, who never fully recovered from his stroke.

In 1918 Wheeler decided to resign from her position at Mount Holyoke College and accept an associate professorship at Bryn Mawr College. She felt that Bryn Mawr offered great potential for her career advancement. The possibility of teaching advanced mathematics to graduate students intrigued her, and there was the prospect of being promoted to chairperson when Charlotte Angas Scott* retired. Professionally, her career at Bryn Mawr was successful. She became chairperson in 1924 and full professor in 1925. Except for brief periods, Wheeler remained at Bryn Mawr as chairperson and teacher until her own retirement in 1948.

Wheeler's personal life during the Bryn Mawr years was not a consistently happy one. She lost her father in 1920 and her husband several months later. There was a brief but happy second marriage, followed by the death of her second husband in 1932. In 1935 her mother died. Later that same year, Emmy Noether*, her colleague and new-found friend, also died suddenly. All of these events took their toll on Wheeler.

During Wheeler's second marriage, to Arthur Leslie Wheeler, a classics scholar, the couple lived in Princeton. Wheeler gave up her administrative duties at Bryn Mawr but continued lecturing on a part-time basis. She had more time to devote to her own research and could participate in the stimulating mathematical environment at Princeton University. Summers the Wheelers spent in the Adirondacks at a place they built and called "Q.E.D.," a name appropriate in the light of both of their careers. Following her husband's death, Wheeler returned to live and work full-time at Bryn Mawr.

Retirement for Wheeler in 1948 did not mean withdrawal from all mathematical activity. Despite recurring severe bouts of arthritis, she kept abreast of new developments and attended mathematical meetings. She remained in contact with many of her students, taking great pride in their achievements. She traveled, spending most of her summers in the Adirondacks, where she enjoyed various outdoor activities.

Wheeler suffered a stroke early in 1966. Never recovering, she died a few months later, on March 26, at the age of eighty-two. According to her wishes, she was buried beside Alexander Pell, in the Lower Merion Baptist Church Cemetery at Bryn Mawr.

Wheeler was highly respected professionally during her lifetime. Of the 211 mathematicians ever starred in *American Men of Science*, only three were women. One of them was Wheeler. Such starring was an honor reserved for those considered prominent in their field of activity by their contemporaries. In 1926 she was elected to Phi Beta Kappa. She received honorary doctorates from the New Jersey College for Women (now Douglass College of Rutgers University) (1932) and Mount Holyoke College (1937). In 1940 she was singled out as one of the one hundred American women to be acclaimed by the Women's Centennial Congress as having succeeded in careers not open to women a century before.

WORK

When Wheeler was studying at Göttingen, the most influential mathematician there was David Hilbert. In the early 1900s, Hilbert's work and interest evolved around integral equations, and he attached a great deal of importance to the subject. As a result, many mathematicians at Göttingen and throughout the world, among them Wheeler, were inspired to pursue further investigations in this area. Numerous papers were published. As the years passed, interest declined, and many of the results obtained passed into relative obscurity. An outgrowth of the work on integral equations was the development of a field in mathematics known as functional analysis, dealing with transformations, or operators, acting on functions.

Wheeler's research work spanned this period when the study of integral equations per se was at its peak of popularity and functional analysis was in its infancy. She regarded her work as being centered on "linear algebra of infinitely many variables." Her interest derived from possible applications of linear algebra to both differential and integral equations. Particularly noteworthy were her results on biorthogonal systems of functions. Some of the results she published were extended and generalized in the work of her own doctoral students at Bryn Mawr.

In 1927 Wheeler herself attempted to summarize her work and its overall importance in a series of invited lectures on the theory of quadratic forms in infinitely many variables. Unfortunately, these so-called Colloquium Lectures, presented during an American Mathematical Society meeting, were never published; but a detailed outline of the topics covered is found in an abstract written by T. H. Hildebrandt. In all the years that the Colloquium Lectures have been given at American Mathematical Society meetings, only three lecturers have been women: Wheeler in 1927, Julia Robinson* in 1980, and Karen K. Uhlenbeck in 1985.

Wheeler drew accolades for her teaching throughout her career. Despite personal pressures and research commitments, she found time and even money to give to her students. Frequently she would invite graduate students to visit her summer home, where she provided them with encouragement and research time. Students felt free to talk to her about both personal and academic problems. Often she would take students to professional meetings at neighboring colleges and universities and urge them to participate actively.

As an administrator, Wheeler strove to enhance the national and worldwide reputation of the Bryn Mawr mathematics department. She tried to create an atmosphere in which students and faculty had ample opportunity for professional growth and development. When the Depression cut into available funds at the college, she nonetheless reduced teaching loads whenever possible so that faculty could find time for research.

Wheeler was instrumental in offering professional and political asylum at Bryn Mawr to the eminent German-Jewish algebraist Emmy Noether. A group of qualified Bryn Mawr students was assembled to take part in advanced algebraic seminars with Noether. Wheeler laid plans to involve Noether in an exchange of graduate mathematics courses with the University of Pennsylvania. Unfortunately, these plans never materialized because of Noether's unexpected death following surgery in 1935, less than two years after her arrival in America.

Wheeler did not confine her professional activities to her own research or to Bryn Mawr College. She was an active participant in such national professional organizations as the American Mathematical Society and the Mathematical Association of America. From 1927 to 1945 she served as an editor of the *Annals of Mathematics*. She worked on a College Entrance Examination Board committee which formulated basic guidelines for testing the mathematical potential of college-bound students (1933–1935). She was among those who petitioned for the establishment of the *Mathematical Reviews* in 1939, when the German abstract and review journal *Zentralblatt für Mathematik und ihre Grenzgebiete* became a victim of Nazi policy.

BIBLIOGRAPHY

Works by Anna Johnson Pell Wheeler

Mathematical Works

"The extension of the Galois theory to linear differential equations." Master's thesis, University of Iowa, 1904.

"On an integral equation with an adjoined condition." *Bulletin of the American Mathematical Society* 16 (1909/1910): 412–415.

"Existence theorems for certain unsymmetric kernels." *Bulletin of the American Mathematical Society* 16 (1909/1910): 513–515.

"Biorthogonal systems of functions." *Transactions of the American Mathematical Society* 12 (1911): 135–164.
Part I of Wheeler's doctoral thesis.

"Applications of biorthogonal systems of functions to the theory of integral equations." *Transactions of the American Mathematical Society* 12 (1911): 165–180.
Part II of Wheeler's doctoral thesis.

"Non-homogeneous linear equations in infinitely many unknowns." *Annals of Mathematics* (2) 16 (1914/1915): 32–37.

(with R. L. Gordon) "The modified remainders obtained in finding the highest common factor of two polynomials." *Annals of Mathematics* (2) 18 (1916/1917): 188–193.

"Linear equations with unsymmetric systems of coefficients." *Transactions of the American Mathematical Society* 20 (1919): 23–39.

"A general system of linear equations." *Transactions of the American Mathematical Society* 20 (1919): 343–355.

"Linear equations with two parameters." *Transactions of the American Mathematical Society* 23 (1922): 198–211.

"Linear ordinary self-adjoint differential equations of the second order." *American Journal of Mathematics* 49 (1927): 309–320.

"Spectral theory for a certain class of nonsymmetric completely continuous matrices." *American Journal of Mathematics* 57 (1935): 847–853.

Works about Anna Johnson Pell Wheeler

Case, Bettye, ed. "Anna Johnson Pell Wheeler (1883–1966), Colloquium Lecturer, 1927. Proceedings of the Symposium held on August 20, 1980, at Ann Arbor, MI." *Association for Women in Mathematics Newsletter* 12 (4) (July-August 1982): 4–13.

Summary of a symposium at which Wheeler's life and achievement were described and glowing tributes from former students and colleagues were presented. Several previously unpublished photographs are included.

Grinstein, Louise S., and Paul J. Campbell. "Anna Johnson Pell Wheeler: Her life and work." *Historia Mathematica* 9 (1982): 37–53.

Detailed account of Wheeler's life and achievements. An earlier version was published in the *Association for Women in Mathematics Newsletter* 8 (3) (September 1978): 14–16, 8 (4) (November 1978): 8–12.

Hildebrandt, T. H. "Abstract of The 'theory of quadratic forms in infinitely many variables and applications.' " *Bulletin of the American Mathematical Society* 33 (1927): 664–665.

Summary of Wheeler's Colloquium Lectures.

GRACE CHISHOLM YOUNG (1868–1944)

Sylvia M. Wiegand

BIOGRAPHY

In 1895 Grace Chisholm Young, an Englishwoman, became the first woman to receive a doctorate in any field in Germany. (Sofia Kovalevskaia* had received her degree in absentia in 1874.) She and her husband, William Henry Young, had a unique mathematical marriage which resulted in a combined total of about 220 mathematical articles and several books (as well as six children).

Grace Young was born at Haslemere (near London) on March 15, 1868, the youngest of four children; the other children, Hugh, Marion, and Helen, were also born in the 1860s. Her father, Henry William Chisholm, was fifty-nine, and her mother, Anna Louisa Bell, was forty-four. Henry Chisholm was a Warden of the Standards, an important position in the British government; he worked as a civil servant for fifty-four years.

Young was educated at home by her mother and a governess; nevertheless, she managed to pass the Cambridge Senior Examination in 1885 at the age of seventeen. Young's brother went to Oxford, but at that time women rarely went to a university. Girton College, associated with Cambridge University, was the first institution in England dedicated to educating women at the university level, and it had been in existence only since 1869. At first Young was encouraged to spend her time helping the poor and otherwise "making herself useful." However, she had great initiative and desire for learning, so she entered Girton in 1889. In the Cambridge Tripos Part I examination in 1892, Young scored the equivalent of a first class; and then, in response to a challenge, she took the Oxford examination unofficially and obtained the highest mark for all students at Oxford that year.

Young went to Göttingen University in Germany to continue her studies, because it would have been impossible in England. At that time Göttingen was one of the major centers of mathematical activity in the world, and Felix Klein was the leading mathematician there. His name is still well known; the Klein bottle (named for him) is a four-dimensional figure with no inside surface. A letter written by Young to her old college friend at Girton describes the situation at Göttingen:

Professor Klein's attitude is this, he will not countenance the admission of any woman who has not already done good work, and can bring him proof of the same in the form of degrees or their equivalent, or letters from professors of standing and further he will not take any steps till he has assured himself by a personal interview of the solidity of her claims. Prof. Klein's view is moderate. There are members of the Faculty here who are more eagerly in favor of the admission of women and others who disapprove altogether. (Cartwright 1944, 186–187)

Young earned the Ph.D. magna cum laude at age twenty-seven; the following year she married William Henry Young, an Englishman who had been her tutor at Girton before she went to Göttingen. Will Young served as president of the London Mathematical Society from 1922 to 1924, and he was president of the International Union of Mathematicians in 1929. Among other things, he is famous for his discovery (independent of Henri Lebesgue) of the integral, and his work on Fourier series and cluster sets.

The pattern of their life together was that Will traveled to and from their family home in Switzerland to earn a living, while Grace Young brought up the children and followed her other interests; and both of them worked intensely on mathematics. Among Grace's other interests were medicine, languages, and music. She completed all the requirements for a medical degree except the internship (her medical practice was therefore limited to the family). She knew six languages and taught them to the children, to whom she also communicated her love of music. Each child played an instrument, and the family gave informal concerts together.

A few years after the marriage, Grace and Will exchanged roles. Previously Grace had been the researcher of the pair, but she became so impressed by his creativity that she unofficially became his scribe. She wrote up his papers for publication, often filling in proofs and correcting mistakes. In short, Grace helped a great deal with papers signed by Will; but, more than that, he would probably have accomplished very little without her, and he realized it. Will certainly had a profusion of ideas and great intelligence, but he would not have had the time nor the temperament to carry them through. An illustration of the kind of help she gave him is given by a footnote to one of his papers (W. Young 1914, 110):

Various circumstances have prevented me from composing the present paper myself. The substance of it only was given to my wife, who has kindly put it into form. The careful elaboration of the argument is due to her.

Also, Will wrote to Grace outlining his view of their situation:

I hope you enjoy this working for me. On the whole I think it is, at present at any rate, quite as it should be, seeing that we are responsible only to ourselves as to division of laurels. The work is not of a character to cause conflicting claims. I am very happy that you are getting on with the ideas. I feel partly as if I were teaching you, and setting you problems which I could not quite do myself but could enable you to. Then again I think of myself as like Klein, furnishing the steam required—the initiative, the guidance. But I feel confident too that we are rising *together* to new heights. You do need a good deal of criticism when you are at your best, and in your best working vein.

The fact is that our papers ought to be published under our joint names, but if this were done neither of us get the benefit of it. No. Mine the laurels now and the knowledge. Yours the knowledge only. Everything under my name now, and later when the loaves and fishes are no more procurable in that way, everything or much under your name.

There is my programme. At present you can't undertake a public career. You have your children. I can and do. Every post which brings an answer from you to my last request or suggestion gives me a pleasurable excitement. Life here is more interesting with such stimulants. I am kept working and thinking, too, myself. Everything seems to say we are on the right track just now. But we must flood the societies with papers. They need not all of them be up to the continental standard, but they must show knowledge which others have not got and they must be numerous. (Grattan-Guinness 1972, 141–142)

In addition, Young's daughter Cecily has written about Grace's assistance to Will:

Another famous partnership, that of George Eliot and Lewes, can be taken as in many respects the counterpart of that of my parents. There it was the man who took the brunt of life off the woman's shoulders and spent his creative energies in fostering her genius. This my mother clearly appreciated.

When all is said, it remains that my father had ideas and a wide grasp of subjects, but was by nature undecided; his mind worked only when stimulated by the reactions of a sympathetic audience. My mother had decision and initiative and the stamina to carry an undertaking to its conclusion. Her skill in understanding and in responding, and her pleasure in exercising this skill led her naturally into the position she filled so uniquely. If she had not had that skill, my father's genius would probably have been abortive, and would not have eclipsed hers and the name she had already made for herself. (Wiegand 1977, 7)

In the spring of 1940, Young left Will in Switzerland while she accompanied two of their grandchildren to England, intending to rejoin him in a few days. Due to the collapse of France in World War II, they were not able to see each other again; Will became depressed and senile in his isolation in Switzerland and died in 1942. Two years later, in England, Young suffered a heart attack and died at age seventy-six. The Fellows of Girton College had just recommended that she be awarded an honorary degree; they regretted that she died before the degree could be awarded.

Of the Young's six children, the oldest, Francis Chisholm Young, died in World War I. The second child, Rosalind (Cecily) Tanner, born in 1900, is a mathematician and historian; another daughter, Janet Michael (born in 1901), fulfilled her mother's dream of becoming a medical doctor; and Helen Marion Canu (1903–1940), the last daughter, studied graduate-level mathematics. The two youngest sons, Lawrence Chisholm Young (1904) and Patrick Chisholm Young (1908), became a mathematician and a chemist, respectively.

WORK

(This discussion of Grace Young's work will be limited to articles in her name.)

Young's dissertation was on "The algebraic groups of spherical trigonometry." Some parts of her thesis are mentioned in Klein's book, *Elementary Mathematics from an Advanced Standpoint* (Vol. 1, p. 179). To each spherical triangle on the unit sphere, Klein associates a point of 12–space as follows:

The figure corresponds to the point $(\cos a, \cos b, \cos c, \cos \alpha, \cos \beta, \cos \gamma, \sin a, \ldots \sin \gamma)$ in $\mathbf{R}_{12}$.

If M_3 is the image of the set of all spherical triangles, then M_3 is a three-dimensional algebraic set of $\mathbf{R}_{12}$. Klein found nine identities satisfied by M_3, and then went on to say:

One could gain familiarity with these things by consulting investigations which have been made in exactly the same direction but in which the questions have been put somewhat differently. These appear in the Göttingen dissertation, 1894, of Miss Chisholm (now Mrs. Young), who by the way, was the first woman to pass the normal examination in Prussia for the doctor's degree.

Klein describes Young's work briefly: she considered an image of the spherical triangles in $\mathbf{R}_6$ and completely characterized this M_3.

Young's most important independent work appears in a group of papers published from 1914 to 1916, in which she studied derivates of real functions. In 1915 Girton College awarded her the Gamble Prize for one of these papers, "On infinite derivates." Her introduction to the essay is exuberant and imaginative: "Away with your ordinary curves, the wild atom will none of them." Young's 1916 paper in *Proceedings of the London Mathematical Society* gives her part of the following theorem, now known as the Denjoy-Saks-Young theorem: First we define the *upper right Dini derivate*

$$D^+ f(t_0) = \limsup_{h \to 0^+} \frac{f(t_0 + h) - f(t_0)}{h};$$

$D_+ f(t_0)$, $D^- f(t_0)$, $D_- f(t_0)$ are defined similarly.

Theorem: Except at a set of measure zero, there are three possible dispositions of the derivates of a function $f(x)$, either

(i)   they are all equal and the function is differentiable or,

(ii)   the upper derivates on each side are $+\infty$ and the lower derivates on each side are $-\infty$, or

(iii) the upper derivate on one side is $+\infty$, the lower derivate on the other side is $-\infty$ and the two remaining extreme derivates are finite and equal.

According to Friedrich Riesz and Béla Sz. Nagy, the theorem was proved for continuous $f(x)$ by Arnaud Denjoy and Young independently; Young proved it for measurable $f(x)$, then Stanislaw Saks generalized to all $f(x)$. Lloyd Jackson, an analyst at the University of Nebraska, once mentioned that this theorem was one of his favorites, and it was extremely useful to him in his work, because eliminating options (ii) and (iii) is sufficient to show that a function is differentiable.

In 1905 a geometry book was published in both Youngs' names, but it seems likely that it was written by Grace, because the German edition was published under her name alone. In those days the study of geometry was limited to theorems for the plane; but Young's book included a lot of paper-folding patterns for three-dimensional figures, as well as pictures of the completed figures. The book was intended for elementary school children; and in fact, seven-year-old son Frank helped her with some parts.

Will and Grace Young jointly published a book entitled *The Theory of Sets of Points* in 1906, which was the first of its kind. Set theory was not popular with most mathematicians at that time, but Georg Cantor was very enthusiastic about the book:

It was with great joy that I received the day before yesterday the copy you have most kindly sent to me of your joint work with your husband, "The Theory of Sets of Points". My sincerest thanks to you both.

It is a pleasure for me to see with what diligence, skill and success you have worked and I wish you, in your further researches in this field as well, the finest results, which, with such depth and acuteness of mind on both your parts, you cannot fail to attain. (From the Preface to the Second Edition, by R.C.H. Tanner.)

The authors commented on the importance of set theory in the original preface to the book:

In subjects as wide apart as Projective Geometry, Theory of Functions of a Complex Variable, the Expansions of Astronomy, Calculus of Variations, Differential Equations, mistakes have in fact been made by mathematicians of standing, which even a slender grasp of the Theory of Sets would have enabled them to avoid.

Two joint papers by Grace and Will Young are referred to in Collingwood and Lohwater's book *The Theory of Cluster Sets* (1966, 15, 80). These papers and some signed by Will were important to the development of the theory of cluster sets and prime sets. The titles of some other papers by Young in the bibliography show her diversity of interests, including astronomy, Plato, and the history of the Pythagorean theorem.

In addition to Young's mathematical works, she wrote two books for children, which were lessons on elementary biology (they included cell structure seen under a microscope and contained the story of a family like the Youngs). She worked for five years on a sixteenth-century historical novel (unpublished) called *The Crown of England.*

NOTE BY THE AUTHOR

My father is Laurence Chisholm Young, the fifth child of Grace Chisholm and William Henry Young. In 1970 he retired from the University of Wisconsin, where he had been on the faculty of the mathematics department for twenty-eight years. I am an associate professor of mathematics at the University of Nebraska, the only grandchild to earn a Ph.D. in mathematics. A great grand-daughter of W. H. Young's sister Hepsibah, Hilary Priestly, is a mathematician at Oxford.

Grace Chisholm Young died before I was born, so, unfortunately, we never met. The presence of so many mathematicians in my family (and particularly women mathematicians) has been inspirational for me. Growing up with a tradition of mathematics for women made it seem a natural thing to do and provided helpful role models that most women do not have.

The main source for this essay is Grattan-Guinness (1972).

BIBLIOGRAPHY

Works by Grace Chisholm Young

Mathematical Works

"Algebraisch-gruppentheoretische Untersuchungen zur sphärischen Trigonometrie." Ph.D. diss., University of Göttingen, 1895 (as Grace Chisholm).
"On the curve $y = (x^2 + \sin^2 \psi)^{-3/2}$, and its connection with an astronomical problem." *Monthly Notices, Royal Astronomical Society* 57 (1897): 379–387 (as Mrs. W. H. Young [Miss Grace Chisholm]).
"Sulla varietà razionali normale M^4_3 di S_6 rappresentante della trigonometria sferica." *Atti della Accademia Reale delle Scienze di Torino* 34 (1898): 429–438. (The cumulative pagination is 587–596.)
"On the form of a certain Jordan curve." *Quarterly Journal of Pure and Applied Mathematics* 37 (1905): 87–91.
"A note on derivates and differential coefficients." *Acta Mathematica* 37 (1914): 141–154.
"On infinite derivates." *Quarterly Journal of Pure and Applied Mathematics* 47 (1916): 127–175.
Young won the Gamble Prize for this paper on continuous non-differentiable functions.
"Sur les nombres dérivés d'une fonction." *Comptes rendus hebdomadaires des séances de l'Académie des Sciences* 162 (1916): 380–382.

"On the derivates of a function." *Proceedings of the London Mathematical Society* (2) 15 (1916): 360–384; corrections, (2) 19 (1921): 152.

"Démonstration du lemme de Lebesgue sans l'emploi des nombres de Cantor." *Bulletin des Sciences Mathématiques* (2) 43 (1919): 245–247.

"A note on a theorem of Riemann's." *Messenger of Mathematics* 49 (1919–1920): 73–78.

"On the partial derivates of a function of many variables." *Proceedings of the London Mathematical Society* (2) 20 (1922): 182–188.

"On the solution of a pair of simultaneous Diophantine equations connected with the nuptial number of Plato." *Proceedings of the London Mathematical Society* (2) 23 (1924): 27–44.

"Pythagore, comment a-t-il trouvé son théorème?" *L'Enseignement mathématique* (1) 25 (1926): 248–255.

"On functions possessing differentials." *Fundamenta Mathematicae* 14 (1929): 61–94.

Joint works with W. H. Young

The First Book of Geometry. London: Dent, 1905. Reprinted. New York, 1969. German translation. Leipzig, 1908. Italian translation. Turin, 1911. Hebrew translation. Dresden, 1921.

The Theory of Sets of Points. Cambridge, England: Cambridge University Press, 1906. Reprint. New York, 1972.

"Note on Bertini's transformation of a curve into one possessing only nodes." *Atti della Accademia Reale delle Scienze di Torino* 42 (1906): 82–86.

"An additional note on derivates and the theorem of the mean." *Quarterly Journal of Pure and Applied Mathematics* 40 (1909): 144–145.

"Discontinuous functions continuous with respect to every straight line." *Quarterly Journal of Pure and Applied Mathematics* 41 (1910): 87–93.

"On the determination of a semi-continuous function from a countable set of values." *Proceedings of the London Mathematical Society* (2) 8 (1910): 330–339.

"On the existence of a differential coefficient." *Proceedings of the London Mathematical Society* (2) 9 (1911): 325–335.

"On the theorem of Riesz-Fischer." *Quarterly Journal of Pure and Applied Mathematics* 44 (1913): 49–88.

"On the reduction of sets of intervals." *Proceedings of the London Mathematical Society* (2) 14 (1914): 111–130.

"Sur la frontière normale d'une région ou d'un ensemble." *Comptes rendus hebdomadaires des séances de l'Académie des Sciences* 163 (1916): 509–511.

"On the internal structure of a set of points in space of any number of dimensions." *Proceedings of the London Mathematical Society* (2) 16 (1917): 337–351.

"On the inherently crystalline structure of a function of any number of variables." *Proceedings of the London Mathematical Society* (2) 17 (1918): 1–16.

"On the discontinuities of monotone functions of several variables." *Proceedings of the London Mathematical Society* (2) 22 (1924): 124–142.

"A time-honoured mystery from the Meno of Plato." *O Instituto* 78 (1929): 20pp.

Works about Grace Chisholm Young

Cartwright, M. L. "Grace Chisholm Young." *Journal of the London Mathematical Society* 19 (1944): 185–192.

Grattan-Guinness, I. "A joint bibliography of W. H. and G. C. Young." *Historia Mathematica* 2 (1975): 43–58.

————. "A mathematical union: William Henry and Grace Chisholm Young." *Annals of Science* 29 (1972): 105–186.

Includes many of the Youngs' letters and autobiographical notes. There are appealing descriptions by Grace of her final oral, of obtaining official permission for the Ph.D., of her childhood, and of her children.

Wiegand, Sylvia. "Grace Chisholm Young." *Association for Women in Mathematics Newsletter* 7 (3) (May–June 1977): 5–10.

Other References

Collingwood, E. F., and A. J. Lohwater. *The Theory of Cluster Sets*. Cambridge, England: Cambridge University Press, 1966.

Young, W. H. "On integration with respect to a function of bounded variation." *Proceedings of the London Mathematical Society* (2) 13 (1914): 109–150.

APPENDICES

Appendix A
BIOGRAPHEES IN CHRONOLOGICAL ORDER BY BIRTHDATE

```
                                    | 1816                                                      1987 |

Hypatia (370?-415)
Châtelet (1706-1749)
Agnesi (1718-1799)
Germain (1776-1831)         ****
Somerville (1780-1872)      ********************
Lovelace (1815-1852)        ************
Litvinova (1845-1919?)                    *********************
Ladd-Franklin (1847-1930)                 *********************
Kovalevskaia (1850-1891)                  **************
Hayes (1851-1930)                         ********************
Scott (1858-1931)                             ******************
Stott (1860-1940)                             *******************
Merrill (1864-1949)                               ******************
Young (1868-1944)                                 ******************
Maddison (1869-1950)                              *******************
Newson (1869-1959)                                    ********************
Sinclair (1878-1955)                                  ******************
Noether (1882-1935)                                       **************
Wheeler (1883-1966)                                       ***********************
Sperry (1885-1967)                                        ***********************
```

Kendall (1889-1965)

Geiringer von Mises (1893-1973)

Janovskaja (1896-1966)

Kochina (1899-   )

Cox (1900-1978)

Bari, N. K. (1901-1961)

Kramer (1902-1984)

Rees (1902-   )

Flügge-Lotz (1903-1974)

Péter (1905-1977)

Fenchel (1905-1983)

Hopper (1906-   )

Taussky-Todd (1906-   )

Macintyre (1910-1960)

Neumann (1914-1971)

Bernstein (1914-   )

Bari, R. (1917-   )

Robinson (1919-1985)

Morawetz (1923-   )

Granville (1924-   )

Rudin (1924-   )

Karp (1926-1972)

Weiss (1930-1966)

Note: Each star denotes three years.

Appendix B
BIOGRAPHEES BY PLACE OF ORIGIN, HIGHEST EDUCATION, PLACE OF WORK, AND FIELD OF MATHEMATICAL WORK

Name	Origin	Education	Place of Work	Field
Agnesi	Italy	Tutoring from professor at Pavia U.	Italy	Analysis
Bari, N.	Russia	Ph.D., Moscow (1926) D.Phys.Math.Sci, Moscow (1935)	USSR	Trigonometric series
Bari, R.	New York	Ph.D., Johns Hopkins (1966)	USA	Graph theory
Bernstein	Illinois	Ph.D., Brown (1939)	USA	Applied mathematics
Châtelet	France	Private tutor, France	France	Analysis
Cox	Iowa	M.S., Iowa State (1931); study at UC-Berkeley (1931–1933)	Institute of Statistics, North Carolina	Design of experiments
Fenchel	Germany	Four years at U. Berlin	Denmark	Nonabelian groups (algebra)
Flügge-Lotz	Germany	Doktor-Ingenieur, Hanover (1929)	Germany and Stanford University	Engineering mechanics, aeronautics, automatic control
Geiringer von Mises	Austria	Ph.D., Vienna (1917) D.Sc., Wheaton (1960)	Wheaton College	Trigonometric series, probability theory, applied mathematics
Germain	France	École central des travaux publics	France	Number theory, elasticity
Granville	Washington D.C.	Ph.D., Yale (1949)	USA	Complex analysis, teacher education
Hayes	Ohio	A.B., Oberlin (1878)	Wellesley College	Applied mathematics
Hopper	New York	Ph.D., Yale (1934)	U.S. Navy	Computer science
Hypatia	Egypt	The Museum, Alexandria	Egypt	Geometry, number theory, astronomy
Janovskaja	Russian Poland	Ph.D., Moscow (1935)	USSR	History of logic
Karp	Michigan	Ph.D., Southern California (1959)	U. Maryland	Mathematical logic
Kendall	Colorado	Ph.D., Chicago (1921)	U. of Colorado	Linear algebra, differential geometry

Name	Region	Degree	Location	Research areas
Kochina	Russia	D.Phys.Math.Sci., Moscow (1940)	Moscow and Siberia	Hydrodynamics, differential equations
Kovalevskaia	Russia	Ph.D., Göttingen (1874)	France, Germany, Sweden	Analysis, mechanics, mathematical physics
Kramer	New York	Ph.D., Columbia (1930)	Thomas Jefferson High School, Brooklyn	Complex analysis, history of mathematics
Ladd-Franklin	Connecticut	Ph.D. Johns Hopkins [1882] (1926) LL.D., Vassar College (1887)	USA	Symbolic logic
Litvinova	Russia	Ph.D., Bern (1878)	Russia	Function theory, pedagogy, biography
Lovelace	England	Private study and tutors, England	England	Computing
Macintyre	Scotland	Ph.D., Aberdeen (1949)	Scotland, Cincinnati University	Analysis
Maddison	England	Ph.D., Bryn Mawr (1896)	Bryn Mawr College	Algebraic geometry
Merrill	New Jersey	Ph.D., Yale (1903)	Wellesley College	Analysis
Morawetz	Toronto, Canada	Ph.D., New York U. (1951)	Courant Institute	Applications of differential equations
Neumann	Germany	D.Phil., Oxford (1944) D.Sc., Oxford (1955)	England and Australia	Combinatorial group theory
Newson	Illinois	Ph.D., Göttingen (1897)	Kansas and Illinois	Differential equations
Noether	Germany	Ph.D., Erlangen (1907)	Göttingen, Germany	Modern abstract algebra
Péter	Hungary	Ph.D., Eötvös Loránd U. (1935) Dr. with the Academy (1952)	Hungary	Mathematical logic
Rees	Ohio	Ph.D., Chicago (1932)	USA	Algebra, analysis, applied mathematics
Robinson	Missouri	Ph.D., UC-Berkeley (1948)	USA	Mathematical logic
Rudin	Texas	Ph.D., Texas (1949)	U. Wisconsin	Topology
Scott	England	D.Sc., London (1885)	Bryn Mawr College	Algebraic geometry
Sinclair	Massachusetts	Ph.D., Chicago (1908)	Oberlin College	Calculus of variations
Somerville	Scotland	Private study, London	England and Italy	Celestial mechanics

Sperry	Massachusetts	Ph.D., Chicago (1916)	UC-Berkeley	Projective differential geometry
Stott	Ireland	none past age 16	London	Geometry
Taussky-Todd	Austro-Hungary	Ph.D., Vienna (1930)	Cal-Tech	Number theory and matrices
Weiss	Kansas	Ph.D., Chicago (1957)	USA	Analysis
Wheeler	Iowa	Ph.D., Chicago (1910)	Bryn Mawr College	Functional analysis
Young	England	Ph.D., Göttingen (1895)	Switzerland	Algebraic geometry, analysis

Appendix C
REFERENCES IN BIOGRAPHICAL DICTIONARIES AND OTHER COLLECTIONS

Note: A Key to Title Codes appears at the end of this appendix.

Agnesi   Alic, Archibald, Britannica (11th), CG, Coolidge, DcScB, Fang, Gomes, Hale, Iacobacci, IntDcWomB, Ireland, Jacotin, Loria, May, Mozans, NCE, Osen, Perl, Poggendorf, Poole, Rebière, Tee, Valentin, WorWhoSci, WS, Zen

Bari, N. K.   CG, Fang, May, Poggendorf, WS, Zen

Bari, R.   DWM73,–81

Bernstein   AmM&WS73,–76,–79,–82, DWM73,–81, LEduc74, WhoAm74, WhoAmW64,–66,–68,–70,–72,–74,WhoWorJ72

Châtelet   Alic, Britannica (15th), CG, Coolidge, DcScB, Fang, Hale, IntDcWomB, Ireland, LinLibL, Loria, May, Mozans, Osen, OxFr, Perl, Poggendorf, Rebière, REn, Tee, Valentin, WorWhoSci, WS, Zen

Cox   AmM&WS73, WhAm81, WhoAm78, WhoAmW58,–61,–64, WomBkWorRec, WS

Fenchel

Flügge-Lotz   AmM&WS73, NewYTBS74, NotAW80, Siegel, WhAm76, WhoAmW70, WomBkWorRec, WomPar, WS

Geiringer   CG, Dresden, Ireland, NotAW80, Siegel (under von Mises), WomPar, WS

Germain   Alic, Archibald, Britannica (15th), CG, Coolidge, DcScB, Eneström-II, Gomes, Hale, Iacobacci, IntDcWomB, Ireland, Jacotin, Loria, May, Michaud, Möbius, Mozans, Osen, Perl, Poggendorf, Rebière, Tee, Valentin, WorWhoSci, WS, Zen

Granville   Newell, WND, WomPar (under Collins)

Hayes   AmM&WS27,–33, CG, DcNAA, Ireland, OhA&B, Rebière, Siegel, TwCBDA, WhAm43, WhNAA, WomPar, WomWWA, WS

Hopper   AmM&WS73,–76,–79,–82, DWM73,–81, GoodHs, IntDcWomB, NewYTBE71, Owens, WhoAm74,–76,–78,–82, WhoAmW58, –61,–64,–66,–70,–72,–74, WomBkWorRec,WS

Hypatia   Adelman, Alic, Archibald, AsBiEn, Britannica (11th, 15th), Cantor, CG, Coolidge, DcScB, Gomes, GoodHs, Hale, Hays, Iacobacci, IntDCWomB, Ireland, Jacotin, LinLibL, LinLibS, Loria, May, Michaud, Mozans, NewC, Osen, Pauly, Perl, Poggendorf, Poole, Rebière, REn, Schmidt, Tee, WorWhoSci, WS, Zen

Janovskaja   CG, WS, Zen

Karp   AmM&WS73, CG, WhoAmW66, -68, WS, Zen

Kendall   AmM&WS61, AmWom, CG, Owens, WS, Zen

Kochina   IntWW74,–75,–76,–77, Ireland, Zen

Kovalevskaia	Adelman, Alic, Archibald, Bell, BiD&SB, Britannica (11th, 15th), CasWL, CG, Coolidge, DcScB, Eneström-I, Gomes, Iacobacci, IntDcWomB, Ireland, Jacotin, Loria, May, Möbius, Mozans, Osen, Perl, Poggendorf, Poole, Rebière, Riches, Schmidt, Valentin, WND, WorWhoSci, WS, Zen
Kramer	AmM&WS73,–76,–79, ConAu83 (vol. 107), DWM73,–81, Owens, WhoAmW64,–74,–75,–77
Ladd-Franklin	AmBi, AmM&WS27,–33, BiCAW, Britannica (15th), CG, DcAmB, DcNAA, Eells, Ireland (under Franklin), LibW, May, NatCAB26, -B, NotAW, Poggendorf, Rebière, Siegel, TwCBDA, Valentin, WhAm43, WhNAA, WomPar, WorWhoSci, WS
Litvinova	WS, Zen
Lovelace	Alic, CG, IntDcWomB, Jacotin, Michaud, NewC, Perl, Poole, Rebière, Tee, WND, WS, Zen
Macintyre	CG, May, NatCAB48, WomPar, WS
Maddison	AmM&WS49, CG, Eels, Eneström–II, Owens, Poggendorf, Rebière, Siegel, Valentin, WomWWA, WS
Merrill	AmM&WS49, AmWom, BiDAmEd, CG, DcNAA, NatCAB42, Owens, Siegel, WomPar, WomWWA, WS
Morawetz	AmM&WS73,–76,–79,–82, DWM73,–81, WhoAm82, WhoAmW81, WS
Neumann	CG, Kramer, WomBkWorRec, WorWhoSci, WS
Newson	AmM&WS55,–61, AmWom, CG, Owens, Poggendorf, Rebière, Siegel, Valentin, WomWWA, WS
Noether	Britannica (15th), CG, DcScB, Iacobacci, IntDcWomB, Jacotin, Jones, May, Osen, Perl, Poggendorf, Siegel, Wer, WhoNG, WND, WomBkWorRec, WorWhoSci, WS, Zen
Péter	CG, WS
Rees	AmM&WS73,76,–79,–82, CurBio57, DWM81, IntWW74,–75, –76,–77,–78, Ireland, Jones, Owens, WhoAm74,–76,–78,–82, WhoAmW58,–61,–64,–66,–68,–70,–72,–74, WomBkWorRec, WomPar, WS
Robinson	AmM&WS82, DWM81, WhoAm78, WS
Rudin	AmM&WS76,–79,–82, DWM73,–81, WhoAm82, WS
Scott	AmM&WS27,–33, BiDAmS, CG, DcNAA, Eneström–II, IntDcWomB, Ireland, May, NotAW, Osen, Poggendorf, Rebière, Siegel, Valentin, WhAm43, WomBkWorRec, WomPar, WomWWA, WS
Sinclair	AmM&WS55,–61, AmWom, CG, Owens, Poggendorf, WS
Somerville	Adelman, Alic, Alli, BibD, BiD&SB, BrAu19, Britannica, CG, Chambr3, Coolidge, DcEnL, DcScB, DiNB, EvLB, Hale, IntDcWomB, Ireland, Jacotin, May, Mozans, Osen, Perl, Poggendorf, Poole, Rebière, Tee, Valentin, Walford, WND, WorWhoSci, WS, Zen

Sperry	AmM&WS38,−61, AmWom, CG, Owens, WhoAmW58, WS
Stott	CG, WS
Taussky-Todd	AmM&WS73,−76,−79, DWM73,−81, IntAu&W77, WhoAm78, WhoAmW74,−75, WhoWest82, WS
Weiss	CG, WS
Wheeler	AmM&WS55, BiDAmEd, CG, NotAW80, Owens, Poggendorf, Siegel, WhoAm51, WomPar, WS
Young	CG, Eneström−II, Perl, Poggendorf, Rebière, WhLit, Who44, WS

KEY TO TITLE CODES

(Some of the title codes are from *Biography and Genealogy Master Index*, 2nd ed., and *1983 Supplement*, edited by Miranda C. Herbert and Barbara McNeil. Detroit: Gale Research Company, 1980, 1983.)

Adelman	Adelman, Joseph Ferdinand Gottlieb. *Famous Women*. New York: Lonow, 1926.
Alic	Alic, Margaret. *Hypatia's Heritage*. London: The Women's Press Limited, 1986.
Alli	Allibone, S. Austin. *A Critical Dictionary of English Literature and British and American Authors Living and Deceased from the Earliest Accounts to the Latter Half of the Nineteenth Century*. 3 vols. Philadelphia: J. B. Lippincott & Co., 1858−1871. Reprint. Detroit: Gale Research Co., 1965.
AmBi	Preston, Wheeler. *American Biographies*. New York: Harper & Brothers Publishers, 1940. Reprint. Detroit: Gale Research Co., 1974.
AmM&WS	*American Men and Women of Science. Physical and Biological Sciences* (formerly *American Men of Science*). Edited by Jaques Cattell. New York: R. R. Bowker Co., 1927, 1933, 1938, 1949, 1955, 1961, 1971−1973, 1976−1978, 1979, 1982.
AmWom	*American Women; The Official Who's Who Among the Women of the Nation*. 3 vols. Edited by Durward Howes. Los Angeles: American Publications, 1935−1940. Consolidated and reprinted as *American Women 1935−1940: A Composite Biographical Dictionary*. Detroit: Gale Research Co., 1981.
Archibald	Archibald, R. C. "Women as mathematicians and astronomers." *American Mathematical Monthly* 25 (1918): 136−139.
AsBiEn	*Asimov's Biographical Encyclopedia of Science and Technology*. 2nd revised edition. Edited by Isaac Asimov. New York: Doubleday, 1982.

Bell   Bell, Eric Temple. *Men of Mathematics*. New York: Simon and Schuster, 1937.

BibD   *The Bibliophile Dictionary*. Originally published as Volumes 29 and 30 of *The Bibliophile Library of Literature, Art, and Rare Manuscripts*. Compiled and arranged by Nathan Haskell Dole, Forrest Morgan, and Caroline Ticknor. New York and London: International Bibliophile Society, 1904. Reprint. Detroit: Gale Research Co., 1966.

BiCAW   *The Biographical Cyclopaedia of American Women*. 2 vols. Vol. 1: Compiled under the supervision of Mabel Ward Cameron. New York: Halvord Publishing Co., Inc., 1924. Vol. 2: Compiled under the supervision of Erma Conkling Lee. New York: Franklin W. Lee Publishing Corp., 1925. Reprint (both volumes). Detroit: Gale Research Co., 1974.

BiDAmEd   *Biographical Dictionary of American Educators*. 3 vols. Edited by John F. Ohles. Westport, Conn.: Greenwood Press, 1978.

BiDAmS   Elliott, Clark A. *Biographical Dictionary of American Science, the Seventeenth through the Nineteenth Centuries*. Westport, Conn.: Greenwood Press, 1979.

BiD&SB   *Biographical Dictionary and Synopsis of Books Ancient and Modern*. Edited by Charles Dudley Warner. Akron, Ohio: Werner Co., 1902. Reprint. Detroit: Gale Research Co., 1965.

BrAu   *British Authors before 1800: A Biographical Dictionary*. Edited by Stanley J. Kunitz and Howard Haycraft. New York: H. W. Wilson Co., 1952.

Britannica   *Encyclopaedia Britannica*. 11th ed. Cambridge, England: Cambridge University Press, 1910–1911. *The New Encyclopaedia Britannica*. 15th ed. Chicago: Encyclopaedia Britannica, Inc., 1974.

Cantor   Cantor, Moritz. *Vorlesungen über Geschichte der Mathematik*. 3 vols. Leipzig: Teubner, 1922.

CasWL   *Cassell's Encyclopaedia of World Literature*. Edited by S. H. Steinberg in two volumes. Revised and enlarged in three volumes by J. Buchanan-Brown. New York: William Morrow & Co., 1973.

CG   Campbell, Paul J., and Louise S. Grinstein. "Women in mathematics: A preliminary selected bibliography." *Philosophia Mathematica* 13/14 (1976/77): 171–203 + errata from first author.

Chambr   *Chambers's Cyclopaedia of English Literature*. 3 vols. Edited by David Patrick, revised by J. Liddell Geddie. Philadelphia: J. B. Lippincott Co., 1938. Reprint. Detroit: Gale Research Co., 1978.

ConAu   *Contemporary Authors*. 118 vols. Detroit: Gale Research Co., 1967–1986.

Coolidge   Coolidge, Julian L. "Six female mathematicians." *Scripta Mathematica* 17 (1951): 20–31.

CurBio   *Current Biography Yearbook*. New York: H. W. Wilson Co., 1940–1980.

DcAmB | *Dictionary of American Biography.* 20 vols. and 6 supplements. Edited under the auspices of the American Council of Learned Societies. New York: Charles Scribner's Sons, 1928–1936, 1944, 1958, 1973, 1974, 1977, 1980.

DcEnL | Adams, W. Davenport. *Dictionary of English Literature: Being a Comprehensive Guide to English Authors and Their Works.* 2nd ed. London: Cassell Petter & Galpin, n.d. Reprint. Detroit: Gale Research Co., 1966.

DcNAA | *A Dictionary of North American Authors Deceased before 1950.* Compiled by W. Stewart Wallace. Toronto: Ryerson Press, 1951. Reprint. Detroit: Gale Research Co., 1968.

DcScB | *Dictionary of Scientific Biography.* 14 vols. and supplement. Edited by Charles Coulston Gillispie. New York: Charles Scribner's Sons, 1970–1976, 1978.

DiNB | *Dictionary of National Biography.* 63 vols. Edited by Leslie Stephen and Sidney Lee. London: Smith, Elder, & Co., 1885–1901. With 7 supplements covering 1901–1960.

Dresden | Dresden, Arnold. "The migration of mathematicians." *American Mathematical Monthly* 49 (1942): 415–429.

DWM | *Directory of Women in the Mathematical Sciences.* Committee on Women in Mathematics, September 1981. *Directory* of *Women Mathematicians.* American Mathematical Society, 1973.

Eells | Eells, Walter Crosby. "American doctoral dissertations on mathematics and astronomy written by women in the 19th century." *Mathematics Teacher* 50 (1957): 374–376.

Eneström–I | Eneström, Gustaf. "Bio-bibliographie der 1881–1900 verstorbenen Mathematiker." *Bibliotheca Mathematica* 2 (1901): 326–350.

Eneström–II | Eneström, Gustaf. "Note bibliographique sur les femmes dans les sciences exactes." *Bibliotheca Mathematica* 10 (1896): 73–76.

EvLB | *Everyman's Dictionary of Literary Biography, English and American.* Rev. ed. Compiled after John W. Cousin by D. C. Browning. London: J. M. Dent & Sons Ltd.; New York: E. P. Dutton & Co., 1960.

Fang | Fang, J. *Mathematicians from Antiquity to Today. I: A-C.* Hauppauge, N.Y.: Paideia, 1972.

Gomes | Gomes Teixeira, Francisco. "Conferências sôbre quatro mulheres célebres na História da Matemática." In *Panegíricos e Conferencias,* 195–228. Coimbra, Portugal: Imprensa da Universidade, 1925.

GoodHs | *The Good Housekeeping · Woman's Almanac.* Edited by Barbara McDowell and Hana Umlauf. New York: Newspaper Enterprise Association, Inc., 1977.

Hale | Hale, Sarah Josepha. *Woman's Record: or Sketches of All Distinguished Women from "the beginning" till A.D. 1850.* New York: Harper, 1853.

Hays | Hays, Mary. *Female Biography.* London: Richard Phillips, 1803.

Iacobacci   Iacobacci, Rora F. "Women of mathematics." *Arithmetic Teacher* 17 (1970): 316–324; also in *Mathematics Teacher* 63 (1970): 329–337.

IntAu&W   *The International Authors and Writers Who's Who*. 8th ed. Edited by Adrian Gaster. Cambridge, England: International Biographical Centre, 1977.

IntDcWomB   *The International Dictionary of Women's Biography*. Edited by Jennifer S. Uglow and Frances Hinton. New York: Continuum, 1982.

IntWW   *The International Who's Who*. London: Europa Publications Ltd., 1974, 1975, 1976, 1977, 1978. Distributed by Gale Research Co., Detroit, Mich.

Ireland   Ireland, Norma Olin. *Index to Women of the World from Ancient to Modern Times: Biographies and Portraits*. Westwood, Mass.: F. W. Faxon Co., 1970.

Jacotin   Dubreil-Jacotin, Marie-Louise. "Women mathematicians." In *Great Currents of Mathematical Thought*, edited by F. LeLionnais, vol. 1, 268–280. New York: Dover, 1970. Translation of revised and enlarged 1962 edition of *Les Grands Courants de la Pensée Mathématique*. Paris: Librairie Scientifique et Technique, 1948.

Jones   Jones, Phillip S. "Women in American mathematics—20th century." *Mathematics Teacher* 50 (1957): 376–378.

Kramer   Kramer, E. E. "Six more female mathematicians." *Scripta Mathematica* 23 (1957): 83–95. In revised form in *The Nature and Growth of Modern Mathematics*, 704–714. New York: Hawthorn Books, 1970.

LEduc   *Leaders in Education*. 5th ed. Edited by Jaques Cattell Press. New York: R. R. Bowker Co., 1974.

LibW   *Liberty's Women*. Edited by Robert McHenry. Springfield, Mass.: G. & C. Merriam Co., Publishers, 1980.

LinLibL   *The Lincoln Library of Language Arts*. 3rd ed. 2 vols. Columbus, Ohio: Frontier Press Co., 1978.

LinLibS   *The Lincoln Library of Social Studies*. 8th ed. 3 vols. Columbus, Ohio: Frontier Press Co., 1978.

Loria   Loria, Gino. "Les femmes mathématiciennes." *Revue Scientifique* (4) (20) (1903): 385–392.

May   May, Kenneth O. *Bibliography and Research Manual of the History of Mathematics*. Toronto and Buffalo: University of Toronto Press, 1973.

Michaud   *Biographie Universelle Ancienne et Moderne*. Paris: Desplaces, 1854–1857.

Möbius   Möbius, Paul Julius. "Beiträge zur Kenntnis des Mathematischen Talentes. C. Ueber die mathematischen Weiber." In *Ueber die Anlage zur Mathematik*, 77–86. Leipzig: Barth, 1900.

Mozans	Mozans, H. J. (pseudonym for John Augustine Zahm). *Women in Science*. New York and London: Appleton, 1913. Reprint. Cambridge, Mass.: MIT Press, 1974.
NatCAB	*The National Cyclopaedia of American Biography*. 57 vols. New York and Clifton, N.J.: James T. White & Co., 1892–1977. Reprint. Vols. 1–50. Ann Arbor: University Microfilms, 1967–1971.
NCE	*New Catholic Encyclopedia*. New York: McGraw-Hill, 1967.
NewC	*The New Century Handbook of English Literature*. Rev. ed. Edited by Clarence L. Barnhart with the assistance of William D. Halsey. New York: Appleton-Century-Crofts, 1967.
Newell	*Black Mathematicians and Their Works*. Edited by Virginia K. Newell et al. Ardmore, Pa.: Dorrance, 1980.
NewYTBE	*The New York Times Biographical Edition: A Compilation of Current Biographical Information of General Interest*. New York: Arno Press, 1970–1973. Continued by *The New York Times Biographical Service*.
NewYTBS	*The New York Times Biographical Service: A Compilation of Current Biographical Information of General Interest*. New York: Arno Press, 1974–1979. A continuation of *The New York Times Biographical Edition*.
NotAW	*Notable American Women, 1607–1950: A Biographical Dictionary*. 3 vols. Edited by Edward T. James. Cambridge, Mass.: Belknap Press of Harvard University Press, 1971.
NotAW80	*Notable American Women: The Modern Period*. Edited by Barbara Sicherman and Carol Hurd Green. Cambridge, Mass.: Belknap Press of Harvard University Press, 1980.
OhA&B	*Ohio Authors and Their Books: Biographical Data and Selective Bibliographies for Ohio Authors, Native and Resident, 1796–1950*. Edited by William Coyle. Cleveland and New York: World Publishing Co., 1962.
Osen	Osen, Lynn M. *Women in Mathematics*. Cambridge, Mass.: MIT Press, 1974.
Owens	"Women in Mathematics Questionnaires." In Helen Brewster Owens Collection, Schlesinger Library of Radcliffe College, Cambridge, Mass., 1937, 1940.
OxFr	*The Oxford Companion to French Literature*. Corrected ed. Compiled and edited by Sir Paul Harvey and J. E. Heseltine. Oxford: Clarendon Press, 1966.
Pauly	Pauly, August Friedrich von, and G. Wissowa. *Paulys Real-encyclopädie der Classischen Altertumwissenschaft*. Stuttgart, 1894–1919.
Perl	Perl, Teri. *Math Equals: Biographies of Women Mathematicians + Related Articles*. Menlo Park, Calif.: Addison-Wesley, 1978.
Poggendorf	Poggendorf, Johann Christian. *Biographisch-Literarisches Handwörterbuch zur Geschichte der exakten Wissenschaften*. Leipzig: Barth

	(vols. 1–4), Verlag Chemie (vols. 5–6), 1863–1936. Ann Arbor: Edwards Brothers, 1936. Berlin: Akademie-Verlag (vol. 7), 1981– 1984.
Poole	Poole, W. F. *Poole's Index to Periodical Literature 1802–1881*. Boston: Houghton, Mifflin, and Co., 1882. Rev. ed., 1893. With 5 supplements covering 1882–1907.
Rebière	Rebière, Alphonse. *Les Femmes dans la Science*. 2nd ed. Paris: Nony, 1897.
REn	Benet, William Rose. *The Reader's Encyclopedia*. 2nd ed. New York: Thomas Y. Crowell Co., 1965.
Riches	Riches, Phyllis M. *An Analytical Bibliography of Universal Collected Biography*. London: The Library Association, 1934.
Schmidt	*400 Outstanding Women of the World*. Edited by Minna M. Schmidt. Chicago: M. M. Schmidt, 1933.
Siegel	Siegel, Patricia Joan, and Kay Thomas. *Women in the Scientific Search: An American Bio-bibliography, 1724–1979*. Metuchen, N.J.: Scarecrow, 1985.
Tee	Tee, Garry J. "The pioneering women mathematicians," *The Mathematical Intelligencier* 5(4) (1983): 27–36.
TwCBDA	*The Twentieth Century Biographical Dictionary of Notable Americans*. 10 vols. Edited by Rossiter Johnson. Boston: The Biographical Society, 1904. Reprint. Detroit: Gale Research Co., 1968.
Valentin	Valentin, G. "Die Frauen in den exakten Wissenschaften." *Bibliotheca Mathematica* 9 (1895): 65–76.
Walford	Walford, Lucy Bethia (Colquhoun). *Four Biographies from Blackwood*. London: Blackwood, 1888.
Wer	*Degeners Wer Ist's?* 10th ed. Berlin: Verlag Herrmann Degener, 1935.
WhAm	*Who Was Who in America*. 8 vols. plus index. Chicago: A. N. Marquis Co., 1943–1985.
WhLit	*Who Was Who in Literature, 1906–1934*. 2 vols. Gale Composite Biographical Dictionary Series, No. 5. Detroit: Gale Research Co., 1979.
WhNAA	*Who Was Who among North American Authors, 1921–1939*. Compiled from *Who's Who among North American Authors*, Vols. 1–7, 1921–1939. 2 vols. Gale Composite Biographical Dictionary Series, No. 1. Detroit: Gale Research Co., 1976.
Who	*Who's Who*. An annual biographical dictionary. New York: St. Martin's Press; London: A. & C. Black, Ltd.
WhoAm	*Who's Who in America*. Chicago: Marquis Who's Who, Inc., 1951, 1974, 1976, 1978, 1982.
WhoAmW	*Who's Who of American Women*. Chicago: Marquis Who's Who,

	Inc., 1958, 1961, 1964, 1966, 1968, 1970, 1972, 1974, 1975, 1977, 1981.
WhoNG	Wistrion, Robert S. *Who's Who in Nazi Germany*. New York: Macmillan, 1982.
WhoWest	*Who's Who in the West*. Chicago: Marquis Who's Who, Inc., 1982.
WhoWorJ	*Who's Who in World Jewry: A Biographical Dictionary of Outstanding Jews*. Edited by I. J. Carmin Karpman. New York: Pitman Publishing Corp., 1972.
WND	Perl, Teri and Joan M. Manning. *Women, Numbers and Dreams*. Santa Rosa, Cal.: National Women's History Project (P.O. Box 3716, Santa Rosa, Calif. 95402), 1982.
WomBkWorRec	*The Women's Book of World Records and Achievements*. Edited by Lois Decker O'Neill. Garden City, N.Y.: Anchor, 1979.
WomPar	Herman, Kali. *Women in Particular: An Index to American Women*. Phoenix, Ariz.: Oryx Press, 1984.
WomWWA	*Woman's Who's Who of America*. Edited by John William Leonard. New York: American Commonwealth Co., 1914. Reprint. Detroit: Gale Research Co., 1976.
WorWhoSci	*World Who's Who in Science*. Edited by Allen G. Debus. Chicago: Marquis Who's Who, Inc., 1968.
WS	Herzenberg, Caroline L. *Women Scientists from Antiquity to the Present: An Index*. West Cornwall, Conn.: Locust Hill Press, 1986.
Zen	Zenkezich, I. G. *The Fate of Talent (Essays About Women Mathematicians)* (in Russian). Briansk: Pedagogicheskoe Obshchestzo RFSFR, 1968.

NAME INDEX

Page numbers in *italics* refer to main entries in the sourcebook.

SUBJECT INDEX

ABOUT THE CONTRIBUTORS

HAJNAL ANDRÉKA was a student of Rózsa Péter and is Senior Research Fellow of the Mathematical Institute of the Hungarian Academy of Sciences and a close collaborator of I. Németi. Her research areas are mathematical theories of logic, algebraic logic, and universal algebra. Her publications include a joint book with L. Henkin, J. D. Monk, I. Németi, and A. Tarski (*Cylindric Set Algebras*, 1981) and about forty research papers.

IRVING H. ANELLIS received his Ph.D. in 1977 and is Professor of Mathematics at Iowa State University. He is an assistant editor of *Philosophia Mathematica*. He works in history and philosophy of logic and mathematics. Currently he is writing a history of mathematical logic in the USSR.

DOUGLAS E. CAMERON is Professor of Mathematics at the University of Akron. He is one of the West's foremost experts on modern Russian mathematics history. His research into the origins of topology led him to make two extended visits to the Soviet Union interviewing individuals about their memories of the Luzitania era.

PAUL J. CAMPBELL received a Ph.D. in mathematical logic from Cornell University in 1971 and is Associate Professor of Mathematics and Computer Science at Beloit College. He is Editor of *The UMAP Journal*, Reviews Editor for *Mathematics Magazine*, and a member of the Board of Governors of the Mathematical Association of America.

H.S.M. COXETER, F.R.S., was born in London and educated in Cambridge and Princeton; he has been awarded seven honorary degrees and is Professor Emeritus at the University of Toronto. He is the author of *Introduction to Geometry*, *Projective Geometry*, *The Real Projective Plane*, *Non-Euclidean Geometry*, *Twelve Geometric Essays*, *Regular Polytopes*, and *Regular Complex Polytopes*.

FLORENCE D. FASANELLI is a mathematics teacher with a special interest in the relations between the history and pedagogy of mathematics. She has a background in mathematics and art history, connections between which have drawn her to develop materials for the classroom.

WILHELM FLÜGGE was the husband of Irmgard Flügge-Lotz. He is Professor Emeritus of Applied Mechanics at Stanford University and the author of several books on shell design and analysis.

PHYLLIS FOX is a computer scientist with special interest in scientific computing and numerical software. She has degrees in mathematics and electrical engineering, including a Ph.D. in mathematics. She was Professor of Computer Science at New Jersey Institute of Technology (1964–1973) and a Member of Technical Staff at Bell Laboratories (1973–1983). She is a consultant to Bell Communications Research.

MARY W. GRAY is Professor of Mathematics, Statistics, and Computer Science at American University, Washington, D.C. Trained as an algebraist, she does research on applications of statistics to policy analysis and in litigation, and on legal issues in computing. She is also a member of the District of Columbia and U.S. Supreme Court Bars.

JUDY GREEN is Associate Professor of Mathematics at Rutgers University-Camden and Honorary Research Associate in History of Mathematics at the National Museum of American History, Smithsonian Institution. She earned her Ph.D. at the University of Maryland in 1972 in mathematical logic. Her research interests and publications concern pre–World War II American women in mathematics and the history of logic.

LOUISE S. GRINSTEIN received a Ph.D. from Columbia University in mathematics education. She has worked in industry as a computer programmer and systems analyst and is Professor of Mathematics at Kingsborough Community College of the City University of New York. She is the coeditor of *Calculus: Readings from the Mathematics Teacher* (1977). The present volume's contribution is based on the article "Anna Johnson Pell Wheeler: Her life and work." *Historia Mathematica* 9 (1982): 37–53.

CLAUDIA HENRION graduated from Stanford in 1980, was awarded a Danforth Graduate Fellowship, and received a Ph.D. in mathematics from Dartmouth in 1985. She is Assistant Professor of Mathematics at Middlebury College.

ELSE HØYRUP is Research Librarian in Mathematics at Roskilde University Library, Denmark. Her research area is women in science and technology. With Jens Høyrup she is the author of *Mathematics in Society* (1973, in Danish), *Women: Work and Intellectual Development* (1974, in Danish), and *Women and Mathematics, Science, and Engineering: A Bibliography* (1978).

ROSEMARY McCROSKEY KARR is Assistant Professor of Mathematics, Statistics, and Computer Science at Eastern Kentucky University. Her primary interest is in topics related to training and retraining elementary mathematics teachers.

HUBERT KENNEDY is the editor/translator of *Selected Works of Giuseppe Peano* (1973), author of *Peano: Life and Works of Giuseppe Peano* (1980; Italian translation 1983), and translator of the novel *The Hustler* (1984) from the German original of John Henry Mackay. Currently a consulting editor of the *Journal of Homosexuality*, he is preparing a biography of Karl Heinrich Ulrichs (1825–1895), pioneer of the modern gay movement.

PATRICIA CLARK KENSCHAFT is Associate Professor of Mathematics at Montclair

State College. She has written mathematics texts for nontechnical majors and research papers about underrepresented groups in mathematics. She is founder and President of the New Jersey Section of the Association for Women in Mathematics, and an officer in the New Jersey Section of the Mathematical Association of America.

AMY C. KING is Professor of Mathematics at Eastern Kentucky University. Her primary interest is in complex analysis, but she has also published works in the history of mathematics, including one concerning doctorates received by women in the mathematical sciences. The chapter on Hopper in this volume is dedicated to the memory of her husband, Dr. Don R. King, who spent countless hours helping with its organization and many revisions.

ANN HIBNER KOBLITZ is the author of *A Convergence of Lives. Sofia Kovalevskaia: Scientist, Writer, Revolutionary* (1984). She is co-chair of the Women's Committee of the History of Science Society, and has a grant from the National Science Foundation to work on a study of the first generation of Russian women to enter the sciences.

JEANNE LaDUKE is Associate Professor of Mathematics at DePaul University. She received her Ph.D. from the University of Oregon and has published research articles in abstract harmonic analysis and in the history of American mathematics.

SALLY IRENE LIPSEY, retired from the Department of Mathematics at Brooklyn College of the City University of New York, is the author of *Mathematics for Nursing Science* and many journal articles. Her research focused on the improvement of teaching, especially by means of applications, and on the problem of women and mathematics. She would like to acknowledge the excellent help of Benedict T. Lassar and Martha H. Kramer in supplying useful information for her essay.

EDITH H. LUCHINS is Professor of Mathematical Sciences at Rensselaer Polytechnic Institute. She did undergraduate work at Brooklyn College, where she was introduced to the history of mathematics by Professor Carl Boyer, and graduate work at New York University (the Courant Institute) and at the University of Oregon. An NSF grant in 1974–1976 on why there are so few women mathematicians led to an interview with Olga Taussky-Todd. Luchins teaches algebra and number theory and fancies herself a poet.

ANN MOSKOL is Associate Professor of Mathematics and Computer Science at Rhode Island College. Her diverse interests include applied mathematics, mathematics education, and computer science. She is currently directing a grant (the Rhode Island Mathematics Excellence Program) to develop in-service packages for mathematics teachers, and researching the educational uses of artificial intelligence software packages for microcomputers.

IAN MUELLER is Professor of Philosophy and the Conceptual Foundations of Science at the University of Chicago. He has published *Philosophy of Mathematics and Deductive Structure in Euclid's Elements* (1981) and numerous articles on Greek philosophy and its interaction with Greek science.

M. F. NEWMAN is a Senior Fellow in Mathematics at the Australian National University.

He was a student and colleague of Hanna Neumann. His main mathematical interests are research and education. His research is in the theory of groups, with special emphasis on the use of computers. His essay is based on the longer works, Newman (1973) and Newman and Wall (1974), for which in turn Neumann's family (especially Bernhard), friends, and colleagues provided much useful information.

MARYJO NICHOLS is Associate Professor of Mathematics at the University of Detroit, where she has been teaching since 1957. She is a frequent speaker at mathematics conferences and has been President of the Detroit Council of Teachers of Mathematics. Her interests are number theory and the history of mathematics.

GOTTFRIED E. NOETHER is the son of the mathematician Fritz Noether, Emmy Noether's younger brother. He is Professor Emeritus in the Department of Statistics of the University of Connecticut and is the author of some forty papers and three books, primarily in the field of nonparametric statistics.

ELIZABETH CHAMBERS PATTERSON is Professor of Physics at Albertus Magnus College. She is the author of two books on Mary Somerville, as well as of *John Dalton and the Atomic Theory: The Biography of a Natural Philosopher* (1970).

JAMES D. PATTERSON is Professor of Physics and Space Sciences at the Florida Institute of Technology. From 1963 to 1984 he was at the South Dakota School of Mines and Technology. Theoretical solid state physics is his area of research interest, and he is the author of *Introduction to the Theory of Solid State Physics* (1971).

GEORGE W. PHILLIPS is Assistant Professor of Russian and European history at the John Jay College of Criminal Justice, of the City University of New York. He specializes in the history of Imperial Russia (late nineteenth and early twentieth centuries) and the history of the Soviet Union. He would like to acknowledge the generous help of Professor Esther R. Phillips, of the Department of Mathematics and Computer Science of Lehman College, City University of New York, who did the analysis of Kochina's mathematical work; and of librarians at (1) the Mina Rees Library at the Graduate Center of City University of New York; (2) Science and Technology Division and the Slavonic Division of the New York Public Library; and (3) Engineering Societies Library in New York City.

KAREN D. RAPPAPORT is the Research Supervisor for Computer and Mathematics Services at Celanese Research Company. She received her Ph.D. from New York University. In addition to her work in scientific computing and its applications, her interests include the history of women in mathematics, exploratory data analysis, and perturbation theory.

CONSTANCE REID, the sister of Julia Robinson, is the author of *From Zero to Infinity, A Long Way from Euclid, Hilbert, Courant in Göttingen and New York, Neyman—From Life*, and *Hilbert-Courant*. She is also the editor of *International Congresses, An Illustrated History* and *More Mathematical People*. Her contribution is based on "The Autobiography of Julia Robinson," which will appear in *More Mathematical People*, edited by Donald J. Albers, G. L. Alexanderson, and Constance Reid, in 1987. Technical material on Robinson's mathematical work was added by R. M. Robinson (Julia Robinson's husband).

JALEH REZAIE is Assistant Professor of Mathematics, Statistics, and Computer Science at Eastern Kentucky University.

JOAN L. RICHARDS is Assistant Professor of History of Science at Brown University. Her research interests lie primarily in the development of mathematics in the nineteenth century and the interactions between mathematical and other forms of thought. She is completing a book on the reception of non-Euclidean geometry in Victorian Britain, and beginning a study of the interactions of historical and mathematical thought in France and England after the French Revolution.

RAPHAEL M. ROBINSON was Julia Robinson's husband. He is Professor Emeritus of Mathematics at the University of California at Berkeley.

ALICE SCHAFER retired from Wellesley College as the Helen Day Gould Professor of Mathematics and is now Lecturer in Mathematics at Simmons College. She was the second president of the Association for Women in Mathematics (1973–1975). Her main research interest is group theory.

TINA SCHALCH graduated in 1986 from Eastern Kentucky University with a double major in mathematics and computer science. She is a member of the Association for Computing Machinery and Kappa Mu Epsilon.

LAUREL G. SHERMAN is an Affiliate Scholar at Oberlin College, Oberlin, Ohio. She has a research interest in women in the history of science and mathematics. Her writing includes science book reviews for several city newspapers and science and mathematics textbooks for grades K-12.

JOAN SPETICH received a master's degree in mathematics in 1986 from the University of Akron, with a thesis on Nina Bari's research on trigonometric series.

JOHN R. SPREITER is Professor of Applied Mechanics and Aeronautics and Astronautics at Stanford University. From 1943 to 1968 he was a Research Scientist at NASA (previously NACA) Ames Research Center. For the last six of those years, he was Chief of the Theoretical Studies Branch of the Space Sciences Division. He was the first student of Irmgard Flügge-Lotz after she arrived at Stanford in 1948 and was appointed to be her successor when she retired.

RUTH REBEKKA STRUIK is Professor of Mathematics at the University of Colorado in Boulder. She received her Ph.D. in 1955 from New York University; Wilhelm Magnus was her thesis director. Her research interests have been primarily in group theory. She would like to express appreciation for information received from those who personally knew Kendall; librarians at the Schlesinger Library at Radcliffe College; Charlotte Smokler; Jeanne LaDuke; and the personnel at the Colorado Historical Society.

GARRY J. TEE is a Senior Lecturer in the Department of Computer Science at the

University of Auckland, New Zealand. He has published researches into numerical analysis and the history of science, including "The pioneering women mathematicians" (*The Mathematical Intelligencer* 5 [4] [1983]: 27–36) and "Sof'ya Vasil'yeva Kovalevskaya" (*Mathematical Chronicle* [1977]: 113–139).

GUIDO WEISS is Professor of Mathematics at Washington University. His research interests are in complex and real analysis. In 1967 he won the Chauvenet Prize of the Mathematical Association of America for excellence in mathematical exposition.

BETSEY S. WHITMAN is Professor and Chairperson of Mathematics at Florida A&M University, where she has taught mathematics and mathematics education since 1967. Her research interests include intuitive equation solving and women in mathematics.

SYLVIA M. WIEGAND is Associate Professor of Mathematics at the University of Nebraska in Lincoln. She received her Ph.D. from the University of Wisconsin in 1972; her research areas are ring theory and commutative algebra. Professor Wiegand's family is full of mathematicians: her grandmother, Grace Chisholm Young; grandfather, William Henry Young; father, Laurence Chisholm Young; aunt, Rosalind Cecily Tanner; some distant cousins; and her husband, Roger Wiegand.

JOEL E. WILSON is Assistant Professor of Mathematics, Statistics and Computer Science at Eastern Kentucky University. His primary interests are teaching undergraduate mathematics and computer science.